Study Guide to
Byrd & Chen's
Canadian
Tax
Principles
2006-2007
Edition

CLARENCE BYRD
Athabasca University

IDA CHEN
Clarence Byrd Inc.

PEARSON
Prentice Hall

Toronto

D1517125

ISBN-10: 0-13-232531-4
ISBN-13: 978-0-13-232531-8
This ISBN is shared with the text (*Byrd & Chen's Canadian Tax Principles*, 2006–2007 Edition).

Editor-in-Chief: Gary Bennett
Executive Editor: Samantha Scully
Executive Marketing Manager: Cas Shields
Developmental Editor: Jose Sevilla
Production Editor: Marisa D'Andrea
Production Coordinator: Deborah Starks
Art Director: Mary Opper
Cover Design: Anthony Leung

1 2 3 4 5   11 10 09 08 07

Printed and bound in Canada.

PEARSON
Prentice
Hall

Preface

Web Site

The web site for this book can be found at:

www.pearsoned.ca/byrdchen/ctp2007/

This web site contains many features designed to enhance the usefulness of the text (see Introduction, page vii). Please check the web site for additions or corrections to the text before using this book.

Content

Your textbook is accompanied by this Study Guide. Solutions to both the Exercises and the Self Study Problems and Cases will be found in this Guide. Additional features of the Study Guide that have been well received by our users are detailed guidance on how to work through each Chapter (the How To Work Through The Chapter lists) and a guide for reviewing the basic concepts that you should have mastered on completion of each Chapter (the list of Objectives).

This Study Guide contains two sample personal tax returns (Chapter 6 and Chapter 14) and one sample corporate tax return (Chapter 16). Only limited schedules are printed in the Study Guide. The complete returns are available on the Student CD-ROM.

The Glossary of tax terms can be found at the back of this Study Guide.

Using The Solutions

With respect to the problem solutions that are included in this book, the header at the top of each page identifies the solution on the page. The page numbers in this Companion Study Guide have been numbered with the prefix "S-" to distinguish them from the page numbers of the text. As always, we encourage you to attempt to solve each Exercise or Self Study Problem prior to consulting these solutions. It is our opinion that one of the most unfortunate misconceptions that many students have, is the belief that simply reading through a solution is a learning experience. It is not!

We welcome any corrections or suggestions for additions or improvements. These can be sent to us at:

Clarence Byrd Inc.
139 Musie Loop Road, Chelsea, Quebec   J9B 1Y6
e-mail address: ichen@byrdinc.ca

August, 2006   Clarence Byrd, Athabasca University
                                                    Ida Chen, Clarence Byrd Inc.

Table Of Contents

Introduction

Web Site

The web site for this book can be found at:

www.pearsoned.ca/byrdchen/ctp2007/

Here you will find:

- Glossary Flashcards and Key Terms Self-Tests
- Updates and corrections to the textbook and Study Guide
- PowerPoint slides for Chapters 15 to 19
- Links to other relevant web sites
- A short on-line survey ($100 cash prize available)
- Instructions on how to install the 2006 ProFile program and download updated sample tax returns and Cases when the updated ProFile software is available in January, 2007
- A "Guide to Using Your Student CD-ROM"

Glossary

At the back of this Study Guide is a comprehensive Glossary that carefully defines more than 500 tax terms that are used throughout the text. Tied to this important resource, at the end of each chapter, you will find a list of the Key Terms that were used in that chapter. This provides an additional resource for reviewing the text material in that, by reviewing this list, you can ensure that you are familiar with all of the concepts that are presented in the chapter. These Key Terms are listed at the end of each chapter without definitions.

Study Guide On Student CD-ROM

For your convenience, we have included the Study Guide for Chapters 1 to 14 on the Student CD-ROM in PDF format. To assist you in navigating through the electronic version of this Study Guide, we have provided bookmarks that are set to automatically show when you first open the file. You will be able to expand or collapse the table of contents branches and jump to any solution by clicking on the solution number with your mouse. For example, by clicking on " Solution To Self Study Problem Two-3" in the expanded CHAPTER 2 Table of Contents, you will jump to the solution for Self Study Problem Two-3.

To hide the bookmarks, choose the "Hide Bookmarks" option under the Window menu (Hotkey is F5).

CHAPTER ONE

How To Work Through Chapter One

Web Site
As a reminder, the web site for this book can be found at:

www.pearsoned.ca/byrdchen/ctp2007/

Here you will find:

- Glossary Flashcards and Key Terms Self-Tests
- Updates and corrections to the textbook and Study Guide
- PowerPoint slides for Chapters 15 to 19
- Links to other relevant websites
- A "Guide to Using Your Student CD-ROM"
- A short on-line survey ($100 cash prize available)
- Instructions on how to install the 2006 ProFile program and download updated sample tax returns and Cases when the updated ProFile software is available in January, 2007

We recommend the following approach in dealing with the material in this chapter:

The Canadian Tax System

☐   Read the text pages 1 (from paragraph 1-1) through 3 (through paragraph 1-8).

☐   Complete Exercise One-1 on page 3 of the text. The solution is on page S-2 of this Study Guide. All solutions to Exercises and Self Study Problems and Cases can be found in this Study Guide and the page numbers all start with the prefix S-.

☐   Read the text pages 3 (from paragraph 1-9) and 4 (through paragraph 1-13).

☐   Complete Exercise One-2 on page 4 of the text. The solution is on page S-2.

☐   Read the text pages 4 (from paragraph 1-14) and 5 (through paragraph 1-22).

☐   Complete Exercise One-3 on page 6 of the text. The solution is on page S-2.

☐   Read the text pages 6 (from paragraph 1-23) through 10 (through paragraph 1-39).

Introduction To The Income Tax Act And Its Structure

☐   Read the text pages 11 (from paragraph 1-40) through 18 (through paragraph 1-70).

To Complete This Chapter

☐   Review the Key Terms Used In This Chapter on page 18 of the text. Consult the Glossary for the meaning of any key terms you do not know.

☐   Review the Glossary Flashcards and complete the Key Terms Self-Test for the Chapter. These features can be found in two places, on your Student CD-ROM under the heading "Key Term Practice" and on the web site.

☐   Review the Learning Objectives of the Chapter found on page S-3 of this Study Guide.

☐   As a review, we recommend that you view the PowerPoint Slides for Chapter One that are on your Student CD-ROM. If you do not have access to the Microsoft PowerPoint program, the PowerPoint Viewer program can be installed from the Student CD-ROM.

Unlike the other Chapters in this book, there are no Self Study Problems to be completed.

Solution to Chapter One Exercises

Exercise One - 1 Solution
Income tax returns would have to be filed by Max Jordan, the Jordan family trust, and Jordan Enterprises Ltd.

Exercise One - 2 Solution

Federal Tax Payable [(15.25%)($27,000)]	$4,118
Provincial Tax Payable [(7.5%)($27,000)]	2,025
Total Tax Payable [(15.25% + 7.5%)($27,000)]	$6,143

Exercise One - 3 Solution
Margie's GST and provincial sales tax paid total $24,080 [(6% + 8%)($172,000)]. Based on her Taxable Income of $895,000, this would represent an effective rate of 2.7 percent ($24,080 ÷ $895,000).

Jane's GST and provincial sales tax paid total $3,850 [(6% + 8%)($27,500)]. On her Taxable Income of $18,000, this would be an effective rate of 21.4 percent ($3,850 ÷ $18,000).

Chapter One Learning Objectives

After completing Chapter 1, you should be able to:

1. List some of the different bases that can be used by the various levels of government to assess taxes (paragraphs 1-1 through 1-4).

2. List all of the types of entities that are subject to paying federal income taxes (paragraphs 1-5 through 1-8).

3. Explain the relationship between the assessment of income taxes at the federal level and the assessment of income taxes at the provincial level (paragraphs 1-9 through 1-19).

4. List some of the ways that taxation is used to achieve economic objectives (paragraph 1-20).

5. Describe the differences between progressive, regressive, and flat tax systems, including some of the advantages and disadvantages of each system (paragraphs 1-21 through 1-29).

6. Discuss the issue of who ultimately pays the cost of various types of taxes (paragraphs 1-30 and 1-31).

7. Explain the nature of tax expenditures (paragraphs 1-32 through 1-36).

8. Evaluate issues in tax policy on the basis of the qualitative characteristics of tax systems (paragraphs 1-37 through 1-39).

9. Describe the general structure of the *Income Tax Act* (paragraphs 1-40 through 1-54).

10. List and explain the nature of other sources of income tax legislation (paragraphs 1-55 through 1-64).

11. Describe other sources of income tax information (paragraphs 1-65 through 1-70).

CHAPTER TWO

How To Work Through Chapter Two

We recommend the following approach in dealing with the material in this chapter:

Introduction To Procedures And Administration
☐ Read the text pages 23 through 28 (through paragraph 2-33).

☐ Complete Exercise Two-1 on page 28 of the text. The solution is on page S-7.

☐ Read the text pages 28 (from paragraph 2-34) and 29 (through paragraph 2-36).

☐ Complete Exercise Two-2 on page 29 of the text. The solution is on page S-7.

Instalment Payments For Individuals
☐ Read the text pages 29 (from paragraph 2-37) through 31 (through paragraph 2-49).

☐ Complete Exercises Two-3 through Two-5 on page 31 of the text. The solutions are on page S-7.

☐ Complete Self Study Problem Two-1 on page 51 of the text. The solution is on page S-8.

Interest And Penalties For Individuals
☐ Read the text pages 31 (from paragraph 2-50) through 33 (through paragraph 2-60).

☐ Complete Exercise Two-6 on page 33 of the text. The solution is on page S-7.

☐ Read the text page 33 (paragraphs 2-61 and 2-62).

Returns And Payments For Corporations
☐ Read the text pages 34 (from paragraph 2-63) and 35 (through paragraph 2-66).

☐ Complete Exercises Two-7 and Two-8 on page 35 of the text. The solutions are on page S-7.

☐ Complete Self Study Problems Two-2 and Two-3 on pages 51 and 52 of the text. The solutions are on pages S-8 and S-9.

Due Date For Balance Owing For Corporations
☐ Read the text page 35 (paragraph 2-67).

☐ Complete Exercise Two-9 on page 35 of the text. The solution is on page S-8.

☐ Complete Self Study Problem Two-4 on page 52 of the text. The solution is on page S-10.

Interest And Penalties For Corporations
☐ Read the text pages 35 (from paragraph 2-68) and 36 (through paragraph 2-69).

Returns And Payments For Trusts
☐ Read the text page 36 (paragraphs 2-70 through 2-73).

General Administrative Issues
☐ Read the text pages 36 (from paragraph 2-74) through 40 (through paragraph 2-95).

☐ Complete Self Study Problem Two-5 on page 52 of the text. The solution is on page S-10.

Appeals

☐ Read the text pages 40 (from paragraph 2-96) and 41 (through paragraph 2-107).

☐ Complete Exercise Two-10 on page 41 of the text. The solution is on page S-8.

☐ Read the text pages 41 (from paragraph 2-108) and 42 (through paragraph 2-115).

Tax Evasion, Avoidance, And Planning

☐ Read the text pages 43 (from paragraph 2-116) through 46 (through paragraph 2-134).

Collection And Enforcement

☐ Read the text pages 46 (from paragraph 2-135) through 48 (through paragraph 2-146).

Fairness Package

☐ Read the text pages 48 (from paragraph 2-147) and 49 (through paragraph 2-153).

To Complete This Chapter

☐ Review the Key Terms Used In This Chapter on page 49 of the text. Consult the Glossary for the meaning of any key terms you do not know.

☐ Review the Glossary Flashcards and complete the Key Terms Self-Test for the Chapter. These features can be found in two places, on your Student CD-ROM under the heading "Key Term Practice" and on the web site.

☐ Review the Learning Objectives of the Chapter found on pages S-11 and S-12 of this Study Guide.

☐ As a review, we recommend that you view the PowerPoint Slides for Chapter Two that are on your Student CD-ROM. The PowerPoint Viewer program can be installed from the Student CD-ROM.

Solution to Chapter Two Exercises

Exercise Two - 1 Solution
While Mr. Katarski's 2006 tax return does not have to be filed until June 15, 2007, his tax liability must be paid by April 30, 2007 in order to avoid the assessment of interest.

Exercise Two - 2 Solution
Ms. Sally Cheung's 2006 tax return must be filed by the later of six months after the date of her death and her normal filing date. As she has business income, her normal filing date is June 15. The later of the two dates would be August 15, 2007, six months after the date of her death. Her final return for 2007 would be due on June 15, 2008.

Exercise Two - 3 Solution
She is not required to make instalment payments as long as her actual 2006 net tax owing is less than $2,000.

Exercise Two - 4 Solution
As his net tax owing in the current year and one of the two preceding years is in excess of $2,000, he is required to make instalment payments. The minimum amount would be based on the preceding taxation year's net tax owing of $1,500, and would be $375 per quarter.

Exercise Two - 5 Solution
Use of the estimate for the current year of $32,000 would provide the lowest total instalments for the year. The required payments would be $8,000 in each quarter and they would be due on March 15, June 15, September 15 and December 15. While the second preceding year has the lowest net tax owing, if this were used for the first two quarters, the third and fourth quarter payments would have to bring the total amount to the net tax owing for the first preceding year, a total of $37,000. If $37,000 in instalments had been paid, the CRA would not pay interest on the overpayment of $5,000 ($37,000 - $32,000).

Exercise Two - 6 Solution
Given the size of her net tax owing, ITA 163.1 will not be applicable and there will be no penalties for late instalments. However, a penalty of 7 percent of taxes payable will be assessed for filing two months late (5 percent, plus 1 percent per month). If, in one of the three preceding taxation years she has committed a similar offence, the penalty would be 14 percent (10 percent, plus 2 percent per month).

Exercise Two - 7 Solution
The first two instalments would be due on the last day of January and February, 2006. They would be based on the second preceding year and would be $4,333 each ($52,000 ÷ 12). The remaining 10 instalments would be based on the preceding year, less the $8,666 paid in the first two instalments. The amount would be $8,033 [($89,000 - $8,666) ÷ 10] and the instalments would be due on the last day of each month for March to December, 2006.

Exercise Two - 8 Solution
The minimum instalments would be based on the estimated taxes payable for the current year. The amount would be $5,583 ($67,000 ÷ 12) and the instalments would be due on the last day of each month in 2006. Note that, if the estimate of tax payable for 2006 is too low, interest will be assessed on the deficiency.

Exercise Two - 9 Solution

Radco Inc.'s tax return is due six months after the fiscal year end, on July 31, 2006. Unless Radco is able to claim the small business deduction, the final payment on their taxes must be made two months after their year end, on March 31, 2006. If they are eligible for the small business deduction, they can defer the final payment for an additional month, to April 30, 2006.

Exercise Two - 10 Solution

The notice of objection must be filed by the later of:

- 90 days after the date of mailing of the reassessment (August 13, 2008); or
- one year after the due date for filing the return that is being reassessed (April 30, 2008).

The later of these two dates is August 13, 2008.

Solution to Self Study Problem Two - 1

Need For Instalments   Instalments are required when an individual's "net tax owing" exceeds $2,000 in the current year and in either of the two preceding years. In somewhat simplified terms, "net tax owing" is defined as the combined federal and provincial taxes payable, less amounts withheld under ITA 153. Mr. Gore's net tax owing for 2006 is $4,000 ($17,000 - $13,000). In addition, the amount for 2004 is $2,500 ($14,000 - $11,500). As both of these amounts are in excess of $2,000, Mr. Gore would be required to pay instalments.

Amounts   The amount of the instalments could be based on the net tax owing for 2005 or 2006. In addition, the first two 2006 instalments could be based on the net tax owing for 2004. However, since net tax owing for 2005 is nil, the best solution for Mr. Gore is to use that year. This means that, even though Mr. Gore meets the requirements for making instalment payments, the minimum amount of the required instalments would be nil.

If Mr. Gore did have to pay instalments, the due dates would have been March 15, June 15, September 15 and December 15.

Solution to Self Study Problem Two - 2

There are three possible payment schedules that could be used by Amalmor Inc. in this situation. The amounts involved are calculated as follows:

Current Year Base   The payments could be 1/12th of the estimated taxes payable for the current year. This amount would be $7,917 ($95,000/12).

Previous Year Base   The payments could be 1/12th of the taxes that were paid in the immediately preceding year. This amount would be $6,667 ($80,000/12).

Previous And Second Previous Years   A final alternative would be to base the first two payments on 1/12th of the taxes paid in the second previous year, with the remaining ten payments based on the previous year total, less the amounts paid in the first two instalments. The first two amounts would be $5,208 ($62,500/12), or a total of $10,416. In the remaining 10 months of the year, the payments would be $6,958 [($80,000 - $10,416)/10].

The last alternative involves the same total as using the previous year as a base. However, this alternative is preferable to using the previous year as a base as it provides for lower payments in the first two months. The instalments would be due on the last day of each month in 2006. Note that any remaining taxes payable must be paid within two months of the Company's year end (three months for companies that qualify for the small business deduction).

Solution to Self Study Problem Two - 3

Case One

A. The net tax owing in the current year is nil and, as a consequence, no instalments are required for 2006.

B. Given that instalments are not required, the minimum instalment would be nil.

Case Two

A. The net tax owing for the current year is $2,885. In addition, the net tax owing in 2005 was $5,216. As the net tax owing for the current year and one of the two preceding years exceeds $2,000, instalment payments are required.

B. The best alternative for instalment payments would be to use the current year estimate. This would result in required instalment payments of $721 ($2,885 ÷ 4) to be paid on March 15, June 15, September 15, and December 15. If the estimated taxes payable are below actual taxes payable for 2006, instalment interest may be charged.

The alternative that will be used by the CRA in its instalment notices will be based on the net tax owing for 2004 of $1,820 ($23,540 - $21,720) for the first two instalments. These instalment payments would be $455 per quarter, $266 lower than the $721 required using the current year as the instalment base. However, the third and fourth payments would be $2,153 {[$5,216 - (2)($455)] ÷ 2}. As this is $1,432 higher than the $721 required using the current year's net tax owing, the small savings in the first two quarters would quickly be wiped out and the taxpayer would wind up paying a much larger total ($5,216 vs. $2,885).

Case Three

A. Corporations are required to make instalment payments unless the taxes paid in the preceding taxation year or the estimated taxes payable for the current year are less than $1,000.

B. The best choice would be to use the previous year. This would result in instalment payments of $956 ($11,466 ÷ 12) to be paid at the end of each month beginning January 31.

Case Four

A. Corporations are required to make instalment payments unless the taxes paid in the preceding taxation year or the estimated taxes payable for the current year are less than $1,000.

B. The best choice is to use the current year as the base. This would result in instalment payments of $2,060 ($24,718 ÷ 12) to be paid at the end of each month beginning January 31. If 2004 is used as the base, the first two instalments would be $1,962 ($23,540 ÷ 12), somewhat less than the $2,060 amount required using the current year. However, the remaining 10 instalments would be a much higher $2,864 {[$32,560 - (2)($1,962)] ÷ 10}.

Solution to Self Study Problem Two - 4

The three taxable entities are individuals, corporations, and trusts. The required information for each is as follows:

Individuals   For individuals without business income, the taxation year is the calendar year and the filing deadline is April 30 of the following year. Individuals with business income, and their spouse or common-law partner, have an extended filing deadline of June 15. Instalment payments for all individuals, if required, are to be made quarterly on March 15, June 15, September 15, and December 15.

Corporations   Corporations can choose any fiscal year that does not exceed 53 weeks. The filing deadline is six months after the year end and instalments, when required, must be made on a monthly basis.

Trusts   Testamentary trusts can choose any fiscal year not exceeding 12 months. Their filing deadline is 90 days after the year end and they are not required to pay instalments. Inter vivos trusts must use a calendar year. They are also required to file within 90 days of the year end and quarterly instalment payments are required under the same rules as those used by individuals. However, this requirement appears to be waived on an administrative basis.

Solution to Self Study Problem Two - 5

With respect to resolving the dispute, a first step may involve nothing more than a call to the CRA to discuss the matter. If Mr. Coffee feels that there has been a misunderstanding that can be resolved by providing a more detailed explanation of the relevant facts, this may be the only step required. However, in some cases more formal steps will be necessary and they can be outlined as follows:

Notice of Objection   As the reassessment relates to the previous year's tax return, it is within the three year time limit and, therefore, a legitimate procedure for the Minister. This means that within 90 days of the mailing date on the notice of reassessment or (as Mr. Coffee is an individual) one year from the due date for the return under reassessment, a notice of objection can be filed. This objection, or Form T400A, should be sent by registered mail and should explain the facts and reasons why Mr. Coffee does not agree with the reassessment.

Tax Court of Canada   If there is an adverse decision on the notice of objection, Mr. Coffee has up to 90 days after the mailing date of the response to the notice of objection to appeal to the Tax Court of Canada. Alternatively, if he does not receive a response to his notice of objection within 90 days, he will then be able to appeal to the Tax Court of Canada. As the amount involved is only $5,000, it would probably be advisable for Mr. Coffee to choose the informal procedures.

Federal Courts   If Mr. Coffee has elected the informal Tax Court of Canada procedures, no appeal of an adverse decision is possible. An appeal to the Federal Court - Appeals Division would, however, be possible if an adverse decision was rendered under the general procedures. In theory, an adverse decision by the Federal Court could be appealed to the Supreme Court of Canada. However, this can only happen if the Federal Court recommends it or the Supreme Court authorizes such action. This would be extremely unlikely given the amount involved.

If you are to become involved in representing Mr. Coffee's interest in this matter, a signed Consent Form, T1013, which would give you authorization to discuss the case with the CRA would have to be on file with the CRA.

Chapter Two Learning Objectives

After completing Chapter 2, you should be able to:

1. Explain the nature of and need for source deductions (paragraphs 2-8 through 2-24).

2. Demonstrate a basic understanding of the situations in which an individual is required to file an income tax return (paragraphs 2-25 through 2-30).

3. List the dates on which income tax returns must be filed by individuals (paragraphs 2-31 through 2-36).

4. Explain the circumstances which result in an individual having to make income tax instalment payments (paragraphs 2-37 through 2-41).

5. Calculate the amount of any income tax instalment payments required for individual taxpayers (paragraphs 2-42 through 2-49).

6. Explain how the prescribed interest rate is used to calculate interest on late or insufficient income tax instalments for individuals (paragraphs 2-50 through 2-56).

7. Calculate the penalties that will be assessed for the late filing of individual income tax returns (paragraphs 2-57 through 2-60).

8. Identify the dates on which balances owing by individuals are due (paragraphs 2-61 and 2-62).

9. Identify the dates on which income tax returns must be filed by corporations (paragraph 2-63).

10. Calculate the amount of income tax instalment payments required for corporations (paragraphs 2-64 through 2-66).

11. Identify the dates on which balances owing by corporations are due (paragraph 2-67).

12. Explain how the prescribed interest rate is used to calculate interest on late or insufficient income tax instalments for corporations (paragraph 2-68).

13. Calculate the penalties that will be assessed for the late filing of corporate income tax returns (paragraph 2-69).

14. Demonstrate a basic understanding of the provisions regarding returns and payments for trusts (paragraphs 2-70 through 2-73).

15. Describe the assessment, reassessment and adjustments to income tax returns for all taxpayers (paragraphs 2-87 through 2-96).

16. Explain the procedures for filing a notice of objection (paragraphs 2-97 through 2-107).

17. Describe further appeals procedures, including those made to the Tax Court of Canada, the Federal Court of Appeals, and the Supreme Court of Canada (paragraphs 2-108 through 2-115).

18. Explain the difference between tax avoidance and tax evasion, including the concepts involved in the General Anti-Avoidance Rule (paragraphs 2-116 through 2-134).

19. Demonstrate a basic understanding of the avenues of collection and enforcement available to the CRA (paragraphs 2-135 through 2-141).

20. Describe the penalties applicable to tax preparers and promoters (paragraphs 2-142 through 2-146).

21. Demonstrate a basic understanding of the provisions of the fairness package (paragraphs 2-147 through 2-153).

CHAPTER THREE

How To Work Through Chapter Three

We recommend the following approach in dealing with the material in this chapter:

Introduction To Liability For Income Tax

☐ Read the text pages 57 (from paragraph 3-1) through 59 (through paragraph 3-10).

☐ Complete Exercise Three-1 on page 59 of the text. The solution is on page S-15.

☐ Complete Self Study Problem Three-1 on page 74 of the text. The solution is on page S-16.

Temporary Absences

☐ Read the text pages 59 (from paragraph 3-11) and 60 (through paragraph 3-14).

☐ Complete Exercise Three-2 on page 60 of the text. The solution is on page S-15.

Part Year Residence

☐ Read the text pages 60 (from paragraph 3-15) and 61 (through paragraph 3-16).

☐ Complete Exercise Three-3 on page 61 of the text. The solution is on page S-15.

Sojourners And Other Deemed Residents

☐ Read the text pages 61 (from paragraph 3-17) and 62 (through paragraph 3-23).

☐ Complete Exercises Three-4 and Three-5 on page 62 of the text. The solutions are on page S-15.

☐ Complete Self Study Problems Three-2, Three-3, and Three-4 on pages 74 and 75 of the text. The solutions are on page S-17.

Residence Of Corporations

☐ Read the text page 63 (paragraphs 3-24 through 3-27).

☐ Complete Exercises Three-6 and Three-7 on page 63 of the text. The solutions are on page S-15.

Residence Of Trusts

☐ Read the text page 64 (paragraph 3-28).

Taxation Of Non-Residents

☐ Read the text pages 64 (from paragraph 3-29) and 65 (through paragraph 3-35).

☐ Complete Exercise Three-8 on page 65 of the text. The solution is on page S-15.

The Concept Of Income

☐ Read the text pages 65 (from paragraph 3-36) and 67 (through paragraph 3-50).

Computing Net Income For Tax Purposes

☐ Read the text pages 67 (from paragraph 3-51) through 70 (through paragraph 3-67).

☐ Complete Exercises Three-9 through Three-11 on page 70 of the text. The solutions are on page S-16.

☐ Complete Self Study Problems Three-5 and Three-6 on pages 75 and 76 of the text. The solutions are on pages S-18 through S-20.

Principles Of Tax Planning

☐ Read the text pages 70 (from paragraph 3-68) through 72 (through paragraph 3-81).

☐ Complete Exercises Three-12 and Three-13 on pages 72 and 73 of the text. The solutions are on page S-16.

To Complete This Chapter

☐ Review the Key Terms Used In This Chapter on page 73 of the text. Consult the Glossary for the meaning of any key terms you do not know.

☐ Review the Glossary Flashcards and complete the Key Terms Self-Test for the Chapter. These features can be found in two places, on your Student CD-ROM under the heading "Key Term Practice" and on the web site.

☐ Review the Learning Objectives of the Chapter found on page S-21 of this Study Guide.

☐ As a review, we recommend that you view the PowerPoint Slides for Chapter Three that are on your Student CD-ROM. The PowerPoint Viewer program can be installed from the Student CD-ROM.

Solution to Chapter Three Exercises

Exercise Three - 1 Solution
By retaining his residence, he has maintained one of the primary residential ties. However, the fact that he was not able to sell the property, accompanied by the long-term lease to a third party, would probably be sufficient evidence that this is not a significant residential tie. The retention of his membership in the Ontario Institute Of Chartered Accountants would be viewed as a secondary residential tie. However, it is unlikely that this tie would be sufficient to cause Mr. Farr to be viewed as a Canadian resident.

Exercise Three - 2 Solution
Jane did, in fact, sever most of her residential ties with Canada. This would suggest that she would not be considered a Canadian resident during the 26 months that she worked in Florida. However, the fact that she returned frequently to visit her boyfriend might lead the CRA to assess her on the basis of being a Canadian resident during this period. However, it is not clear that such an assessment would be successful.

Exercise Three - 3 Solution
Mark would be taxed on his worldwide income for the part of the year that he was resident in Canada. This would be the period January 1 through June 15, the date that his wife and children fly to the U.S. June 15 would be latest of: the date that Mark leaves Canada (February 1), the date that Mark establishes U.S. residency (February 1), and the date that his wife and children depart Canada (June 15). It is unlikely that the fact that his house was not sold until a later date would influence his residence status.

Exercise Three - 4 Solution
Mr. Kirsh will be a part year resident and liable for Canadian taxes on his worldwide income, including any income on the U.S. bank accounts, for the period September 1 through December 31 of the current year.

Exercise Three - 5 Solution
While Ms. Blakey is the child of a Canadian High Commissioner, it appears that she is no longer a dependant of this individual. It would also appear that she has income in excess of the base for the basic personal tax credit for 2006 of $9,039. As a consequence, she would not be considered a deemed resident under ITA 250(1).

Exercise Three - 6 Solution
Roswell Ltd. would be considered to be a resident of Canada for tax purposes because the "mind and management" of the company appear to be located in Kemptville, Ontario.

Exercise Three - 7 Solution
As the Company was incorporated in Canada after April 26, 1965, it would be deemed to be a Canadian resident under ITA 250(4).

Exercise Three - 8 Solution
She is not correct. Under ITA 2(3) she would be subject to Canadian taxes on employment income earned in Canada.

Exercise Three - 9 Solution

His Net Income For Tax Purposes would be $38,000 ($42,000 + $24,000 - $13,000 - $15,000).

Exercise Three - 10 Solution

Her Net Income For Tax Purposes would be nil. She would have a non-capital loss carry over of $10,480 ($33,240 + $24,750 - $19,500 - $48,970).

Exercise Three - 11 Solution

Her Net Income For Tax Purposes would be $7,894 ($42,680 + Nil - $8,460 - $26,326). She would have an allowable capital loss carry over of $5,880 ($27,400 - $33,280).

Exercise Three - 12 Solution

Mr. Chung is involved in income splitting, tax deferral, and possibly tax avoidance. He is getting the deduction from taxable income now and his wife will be taxed on the income in the future. All RRSP contributions normally create a tax deferral. The contribution will be deductible and the earnings on the contribution will accumulate on a tax free basis. However, all of these amounts will be taxable when they are withdrawn from the plan. There may also be tax avoidance. This will happen if his spouse is taxed at a lower rate than is currently applicable to Mr. Chung when the funds become taxable to her.

Exercise Three - 13 Solution

As the dental plan is a benefit that can be received by Mr. Green without being taxed (private health care), tax avoidance is illustrated.

Solution to Self Study Problem Three - 1

A. Jane Smith would be deemed a Canadian resident because she is a dependent child of a Canadian ambassador [ITA 250(1)(f)].

B. Marvin Black would not be considered a resident of Canada as he does not live in Canada. However, he would be subject to Canadian taxation on the employment income earned in Canada [ITA 2(3)(a)]. Paragraph 21 of IT-221R3 makes it clear that time spent earning employment income in Canada does not count as sojourning in Canada.

C. John Leather would be considered a resident of Canada for the part of the year until September 12. As his presence in Canada during the first part of the year was not on a part time basis, he would not fall under the sojourning rules.

D. Members of the Canadian armed forces are deemed to be Canadian residents without regard to where they actually live. As Francine Donaire is exempt from French taxation due to her relationship to a deemed resident, she is a deemed resident of Canada [ITA 250(1)(g)].

E. More information would be required here. Robert would either be a part year resident of Canada or, alternatively, a non-resident earning employment income in Canada, depending on the nature of his stay in the country. If he, in fact, established residential ties in Canada, it is possible that he would be viewed as a resident during his short stay. The importance of this is that, under this interpretation of the facts, he would be subject to Canadian income tax on his worldwide income, not just his Canadian employment income.

F. The fact that Susan Allen is a Canadian citizen is irrelevant to the determination of residency. Since she appears to have no residential ties with Canada, she would not be considered a Canadian resident.

Solution to Self Study Problem Three - 2

A. As AMT Ltd. was incorporated prior to April 27, 1965, it is not automatically considered to be a resident of Canada under ITA 250(4)(a). However, based on the fact that the mind and management was in Canada subsequent to that date, it was a resident of Canada subsequent to April 26, 1965. As a consequence, it would still be deemed a Canadian resident under ITA 250(4)(c).

B. UIF Inc. was not incorporated in Canada and its mind and management are not currently within Canada. Therefore, UIF Inc. would not be considered a Canadian resident.

C. BDT Ltd. would be deemed a Canadian resident under ITA 250(4)(a). This is because it was incorporated in Canada subsequent to April 26, 1965.

D. While QRS Inc. was not incorporated in Canada, it would appear that its mind and management are located in Ontario. This would result in QRS Inc. being treated as a Canadian resident.

Solution to Self Study Problem Three - 3

A. Molly London would be considered a part year resident of Canada until October 31, the date of her departure. As her presence in Canada during the first part of the year was on a full time basis, she would not fall under the sojourning rules.

B. Daryl Bennett would not be considered a Canadian resident. He sojourned in Canada for less than 183 days. He would therefore not be considered a deemed resident by the sojourner rule. As his residential ties appear to be in the U.S., he would be a U.S. resident. His Canadian citizenship would not affect his residency status.

C. While Tweeks Inc. was not incorporated in Canada, it would appear that its mind and management are located in Quebec. This would result in Tweeks Inc. being treated as a Canadian resident.

D. Bordot Industries would be deemed a Canadian resident under ITA 250(4)(a). This is because it was incorporated in Canada subsequent to April 26, 1965.

Solution to Self Study Problem Three - 4

Mr. Aiken And Mr. Baker Assuming that their respective moves were permanent in nature, both Mr. Aiken and Mr. Baker would be treated as part year residents. This means that they would be considered residents of Canada only for that portion of the year that they were actually in Canada. As a result, they will be liable for Canadian taxes only for a part of the current year. Deductions and credits are determined in accordance with ITA 114 and ITA 118.91.

Mr. Chase While Mr. Chase was in Canada for the same number of days as the other individuals, the fact that he was present only on a temporary basis makes him subject to the sojourning rule. Under this rule [see ITA 250(1)(a)], he will be considered a resident for the full year if he sojourns in Canada for 183 days or more during any calendar year. As Mr. Chase was present for 192 days, he would be viewed as a Canadian resident throughout the year and would be subject to Canadian income taxes on his worldwide income. The Canada-U.S. tax agreement would have to be taken into consideration in this case.

Solution to Self Study Problem Three - 5

Case A   The Case A solution would be calculated as follows:

Income Under ITA 3(a):		
Employment Income	$34,000	
Income From Property	21,000	$55,000
Income Under ITA 3(b):		
Taxable Capital Gains	$42,000	
Allowable Capital Losses	(57,000)	Nil
Balance From ITA 3(a) and (b)		$55,000
Subdivision e Deductions		(5,500)
Balance From ITA 3(c)		$49,500
Deduction Under ITA 3(d):		
Business Loss		(36,000)
Net Income For Tax Purposes (Division B Income)		$13,500

Miss Bain would have a carry over of unused allowable capital losses in the amount of $15,000 ($57,000 - $42,000).

Case B   The Case B solution would be calculated as follows:

Income Under ITA 3(a):		
Employment Income	$18,500	
Income From Property	12,000	$30,500
Income Under ITA 3(b):		
Taxable Capital Gains	$ 9,000	
Allowable Capital Losses	(12,000)	Nil
Balance From ITA 3(a) and (b)		$30,500
Subdivision e Deductions		(10,500)
Balance From ITA 3(c)		$20,000
Deduction Under ITA 3(d):		
Business Loss		(28,200)
Net Income For Tax Purposes (Division B Income)		Nil

As Miss Bain's business loss exceeds the balance from ITA 3(c), her Net Income For Tax Purposes (Division B income) is nil. This means there would be a carry over of unused business losses in the amount of $8,200 ($28,200 - $20,000) and of unused allowable capital losses in the amount of $3,000 ($12,000 - $9,000).

Solution to Self Study Problem Three - 6

Case A   The Case A solution would be calculated as follows:

Income Under ITA 3(a):		
Employment Income	$45,000	
Income From Property	15,000	$60,000
Income Under ITA 3(b):		
Taxable Capital Gains	$25,000	
Allowable Capital Losses	(10,000)	15,000
Balance From ITA 3(a) And b)		$75,000
Subdivision e Deductions		(5,000)
Balance From ITA 3(c)		$70,000
Deduction Under ITA 3(d):		
Business Loss		(20,000)
Net Income For Tax Purposes (Division B Income)		$50,000

In this Case, there are no carry overs from the current year.

Case B   The Case B solution would be calculated as follows:

Income Under ITA 3(a):		
Employment Income	$17,000	
Income From Property	12,000	$29,000
Income Under ITA 3(b):		
Taxable Capital Gains	$22,000	
Allowable Capital Losses	(8,000)	14,000
Balance From ITA 3(a) And (b)		$43,000
Subdivision e Deductions		(6,000)
Balance From ITA 3(c)		$37,000
Deduction Under ITA 3(d):		
Business Loss		(42,000)
Net Income For Tax Purposes (Division B Income)		Nil

In this Case, Mr. Haynes' will have an unused business loss carry over from the current year of $5,000 ($42,000 - $37,000).

Case C The Case C solution would be calculated as follows:

Income Under ITA 3(a):		
Employment Income	$24,000	
Income From Property	47,000	$71,000
Income Under ITA 3(b):		
Taxable Capital Gains	$22,000	
Allowable Capital Losses	(73,000)	Nil
Balance From ITA 3(a) And (b)		$71,000
Subdivision e Deductions		(4,000)
Balance From ITA 3(c)		$67,000
Deduction Under ITA 3(d):		
Business Loss		(48,000)
Net Income For Tax Purposes (Division B Income)		$19,000

In this Case, Mr. Haynes will have a carry over from the current period of unused allowable capital losses in the amount of $51,000 $73,000 - $22,000).

Case D The Case D solution would be calculated as follows:

Income Under ITA 3(a):		
Employment Income	$18,000	
Income From Property	7,000	$25,000
Income Under ITA 3(b):		
Taxable Capital Gains	$13,000	
Allowable Capital Losses	(18,000)	Nil
Balance From ITA 3(a) And (b)		$25,000
Subdivision e Deductions		(12,000)
Balance From ITA 3(c)		$13,000
Deduction Under ITA 3(d):		
Business Loss		(20,000)
Net Income For Tax Purposes (Division B Income)		Nil

In this Case, Mr. Haynes has a carry over from the current year of unused business losses in the amount of $7,000 ($20,000 - $13,000) and of unused allowable capital losses in the amount of $5,000 ($18,000 - $13,000).

Chapter Three Learning Objectives

After completing Chapter 3, you should be able to:

1. Demonstrate a basic understanding of the charging provisions of the *Income Tax Act* (paragraphs 3-1 through 3-4).

2. Determine the residence of an individual based on an evaluation of primary and secondary residential ties (paragraphs 3-5 through 3-10).

3. Evaluate the residency status of an individual who is temporarily absent from Canada (paragraphs 3-11 through 3-14).

4. Explain the rules associated with the taxation of individuals in years in which they immigrate to Canada or emigrate from Canada (paragraphs 3-15 and 3-16).

5. Identify the types of individuals who will be deemed to be Canadian residents without regard to their actual physical location (paragraphs 3-17 through 3-23).

6. Determine the residence of corporations (paragraphs 3-24 through 3-27).

7. Determine the residence of trusts (paragraph 3-28).

8. List the three circumstances that will result in non-residents being subject to Canadian income taxes (paragraphs 3-29 through 3-34).

9. Describe, in general terms, the various views of income that are held by economists, accountants, and tax authorities (paragraphs 3-36 through 3-50).

10. Calculate Net Income For Tax Purposes by applying the rules found in Section 3 of the *Income Tax Act* (paragraphs 3-51 through 3-67).

11. Demonstrate a basic understanding of the concept of tax planning (paragraphs 3-68 through 3-70).

12. Explain and provide examples of tax avoidance or reduction (paragraphs 3-71 through 3-73).

13. Explain and provide examples of tax deferral (paragraphs 3-74 through 3-77).

14. Explain and provide examples of income splitting (paragraphs 3-78 through 3-81).

CHAPTER FOUR

How To Work Through Chapter Four

We recommend the following approach in dealing with the material in this chapter:

Introduction
☐   Read the text page 81 (paragraphs 4-0 through 4-3).

Transaction Tax Concepts
☐   Read the text pages 82 (from paragraph 4-4) through 85 (through paragraph 4-23).

☐   Complete Exercise Four-1 on page 85 of the text. The solution is on page S-25.

☐   Complete Self Study Problem Four-1 on page 105 of the text. The solution is on pages S-26 and S-27.

Commercial Activity
☐   Read the text page 86 (from paragraph 4-24 through paragraph 4-31).

Accounting And The GST
☐   Read the text page 87 (from paragraph 4-32 through 4-36).

Concept Of Supply
☐   Read the text pages 87 (from paragraph 4-37) through 89 (through paragraph 4-48).

Liability For GST
☐   Read the text pages 89 (from paragraph 4-49) and 90 (through paragraph 4-58).

Small Suppliers Exemption
☐   Read the text pages 91(from paragraph 4-59) and 92 (through paragraph 4-64).

☐   Complete Exercise Four-2 on page 92 of the text. The solution is on page S-25.

☐   Read the text page 92 (paragraph 4-65).

☐   Complete Self Study Problems Four-2 and Four-3 on pages 105 and 106 of the text. The solutions are on page S-27.

Input Tax Credits
☐   Read the text pages 92 (from paragraph 4-66) through 95 (through paragraph 4-79).

☐   Complete Exercises Four-3 through Four-5 on pages 95 and 96 of the text. The solutions are on page S-25.

☐   Complete Self Study Problem Four-4 on page 106 of the text. The solution is on page S-28.

Relief For Small Businesses
☐   Read the text pages 96 (from paragraph 4-80) through 98 (through paragraph 4-89).

☐   Complete Exercises Four-6 and Four-7 on page 98 of the text. The solutions are on page S-26.

Simplified Input Tax Credit Method

☐ Read the text pages 98 (from paragraph 4-90) and 99 (through paragraph 4-93).

☐ Complete Exercise Four-8 on page 99 of the text. The solution is on page S-26.

☐ Complete Self Study Problem Four-5 on pages 106 and 107 of the text. The solution is on page S-28.

Procedures And Administration

☐ Read the text pages 99 (from paragraph 4-94) through 103 (through paragraph 4-121).

Specific Applications

☐ Read the text page 103 (paragraphs 4-122 and 4-123).

Harmonized Sales Tax (HST)

☐ Read the text page 104 (from paragraphs 4-124 through 4-128).

To Complete This Chapter

☐ Review the Key Terms Used In This Chapter on page 104 of the text. Consult the Glossary for the meaning of any key terms you do not know.

☐ Review the Glossary Flashcards and complete the Key Terms Self-Test for the Chapter. These features can be found in two places, on your Student CD-ROM under the heading "Key Term Practice" and on the web site.

☐ Review the Learning Objectives of the Chapter found on page S-29 of this Study Guide.

☐ As a review, we recommend that you view the PowerPoint Slides for Chapter Four that are on your Student CD-ROM. The PowerPoint Viewer program can be installed from the Student CD-ROM.

Solution to Chapter Four Exercises

Exercise Four - 1 Solution
Under a VAT system, the 5 percent would be applied to the value added, resulting in a tax of $7,600 [(5%)($416,000 - $264,000)]. Alternatively, under a GST system, $20,800 [(5%)($416,000)] would be owing on sales, but would be offset by an input tax credit of $11,650 [(5%)($233,000)] on purchases. The net tax owing in this case would be $9,150. The fact that the tax is larger under the GST system reflects the fact that the cost of goods sold exceeded the purchases of goods by $31,000.

Exercise Four - 2 Solution
As Ms. Salome's sales exceed $30,000 in the third quarter, she will be required to begin collecting GST on the first sale in that quarter that exceeds the $30,000 threshold. This means she will have to begin collecting GST sometime between July 1 and September 30.

As Mr. Laughton's sales accumulate to more than $30,000 by the end of the second quarter, he will have to begin collecting GST on August 1, the first day of the second month of the third quarter.

Exercise Four - 3 Solution
The GST payable would be calculated as follows:

Sales [(6%)($1,223,000)]	$73,380
Input Tax Credits:	
Purchases [(6%)($843,000 + $126,000)]	(58,140)
Salaries, Interest, And Amortization	Nil
GST Payable For The Quarter	$15,240

Exercise Four - 4 Solution
The GST payable would be calculated as follows:

Sales [6%)($124,000)]	$7,440
Input Tax Credits:	
Rent [(6%)($25,800)]	(1,548)
Assistant's Salary	Nil
Capital Expenditures [(6%)($36,000 + $20,000)]	(3,360)
GST Payable For The Year	$2,532

Exercise Four - 5 Solution
The pro rata input tax credit for the land and building acquisition would be $28,800 [(6%)(40%)($1,200,000)]. There would be no input tax credit for the office equipment as it is used less than 50 percent for taxable supplies.

Exercise Four - 6 Solution

The total GST included sales for the quarter would be $45,050 [(106%)($42,500)]. The purchases made do not affect the Quick Method calculation since they are non-capital. The GST payable under the Quick Method would be calculated as follows:

First $30,000 (GST Inclusive) At 1.2%	$360
Remaining $15,050 ($45,050 - $30,000) At 2.2%	331
GST Payable For The Quarter	$691

Exercise Four - 7 Solution

If the Quick Method is not used, the GST payable (refund) would be calculated as follows:

Sales [(6%)($56,100)]	$3,366
Input Tax Credits:	
Current Costs [(6%)($23,400)]	(1,404)
Capital Expenditures [(6%)($42,000)]	(2,520)
GST Payable (Refund) For The Quarter	($ 558)

Alternatively, under the Quick Method, GST included sales would be $59,466 [(106%)($56,100)], and the calculation would be as follows:

First $30,000 (GST Inclusive) At 1.2%	$ 360
Remaining $29,466 ($59,466 - $30,000) At 2.2%	648
Subtotal	$1,008
Input Tax Credit - Capital Expenditures [(6%)($42,000)]	(2,520)
GST Payable (Refund) For The Quarter	($1,512)

As the Quick Method produces a larger refund, it would be the preferable method. Note that input tax credits on capital expenditures are available, even when the Quick Method is used.

Exercise Four - 8 Solution

Using the simplified method, the GST payable (refund) would be calculated as follows:

Sales [(6%)($318,000 ÷ 1.06)]	$18,000
Input Tax Credits On Purchases And Personal Capital Property	
[6/106][$190,800 + ($50,000)(106%)]	(13,800)
Input Tax Credits On Real Capital Property [(6%)($150,000)]	(9,000)
GST Payable (Refund) For The Year	($ 4,800)

Solution to Self Study Problem Four - 1

First, determine the selling price at each turnover.

Vendor	Cost	Value Added	Selling Price
Manufacturer	$100	$ 50	$150
Wholesaler	150	75	225
Distributor	225	113	338
Retailer	338	169	507

Under the normal GST system, a 6 percent tax is applied on the selling price at each stage and the business gets an input tax credit for the tax paid on purchased inputs. The net result is that all payments of GST by vendors are refunded as input tax credits, so there is no net out-of-pocket cost (other than administration) to vendors from the GST. The consumer bears the full cost of the tax by paying $30 [($507)(6%)] with no opportunity to get an input tax credit.

Turnover Tax Calculation

The turnover tax is similar to the GST, as it applies to revenue. However, the turnover tax is significantly different as there is no input tax credit for tax paid at each stage on purchased goods (inputs). The tax is passed on to the purchasers in the chain, resulting in pyramiding of the tax. Because of the multiple times goods get taxed, to raise the same amount of tax revenue, the turnover tax rate of 2.46 percent (as shown in the following calculation) is much lower than the 6 percent GST rate.

$$[(\$150)(X\%)] + [(\$225)(X\%)] + [(\$338)(X\%)] + [(\$507)(X\%)] = \$30$$
$$[(\$150 + \$225 + \$338 + \$507)(X\%)] = \$30$$
$$[(\$1,220)(X\%)] = \$30$$
$$X\% = \$30 \div \$1,220$$
$$X\% = 2.46\%$$

Solution to Self Study Problem Four - 2

Businesses are required to register for the GST if taxable revenues for the current calendar quarter or previous four quarters exceed $30,000. As revenues for the four quarters ending September 30, 2006 were under the $30,000 threshold, the business was not required to collect GST in the quarter ending December 31, or in the month of January, 2007.

However, the small supplier threshold was exceeded at the end of December, 2006, with revenues for the four quarters then ending totaling $36,500 ($29,000 - $4,000 + $11,500). Therefore, Chantelle Chance is required to start collecting GST on the first day of the second month following the quarter in which the $30,000 threshold is reached. This means that collections will begin on February 1, 2007. Application to register to collect GST, however, should be made within 30 days, or by March 2, 2007.

Solution to Self Study Problem Four - 3

The required GST remittance for Bombardeaux is based on Canadian GST included sales, and is calculated as follows:

First $30,000 at 3.3 Percent	$ 990
Remaining $44,200 ($74,200 - $30,000) At 4.3 Percent	1,901
Subtotal	$2,891
Input Tax Credit (GST Paid On Capital Expenditures) [(6%)($20,000)]	(1,200)
GST Remittance	$1,691

Solution to Self Study Problem Four - 4

The GST refund for Lassen Ltd. for the current year would be calculated as follows:

GST Collected [(6%)($5,700,000 - $1,200,000 - $2,400,000)]	$126,000	
Input Tax Credits:		
Purchases [(6%)($2,600,000 - $200,000)]		(144,000)
Depreciation And Amortization		Nil
Salaries And Wages		Nil
Other Operating Expenses [(6%)($370,000)]		(22,200)
Accrued Interest		Nil
Building [(6%)(40%)($3,000,000)]		(72,000)
Other Capital Expenditures		Nil
GST Payable (Refund)		($112,200)

Notes:

- The fact that purchases on which GST was paid ($2,400,000) exceed fully taxable sales ($2,100,000) could be the result of zero-rated sales. Some zero-rated supplies involve selling items on which GST is paid. An example of this would be export sales.

- There is no need to depreciate or amortize capital expenditures for GST purposes.

- No GST is paid on salaries or wages and, therefore, no input tax credits are available.

- Input tax credits on real property are available based on a pro rata portion of their usage in providing taxable supplies.

- No input tax credits are available on capital expenditures other than real property if less than 50 percent of their usage is in providing taxable and zero-rated supplies.

- Since no GST is paid on accrued interest, no input tax credits are available.

Solution to Self Study Problem Four - 5

For Part A and Part B, the GST refund for the year would be calculated as follows:

	Part A	Part B
GST Collected [(6%)($1,955,000)]	$117,300	$117,300
Input Tax Credits:		
Purchases [(6%)($1,356,000 - $212,000)]	(68,640)	(68,640)
Depreciation Expense	Nil	Nil
Salaries And Wages	Nil	Nil
Interest Expense	Nil	Nil
Other Operating Expenses [(6%)($162,000)]	(9,720)	(9,720)
Equipment [(6%)($725,000)]	(43,500)	Nil
Building [(6%)(($1,450,000)]	(87,000)	
[(6%)(73%)($1,450,000)]		(63,510)
GST Payable (Refund)	($ 91,560)	($ 24,570)

In Part A, input tax credits are available on both the equipment and the building because 100 percent of their usage is for taxable supplies (fully taxable and zero-rated).

In Part B, there is no input tax credit available on the equipment as it is used less than 50 percent to provide taxable supplies. The building's input tax credit is limited to 73 percent of the GST paid.

Chapter Four Learning Objectives

After completing Chapter 4, you should be able to:

1. Describe the different ways in which transaction taxes can be assessed (paragraphs 4-4 through 4-23).

2. Describe the meaning of commercial activity for GST purposes (paragraphs 4-24 through 4-31).

3. Describe the relationship between amounts determined for accounting purposes and amounts required for the filing of GST returns (paragraphs 4-32 through 4-36).

4. Outline the difference between fully taxable supplies, zero-rated supplies, and exempt supplies (paragraphs 4-37 through 4-45).

5. Identify a few examples of each type of supply (paragraphs 4-37 through 4-45).

6. Demonstrate an understanding of the concept of consideration for GST purposes (paragraphs 4-46 through 4-48).

7. Determine whether or not an entity is required to register for GST (paragraphs 4-49 through 4-65).

8. Apply the rules for calculating input tax credits on current expenditures (paragraphs 4-66 through 4-68).

9. Apply the rules for calculating input tax credits on real estate acquisitions (paragraphs 4-69 through 4-73).

10. Apply the rules for calculating input tax credits on acquisitions of capital property other than real estate (paragraphs 4-69 through 4-73).

11. Demonstrate an understanding of input tax credits as they relate to vendors of exempt and zero-rated supplies (paragraphs 4-74 through 4-79).

12. Apply the quick method of accounting for GST (paragraphs 4-81 through 4-89).

13. Apply the simplified method of accounting for input tax credits (paragraphs 4-90 through 4-93).

14. Outline the basic procedures and administration of the GST (paragraphs 4-94 through 4-121).

15. Briefly describe the listed specific applications of the GST (paragraphs 4-122 and 4-123).

16. Describe the general provisions of the harmonized sales tax (HST) that is applicable to some provinces (paragraphs 4-124 through 4-128).

CHAPTER FIVE

How To Work Through Chapter Five

We recommend the following approach in dealing with the material in this chapter:

General Rules And Bonus Arrangements
☐ Read the text pages 113 (from paragraph 5-1) and 114 (through paragraph 5-10).

☐ Complete Exercise Five-1 on page 114 of the text. The solution is on page S-34.

☐ Read the text page 115 (paragraphs 5-11 and 5-12).

Employee Versus Self-Employed
☐ Read the text pages 115 (from paragraph 5-13) through 118 (through paragraph 5-27).

[handwritten: test]

[handwritten: ① Control ② provider of tools ③ risk / profit]

Basic Inclusions
☐ Read the text pages 118 (from paragraph 5-28) through 121 (through paragraph 5-32).

☐ Complete Exercise Five-2 on page 121 of the text. The solution is on page S-34.

☐ Read the text page 121 (paragraph 5-33).

Tax Planning Considerations
☐ Read the text pages 121 (from paragraph 5-34) and 122 (through paragraph 5-38).

☐ Complete Exercise Five-3 on page 122 of the text. The solution is on page S-34.

☐ Read the text pages 122 and 123 (paragraph 5-39).

GST On Taxable Benefits *[handwritten: (incl)]*
☐ Read the text page 123 (paragraphs 5-40 and 5-41).

☐ Complete Exercise Five-4 on page 123 of the text. The solution is on page S-34.

Board And Lodging
☐ Read the text pages 123 (from paragraph 5-42) and 124 (through paragraph 5-44).

Employer Supplied Automobiles
☐ Read the text pages 124 (from paragraph 5-45) through 128 (through paragraph 5-73).

☐ Complete Exercise Five-5 on page 128 of the text. The solution is on page S-34.

☐ Read the text pages 128 (from paragraph 5-74) and 129 (through paragraph 5-79).

☐ Complete Exercise Five-6 on page 129 of the text. The solution is on page S-34.

☐ Read the text pages 129 and 130 (paragraph 5-80).

☐ Complete Self Study Problems Five-1 and Five-2 on pages 156 and 157 of the text. The solutions are on page S-38 through S-40.

Allowances
☐ Read the text pages 130 (from paragraph 5-81) through 132 (through paragraph 5-91).

☐ Complete Exercises Five-7 and Five-8 on page 132 of the text. The solutions are on page S-35.

☐   Read the text pages 132 (from paragraph 5-92) and 133 (through paragraph 5-95).

☐   Complete Exercise Five-9 on page 133 of the text. The solution is on page S-35.

Employee Insurance Benefits

☐   Read the text pages 133 (from paragraph 5-96) and 134 (through paragraph 5-101).

☐   Complete Exercise Five-10 on page 134 of the text. The solution is on page S-35.

☐   Read the text pages 134 (from paragraph 5-102) and 135 (through paragraph 5-104).

Loans To Employees

☐   Read the text pages 135 (from paragraph 5-105) and 136 (through paragraph 5-108).

☐   Complete Exercise Five-11 on page 136 of the text. The solution is on page S-35.

☐   Read the text pages 136 (from paragraph 5-109) through 138 (through paragraph 5-116).

☐   Complete Exercise Five-12 on page 138 of the text. The solution is on page S-36.

☐   Complete Self Study Problem Five-3 on page 157 of the text. The solution is on pages S-40 and S-41.

Stock Options - General Rules

☐   Read the text pages 138 (from paragraph 5-117) through 141 (through paragraph 5-132).

Stock Options - Public Companies

☐   Read the text pages 141 and 142 (paragraph 5-133).

☐   Complete Exercise Five-13 on page 142 of the text. The solution is on page S-36.

Stock Options - Canadian Controlled Private Corporations (CCPCs)

☐   Read the text pages 142 (from paragraph 5-134) and 143 (through paragraph 5-138).

☐   Complete Exercise Five-14 on page 143 of the text. The solution is on pages S-36 and S-37.

☐   Read the text page 143 (paragraph 5-139).

Stock Options - Deferral On Publicly Traded Shares

☐   Read the text pages 143 (from paragraph 5-140) through 145 (through paragraph 5-145).

☐   Complete Exercises Five-15 and Five-16 on page 145 of the text. The solutions are on page S-37.

☐   Read the text pages 145 and 146 (paragraph 5-146).

☐   Complete Exercise Five-17 on page 146 of the text. The solution is on page S-37.

☐   Complete Self Study Problem Five-4 on pages 157 and 158 of the text. The solution is on pages S-41 and S-42.

Other Inclusions

☐   Read the text pages 146 (from paragraph 5-147) and 147 (through paragraph 5-155).

Specific Deductions

☐   Read the text pages 147 (from paragraph 5-156) through 151 (through paragraph 5-171).

☐   Complete Exercise Five-18 on page 151 of the text. The solution is on page S-37.

☐   Read the text pages 151 (from paragraph 5-172) through 153 (through paragraph 5-180).

☐   Complete Self Study Problems Five-5 through Five-8 on pages 158 through 161 of the text. The solutions are on pages S-43 through S-47.

Employee And Partner GST Rebate

☐   Read the text pages 153 (from paragraph 5-181) and 154 (through paragraph 5-192).

To Complete This Chapter

☐   Review the Key Terms Used In This Chapter on page 155 of the text. Consult the Glossary for the meaning of any key terms you do not know.

☐   Review the Glossary Flashcards and complete the Key Terms Self-Test for the Chapter. These features can be found in two places, on your Student CD-ROM under the heading "Key Term Practice" and on the web site.

☐   Review the Learning Objectives of the Chapter found on page S-45 of this Study Guide.

☐   As a review, we recommend that you view the PowerPoint Slides for Chapter Five that are on your Student CD-ROM. The PowerPoint Viewer program can be installed from the Student CD-ROM.

Solution to Chapter Five Exercises

Exercise Five - 1 Solution
The bonus will be taxed in Mr. Neelson's hands in the year of receipt. This means that it will be included in his 2007 tax return. With respect to Neelson Inc., the bonus is not payable until more than 180 days after the September 30 fiscal year end. As a consequence, the Company will not be able to deduct the bonus in the year ending September 30, 2006. It will be deducted in the year ending September 30, 2007.

Exercise Five - 2 Solution
The tax consequences of the various items would be as follows:

- IT-470R indicates that such benefits would not be taxable to John.
- It could be argued that this is "general employment-related training" as described in T-470R. If the argument is successful, the payment would not be taxable to John. If unsuccessful, the $2,000 would be a taxable benefit.
- While IT-470R indicates that uniforms or special clothing is not a taxable benefit, it is unlikely that business clothing would fall into this category. The $8,500 would probably be included in John's income as a taxable benefit.
- The $450 gift could be received tax free.
- ITA 6(1)(a) indicates that such benefits are not taxable.

Exercise Five - 3 Solution
From Jill's point of view, the best alternative is probably the dental plan. Its value is significantly enhanced by the fact that it can be received without tax consequences. The annual vacation trip is clearly a taxable benefit. Since the birthday gift has a value in excess of $500, Jill would have a taxable benefit for the fair market value of the season's tickets.

Exercise Five - 4 Solution
Ms. Correli's taxable benefit would be $4,770, the $4,500 cost of the trip, plus the additional $270 in GST.

Exercise Five - 5 Solution
The basic standby charge would be $6,900 [(2%)($28,750)(12)]. As her employment related driving is more than 50 percent of the total (16,000 out of 28,000), she can use the reduced standby charge calculation. Since her personal kilometers driven total 12,000 (28,000 - 16,000), the reduced amount would be $4,139 [(12,000 ÷ 20,004)($6,900)].

The operating cost benefit could be calculated as $2,640 [($0.22)(12,000)]. However, as her employment related use is greater than 50 percent, Mrs. Lee can use the alternative operating cost benefit calculation based on one-half the standby charge. This would produce a value of $2,070 [(1/2)($4,139)] and a minimum total benefit of $6,209 ($4,139 + $2,070).

Exercise Five - 6 Solution
The basic standby charge would be $4,389 [(2/3)($7,182)(11/12)]. The 11 is 325/30 rounded to the nearest whole number and represents the months available for use. As his employment related driving exceeds 50 percent of the total, this standby charge can be reduced. The reduced amount would be $718 [($4,389)(3,000/18,337)]. The 18,337 is based on multiplying 1,667 kilometers per month by the 11 months the car is available.

Mr. Forthwith's operating cost benefit could be calculated as $660 [($0.22)(3,000)], resulting in a total taxable benefit of $1,378 ($718 + $660). However, as his employment related use is greater than 50 percent, Mr. Forthwith can use the alternative operating cost benefit calculation based on one-half the standby charge. This gives an operating cost benefit of $359 [(1/2)($718)] and a minimum total benefit of $1,077 ($718 + $359).

Exercise Five - 7 Solution

She will have to include the $3,600 allowance that was received from her employer. She can deduct the employment related portion of her actual automobile costs against this amount. This would be $1,936 [($7,150)(6,500/24,000)]. The net inclusion would be $1,664 ($3,600 - $1,936).

Exercise Five - 8 Solution

As the milage allowance paid by the employer was based on the number of employment related kilometers driven, the $3,500 [(35,000 Km.)($0.10)] will not be included on his T4 Information Return and, as a consequence, it does not have to be included in his employment income. However, he will not be able to deduct his actual costs of owning and operating the automobile.

In this example, Mr. Lorenz's actual cost would be $11,900 [($5,400 + $15,000)(35,000/60,000)], well in excess of the allowance of $3,500. While Mr. Lorenz could attempt to include the allowance in income and deduct the actual costs, this approach is likely to be disallowed by the CRA.

Exercise Five - 9 Solution

The hotel allowance would appear to be reasonable and would not be included in Ms. Ohm's T4. Given this, it will not be included in her net employment income. Even though her actual costs of $18,300 are in excess of the $16,400 allowance, it would be difficult for Ms. Ohm to argue that the $200 figure is not reasonable. Given this, she does not have the choice of including the $16,400 in income and deducting the actual amount of $18,300.

As the milage charge is based on kilometers, it will not be included in her T4. In addition, since the amount appears to be reasonable in terms of actual costs, she does not have the choice of including it in income and deducting the actual costs. In fact, it would not be to Ms. Ohm's advantage to do so as her actual costs would be $2,880 [($7,200)(9,400/23,500)], which is less than the $3,666 reimbursement she received.

No amounts would be included in Ms. Ohm's net employment income and no amounts would be deductible.

Exercise Five - 10 Solution

As his employer contributes to the plan, the $5,250 in benefits received during the year will be included in his employment income. This can be offset by the $600 in non-deductible contributions that he made during 2005 and 2006, leaving a net inclusion of $4,650.

Exercise Five - 11 Solution

Whether or not the loan qualified as a home relocation loan would make no difference in the calculation of Mrs. Caldwell's taxable benefit. The only difference would be the availability of a deduction from Taxable Income in the case of the home relocation loan.

The ITA 80.4(1) benefit would be $3,750 [($100,000)(4%)(1/4) + ($100,000)(5%)(1/4) + ($100,000)(3%)(2/4)]. As this is a home purchase loan, the annual benefit cannot exceed the benefit that would result from applying the 4 percent rate that was in effect when the loan was made. This benefit would be $4,000 [($100,000)(4%)]. Note that the 4 percent rate is not compared to the prescribed rate on a quarter-by-quarter basis, but on an annual basis. The lower figure of $3,750 would then be reduced by the $2,000 in interest paid [($100,000)(2%)], resulting in a net benefit of $1,750.

Exercise Five - 12 Solution

In the absence of the interest free loan, the employee would borrow $125,000 at 6 percent, requiring an annual interest payment of $7,500. The after tax cash outflow associated with the employer providing sufficient additional salary to carry this loan would be calculated as follows:

Required Salary [$7,500 ÷ (1.00 - .42)]	$12,931
Reduction In Corporate Taxes At 35 Percent	(4,526)
After Tax Cash Flow - Additional Salary	$ 8,405

Alternatively, if the loan is provided, the employee will have a taxable benefit of $2,500 [(2%)($125,000)], resulting in taxes payable of $1,050 [(42%)($2,500)]. To make this situation comparable to the straight salary alternative, the employer will have to provide the employee with both the loan amount and sufficient additional salary to pay the taxes on the imputed interest benefit. The amount of this additional salary would be $1,810 [$1,050 ÷ (1.00 - .42)]. The employer's after tax cash flow associated with providing the additional salary and the loan amount would be calculated as follows:

Required Salary [$1,050 ÷ (1.00 - .42)]	$1,810
Reduction In Corporate Taxes At 35 Percent	(634)
After Tax Cost Of Salary	$1,176
Employer's Lost Earnings [(7%)(1.00 - .35)($125,000)]	5,688
After Tax Cash Flow - Loan	$6,864

Given these results, providing the loan appears to be the better alternative.

Exercise Five - 13 Solution

At time of exercise, he will have an employment income benefit of $21,250 [($31.50 - $23.00)(2,500 Shares)]. As he sells the shares prior to the end of the year, deferral of the employment income is not possible. As the option price at issue exceeded the fair market value at issue, Mr. Guise will be able to deduct $10,625 [(1/2)($21,250)] in the determination of Taxable Income. These results are summarized in the following table:

Employment Income Inclusion [($31.50 - $23.00)(2,500)]	
= Increase In Net Income For Tax Purposes	$21,250
ITA 110(1)(d) Deduction [(1/2)($21,250)]	(10,625)
Increase In Taxable Income	$10,625

In addition, there will be an allowable capital loss of $4,375 [($31.50 - $28.00)(2,500 Shares)(1/2)]. Mr. Guise will only be able to deduct this loss in 2006 to the extent that he has taxable capital gains on other dispositions. It cannot be deducted against the employment income inclusion.

Exercise Five - 14 Solution

At the time the shares are sold, there will be an employment income benefit of $58,500 [($75.00 - $42.50)(1,800 Shares)]. As the option price of $42.50 was below the fair market value of $45 at the time the options were issued, there is no deduction under ITA 110(1)(d). Although she might have been eligible for the deduction under ITA 110(1)(d.1), she did not hold the shares for the required two years. These results are summarized in the following table:

Employment Income Inclusion [(($75.00 - $42.50)(1,800)]	
= Increase In Net Income For Tax Purposes	$58,500
ITA 110(1)(d) Deduction	N/A
ITA 110(1)(d.1) Deduction	N/A
Increase In Taxable Income	$58,500

When she sells the shares, she will have an allowable capital loss of $23,400 [($49.00 - $75.00)(1,800 Shares)(1/2)]. Ms. Van will only be able to deduct this loss in 2006 to the extent that she has taxable capital gains on other dispositions. It cannot be deducted against the employment income inclusion.

Exercise Five - 15 Solution

The specified value of the shares involved with these options is $20,000 [(1,000)($20)]. As this is well below the $100,000 annual limit specified under ITA 7(8), she can defer all of the $22,000 [(1,000)($45 - $23)] employment benefit that is measured at the time of exercise. This means that the 2006 Net Income For Tax Purposes and Taxable Income inclusion will be nil.

As the shares are sold in 2007, the $22,000 employment income benefit will be recognized in that year, increasing Net Income For Tax Purposes by $22,000. There will also be a 2007 deduction of $11,000 [(1/2)($22,000)] under ITA 110(1)(d) in the calculation of Taxable Income. The 2007 net effect on Taxable Income is $11,000 ($22,000 - $11,000). She will also have a 2007 allowable capital loss of $1,500 [(1,000)($42 - $45)(1/2)]. Ms. Masterson will only be able to deduct this loss in 2007 to the extent that she has taxable capital gains on other dispositions. It cannot be deducted against the employment income inclusion.

Exercise Five - 16 Solution

The Net Income For Tax Purposes and Taxable Income amounts for 2006 and 2007 would be identical to those in Exercise Five-15. The only difference is that no election is required to defer the 2006 employment income inclusion.

Exercise Five - 17 Solution

The specified value of the shares that vested in 2006 is $120,000 [(10,000)($12)]. This means that the ITA 7(8) election can only be made on 8,333 of the shares [(10,000 Shares)($100,000 ÷ $120,000)]. This results in a deferral of $166,660 [(8,333)($32 - $12)] and an income inclusion of $33,340 [(10,000 - 8,333)($32 - $12)].

The specified value of the shares that vested in 2007 is $180,000 [(15,000)($12)]. As was the case in 2006, the ITA 7(8) election can only be made on 8,333 of the shares [(15,000 Shares)($100,000 ÷ $180,000)], resulting in a deferral of $166,660 [(8,333)($32 - $12)] and an income inclusion of $133,340 [(15,000 - 8,333)($32 - $12)]. This information will be reflected in Mr. Traverse's 2008 T4 as a special item of deferred income of $333,320 ($166,660 + $166,660) and an employment income inclusion of $166,680 ($33,340 + $133,340). These two amounts total $500,000 ($333,320 + $166,680), the current and deferred employment income created by exercising the options [(25,000)($32 - $12)].

Exercise Five - 18 Solution

The potential deduction is $27,100 [$8,000 + (1/2)($12,000) + $13,100]. However, this total exceeds his commission income and cannot be deducted under ITA 8(1)(f). If he deducts under ITA 8(1)(h), there is no limit on the total. However, he cannot deduct the advertising or the entertainment. As the travel costs that are deductible under ITA 8(1)(h) exceed the $12,200 limited deduction under ITA 8(1)(f), his maximum deduction is the $13,100 in travel costs that can be deducted under ITA 8(1)(h).

Solution to Self Study Problem Five - 1

Acura TL   The taxable benefit on this vehicle would be calculated as follows:

Standby Charge [(2%)(5)($39,000 + $2,730 + $2,340)(3,400 ÷ 8,335)]	$1,798
Operating Cost Benefit - Lesser Of:	
• [(3,400)($0.22)] = $748	
• [(1/2)($1,798)] = $899	748
Total Benefit On Acura TL	$2,546

With employment related usage at more than 50 percent of the total, Ms. Vines is eligible for the reduced standby charge calculation. Ms. Vines could have calculated the operating cost benefit as one-half of the standby charge, or $899, as employment related usage was more than 50 percent of total usage. The use of the alternative $0.22 per kilometer results in a lower operating cost benefit.

Ford Crown Victoria   The taxable benefit on this vehicle is calculated as follows:

Standby Charge [(2/3)(6)($699 - $100)]	$2,396
Operating Cost Benefit - Lesser Of:	
• [(14,600)($0.22)] = $3,212	
• [(1/2)($2,396)] = $1,198	1,198
Total Benefit On Ford Crown Victoria	$3,594

As the car was driven more than 50 percent for employment related purposes, a reduction in the standby charge is available. However, her total personal use kilometers exceed 10,002 [(6)(1,667)] and as a result the reduction is nil [($2,396)(10,002/10,002)]. The $100 insurance included in the monthly lease payment is removed from the standby charge calculation as it is an operating cost.

As the car was driven more than 50 percent for employment related purposes, Ms. Vines can calculate the operating cost benefit as either one-half of the standby charge or $0.22 per kilometer of personal use. As the $0.22 per kilometer calculation results in a benefit of $3,212, the one-half standby charge approach is preferable. To use this approach, Ms. Vines must notify her employer before the end of the year.

Total Benefit   The total taxable benefit would be calculated as follows:

Total Benefit - Acura	$2,546
Total Benefit - Ford	3,594
Reimbursement To Company [($0.10)(3,400 Km + 14,600 Km)]	(1,800)
Total Taxable Benefit	$4,340

Notes:

- The taxable benefit calculation is not influenced by restrictions on the amount that the Company can deduct with respect to the Acura.

- Calculation of the operating cost benefits is not influenced by the employer's actual operating costs.

Solution to Self Study Problem Five - 2

Mr. Sam Stern The taxable benefit for the president of the Company would be calculated as follows:

Standby Charge [(2%)(8)($78,000)]	$12,480
Operating Cost Benefit [(32,000)($0.22)]	7,040
Taxable Benefit	$19,520

As Mr. Stern did not drive the car more than 50 percent for employment related purposes, no reduction in the standby charge is available. Since his employment related use was not more than 50 percent, he cannot use the alternative calculation of the operating cost benefit.

Ms. Sarah Blue The taxable benefit for the marketing vice president would be calculated as follows:

Standby Charge [(2/3)(12)($900)(5,000/20,004)]	$1,800
Operating Cost Benefit - Lesser Of:	
• [(5,000)($0.22)] = $1,100	
• [(1/2)($1,800)] = $900	900
Taxable Benefit	$2,700

As employment related driving was more than 50 percent, Ms. Blue can reduce the standby charge on the basis of actual personal usage.

Mr. John Stack The taxable benefit for the finance vice president would be calculated as follows:

Standby Charge [(2%)(12)($48,000)(10,000/20,004]	$5,759
Operating Cost Benefit - Lesser Of:	
• [(10,000)($0.22)] = $2,200	
•](1/2)($5,759)] = $2,880	2,200
Payment For Use Of Company Car	(7,000)
Taxable Benefit	$ 959

Mr. Stack's employment related driving was more than 50 percent of the total and, as a consequence, he can reduce his standby charge on the basis of actual personal milage.

Mr. Alex Decker The taxable benefit for the industrial relations vice president would be calculated as follows:

Standby Charge [(2/3)(10)($500)(8,500/16,670)]	$1,700
Operating Cost Benefit - Lesser Of:	
• [(8,500)($0.22)] = $1,870	
• [(1/2)($1,700)] = $850	850
Taxable Benefit	$2,550

As Mr. Decker's employment related driving is more than 50 percent of the total, he can reduce his standby charge on the basis of actual personal milage. While the $10,000 deposit will affect the deductibility of the lease payments by the employer, it does not influence the calculation of the taxable benefit to Mr. Decker.

Tax Planning   With respect to the tax planning of management compensation, two points can be made. First, the question of providing company cars as a method of compensation should be examined on a case-by-case basis. In situations where a car is owned by the Company and provided to an executive for a fairly long period of time, the taxable benefit assessed may exceed the value of the benefit. For example, over five years, the taxable benefit without regard for operating costs on Mr. Stern's Mercedes could total $93,600 [(2%)(60)($78,000)]. This is more than $15,000 in excess of the cost of the car. With the limitations on the deductibility of CCA and leasing costs on cars, the after tax cost to the Company of owning and leasing luxury cars can be very high. While a complete analysis of this issue will depend on a number of variables, it is possible that some of these executives would be better off receiving additional amounts of salary and billing the Company for employment related mileage driven in their own cars.

The second point to be made here is that, except in situations where the car is kept for very short periods of time, the employee will be allocated a smaller taxable benefit if the Company were to lease the car rather than buy it. In general, monthly lease payments on a three year lease will tend to be between 2 percent and 2.5 percent of the capital cost of the car. As the leasing standby charge is based on two-thirds of the monthly lease payment, it is clear that the standby charge under this type of arrangement will be less than the 2 percent per month that is assessed when the Company owns the car. However, for shorter lease terms, the lease payment will be a greater percentage of the capital cost and this relationship may reverse.

Other tax planning techniques would involve any procedure that would reduce the capital cost of purchased cars or the lease payments on leased cars. Such procedures would include high residual values on leasing arrangements and low trade in values assigned to old cars when new ones are purchased. In addition, it might be possible to reduce a taxable benefit, such as the one being allocated to Mr. Stern, by selling his car to a leasing company with an immediate leaseback arrangement. Although large refundable deposits on leasing arrangements would reduce the lease payment and therefore the standby charge, there would be a tax cost to the employer (see Chapter 8).

Solution to Self Study Problem Five - 3

Approach   The appropriate comparison in evaluating the interest free loan arrangement would be to determine the cost to the Company of providing the loan and then compare this amount with the cost of providing an equivalent benefit in the form of straight salary.

Cost Of Providing Interest Payments On Mortgage   As the problem indicates, Mr. Malone can borrow on a regular mortgage at a rate of interest of 5 percent. This means that the annual interest payments on $200,000 would amount to $10,000. However, Mr. Malone is in the 45 percent tax bracket and, as a consequence, $18,182 ($10,000 ÷ .55) of before tax salary would be required to provide the necessary $10,000 in after tax funds. The annual cost to the Company of this alternative would be as follows:

Gross Salary Increase	$18,182
Reduction In Corporate Taxes (At 40 Percent)	(7,273)
Net Cost To Company	$10,909

Cost Of Providing Interest Free Loan   Mr. Malone would be assessed a taxable benefit on the loan in the amount of imputed interest at the Regulation 4301 rate. The benefit would amount to $6,000 [(3%)($200,000)] for one year. In order to make the two alternatives comparable, it is necessary to recognize that Mr. Malone would pay an additional $2,700 [(45%)($6,000)] in taxes on this benefit and, as a consequence, the Company would have to pay him an additional $4,909 ($2,700 ÷ .55) in salary to provide for this outflow of funds.

Given this, the annual cost to the Company of the loan alternative can be calculated as follows:

Gross Salary Increase	$ 4,909
Reduction In Corporate Taxes (At 40 Percent)	(1,964)
Lost Earnings On Funds Loaned (At 18 Percent)	36,000
Corporate Taxes On Imputed Earnings (At 40 Percent)	(14,400)
Net Cost To Company	$24,545

Conclusion On the basis of the preceding analysis, it can be concluded that the Company should provide an additional $18,182 in salary rather than providing Mr. Malone with an interest free loan of $200,000. This alternative results in a net annual cost to the Company which is $13,636 lower.

Alternative Calculation An alternative solution to the question involves calculating the cost to the Company using the value of the interest free loan to Mr. Malone. The annual cost of the mortgage to Mr. Malone is $10,000 [(5%)($200,000)] and the cost of the taxable benefit on the interest free loan is $2,700 [(45%)(3%)(200,000)]. This means the value of the interest free loan to Mr. Malone is $7,300 ($10,000 - $2,700). He would require $13,273 [$7,300 ÷ (1 - .45)] in before tax salary to make up this difference. To the Company, the after tax cost of the additional $13,273 is $7,964 [($13,273)(1 - .4)]. The cost of the interest free loan to the Company, after taxes, is $21,600 [(18%)($200,000)(1 - .4)]. The difference in cost is $13,636 ($21,600 - $7,964) in favour of the increased salary. This is the same result that we arrived at under the first calculation.

Solution to Self Study Problem Five - 4

Case A In 2005, the year in which the options are issued, there would be no tax consequences for Ms. Wu. The tax consequences in 2006 would be as follows:

Fair Market Value At Exercise [(12,000)($31)]	$372,000
Cost Of Shares [(12,000)($22)]	(264,000)
Employment Income Inclusion	
= Increase In Net Income For Tax Purposes	$108,000
Deduction Under ITA 110(1)(d) [(1/2($108,000)]	(54,000)
Increase In Taxable Income	$ 54,000

As Ms. Wu is a specified shareholder, none of this amount can be deferred until the shares are sold.

When the shares are sold in 2007, the tax consequences would be as follows:

Proceeds Of Disposition [(12,000)($28)]	$336,000
Adjusted Cost Base [(12,000)($31)]	(372,000)
Capital Loss	($ 36,000)
Inclusion Rate	1/2
Allowable Capital Loss	($ 18,000)

Ms. Wu will only be able to deduct this loss in 2007 to the extent that she has taxable capital gains on other dispositions. It cannot be deducted against the employment income inclusion.

Case B   In this Case, we have a public company. However, the results are different than in Case A as we are assuming that Ms. Wu is not a specified shareholder. This means that a portion of the gain at the time of exercise can be deferred until the shares are sold. This is limited to the first $100,000 of fair market value of shares at the time the options are granted. As the fair market value of the shares at the time the options are granted is $20 per share, this applies to the gain on 5,000 of the 12,000 shares acquired by Ms. Wu.

As in the previous Case, there would be no tax consequence associated with the issuance of the options in 2005. The 2006 tax consequences would be calculated as follows:

Fair Market Value At Exercise [(12,000)($31)]	$372,000
Cost Of Shares [(12,000)($22)]	(264,000)
Employment Income	$108,000
Available Deferral [(5,000/12,000)($108,000)]	(45,000)
Increase In Net Income For Tax Purposes	$ 63,000
Deduction Under ITA 110(1)(d) [(1/2($63,000)]	(31,500)
Increase In Taxable Income	$ 31,500

When the shares are sold in 2007, the tax consequences would be as follows:

Deferred Employment Income	
= Increase In Net Income For Tax Purposes	$45,000
Deduction Under ITA 110(1)(d) [(1/2)($45,000)]	(22,500)
Increase in Taxable Income	$22,500
Proceeds Of Disposition [(12,000)($28)]	$336,000
Adjusted Cost Base [(12,000)($31)]	(372,000)
Capital Loss	($ 36,000)
Inclusion Rate	1/2
Allowable Capital Loss	($ 18,000)

Ms. Wu will only be able to deduct this loss in 2007 to the extent that she has taxable capital gains on other dispositions. It cannot be deducted against the employment income inclusion.

Case C   In this Case, because Imports Ltd. is a Canadian controlled private corporation, there are no consequences either in 2005, when the options are issued, or in 2006, when they are exercised. When the shares are sold in 2007, there would be an increase in Taxable Income of $54,000 and an allowable capital loss of $18,000. The calculation of these amounts is as in Case A.

Note that in all three Cases, the increase in Taxable Income due to the stock options for 2006 and 2007 totals $54,000.

Solution to Self Study Problem Five - 5

Salary From Maritime Trust [(6/12)($65,000)]		$32,500
Salary From Bolten [(6/12)($50,000)]		25,000
Total Salaries		$57,500
Maritime Trust Stock Options: (Note 1)		
Market Price Of Shares [(5,000)($16)]	$80,000	
Option Price [(5,000)($15)]	(75,000)	5,000
Bolton Financial Services Stock Options (Note 2)		Nil
Taxable Benefit - Car:		
Standby Charge [(2%)(4)($25,000)(6,668/6,668)]	$2,000	
Operating Cost Benefit - Lesser Of:		
• [(10,000)($0.22)] = $2,200		
• [(1/2)($2,000)] = $1,000	1,000	3,000
Taxable Benefit - Loan [(3%)($200,000)(6/12)]		3,000
Net Employment Income		$68,500

Notes:

1. Although there is an election to defer the employment income inclusion on the exercise of publicly traded company stock until the acquired shares are sold, Mr. Jurgens did not make this election.

2. As Bolten Financial Services is a Canadian controlled private corporation, the exercise of the options to purchase its common stock does not result in a taxable benefit at the time of exercise. When the shares are sold, he will have to include the difference between the option price and the fair market value at the time of exercise in employment income.

3. As Mr. Jurgens' employment related milage is more than 50 percent of the total milage, he can make use of the reduced standby charge formula. In this case, however, his personal usage exceeded the 6,668 [(4)(1,667)] kilometer maximum usage allowed by the reduction, so the reduction is nil. His employment related milage is more than 50 percent of the total and, as a consequence, he can elect to calculate the operating cost benefit as 50 percent of the standby charge. Since this amount of $1,000 [(50%)($2,000)] is less than the $2,200 [(10,000)($0.22)] determined through the usual calculation, the $1,000 would be the operating cost benefit.

4. The imputed interest on the interest free loan must be included in employment income under the requirements of ITA 6(9), a benefit which is defined in ITA 80.4(1). Note, however, there is a deduction under ITA 110(1)(j) for the amount of this benefit which relates to an interest free home relocation loan of $25,000. However, this is a deduction in the calculation of Taxable Income and will not affect the amount of net employment income.

5. The interest and dividend income is not included in the calculation of net employment income.

Solution to Self Study Problem Five - 6

Mr. Barth's net employment income for the year would be calculated as follows:

Gross Salary	$ 82,500
Bonus (Note One)	20,000
Registered Pension Plan Contributions	(3,200)
Professional Dues	(1,800)
Stock Option Benefit (Note Two)	3,000
Automobile Benefit (Note Three)	3,220
Counseling Benefit (Note Four)	1,500
Imputed Interest Benefit (Note Five)	750
Net Employment Income	$105,970

Note One   As the bonus is not payable until more than three years after the end of the employer's taxation year, it is a salary deferral arrangement and must be included in income under ITA 6(11).

Note Two   As Mr. Barth's employer is a public company, the employment income inclusion for stock options would normally occur when the options were exercised in 2005. This amount would have been $3,000 [($18 - $15)(1,000)]. However, the specified value of the securities is $12,000 [(1,000)($12)], well below the $100,000 limit on amounts that can be deferred. As a consequence, the $3,000 income inclusion can be deferred until the shares are sold. As the shares are sold in 2006, the $3,000 must be taken into net employment income in that year. We would also note that Mr. Barth is eligible for the ITA 110(1)(d) deduction of one-half the stock option benefit. However, it is a deduction in the calculation of Taxable Income and will not affect the amount of net employment income.

Note Three   Since Mr. Barth's employment related usage is not more than 50 percent, there is no reduction of the full standby charge. The automobile benefit is calculated as follows:

Standby Charge [(2%)(10)($27,500)]	$5,500
Operating Cost Benefit [(6,000)($0.22)]	1,320
Total Before Payments	$6,820
Payments Withheld	(3,600)
Taxable Benefit	$3,220

Note Four   IT-470R indicates that counseling services, with the exception of those items specified under ITA 6(1), are considered taxable benefits. The items specified under ITA 6(1) are counseling with respect to mental or physical health or with respect to re-employment or retirement. As a consequence, the counseling on personal finances is a taxable benefit.

Note Five   The imputed interest benefit is calculated as follows:

Basic Benefit [($150,000)(3%)(3/12)]	$1,125
Interest Paid	(375)
Taxable Benefit	$ 750

Note Six   Other items and the reasons for their exclusion would be as follows:

- Any income tax withheld is not deductible.
- CPP contributions, EI premiums, and United Way donations create a credit against

taxes payable, but are not deductible in the determination of employment income.
• The payments for personal use of the company car are used in the calculation of the taxable benefit associated with this automobile.

Solution to Self Study Problem Five - 7

Ms. Firth's net employment income for the year would be calculated as follows:

Gross Salary	$ 72,000
Commission Income	14,000
Registered Pension Plan Contributions (Note One)	(3,200)
Disability Insurance Receipts, Less Employee's Premium ($2,000 - $250)	1,750
Automobile Benefit (Note Two)	9,671
Automobile Expenses (Note Two)	(5,728)
Term Life Insurance Benefit [($1,350)(2/3)]	900
Low Interest Loan Benefit [($400,000)(3%) - $3,000]	9,000
Christmas Gift (Note Three)	Nil
Stock Option Benefit [(1,000)($7 - $5)] (Note Four)	2,000
Entertainment Expenses [(50%)($6,500)]	(3,250)
Travel Meals [(50%)($1,300)]	(650)
Lodging	(3,500)
Travel Allowance	3,600
Net Employment Income	$96,593

Note One   Contributions made to a registered pension plan under the terms of the plan are deductible.   The matching contributions made by the employer are not a taxable benefit.

Note Two   The personal benefit on the company car, taking into consideration the month she was in the hospital and unable to make use of the car, would be calculated as follows:

Reduced Standby Charge [(2%)(11)($58,000)(7,000/18,337)]	$ 4,871
Car Allowance	7,200
Operating Costs Benefit	Nil
Total Benefit	$12,071
Less: Payments Withheld By Employer	(2,400)
Taxable Benefit	$ 9,671

The deductible car expenses would be $5,728 [($6,200)(85,000 km/92,000 km)].

Note Three   The December 15, 2001 CRA News Release titled "Gifts And Awards Given By Employers To Their Employees" describes the policy that allows employers to give their employees up to two non-cash gifts per year on a tax free basis, for a variety of special occasions. As the cost of the Christmas gift, including taxes, is less than $500 and the gift is non-cash, it is not a taxable benefit.

Note Four   Although Ms. Firth would qualify for the deduction of one-half of the stock option benefit under ITA 110(1)(d), it is a deduction from Taxable Income and would not affect the calculation of net employment income.

Excluded Items   Other items not included and the reason for their exclusion:

- Federal and provincial income taxes withheld are not deductible.

- The purchase of Canada Savings Bonds is a non-deductible capital expenditure. Any interest charged on the payroll deduction purchase is deductible from Net Income For Tax Purposes, but does not affect employment income.

- The $2,500 membership to the Mountain Tennis Club paid by the Company for Ms. Firth is not a taxable benefit since the primary beneficiary appears to be the Company.

Solution to Self Study Problem Five - 8

Part A As Mr. Worthy's income includes commissions, he has a choice of deducting his expenses under a combination of ITA 8(1)(f), (i), and (j) or, alternatively under a combination of ITA 8(1)(h), (h.1), (i), and (j).

Deductions under ITA 8(1)(f) are limited to the amount of commissions earned. Alternatively, traveling costs and motor vehicle costs other than capital costs can be deducted under ITA 8(1)(h) and ITA 8(1)(h.1). Deductions under these provisions are not limited to commission income. As discussed in the text, he cannot use both ITA 8(1)(f) and the combination of ITA 8(1)(h) and (h.1).

As the deduction under ITA 8(1)(f) is limited by commission income, alternative calculations are required to determine the maximum deduction. These calculations are as follows:

	ITA 8(1)(f)	ITA 8(1) (h) and (h.1)	ITA 8(1) (i) and (j)
Supplies			
Monthly Charge For Residential Line	Nil	Nil	Nil
Long Distance Telephone Charges	Nil	Nil	$ 400
Cellular Phone Airtime	Nil	Nil	800
Office Supplies	Nil	Nil	295
Entertainment			
Deductible Portion [(50%)($2,550)]	$1,275	Nil	Nil
Travel Costs			
Hotels	2,850	$2,850	Nil
Deductible Portion Of Meals			
[(50%)($900)]	450	450	Nil
Automobile Costs:			
Operating Costs [(80%)($2,700)]	2,160	2,160	Nil
Car Interest [(80%)($2,300)]	Nil	Nil	1,840
Car CCA [(80%)($2,450)]	Nil	Nil	1,960
Home Office Costs:			
House Utilities	Nil	Nil	485
House Maintenance	Nil	Nil	255
House Insurance	70	Nil	Nil
Property Taxes	265	Nil	Nil
Capital Cost Allowance - House	Nil	Nil	Nil
Mortgage Interest	Nil	Nil	Nil
Office Furniture			
Interest	Nil	Nil	Nil
Capital Cost Allowance	Nil	Nil	Nil
Total	$7,070	$5,460	$6,035

Mr. Worthy's minimum net employment income can be calculated as follows:

Salary		$65,000
Commissions	$11,000	
Expenses Under ITA 8(1)(f) - Limited To Commissions	(7,070)	3,930
Total		$68,930
Expenses Under ITA 8(1)(i) and (j)		(6,035)
Net Employment Income		$62,895

Expenses in excess of commission income cannot be deducted under ITA 8(1)(f). Since the total of the expenses is less than the commissions of $11,000, they can all be deducted. The deduction of automobile capital costs (CCA and financing costs) under ITA 8(1)(j) is permitted without regard to other provisions used.

Notes:

1. The monthly telephone charge is not deductible. The long distance charges and cellular telephone airtime to clients can be deducted. The deduction for supplies can be deducted under ITA 8(1)(f) or (i). They have been deducted under ITA 8(1)(i), which is not limited by the commission income.

2. Only 50 percent of entertainment and meals when travelling are deductible.

3. ITA 8(1)(f) prohibits the deduction of amounts associated with capital assets except as they are permitted under ITA 8(1)(j) and ITA 8(1)(p). These latter Paragraphs only permit interest or capital cost allowance to be deducted when it is related to an automobile, aircraft, or musical instrument. Therefore, the interest and the capital cost allowance on the house and the office furniture would not be deductible against employment income. This is a good illustration of the importance of distinguishing between employment income and business income. While these amounts cannot be deducted against employment income, they would likely be deductible against business income.

4. As the car is used 20 percent for personal purposes, this proportion of the operating costs, capital cost allowance, and interest costs will not be deductible.

5. The deduction for home office costs has been split between ITA 8(1)(i) and (f). Since the maintenance portion can be deducted under ITA 8(1)(i), it is not limited by the commission income. The insurance and property tax components are limited as they are deducted under ITA 8(1)(f). A limitation, which is not illustrated in this problem, prevents the deduction of home office costs from creating an employment loss. If any of the home office costs had not been deductible during the current year, they could be deducted against employment income in any subsequent year as long as a loss is not created or increased by their deduction.

6. Mr. Worthy's employer must sign Form T2200 certifying that Mr. Worthy is required to incur travel expenses and maintain his own work space. Mr. Worthy must retain this signed form with his records in order to deduct car and home office expenses.

Part B If Mr. Worthy deducted the ITA 8(1)(f) expenses, they would be limited to his commission income of $4,000. Alternatively, he can use the combination of ITA 8(1)(h)and (h.1). His minimum net employment income under both alternatives can be calculated as follows:

	ITA 8(1)(f)	ITA 8(1)(h)(h.1)
Salary	$65,000	$65,000
Commissions	4,000	4,000
Expenses Under ITA 8(1)(f) - Limited To Commissions	(4,000)	Nil
Subtotal	$65,000	$69,000
Expenses Under ITA 8(1)(h) and (h.1)	Nil	(5,460)
Expenses Under ITA 8(1)(i) and (j)	(6,035)	(6,035)
Net Employment Income	$58,965	$57,505

Using the combination of ITA 8(1)(h), (h.1), (i), and (j) produces a lower net employment income figure. Note that when this approach is used, home office costs are limited to utilities and maintenance. Further, there is no deduction for entertainment costs. However, this approach results in deductions totalling $1,460 ($5,460 - $4,000) more than the amount available using ITA 8(1)(f), (i), and (j) due to the effect of the commission income limit.

Chapter Five Learning Objectives

After completing Chapter 5, you should be able to:

1. Explain the basic concept of employment income (paragraphs 5-1 through 5-6).

2. Explain the reasons for using, and rules associated with, bonus arrangements for employees (paragraphs 5-7 through 5-11).

3. Distinguish between an employee and a self-employed individual earning business income (paragraphs 5-13 through 5-27).

4. List the benefits that can be excluded from employment income under ITA 6(1)(a) (paragraph 5-29).

5. List the benefits that must be included in income under the other paragraphs contained in ITA 6(1) (paragraph 5-30).

6. Apply the content of IT-470R with respect to the tax status of the various employee benefits described in the Bulletin (paragraphs 5-31 through 5-39).

7. Explain the basic elements of tax planning for employee benefits (paragraphs 5-34 through 5-39).

8. Describe the effects of GST on taxable benefits (paragraphs 5-40 and 5-41).

9. Explain the treatment of board and lodging benefits (paragraphs 5-42 through 5-44).

10. Calculate the standby charge and operating cost benefits that apply to employees who are provided with an automobile that is leased or owned by their employer (paragraphs 5-45 through 5-80).

11. Explain the basic elements of tax planning for company cars (paragraph 5-80).

12. Explain the tax treatment of allowances that are provided by employers to their employees for travel costs (paragraphs 5-81 through 5-95).

13. Describe the tax status of various types of insurance benefits that are provided by employers to their employees (paragraphs 5-96 through 5-104).

14. Calculate the tax consequences of low-rate or interest free loans to employees (paragraphs 5-105 through 5-116).

15. Calculate the employment income benefits that result from employers granting stock options to their employees (including the exercising of the options and the subsequent sale of the acquired shares) (paragraphs 5-117 through 5-146).

16. Demonstrate a basic understanding of specific other inclusions (paragraphs 5-147 through 5-155).

17. Demonstrate an understanding of deductions against employment income (paragraphs 5-156 through 5-175).

18. Explain the conditions that must be met for employees to deduct home office costs (paragraphs 5-176 through 5-180).

CHAPTER SIX

How To Work Through Chapter Six

We recommend the following approach in dealing with the material in this chapter:

Taxable Income Of Individuals
☐ Read the text pages 169 (from paragraph 6-1) through 172 (through paragraph 6-14).
☐ Complete Exercise Six-1 on page 172 of the text. The solution is on page S-68.
☐ Read the text page 172 (paragraph 6-15).

Federal And Provincial Tax Payable Before Credits
☐ Read the text pages 172 (from paragraph 6-16) through 174 (through paragraph 6-29).
☐ Complete Exercise Six-2 on page 174 of the text. The solution is on page S-68.
☐ Read the text pages 174 (paragraph 6-30) and 175.

Credits Against Tax Payable - Calculating The Amount
☐ Read the text page 175 (paragraphs 6-31 through 6-34).

Personal Tax Credits - ITA 118(1)
☐ Read the text pages 175 (from paragraph 6-35) and 176 (through paragraph 6-38).
☐ Complete Exercise Six-3 on page 176 of the text. The solution is on page S-68.

Tax Credits - Eligible Dependant, Caregiver, And Infirm Dependant Over 17
☐ Read the text pages 177 (from paragraph 6-39) and 178 (through paragraph 6-48).
☐ Complete Exercise Six-4 on page 178 of the text. The solution is on page S-68.
☐ Read the text page 178 (from paragraph 6-49 through paragraph 6-50).
☐ Complete Exercise Six-5 on page 178 of the text. The solution is on page S-68.
☐ Read the text page 179 (from paragraph 6-51 through paragraph 6-53).
☐ Complete Exercise Six-6 on page 179 of the text. The solution is on pages S-68 and S-69.
☐ Read the text page 179 (from paragraph 6-54 through paragraph 6-56).
☐ Complete Exercises Six-7 and Six-8 on page 180 of the text. The solutions are on page S-69.

Age and Pension Income Tax Credits
☐ Read the text page 180 (paragraphs 6-57 and 6-58).
☐ Complete Exercise Six-9 on page 180 of the text. The solution is on page S-69.
☐ Read the text pages 180 (from paragraph 6-59) through 181 (through paragraph 6-63).

Adoption Expenses Credit
☐ Read the text pages 181(from paragraph 6-64) and 182 (through paragraph 6-69).
☐ Complete Exercise Six-10 on page 182 of the text. The solution is on page S-69.

Charitable Donations Credit

- ☐ Read pages 182 (from paragraph 6-70)and 183 (through paragraph 6-79).
- ☐ Complete Exercise Six-11 on page 184 of the text. The solution is on page S-70.

Medical Expense Tax Credit

- ☐ Read the text pages 184 (from paragraph 6-80) through 186 (through paragraph 6-86).
- ☐ Complete Exercise Six-12 on page 186 of the text. The solution is on page S-70.

Refundable Medical Expense Supplement

- ☐ Read the text pages 186 (from paragraph 6-87) and 187 (through 6-89).
- ☐ Complete Exercise Six-13 on page 187 of the text. The solution is on page S-70.

Disability Tax Credit

- ☐ Read the text pages 187 (from paragraph 6-90) and 188 (through paragraph 6-98).
- ☐ Complete Exercise Six-14 on page 189 of the text. The solution is on page S-70.

Education Related Tax Credits

- ☐ Read the text pages 189 (from paragraph 6-99) and 190 (through paragraph 6-107).
- ☐ Complete Exercise Six-15 on page 190 of the text. The solution is on page S-71.

Carry Forward Of Tuition, Education and Textbook Credits

- ☐ Read the text pages 190 (from paragraph 6-108) and 191 (through paragraph 6-110).
- ☐ Complete Exercise Six-16 on page 191. The solution is on page S-71.

Transfer Of Tuition, Education And Textbook Credits

- ☐ Read the text page 191 (from paragraph 6-111) and page 192 (through paragraph 6-115).
- ☐ Complete Exercise Six-17 on page 192 of the text. The solution is on pages S-71 and S-72.

Employment Insurance And Canada Pension Plan Credits

- ☐ Read the text pages 192 (from paragraph 6-116) and 193 (through paragraph 6-122).

Transfers To A Spouse Or Commmon-Law Partner

- ☐ Read the text page 193 (paragraphs 6-123 and 6-124).
- ☐ Complete Exercise Six-18 on page 193 of the text. The solution is on page S-72.
- ☐ Read the text page 194 (from paragraphs 6-125 through 6-127).

Political Contributions Tax Credit

- ☐ Read the text pages 194 (from paragraphs 6-128 through 6-130).
- ☐ Complete Exercise Six-19 on page 194 of the text. The solution is on page S-72.

Labour Sponsored Funds Tax Credit

- ☐ Read the text page 195 (paragraphs 6-131 and 6-132).
- ☐ Complete Exercise Six-20 on page 195 of the text. The solution is on page S-72.

May 2006 Budget Proposed Tax Credits

☐ Read the text pages 195 (from paragraph 6-133) through 196 (through paragraph 6-140).

Refundable GST Credit, Child Tax Benefit, And Social Benefits Repayment

☐ Read the text pages 196 (from paragraph 6-141) through 198 (through paragraph 6-159.

☐ Complete Exercise Six-21 on page 198 of the text. The solution is on page S-72.

Comprehensive Example

☐ Read the text pages 199 (from paragraph 6-160) through 200.

Sample Personal Tax Return For Chapter 6

☐ Read the Sample Personal Tax Return For Chapter 6 found on pages S-54 through S-64 of this Study Guide. The complete sample tax return is available on the Student CD-ROM included with the text in two formats, a T1 ProFile return file and a .PDF file. To view the files, access your Student CD-ROM (not the ProFile Tax Suite CD-ROM) and under the heading "Textbook Support Files", select the option "Tax Return Files".

☐ When the updated Intuit ProFile software is available in January, 2007, updated sample tax returns and updated Cases that use ProFile software, as well as instructions on how to install the updated software program, will be available at:

www.pearsoned.ca/byrdchen/ctp2007

☐ Complete Self Study Problems Six-1 through Six-3 on pages 203 through 206 of the text. The solutions are on pages S-73 through S-79.

Tax Return Software

☐ Read the Suggestions For Working With Profile Software found on pages S-65 through S-67 of this Study Guide.

☐ Complete Self Study Case Six-1 using the ProFile T1 Software. The Self Study Case is on pages 206 through 208 of the text. The condensed solution is on pages S-79 through S-82 of this Study Guide. The complete tax return is available on the Student CD-ROM included with the text in two formats, a T1 ProFile return file and a .PDF file.

This Self Study Case is extended in Self Study Problem Six-3, using 2006 rates and in Self Study Case Fourteen-1.

To Complete This Chapter

☐ Review the Key Terms Used In This Chapter on page 201 of the text. Consult the Glossary for the meaning of any key terms you do not know.

☐ Review the Glossary Flashcards and complete the Key Terms Self-Test for the Chapter. These features can be found in two places, on your Student CD-ROM under the heading "Key Term Practice" and on the web site.

☐ Review the Learning Objectives of the Chapter found on page S-83 of this Study Guide.

☐ As a review, we recommend that you view the PowerPoint Slides for Chapter Six that are on your Student CD-ROM. The PowerPoint Viewer program can be installed from the Student CD-ROM.

Sample Personal Tax Return For Chapter 6

The following simplified example contains a T1 individual income tax return completed using the ProFile T1 Personal Income Tax Program for 2005 tax returns from Intuit Canada. As software for 2006 is not yet available, this example contains 2005 rates and credits.

When the updated Intuit ProFile software is available in January, 2007, the updated 2006 version of this sample return, as well as instructions on how to install the updated software program, will be available on the web site at:

www.pearsoned.ca/byrdchen/ctp2007

Only employment income and tax credits are contained in this version of the example. This example is expanded in Chapter 14 to contain other components of Taxable Income and Tax Payable.

Sample Files On Student CD-ROM

The complete sample tax return is available on the Student CD-ROM included with this book in two versions, a T1 ProFile return file and a .PDF file.

Installation Of ProFile, InTRA and Adobe Reader

In order to view the ProFile return files, you must first install the ProFile program from the ProFile Tax Suite CD-ROM (not the Student CD-ROM) that accompanies this book.

If you also install the InTRA Library, you will be able to right-click from a form in a ProFile return and jump directly to the InTRA commentary related to that form. See the installation instructions for both of these programs at the back of the textbook.

In order to view the complete return, including schedules, as a .PDF file, you must have the Adobe Reader program installed on your computer. If you do not have access to the Adobe Reader program, it can be downloaded and installed for free from the Adobe website (http://www.adobe.com).

To View The Tax Return Files

Insert your Student CD-ROM (not the ProFile Tax Suite CD-ROM) and you should see a splash page that allows you to access the contents of the Student CD-ROM.

Under the heading "Textbook Support Files", is the option to view "Tax Return Files". Select this option and you will see two drop-down lists. To view the ProFile file, select the file "Sample - Chapter 6" from the ProFile drop-down list. To view the .PDF file, select the file "PDF Sample - Chapter 6" from the PDF drop-down list.

How To Increase The Benefits From Viewing The ProFile Files

To get the maximum benefit from using the ProFile program, we strongly advise that you do the T1 tutorials "Getting Started" and "Using the Form Explorer" that are included with the program. The data in the following sample tax return problem can be used in the tutorial.

Two Quick Reference Cards (for ProFile and InTRA) are available on the ProFile Tax Suite CD-ROM in .PDF format.

When viewing the sample return file, we offer the following suggestions:

- Press <F1> on any ProFile form or field to display related information in the help system. In ProFile dialog boxes, click the [?] symbol in the top right corner, then click any element for help on that item. Right-click within a form to see available links to the InTRA Library (if InTRA has been installed).

- By pressing <F4> you will open the Form Explorer. In the categories of forms appearing in the shaded box on the left, if you choose "A. Used" near the bottom of the column, all the forms that have calculations for the return will be shown. You can then double click on the form itself to view it.

- Right clicking on a number in a field shows a variety of options, including the form or schedule where the amount originated from.

- Clicking on "Show Auditor" under the "Audit" list will display any warnings or potential errors.

For students who would like more assistance in using the software, we have provided "Suggestions For Working With ProFile Software" in this Study Guide. The three pages of suggestions and tips can be found following this example.

Sample Problem Data

George Kercher (SIN 527-000-145) is a divorced, semi-retired air force pilot living in Banff, Alberta. George was born on February 24, 1954.

He has been your client for many years. Besides doing his 2005 tax return, he would like you to present any tax planning points that he should consider.

After some discussion with George, you confirm that he has never owned any foreign property. As he has for many years, George authorizes the CRA to provide information to Elections Canada and he authorizes you to e-file his return. He is currently living at 69 Beaver Street in Banff, Alberta T0L 0C0. His home phone number is (111) 111-1111.

He informs you that on February 12, 2005, he received $2 million from his mother's estate. Using some of these funds, George bought a house in Banff. The remainder of the funds were invested with his stockbroker, Bull & Bear Inc. In this Chapter 6 version of the example, assume there is no investment income from these funds.

George supports his two daughters:

- Janice (SIN 527-000-269), born June 6, 1992, is in high school and she had no earnings during the year.

- Willa (SIN 527-000-228) was born on January 22, 1986 and is attending university in Edmonton. Willa had Net Income of $3,300 during 2005.

George loves flying, so for the last two summers he has been flying fire bombers June 1 to September 30 for the provincial forest service fire control squad located in Banff.

He brings you the following receipts and documents:

1. A T4 (included in this example).

2. A T2202A "Tuition And Education Amounts Certificate" for himself from Athabasca University. It showed he was a part time student for 6 months and paid $575 in tuition for 2005.

3. A receipt for $1,000 from the Canadian Wildlife Federation dated December 3, 2005.

4. A statement from the Banff Dental Clinic that he paid a total of $1,200 during 2005. This consisted of $850 for himself on November 24, and $150 for Willa and $200 for Janice on December 15.

5. An instalment statement for 2005 that showed that George had paid the CRA instalments of $1,500 on September 15 and December 15 ($3,000 in total). These were the instalments requested by the CRA for the year due to his self-employed income in the previous year.

Notes To The Chapter 6 Return

1. All GST implications have been ignored in this example.

2. Janice has been claimed as the eligible dependant (See "Dependant" form). This information also appears on Schedule 5. Since Willa is over 17 years of age, she cannot be claimed for the eligible dependant credit.

3. Since Willa is over 17 years of age, her medical expenses are reduced by 3 percent of her Net Income For Tax Purposes. Willa should file a return in order to receive the GST credit. Since Willa did not pay her own dental bill, she cannot claim the refundable medical expense supplement herself.

4. Inheritances are not taxable.

5. Due to his nil Tax Payable, George's $1,000 charitable donation is carried forward.

6. George must use his tuition and education credits in calculating his Tax Payable in the order specified under ITA 118.92. This means he cannot deduct his medical expense credit prior to deducting the tuition and education credits. As a result, although his non-refundable tax credits total more than his federal Tax Payable, George cannot choose to reduce his tuition and education credits in order to carry more of the credits forward.

7. Due to his low Net Income For Tax Purposes, George is eligible for the refundable medical expense supplement. One tax planning point that should be considered since the medical expenses occurred late in the year is whether he should save them for the following year. He may be able to claim them by using the 12 month period ending in the year rule if he has other medical expenses. However, this would affect his refundable medical expense supplement.

8. Given George's large refund, it should be determined why he thought he should pay his instalments. He should try to prevent overpaying instalments in the future if possible.

Printed Return

On the following pages you will find George's T4, his T1 jacket and his Schedule 1 (federal tax calculations). The complete return can be found on the Student CD-ROM.

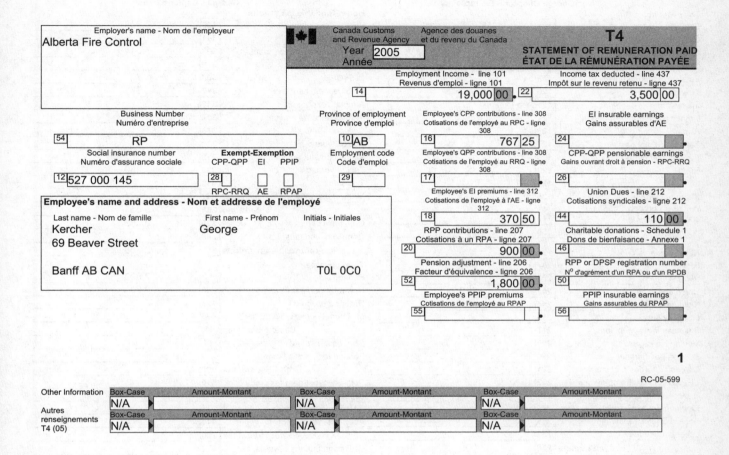

Kercher, George Chapter 6 Example   SIN: 527 000 145
Summary

2005 Tax Summary

Total income
George Chapter 6 Example

Employment *	101	19,000
Old Age Security	113	
CPP/QPP benefits	114	
Other pensions	115	
Employment Insurance	119	
Taxable dividends	120	
Interest	121	
Limited partnership	122	
Rental	126	
Taxable capital gains	127	
Support payments	128	
RRSP	129	
Other	130	
Self-employment *	135	
Workers' compensation and social assistance	147	
Total income	150	19,000

Net income

RPP	207	900
RRSP *	208	
Union and professional dues	212	110
Child care expenses	214	
Disability supports deduction	215	
Business investment loss	217	
Moving expenses	219	
Support payments	220	
Carrying charges and interest	221	
CPP/QPP on self-employment	222	
Exploration and development	224	
Employment expenses	229	
Social benefits repayment	235	
Other deductions *	231	
Net income	236	17,990

Taxable income

Canadian Forces personnel	244	
Home relocation loan	248	
Security options deductions	249	
Other payments deduction	250	
Losses of other years *	251	
Capital gains deduction	254	
Northern residents deductions	255	
Additional deductions	256	
Taxable income	260	17,990

2006 Estimated
George Chapter 6 Example

GST/HST credit	586 00
Child Tax Benefit	3,317 00
RRSP contribution limit	1,600 00

* More than one line is considered

Non-refundable tax credits
George Chapter 6 Example

Basic personal amount	300	8,648
Age amount	301	
Spouse / eligible dependant *	303	7,344
Infirm dependants	306	
CPP/QPP	308	767
Employment Insurance	312	371
Adoption expenses	313	
Pension income amount	314	
Caregiver amount	315	
Disability amount	316	
Interest on student loans	319	
Tuition / education	323	860
Transfers *	318	
Medical expenses	332	561
Subtotal	335	18,551
Credit at 15%	338	2,783
Donations and gifts	349	
Non-refundable tax credits	350	2,783

Total payable

Federal tax	11	2,699
Non-refundable tax credits	350	2,783
Dividend tax credit	425	
Minimum tax carry-over/other *	426	
Basic federal tax	13	
Non resident surtax *	14	
Foreign tax credits / other		
Federal tax	406	
Political/investment tax credit *	410	
Labour-sponsored tax credit	414	
Alternative minimum tax		
Additional tax on RESP	418	
Net federal tax	260	
CPP contributions payable	421	
Social benefits repayment	422	
Provincial/territorial tax	428	
Total payable	435	

Total credits

Income tax deducted *	437	3,500
QC or YT abatement *	440	
CPP overpayment	448	
EI overpayment	450	
Medical expense supplement	452	140
GST/HST rebate	457	
Instalments	476	3,000
Provincial tax credits	479	
Other credits	454	
Total credits	482	6,640

Balance owing (refund)	(6,640)
Combined balance (refund)	(6,640)

Complete Return Available On Student CD-ROM

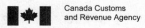 Canada Customs and Revenue Agency | Agence des douanes et du revenu du Canada

T1 GENERAL 2005

Income Tax and Benefit Return

Identification

7

| First name and initial |
| George Chapter 6 Example |
| Last name |
| Kercher |
| Care of |

Mailing address: Apt. No. – Street No. Street name
69 Beaver Street

P.O. Box   R.R.

| City | Prov./Terr. | Postal Code |
| Banff | AB | T0L 0C0 |

Information about your residence

Enter your province or territory of
residence on **December 31, 2005**:   Alberta

Enter the province or territory where you **currently** reside if
it is not the same as that shown
above for your mailing address: _____

If you were self-employed in 2005,
enter the province or territory of
self-employment: Alberta

If you **became** or **ceased** to be a **resident of Canada in 2005**, give the
date of:

Month/Day   Month/Day
entry _____   or   departure _____

Information about you

Enter your social insurance number (SIN) 527 000 145

Year/Month/Day
Enter your date of birth: 1954-02-24

Your language of correspondence: English   Français
Votre langue de correspondance :   X ☐

Your marital status on December 31, 2005:
(see the "Marital status" section in the guide for details)

1 ☐ Married   2 ☐ Living common law   3 ☐ Widowed
4 ☒ Divorced   5 ☐ Separated   6 ☐ Single

Information about your spouse or common-law partner (if you checked box 1 or 2 above)

Enter his or her social insurance number: _____

Enter his or her first name: _____

Enter his or her net income for 2005 to claim
certain credits: (see the guide for details) _____

Check this box if he or she was self-employed in 2005: 1 ☐

If this return is for a deceased
person, enter the date of death: Year/Month/Day

Do not use this area

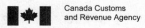 **Elections Canada**   THIS SECTION APPLIES **ONLY** TO CANADIAN CITIZENS.
DO **NOT** ANSWER THIS QUESTION IF YOU ARE NOT A CANADIAN CITIZEN.

As a Canadian citizen, I authorize the Canada Revenue Agency to provide my name, address,
and date of birth to Elections Canada for the National Register of Electors.
Your authorization is required each year. This information will be used only for purposes permitted
under the *Canada Elections Act*.   Yes ☒ 1   No ☐ 2

Goods and services tax/harmonized sales tax (GST/HST) credit application
See the guide for details.
Are you applying for the GST/HST credit?   Yes ☒ 1   No ☐ 2

Your guide contains valuable information to help you complete your return.

**When you come to a line on the return that applies to you, look up the line number
in the guide for more information.**

| Do not use this area | 172 | | | | 171 | | | | | |

Kercher, George Chapter 6 Example   SIN: 527 000 145

2

Please answer the following question

Did you own or hold foreign property at any time in 2005 with a total cost of more than CAN$100,000? (read the "Foreign income" section in the guide for details) **266** Yes ☐ 1   No ☒ 2
If *yes*, attach a completed Form T1135.

If you had dealings with a non-resident trust or corporation in 2005, see the "Foreign income" section in the guide.

As a Canadian resident, you have to report your income from all sources both inside and outside Canada.

Total income

Employment income (box 14 on all T4 slips)		**101**	19,000 00
Commissions included on line 101 (box 42 on all T4 slips)	**102**		
Other employment income		**104**	
Old Age Security pension (box 18 on the T4A(OAS) slip)		**113**	
CPP or QPP benefits (box 20 on the T4A(P) slip)		**114**	
Disability benefits included on line 114 (box 16 on the T4A(P) slip)	**152**		
Other pensions or superannuation		**115**	
Employment Insurance and other benefits (box 14 on the T4E slip)		**119**	
Taxable amount of dividends from taxable Canadian corporations (see the guide)		**120**	
Interest and other investment income (**attach** Schedule 4)		**121**	
Net partnership income: limited or non-active partners only (**attach** Schedule 4)		**122**	
Rental income Gross **160** Net		**126**	
Taxable capital gains (**attach** Schedule 3)		**127**	
Support payments received Total **156** Taxable amount		**128**	
RRSP income (from all T4RSP slips)		**129**	
Other income Specify:		**130**	

Self-employment income (see lines 135 to 143 in the guide)

Business income Gross **162** Net	**135**		
Professional income Gross **164** Net	**137**		
Commission income Gross **166** Net	**139**		
Farming income Gross **168** Net	**141**		
Fishing income Gross **170** Net	**143**		

Workers' compensation benefits (box 10 on the T5007 slip)	**144**	
Social assistance payments	**145**	
Net federal supplements (box 21 on the T4A(OAS) slip)	**146**	

Add lines 144, 145, and 146 (see line 250 in the guide) ▶ **147**

Add lines 101, 104 to 143, and 147
This is your **total income**. **150** 19,000 00

Kercher, George Chapter 6 Example   SIN: 527 000 145

3

Attach your Schedule 1 (federal tax) and Form 428 (provincial or territorial tax) here. Also attach here any other schedules, information slips, forms, receipts, and documents that you need to include with your return.

Net income

Enter your **total income** from line 150			150	19,000	00
Pension adjustment (box 52 on all T4 slips and box 34 on all T4A slips)	**206**	1,800	00		
Registered pension plan deduction (box 20 on all T4 slips and box 32 on all T4A slips)	**207**	900	00		
RRSP deduction (see Schedule 7 and **attach** receipts)	**208**				
Saskatchewan Pension Plan deduction (maximum $600)	**209**				
Annual union, professional, or like dues (box 44 on all T4 slips, or from receipts)	**212**	110	00		
Child care expenses (**attach** Form T778)	**214**				
Disability supports deduction	**215**				
Business investment loss Gross **228** Allowable deduction	**217**				
Moving expenses	**219**				
Support payments made Total **230** Allowable deduction	**220**				
Carrying charges and interest expenses (**attach** Schedule 4)	**221**				
Deduction for CPP or QPP contributions on self-employment and other earnings (**attach** Schedule 8)	**222**		•		
Exploration and development expenses (**attach** Form T1229)	**224**				
Other employment expenses	**229**				
Clergy residence deduction	**231**				
Other deductions Specify:	**232**				
Add lines 207 to 224, 229, 231, and 232. 233		1,010	00 ▶	1,010	00
Line 150 minus line 233 (if negative, enter "0"). This is your **net income before adjustments.** 234				17,990	00
Social benefits repayment (if you reported income on line 113, 119, or 146, see line 235 in the guide)	**235**				•
Line 234 minus line 235 (if negative, enter "0"). If you have a spouse or common-law partner, see line 236 in the guide. This is your **net income.** 236				17,990	00

Taxable income

Canadian Forces personnel and police deduction (box 43 on all T4 slips)	**244**		
Employee home relocation loan deduction (box 37 on all T4 slips)	**248**		
Security options deductions	**249**		
Other payments deduction (if you reported income on line 147, see line 250 in the guide)	**250**		
Limited partnership losses of other years	**251**		
Non-capital losses of other years	**252**		
Net capital losses of other years	**253**		
Capital gains deduction	**254**		
Northern residents deductions (**attach** Form T2222)	**255**		
Additional deductions Specify:	**256**		
Add lines 244 to 256. 257		▶	
Line 236 minus line 257 (if negative, enter "0"). This is your **taxable income. 260**		17,990	00

Use your taxable income to calculate your federal tax on Schedule 1 and your provincial or territorial tax on Form 428.

Kercher, George Chapter 6 Example   SIN: 527 000 145

Refund or Balance owing   4

Net federal tax: enter the amount from line 19 of Schedule 1 (**attach** Schedule 1, even if the result is "0")	420		0 00
CPP contributions payable on self-employment and other earnings (**attach** Schedule 8)	421		
Social benefits repayment (enter the amount from line 235)	422		
Provincial or territorial tax (**attach** Form 428, even if the result is "0")	428		

Add lines 420 to 428
This is your **total payable.** | **435** | 0 00 •

Total income tax deducted (from all information slips)	**437**	3,500 00	•
Refundable Québec abatement	**440**		•
CPP overpayment (enter your excess contributions)	**448**		•
Employment Insurance overpayment (enter your excess contributions)	**450**		•
Refundable medical expense supplement	**452**	140 33	•
Refund of investment tax credit (**attach** Form T2038(IND))	**454**		•
Part XII.2 trust tax credit (box 38 on all T3 slips)	**456**		•
Employee and partner GST/HST rebate (**attach** Form GST370)	**457**		•
Tax **paid** by instalments	**476**	3,000 00	•
Provincial or territorial credits (**attach** Form 479 if it applies)	**479**		•

Add lines 437 to 479
These are your **total credits.** 482 | 6,640 33 ▶ | 6,640 33

Line 435 minus line 482 | (6,640 33)

If the result is negative, you have a **refund**.
If the result is positive, you have a **balance owing**.
Enter the amount below on whichever line applies.

Generally, we do not charge or refund a difference of $2 or less.

Refund **484**   6,640 33 •   Balance owing **485**   •

Amount enclosed **486**   •

┌─ **Direct deposit - Start or change** (see line 484 in the guide) ─┐

You do not have to complete this area every year. Do not complete it this year if your direct deposit information for your refund has not changed.

Refund and GST/HST credit - To start direct deposit or to change account information only, **attach** a "void" cheque or complete lines 460, 461, and 462.

Note: To deposit your **CCTB** payments (including certain related provincial or territorial payments) into the **same** account, also check box 463.

Branch number	Institution number	Account number	CCTB
460	**461**	**462**	**463**
(5 digits)	(3 digits)	(maximum 12 digits)	

Attach to page 1 a **cheque** or **money order** payable to the Receiver General. Your payment is due no later than April 30, 2006.

I certify that the information given on this return and in any documents attached is correct, complete, and fully discloses all my income.

Sign here _____

It is a serious offence to make a false return.

Telephone (111) 111-1111   Date 2006-05-19

490 [X]
Name
Address

Telephone (   )   -

For professional tax preparers only

_____

_____

Do not use **this area**	**487**	**488**					

RC-05-148

Kercher, George Chapter 6 Example   SIN: 527 000 145

T1-2005   Federal Tax   Schedule 1

Complete this schedule to claim your federal non-refundable tax credits and to calculate your net federal tax.

You must attach a copy of this schedule to your return.

Enter your **taxable income** from line 260 of your return 17,990 00 **1**

Use the amount on line 1 to determine which **ONE**
of the following columns you have to complete.

If the amount on line 1 is:	$35,595 or less		more than $35,595 but not more than $71,190		more than $71,190 but not more than $115,739		more than $115,739	
Enter the amount from line 1 above	17,990 00	**2**		**2**		**2**		**2**
Base amount		**3**	35,595 00	**3**	71,190 00	**3**	115,739 00	**3**
Line 2 minus line 3 (this amount cannot be negative)	17,990 00	**4**		**4**		**4**		**4**
Rate	x 15.00 %	**5**	x 22.00 %	**5**	x 26.00 %	**5**	x 29.00 %	**5**
Multiply the amount on line 4 by the rate on line 5	2,698 50	**6**		**6**		**6**		**6**
Tax on base amount	0 00	**7**	5,339 00	**7**	13,170 00	**7**	24,753 00	**7**
Add lines 6 and 7	2,698 50	**8**		**8**		**8**		**8**

Federal non-refundable tax credits

Basic personal amount	**claim $8,648**	**300**	8,648 00
Age amount (if you were born in 1940 or earlier)	**(maximum $3,979)**	**301**	

Spouse or common-law partner amount:

Base amount	8,079 00		
Minus: his or her net income (from page 1 of your return)	0 00		
Result: (if negative, enter "0")	**(maximum $7,344)** ▶	**303**	
Amount for an eligible dependant (**attach** Schedule 5)	**(maximum $7,344)**	**305**	7,344 00
Amount for infirm dependants age 18 or older (**attach** Schedule 5)		**306**	
CPP or QPP contributions:			
through employment from box 16 and box 17 on all T4 slips	**(maximum $1,861.20)**	**308**	767 25 ●
on self-employment and other earnings (**attach** Schedule 8)		**310**	●
Employment Insurance premiums from box 18 on all T4 slips	**(maximum $760.50)**	**312**	370 50 ●
Adoption expenses		**313**	
Pension income amount	**(maximum $1,000)**	**314**	
Caregiver amount (**attach** Schedule 5)		**315**	
Disability amount		**316**	
Disability amount transferred from a dependant		**318**	
Interest paid on your student loans		**319**	
Tuition and education amounts (**attach** Schedule 11)		**323**	860 25
Tuition and education amounts transferred from a child		**324**	
Amounts transferred from your spouse or common-law partner (**attach** Schedule 2)		**326**	

Medical expenses for **self, spouse or common-law partner, and your dependent children born in 1988 or later** (see the guide)	**330**	1,050 00		
Minus: $1,844 or 3% of line 236, whichever is **less**		539 70		
Subtotal (if negative, enter "0")		510 30	(A)	
Allowable amount of medical expenses for **other dependants** (see the calculation at line 331 in the guide and **attach** Schedule 5)	**331**	51 00	(B)	
Add lines (A) and (B).		561 30 ▶	**332**	561 30
Add lines 300 to 326, and 332.	**335**			18,551 30

Multiply the amount on line 335 by 15% =	**338**		2,782 70
Donations and gifts (**attach** Schedule 9)	**349**		
Total federal non-refundable tax credits: Add lines 338 and 349.	**350**		2,782 70

continue

Kercher, George Chapter 6 Example SIN: 527 000 145

Net federal tax

Enter the amount from line 8			2,698 50	**9**
Federal tax on split income (from line 4 of Form T1206)	424		•	**10**
Add lines 9 and 10		2,698 50 ▶	2,698 50	**11**

Enter the amount from line 350	350	2,782 70		
Federal dividend tax credit (13.3333% of the amount on line 120 of your return)	425		•	
Overseas employment tax credit (**attach** Form T626)	426			
Minimum tax carry-over (**attach** Form T691)	427		•	
Add lines 350, 425, 426, and 427		2,782 70 ▶	2,782 70	**12**

Basic federal tax: Line 11 minus line 12 (if negative, enter "0") 429   **13**

Federal foreign tax credit:
Where you **only** have foreign non-business income, calculate your federal foreign tax credit below. Otherwise, use Form T2209, *Federal Foreign Tax Credits*, if you have foreign business income. **Enter on this line the amount you calculated**   **14**

Federal logging tax credit

Federal tax: Line 13 minus line 14 (if negative, enter "0") 406   0 00 **15**

Total federal political contributions (**attach** receipts)	409			
Federal political contribution tax credit (see the guide)	410		•	
Investment tax credit (**attach** Form T2038(IND))	412		•	
Labour-sponsored funds tax credit Net cost 413 Allowable credit 414			•	
Add lines 410, 412, and 414. 416			▶	**16**

Line 15 minus line 16 (if negative, enter "0")
(if you have an amount on line 424 above, see Form T1206) 417   **17**

Additional tax on RESP accumulated income payments (**attach** Form T1172) 418   **18**

Net federal tax: Add lines 17 and 18
Enter this amount on line 420 of your return. 420   0 00 **19**

Federal foreign tax credit: (see lines 431 and 433 in the guide)

Make a separate calculation for each foreign country. Enter on line 14 above the result from line (i) or line (ii), whichever is **less**.

Non-business income tax paid to a foreign country   431   • **(i)**

Net foreign non-business income *   433   **X**   Basic federal tax ***   =   **(ii)**

Net income **

* Reduce this amount by any income from that foreign country for which you claimed a capital gains deduction, and by any income from that country that was, under a tax treaty, either exempt from tax in that country or deductible as exempt income in Canada (included on line 256). Also reduce this amount by the lesser of lines E and F on Form T626.

** Line 236 plus the amount on line 3 of Form T1206, minus the total of the amounts on lines 244, 248, 249, 250, 253, 254, and minus any amount included on line 256 for foreign income deductible as exempt income under a tax treaty, income deductible as net employment income from a prescribed international organization, or non-taxable tuition assistance from box 21 of the T4E slip. If the result is less than the amount on line 433, enter your **Basic federal tax*** on line (ii).

*** Line 429 plus the amount on lines 425 and 426, and minus any refundable Québec abatement (line 440) and any federal refundable First Nations abatement (line 441 on the return for residents of Yukon).

Suggestions For Working With ProFile Software

Before You Start

To get the maximum benefit from using the ProFile tax preparation software program, we strongly advise that you do the T1 tutorials "Getting Started" and "Using the Form Explorer" that are included with the program. The data in the sample tax returns can be used in the tutorial.

We suggest that you install the InTRA Library, so that you will be able to right-click from a form in a ProFile return and jump directly to the InTRA Commentary related to that form.

Two Quick Reference Cards (for ProFile and InTRA) are available on the ProFile Tax Suite CD-ROM in .PDF format.

Sample Tax Returns

Included in this Study Guide are sample tax returns for Chapters 6 and 14. The tax returns contain 2005 data as the 2006 version of the ProFile tax preparation software was not yet available. The ProFile software on the ProFile Tax Suite CD also contains the version for 2005 returns. As a result, the 2005 credits and rates in the sample returns will not be the same as the 2006 figures in the text which can cause confusion for some students.

When the updated Intuit ProFile software is available in January, 2007, the updated 2006 versions of the sample returns, as well as instructions on how to install the updated software program, will be available on the web site at:

www.pearsoned.ca/byrdchen/ctp2007

Before attempting the Self Study Cases, you should review the ProFile files for the sample tax returns and ensure that you are familiar with how the data was entered into the program.

Creating A New T1 Return

To provide some guidance on how to use ProFile to create a simple new personal tax return, we suggest the following approach.

1. Start the ProFile software. Open a new file. Ensure that you have chosen the a new file in the correct software (T1) and year (2005 or 2006 if available).

2. By default, the software will open on the form "Info". Enter all relevant information here. At a minimum, you will need to enter the following information:

    -   Taxpayer's Social Insurance Number (SIN)
    -   Taxpayer's first and last name
    -   Address, city, province, and postal code
    -   Telephone number
    -   Taxpayer's birth date

    If applicable, you will also need to enter any relevant information for the spouse on the "Info" form. At a minimum, the following information will be necessary:

    -   Spouse's Social Insurance Number (SIN)
    -   Spouse's first and last name
    -   Address, city, province, and postal code
    -   Telephone number
    -   Spouse's birth date

3. Using the Form Explorer (F4), go to the Dependant form and enter all relevant information about any eligible dependants. At a minimum, the following information will be necessary:

    - Dependant's Social Insurance Number (SIN)
    - Dependant's first and last name
    - Dependant's relationship to the taxpayer
    - Dependant's birth date
    - Dependant's Net Income
    - Address, city, province, and postal code

    If the Dependant has tuition and education amounts and is not filing a tax return, the education related information should be entered on the Dependant form.

4. Using the Form Explorer (F4), open the relevant information slip form. Enter all relevant information in the appropriate forms. Some common information slip forms are:

    - T3 - Statement of Trust Income
    - T4 - Statement of Remuneration Paid
    - T5 - Statement of Investment Income
    - T2202 - Tuition and Education Amounts
    - T4AOAS - Statement of Old Age Security

5. Enter any other relevant income information on the appropriate forms. These forms may include, but are not limited to, the following:

    - T776 - Statement of Real Estate Rentals
    - T776Asset - T776 Asset Details
    - T776CCA - T776 CCA Details
    - T2032 - Statement of Professional Activities
    - T2032Asset - T2032 Asset Details
    - T2032CCA - T2032 CCA Details

6. Enter any relevant other deduction information on the appropriate forms. These forms may include, but are not limited to, the following:

    - RRSP - RRSP Deduction
    - T777 - Statement of Employment Expenses
    - T778 - Child Care Expense Deduction
    - Support - Support Payments
    - Auto - Motor Vehicle Expenses
    - LossNetCap - Net Capital Losses
    - LossNonCap - Non-Capital Losses

7. Enter any relevant tax credit information on the appropriate forms. These forms may include, but are not limited to, the following:

    - Donations - Charitable Donations
    - Medical - Medical Expenses

8. Enter any remaining relevant information in the appropriate schedule. These schedules may include, but are not limited to, the following:

    - S2 - Federal Amounts Transferred From Your Spouse or Common-Law Partner
      (primarily used if spouse or common-law partner is not filing a tax return)
    - S3Details - Capital Gains Entry
      (this form, not Schedule 3, must be used to input details on capital dispositions)

- S4 - Statement of Investment Income
(much of the information for this schedule will be carried forward from the T3, T5, and other information slips, but a few items such as carrying charges are entered directly on Schedule 4)

9. Use the function "Show Auditor" under the "Audit" list to check for warnings or potential errors.

Tips For Using ProFile Software

- Press the F5 key or choose Spouse from the Form menu to display the return of the spouse.

- Press the F4 key to view the Form Explorer. Choose the form "Summary" to see the tax data of both spouses on the same one page summary. (Second column will be blank for a single taxpayer.)

- Review marks can be used to flag information that should be reviewed. The cell with the review mark will be listed when the Show Auditor feature is turned on.

- A memo and/or a tape can be attached to a cell to provide backup information.

- If you cannot determine where a specific slip or other information should be input, one way to search for the correct form is to open the Form Explorer (F4) and choose the "Key" mode icon in the top right corner of the menu. If you type a key word into the line above the listing of key words, the appropriate form may be found.

- To see the effect of various changes such as province of residence or a change in an RRSP contribution, use the "Snapshot/Variance" feature. Information on this feature is available from the Help menu. Note you must press the "Enter" key for the change to take effect. The data monitor at the bottom of the screen should show the new balance/refund. The difference can also be seen on the "Summary" form. If you open the Auditor (F9) and select the Variance tab you will see a detailed analysis of the changes.

Solution to Chapter Six Exercises

Exercise Six - 1 Solution

The net effect of this home relocation loan on Taxable Income would be as follows:

Taxable Benefit Under ITA 80.4(1)(a) - [(4%)($82,000)]*	$3,280
Reduction For Payments Under ITA 80.4(1)(c) - [(2%)($82,000)]	(1,640)
Total ITA 80.4(1) Benefit	$1,640
ITA 110(1)(j) Deduction - Lesser Of:	
• ITA 80.4(1) Benefit = $1,640	
• [(4%)($25,000)(4/4)]* = $1,000	(1,000)
Net Addition To Taxable Income	$ 640

*Despite the fact that the prescribed rate has increased, the taxpayer can continue to use the rate in effect at the time the loan was made. This can continue for a period of five years. Note that the ITA 110(1)(j) deduction is also based on the rate in effect at the time the loan was made.

Exercise Six - 2 Solution

The required Tax Payable would be calculated as follows:

Federal Tax Payable:		
On First $36,378	$5,548	
On Next $10,322 ($46,700 - $36,378) At 22 Percent	2,271	$7,819
Provincial Tax Payable:		
On First $34,759 At 6.05 Percent	$2,103	
On Next $11,941 ($46,700 - $34,759) At 9.15 Percent	1,093	3,196
Total Tax Payable Before Credits		$11,015

Exercise Six - 3 Solution

The required amount would be calculated as follows:

Basic Personal Amount	$ 8,839
Spousal Amount [$7,505 - ($2,600 - $751)]	5,656
Credit Base	$14,495
Rate	15.25%
Personal Tax Credits	$ 2,210

Exercise Six - 4 Solution

Joan would be entitled to an caregiver tax credit in the amount of $269 {[15.25%][$3,933 - ($15,600 - $13,430)]}.

Exercise Six - 5 Solution

Harold would be entitled to an infirm dependant over 17 tax credit in the amount of $292 {[15.25%][$3,933 - ($7,600 - $5,580)]}. He could not claim the caregiver credit as his daughter does not live with him.

Exercise Six - 6 Solution

As Mr. Litvak is eligible for the eligible dependant credit, he could not take the caregiver tax credit. Given this he would first determine the amount of the eligible dependant credit as follows:

$$\{[15.25\%][\$7,505 - (\$7,500 - \$751)]\} = \$115$$

As his mother's income is below the $13,430 threshold for the caregiver credit, in the absence of ITA 118(4), she would have been eligible for $600, the full amount of the caregiver credit. This means that he will have an additional credit under ITA 118(1)(e) of $485 ($600 - $115). The combination of the eligible dependant credit and the ITA 118(1)(e) credit totals $600, the maximum caregiver credit.

Exercise Six - 7 Solution

ITA 118(4)(d) indicates that, if a taxpayer is entitled to the caregiver credit for a particular individual, the taxpayer cannot claim the infirm dependant over 17 credit for that individual. As his investment income is below the income threshold for the caregiver tax credit, the credit for Suki's son would be calculated as follows:

$$[(15.25\%)(\$3,933 - \text{Nil})] = \$600$$

Exercise Six - 8 Solution *+ don't need to know.*

Her tax credits would be determined as follows:

Basic Personal Amount	$ 8,839
Eligible Dependant (Daughter) [$7,505 - ($1,800 - $751)]	6,456
Caregiver (Son)	3,933
Credit Base	$19,228
Rate	15.25%
Total Credits	$ 2,932

While the eligible dependant credit would have been larger had she claimed it for her son (he has no income above the threshold level), she could not have claimed the caregiver credit for her daughter. She is better off claiming the caregiver credit, plus the decreased eligible dependant credit. As a further alternative, Ms. Forest could have claimed the infirm dependant over 17 credit, instead of the caregiver credit, for her son. However, the credits are for the same amount. As a rule, the caregiver credit should be claimed as it has a higher income threshold.

Exercise Six - 9 Solution

Mr. Smythe's age credit for 2006 would be $134 {[15.25%][$4,066 - (15%)($51,500 - $30,270)]}.

Exercise Six-10 Solution

The maximum adoption expenses tax credit would be calculated as follows:

Cost Of Second China Trip	$ 6,420
Chinese Orphanage Fee	1,600
Canadian Adoption Agency Fee	3,200
Legal Fees	2,700
Total Eligible Expenses	$13,920
Employer Reimbursement	(5,000)
Base For Credit	$ 8,920
Rate	15.25%
Maximum Adoption Expense Credit	$ 1,360

The first trip to China is not eligible for the credit as it was incurred before the adoption period. While the additional medical expenses will likely be available for a medical expenses tax credit, they are not eligible for the adoption expenses credit. You should also note that the expense base for the credit is less than the $10,000 maximum.

Exercise Six - 11 Solution

The credit base for 2006 would be limited to $48,750 [(75%)($65,000)]. However, she chooses to claim $10,000, leaving a carry forward of $90,000 ($100,000 - $10,000). The resulting credit would be:

$200 At 15.25 Percent	$ 31
$9,800 ($10,000 - $200) At 29 Percent	2,842
Total Credit	$2,873

As her income for 2007 is unchanged from 2006, the base for the maximum credit would be the same limit of $48,750 [(75%)($65,000)]. Charitable donations can be carried forward for up to 5 years. As a result, the final year to claim any unused portion of her 2006 donation would be 2011.

Exercise Six - 12 Solution

Amount B Qualifying Expenses ($4,330 + $4,600)	$ 8,930
Amount C	
Lesser of:	
• [(3%)($150,000)] = $4,500	
• 2006 Threshold Amount = $1,884	(1,884)
Subtotal	$ 7,046
Amount D	
Max - Lesser Of:	
• [$8,425 - (3%)($8,250)]* = $8,178	
• Absolute Limit = $10,000	8,178
Allowable Amount Of Medical Expenses	$15,224
Amount A The Appropriate Rate	15.25%
Medical Expense Tax Credit	$ 2,322

* [(3%)($8,250)] is less than $1,884.

Exercise Six - 13 Solution

Ms. Brunt's allowable medical expenses for tax credit purposes would be $5,488 [$6,250 - (3%)($25,400)], resulting in a credit of $837 [(15.25%)($5,488)]. 25/15.25 of this amount or, alternatively, 25 percent of allowable medical expenses, would be $1,372. This means that the refundable supplement would be based on the maximum of $1,000, less a reduction of $163 [(5%)($25,400 - $22,140)], a balance of $837. Given this, she would be eligible for a refund of $293 [(15.25%)($25,400 - $8,839 - $7,505 - $5,488) - $837].

Exercise Six - 14 Solution

John has sufficient other medical expenses to exceed the 3 percent threshold. His income is too high to qualify for the refundable supplement. As Keith has no income, the regular disability credit can be transferred to John. However, as Keith is over 17, the disability supplement is not available. In addition to the disability credit, John will be able to take the caregiver credit, as well as a credit for Keith's medical expenses. Keith's medical expense credit base is limited to the maximum of $10,000. The total credits related to Keith would be as follows:

Disability - Regular Amount	$ 6,741
Caregiver	3,933
Medical Expenses (Absolute Limit)	10,000
Total Credit Base	$20,674
Rate	15.25%
Total Credits Related To Keith	$ 3,153

Exercise Six - 15 Solution

Ms. Bright's education related tax credits would be calculated as follows:

Tuition Amount:		
Total (Including $1,000 Prepayment)	$3,200	
Ineligible Ancillary Fees ($400 - $250)	(150)	$3,050
Education Amount:		
Full Time [(4)($400)]		1,600
Part Time [(2)($120)]		240
Textbook Amount:		
Full Time [(4)($65)]		260
Part Time [(2)($20)]		40
Interest On Student Loan		325
Total Credit Base		$5,515
Rate		15.25%
Total Available Credits		$ 841

Exercise Six - 16 Solution

The available education related credits for the year could be calculated as follows:

Tuition Amount	$4,800
Education Amount [(8)($400)]	3,200
Textbook Amount [(8)($65)]	520
Subtotal From Current Year	$8,520
Rate	15.25%
Credit From Current Year	$1,299
Carry Forward Credit [($300)(15.25/15) - See Note]	305
Total Available Credits	$1,604

The alternative calculation approach that is used in the tax return would be as follows:

Subtotal From Current Year (Preceding Calculation)	$8,520
Carry Forward Amount (See Note)	2,000
Total	$10,520
Rate	15.25%
Total Available Credits	$1,604

Note It is our understanding that the amounts carried forward from years prior to 2006 will be adjusted to reflect the new minimum tax bracket.

Kerri's Tax Payable before deducting education related credits would be $2,007 [(15.25%)($22,000) - $1,348]. This is more than sufficient to absorb the available education related credits and, as a consequence, there would be no carry forward of credits.

Exercise Six - 17 Solution

Income Tax Act Approach Jerry's total available tuition, education, and textbook amount would be $28,615 [$23,500 + (11)($400) +(11)($65)], resulting in a potential credit of $4,364 [(15.25%)($28,615)]. This amount is well in excess of the $763 maximum transfer. However, this maximum must be reduced by Jerry's Tax Payable of $368 [(15.25%)($11,250 - $8,839)]. This will leave a maximum transfer of $395 ($763 - $368) and a carry forward credit of $3,601 ($4,364 - $368 - $395).

Tax Return Approach   Jerry's total available tuition, education, and textbook amount would be $28,615 [$23,500 + (11)($400) + (11)($65)]. This amount is well in excess of the $5,000 maximum transfer. However, this maximum must be reduced by $2,411 ($11,250 - $8,839)], the excess of Jerry's Taxable Income over his basic personal amount. This results in a maximum transfer of $2,589 ($5,000 - $2,411) and a carry forward amount of $23,615 ($28,615 - $2,411 - $2,589).

Exercise Six - 18 Solution

His tax credits would be calculated as follows:

Basic Personal Amount	$ 8,839
Spousal Amount	7,505
Age [$4,066 - (15%)($42,000 - $30,270)]	2,307
Pension Income	2,000
Spousal Age Transfer	4,066
Spousal Tuition, Education, and Textbook Transfer	
[$2,200 + (4 Months)($400) + (4 Months)($65)]	4,060
Credit Base	$28,777
Rate	15.25%
Total Credits	$ 4,388

Exercise Six - 19 Solution

Ms. Unger's $487 credit would be calculated as follows:

	Contributions	Credit Rate	Tax Credit
First	$400	3/4	$300
Next	350	1/2	175
Remaining	35	1/3	12
Maximum Credit	$785		$487

Exercise Six - 20 Solution

The credit will be $450 [(15%)($3,000)]. As his acquisition is less than the $5,000 maximum, the full cost is eligible for the 15 percent federal credit.

Exercise Six - 21 Solution

Ms. Jacobi's income before deducting either the EI repayment or the tax on OAS benefits would be calculated as follows:

Net Employment Income	$50,000
EI Benefits	10,000
OAS Benefits	5,800
Income Before Deductions	$65,800

Dealing first with the EI repayment, Ms. Jacobi would have to repay $3,000 [(30%)($10,000)], which is the lesser of 30 percent of the EI benefits received and $5,115 [(30%)($65,800 - $48,750)].

Using this deduction, the tax on her OAS payments would be $98 [(15%)($65,800 - $3,000 - $62,144)]. As a result, her Net Income For Tax Purposes would be as follows:

Income Before Deductions	$65,800
ITA 60(v.1) Deduction (EI)	(3,000)
ITA 60(w) Deduction (OAS)	(98)
Net Income For Tax Purposes	$62,702

Solution to Self Study Problem Six - 1

Case A   The solution for this Case would be as follows:

Net Income For Tax Purposes And Taxable Income		$50,000

Tax [$5,548 + (22%)($50,000 - $36,378)]		$8,545
Basic Personal Amount	($ 8,839)	
EI	(729)	
CPP	(1,911)	
Canada Employment	(250)	
Credit Base	($11,729)	
Rate	15.25%	(1,789)
Political Contributions Tax Credit		
[(3/4)($400) + (1/2)($350) + (1/3)($250)]		(558)
Federal Tax Payable		$ 6,198

Case B   The solution for this Case is as follows:

Net Income For Tax Purposes And Taxable Income		$50,000

Tax [$5,548 + (22%)($50,000 - $36,378)]		$ 8,545
Basic Personal Amount	($ 8,839)	
Spousal [$7,505 - ($4,650 - $751)]	(3,606)	
EI	(729)	
CPP	(1,911)	
Canada Employment	(250)	
Medical Expenses [$3,150 - (3%)($50,000)]	(1,650)	
Credit Base	($16,985)	
Rate	15.25%	(2,590)
Federal Tax Payable		$ 5,955

As family Net Income For Tax Purposes is greater than $42,140, Stanley Murphy is not eligible for the refundable medical expense supplement.

Case C   The solution for this Case is as follows:

Net Income For Tax Purposes And Taxable Income		$50,000

Tax [$5,548 + (22%)($50,000 - $36,378)]		$ 8,545
Basic Personal Amount	($ 8,839)	
Spousal [$7,505 - ($5,050 - $751)]	(3,206)	
EI	(729)	
CPP	(1,911)	
Canada Employment	(250)	
Transfer From Son (Note)	(5,000)	
Credit Base	($19,935)	
Rate	15.25%	(3,040)
Federal Tax Payable		$ 5,505

Note: The transfer from the son is as follows:

Tuition Fees	$5,400
Base For Education Credit [(8 Months)($400)]	3,200
Base For Textbook Credit [(8 Months)($65)]	520
Total Amount Available	$9,120
Maximum Transfer	(5,000)
Carry Forward (For Albert's Use Only)	$4,120

Albert's Tax Payable is completely eliminated by his basic personal credit. He can transfer a maximum of $5,000 of his education, tuition and textbook amounts to his father. The remaining $4,120 can be carried forward indefinitely, but must be used by Albert.

Case D The solution for this Case is as follows:

Net Income For Tax Purposes and Taxable Income		$41,650
Tax [$5,548 + (22%)($41,650 - $36,378)]		$ 6,708
Basic Personal Amount	($ 8,839)	
Spousal [$7,505 - ($6,500 - $751)]	(1,756)	
Age [$4,066 - (15%)($41,650 - $30,270)]	(2,359)	
Pension	(2,000)	
Spouse's Age	(4,066)	
Spouse's Disability	(6,741)	
Spouse's Pension	(450)	
Credit Base	($26,211)	
Rate	15.25%	(3,997)
Federal Tax Payable		$ 2,711

The Old Age Security and Canada Pension Plan receipts are not eligible for the pension income credit. Helen's Registered Pension Plan receipt is eligible. As Helen Murphy's income is below $30,270, there is no reduction in her age credit.

Case E The solution for this Case can be completed as follows:

Net Income For Tax Purposes And Taxable Income		$50,000
Tax [$5,548 + (22%)($50,000 - $36,378)]		$ 8,545
Basic Personal Amount	($ 8,839)	
Spousal	Nil	
Caregiver (Ahmed)	(3,933)	
EI	(729)	
CPP	(1,911)	
Canada Employment	(250)	
Interest On Student Loan	(375)	
Credit Base	$ 16,037	
Rate	15.25%	(2,446)
Federal Tax Payable		$ 6,099

Stanley would claim the caregiver credit for Ahmed, since Helen would have no Tax Payable after considering her CPP, EI and employment income credit. There would be no credit available for Jaleh as she is not infirm.

Solution to Self Study Problem Six - 2

Part A   Marg has tuition, education and textbook amounts available totalling $10,020 [($400)(8 Months) + ($65)(8 Months) + $6,300]. Her Tax Payable is nil, which can be calculated as follows:

Taxable Income		$12,400
Less:		
Basic Personal Amount	($8,839)	
EI	(441)	
CPP	(232)	
Canada Employment (see Note)	Nil	
Credit Base Before Education related Amounts	($9,512)	
Tuition, Education and Textbook Amounts Claimed		
($12,400 - $9,512)	(2,888)	(12,400)
Subtotal		Nil
Rate		15.25%
Federal Tax Payable		Nil

Note   At this point in time (May, 2006), it appears that the Finance Department has not yet made a decision as to whether the new Canada Employment Credit will affect the calculation of the transfer of education related credits. If the Canada Employment Credit is included, Marg would require $2,638, the transfer amount would be $2,362 and the carry forward amount would still be $5,020.

Marg has an unused tuition, education and textbook amount of $7,132 ($10,020 - $2,888). She can transfer a maximum of $2,112 ($5,000 - $2,888) to her father. This leaves her with a carry forward amount of $5,020 ($10,020 - $2,888 - $2,112).

Note that since her medical expenses were paid for by her father, she cannot claim them herself and they must be transferred to her father. Even if she had paid for them herself and claimed them, she would not increase the transfer to her father as she cannot deduct a medical expense credit prior to deducting her education related credits.

Part B   Mr. Barth's net employment income for the year would be calculated as follows:

Gross Salary	$ 82,500	
Bonus (Note One)	20,000	
Registered Pension Plan Contributions	(3,200)	
Professional Dues	(1,800)	
Stock Option Benefit (Note Two)	3,000	
Automobile Benefit (Note Three)	3,220	
Counseling Benefit (Note Four)	1,500	
Imputed Interest Benefit (Note Five)	750	
Net Employment Income	$105,970	

Note One As the bonus is not payable until more than three years after the end of the employer's taxation year, it is a salary deferral arrangement and must be included in income under ITA 6(11).

Note Two As Mr. Barth's employer is a public company, the employment income inclusion for stock options would normally occur when the options were exercised in 2005. This amount would have been $3,000 [($18 - $15)(1,000)]. However, the specified value of the securities is $12,000 [(1,000)($12)], well below the $100,000 limit on amounts that can be deferred. As a consequence, the $3,000 income inclusion can be deferred until the shares are sold. As the shares are sold in 2006, the $3,000 must be taken into net employment income in that year. There is no capital gain or loss on the sale as the $18,000 proceeds of disposition is equal to his adjusted cost base [($15)(1,000) + $3,000].

Note Three Since Mr. Barth's employment related usage is not more than 50 percent, there is no reduction of the full standby charge. The automobile benefit is calculated as follows:

Standby Charge [(2%)(10)($27,500)]	$5,500
Operating Cost Benefit [(6,000)($0.22)]	1,320
Total Before Payments	$6,820
Payments Withheld	(3,600)
Taxable Benefit	$3,220

Note Four IT-470R indicates that counseling services, with the exception of those items specified under ITA 6(1), are considered taxable benefits. The items specified under ITA 6(1) are counseling with respect to mental or physical health or with respect to re-employment or retirement. As a consequence, the counseling on personal finances is a taxable benefit.

Note Five The imputed interest benefit is calculated as follows:

Basic Benefit [($150,000)(3%)(3/12)]	$1,125
Interest Paid	(375)
Taxable Benefit	$ 750

Taxable Income Mr. Barth's Taxable Income would be calculated as follows:

Net Income For Tax Purposes (Net Employment Income)	$105,970
Stock Option Deduction [(1/2)($3,000)]	(1,500)
Taxable Income	$104,470

Tax Payable   Mr. Barth's Tax Payable would be calculated as follows:

Tax On First $72,756		$ 13,551
Tax On Next $31,714 At 26 Percent		8,246
Federal Tax Before Credits		$ 21,797
Basic Personal Amount	($ 8,839)	
Spousal [$7,505 - ($1,250 - $751)]	(7,006)	
Spouse's Disability	(6,741)	
EI	(729)	
CPP	(1,911)	
Canada Employment	(250)	
Medical Expenses (Note Six)	(2,214)	
Marg's Education, Tuition and Textbook (See Part A)	(2,888)	
Credit Base	($30,578)	
Rate	15.25%	(4,663)
Charitable Donations [(15.25%)($200) + (29%)($2,000 - $200)]		(553)
Net Federal Tax		$ 16,581
Amounts Withheld During Year		(16,000)
Federal Tax Payable		$ 581

Note Six   Allowable medical expenses are as follows:

John And Spouse Medical Expenses ($200+ $3,550)	$3,750
Threshold (Limit Amount)	(1,884)
Subtotal	$1,866
Marg's Medical Expenses - Lesser Of:	
• [$720 - (3%)($12,400)] = $348	
• Absolute Limit = $10,000	348
Allowable Medical Expenses	$2,214

Solution to Self Study Problem Six - 3

The required calculations for Ms. Trubey's balance owing (refund) would be as follows:

Employment Income	$ 60,202
RPP Deduction	(2,406)
Union Dues	(749)
Net And Taxable Income	$ 57,047

Federal Tax On First $36,378		$5,548
Federal Tax On Next $20,669 At 22 Percent		4,547
Gross Federal Tax		$10,095
Basic Personal Amount	($ 8,839)	
Eligible Dependant - Amy	(7,505)	
EI Premiums	(729)	
CPP Contributions	(1,911)	
Canada Employment	(250)	
Caregiver - Marjorie	(3,933)	
Transfer Of Tuition, Education And Textbook - Lesser Of:		
• $5,000		
• [$7,000 + (8)($400) + (8)($65) + (2)($120)		
+ (2)($20)] = $11,000	(5,000)	
Medical Expenses (Note One)	(1,632)	
Credit Base	($29,799)	
Rate	15.25%	(4,544)
Charitable Donations [15.25%)($200) +		
(29%)($175 + $375 + $50 - $200)]		(147)
Net Federal Tax		$ 5,404
Provincial Tax (Given)		2,390
Income Tax Deducted		(19,408)
Instalments Paid (Given)		(2,528)
Balance Owing (Refund)		($14,142)

Note One Allowable medical expenses are as follows:

Eleanor And Minor Child (Amy) Medical Expenses		
($392 + $1,350 + $450 + $1,120)		$3,312
Threshold [(3%)($57,047)]		(1,711)
Subtotal		$1,601
Marjorie's Medical Expenses - Lesser Of:		
• [($50 + $75) - (3%)($5,800)] = Nil		
• Absolute Limit = $10,000		Nil
Diane's Medical Expense - Lesser Of:		
• [$100 - (3%)($2,300)] = $31		
• Absolute Limit = $10,000		31
Allowable Medical Expenses		$1,632

Notes To Eleanor's Tax Return

- Diane transfers the $5,000 maximum education related credits to Eleanor and carries forward the remaining $6,000 [$7,000 + (8)($400) + (8)($65) + (2)($120) + (2)($20) - $5,000].

- Eleanor cannot claim the charitable donation made by Diane, but Diane can carry it forward for up to five years.

- Her daughter, Diane, should file a tax return to make her education related tax credits and charitable donation tax credit available for carry forward. If she does not file, she will not be eligible for the GST credit and she will not benefit from the RRSP deduction room created during the year.

- Her mother, Marjorie, should file a tax return in order to receive the GST credit.

- Eleanor is eligible for the caregiver tax credit for her mother as her income is well below the threshold.

- Since Diane and Marjorie are over 17 years of age, their medical expenses are reduced by 3 percent of their Net Income For Tax Purposes. This means that none of Marjorie's medical expenses can be claimed by Eleanor.

- Eleanor paid too much in instalments. It should be determined why this happened, to try and prevent overpaying instalments again.

Solution to Self Study Case Six - 1

This solution includes selected schedules and worksheets from the ProFile T1 return. Note that the program can only be used to calculate 2005 (not 2006) tax returns, and the problem and solution reflect this fact. The complete tax return is available on the Student CD-ROM (not the ProFile Tax Suite CD-ROM).

Under the heading "Textbook Support Files", is the option to view "Tax Return Files". Select this option and you will see two drop-down lists.

- To view the ProFile file, select the file "Self Study Case 06-1" from the ProFile drop-down list.

- To view the .PDF file, select the file "PDF Self Study Case 06-1" from the PDF drop-down list.

For more information on how to use your Student CD-ROM and the ProFile tax program, refer to the sample tax returns in this Study Guide.

Notes to tax return

- Her daughter, Diane, transfers the $5,000 maximum tuition and education credit to Eleanor and carries forward the remaining $5,400 [$7,000 + (2)($120) + (8)($400) - $5,000].

- Eleanor cannot claim the charitable donation made by Diane, but Diane can carry it forward for up to five years.

- Diane should file a tax return to make her education related tax credits and charitable donation tax credit available for carry forward. If she does not file, she will not be eligible for the GST credit and she will not benefit from the RRSP deduction room created during the year.

- Her mother, Marjorie, should file a tax return in order to receive the GST credit. However, she will need to obtain a Social Insurance Number to do so.

- Eleanor is eligible for the caregiver tax credit for her mother as her income is well below the threshold.

- Since Diane and Marjorie are over 17 years of age, their medical expenses are reduced by 3 percent of their Net Income For Tax Purposes. This means that none of Marjorie's medical expenses can be claimed by Eleanor.

- Eleanor paid too much in instalments. It should be determined why this happened, to try and prevent overpaying instalments again.

Trubey, Eleanor Chap 6 Prob   SIN: 527 000 087
Summary

2005 Tax Summary

Total income		Eleanor Chap 6 Prob
Employment *	101	60,202
Old Age Security	113	
CPP/QPP benefits	114	
Other pensions	115	
Employment Insurance	119	
Taxable dividends	120	
Interest	121	
Limited partnership	122	
Rental	126	
Taxable capital gains	127	
Support payments	128	
RRSP	129	
Other	130	
Self-employment *	135	
Workers' compensation and social assistance	147	
Total income	150	60,202

Net income		
RPP	207	2,406
RRSP *	208	
Union and professional dues	212	749
Child care expenses	214	
Disability supports deduction	215	
Business investment loss	217	
Moving expenses	219	
Support payments	220	
Carrying charges and interest	221	
CPP/QPP on self-employment	222	
Exploration and development	224	
Employment expenses	229	
Social benefits repayment	235	
Other deductions *	231	
Net income	236	57,047

Taxable income		
Canadian Forces personnel	244	
Home relocation loan	248	
Security options deductions	249	
Other payments deduction	250	
Losses of other years *	251	
Capital gains deduction	254	
Northern residents deductions	255	
Additional deductions	256	
Taxable income	260	57,047

2006 Estimated	Eleanor Chap 6 Prob	
GST/HST credit		
Child Tax Benefit	842	00
RRSP contribution limit	2,872	00

* More than one line is considered

Non-refundable tax credits		Eleanor Chap 6 Prob
Basic personal amount	300	8,648
Age amount	301	
Spouse / eligible dependant *	303	7,344
Infirm dependants	306	
CPP/QPP	308	1,861
Employment Insurance	312	761
Adoption expenses	313	
Pension income amount	314	
Caregiver amount	315	3,848
Disability amount	316	
Interest on student loans	319	
Tuition / education	323	
Transfers *	318	5,000
Medical expenses	332	1,632
Subtotal	335	29,093
Credit at 15%	338	4,364
Donations and gifts	349	146
Non-refundable tax credits	350	4,510

Total payable		
Federal tax	11	10,058
Non-refundable tax credits	350	4,510
Dividend tax credit	425	
Minimum tax carry-over/other *	426	
Basic federal tax	13	5,548
Non resident surtax *	14	
Foreign tax credits / other		
Federal tax	406	5,548
Political/investment tax credit *	410	
Labour-sponsored tax credit	414	
Alternative minimum tax		
Additional tax on RESP	418	
Net federal tax	260	5,548
CPP contributions payable	421	
Social benefits repayment	422	
Provincial/territorial tax	428	2,360
Total payable	435	7,908

Total credits		
Income tax deducted *	437	19,408
QC or YT abatement *	440	
CPP overpayment	448	
EI overpayment	450	
Medical expense supplement	452	
GST/HST rebate	457	
Instalments	476	2,528
Provincial tax credits	479	
Other credits	454	
Total credits	482	21,936

Balance owing (refund)		(14,028)
Combined balance (refund)		(14,028)

Complete Return Available On Student CD-ROM

Page 1 of 1

S - 80

Trubey, Eleanor Chap 6 Prob   SIN: 527 000 087

T1-2005   **Federal Tax**   **Schedule 1**

Complete this schedule to claim your federal non-refundable tax credits and to calculate your net federal tax.

You must attach a copy of this schedule to your return.

Enter your **taxable income** from line 260 of your return ___ 57,047 05 **1**

Use the amount on line 1 to determine which **ONE**
of the following columns you have to complete.

If the amount on line 1 is:	$35,595 or less		more than $35,595 but not more than $71,190		more than $71,190 but not more than $115,739		more than $115,739	
Enter the amount from line 1 above		**2**	57,047 05	**2**		**2**		**2**
Base amount		**3**	35,595 00	**3**	71,190 00	**3**	115,739 00	**3**
Line 2 minus line 3 (this amount cannot be negative)	0 00	**4**	21,452 05	**4**		**4**		**4**
Rate	x 15.00 %	**5**	x 22.00 %	**5**	x 26.00 %	**5**	x 29.00 %	**5**
Multiply the amount on line 4 by the rate on line 5		**6**	4,719 45	**6**		**6**		**6**
Tax on base amount	0 00	**7**	5,339 00	**7**	13,170 00	**7**	24,753 00	**7**
Add lines 6 and 7		**8**	10,058 45	**8**		**8**		**8**

Federal non-refundable tax credits

Basic personal amount	claim $8,648	**300**	8,648 00
Age amount (if you were born in 1940 or earlier)	(maximum $3,979)	**301**	

Spouse or common-law partner amount:
Base amount _____ 8,079 00
Minus: his or her net income (from page 1 of your return) _____ 0 00
Result: (if negative, enter "0") (maximum $7,344) ▶ **303**

Amount for an eligible dependant (**attach** Schedule 5)	(maximum $7,344)	**305**	7,344 00
Amount for infirm dependants age 18 or older (**attach** Schedule 5)		**306**	
CPP or QPP contributions: through employment from box 16 and box 17 on all T4 slips	(maximum $1,861.20)	**308**	1,861 00 •
on self-employment and other earnings (**attach** Schedule 8)		**310**	•
Employment Insurance premiums from box 18 on all T4 slips	(maximum $760.50)	**312**	760 50 •
Adoption expenses		**313**	
Pension income amount	(maximum $1,000)	**314**	
Caregiver amount (**attach** Schedule 5)		**315**	3,848 00
Disability amount		**316**	
Disability amount transferred from a dependant		**318**	
Interest paid on your student loans		**319**	
Tuition and education amounts (**attach** Schedule 11)		**323**	
Tuition and education amounts transferred from a child		**324**	5,000 00
Amounts transferred from your spouse or common-law partner (**attach** Schedule 2)		**326**	

Medical expenses for **self, spouse or common-law partner, and your dependent children born in 1988 or later** (see the guide) **330** 3,312 00
Minus: $1,844 or 3% of line 236, whichever is **less** _____ 1,711 41
Subtotal (if negative, enter "0") 1,600 59 (A)
Allowable amount of medical expenses for **other dependants** (see the calculation at line 331 in the guide and **attach** Schedule 5) **331** 31 00 (B)
Add lines (A) and (B). 1,631 59 ▶ **332** 1,631 59

Add lines 300 to 326, and 332. **335** 29,093 09

Multiply the amount on line 335 by 15% = **338** 4,363 96
Donations and gifts (**attach** Schedule 9) **349** 146 00

Total federal non-refundable tax credits: Add lines 338 and 349. **350** 4,509 96
continue

Page 1 of 2

Trubey, Eleanor Chap 6 Prob   SIN: 527 000-087

Net federal tax

Enter the amount from line 8		10,058 45	**9**
Federal tax on split income (from line 4 of Form T1206)	**424**		• **10**
Add lines 9 and 10	10,058 45 ▶	10,058 45	**11**

Enter the amount from line 350	**350**	4,509 96	
Federal dividend tax credit (13.3333% of the amount on line 120 of your return)	**425**		•
Overseas employment tax credit (**attach** Form T626)	426		
Minimum tax carry-over (**attach** Form T691)	**427**		•
Add lines 350, 425, 426, and 427	4,509 96 ▶	4,509 96	**12**

Basic federal tax: Line 11 minus line 12 (if negative, enter "0")   429   5,548 49   **13**

Federal foreign tax credit:
Where you **only** have foreign non-business income, calculate your federal foreign tax credit below. Otherwise,
use Form T2209, *Federal Foreign Tax Credits*, if you have foreign business income. **Enter on this line the**
amount you calculated   **14**

Federal logging tax credit

Federal tax: Line 13 minus line 14 (if negative, enter "0")   406   5,548 49   **15**

Total federal political contributions (**attach** receipts)	**409**		
Federal political contribution tax credit (see the guide)	**410**		•
Investment tax credit (**attach** Form T2038(IND))	**412**		•
Labour-sponsored funds tax credit			
Net cost **413**	Allowable credit **414**		•
Add lines 410, 412, and 414. 416	▶		**16**

Line 15 minus line 16 (if negative, enter "0")
(if you have an amount on line 424 above, see Form T1206)   417   5,548 49   **17**

Additional tax on RESP accumulated income payments (**attach** Form T1172)   418   **18**

Net federal tax: Add lines 17 and 18
Enter this amount on line 420 of your return.   420   5,548 49   **19**

Federal foreign tax credit: (see lines 431 and 433 in the guide)

Make a separate calculation for each foreign country. Enter on line 14 above the result from line (i) or line (ii), whichever is **less**.

Non-business income tax paid to a foreign country	**431**		• **(i)**

Net foreign non-business income *	**433**	X	Basic federal tax ***	= **(ii)**
Net income **				

* Reduce this amount by any income from that foreign country for which you claimed a capital gains deduction, and by any income from that country that was, under a tax treaty, either exempt from tax in that country or deductible as exempt income in Canada (included on line 256). Also reduce this amount by the lesser of lines E and F on Form T626.

** Line 236 plus the amount on line 3 of Form T1206, minus the total of the amounts on lines 244, 248, 249, 250, 253, 254, and minus any amount included on line 256 for foreign income deductible as exempt income under a tax treaty, income deductible as net employment income from a prescribed international organization, or non-taxable tuition assistance from box 21 of the T4E slip. If the result is less than the amount on line 433, enter your **Basic federal tax*** on line (ii).

*** Line 429 plus the amount on lines 425 and 426, and minus any refundable Québec abatement (line 440) and any federal refundable First Nations abatement (line 441 on the return for residents of Yukon).

Chapter Six Learning Objectives

After completing Chapter 6, you should be able to:

1. Calculate federal Tax Payable before the consideration of any tax credits using a supplied schedule of rates and other data (paragraphs 6-1 through 6-30).

2. Calculate the personal tax credits using a supplied schedule of rates and other data (paragraphs 6-31 through 6-56).

3. Calculate the age tax credit using a supplied schedule of rates and other data (paragraphs 6-57 and 6-58).

4. Calculate the pension income tax credit using a supplied schedule of rates and other data (paragraphs 6-59 through 6-63).

5. Calculate the adoption expenses tax credit using a supplied schedule of rates and other data (paragraphs 6-64 through 6-69).

6. Calculate the charitable donations tax credit using a supplied schedule of rates and other data (paragraphs 6-70 through 6-79).

7. Calculate the medical expenses tax credit using a supplied schedule of rates and other data (paragraphs 6-80 through 6-86).

8. Calculate the refundable medical expense supplement using a supplied schedule of rates and other data (paragraphs 6-87 through 6-89).

9. Calculate the disability tax credit using a supplied schedule of rates and other data (paragraphs 6-90 through 6-98).

10. Calculate the education related tax credits using a supplied schedule of rates and other data (paragraphs 6-99 through 6-110).

11. Calculate the amount of education related tax credits that can be transferred to another individual (paragraphs 6-111 through 6-115).

12. Calculate the Employment Insurance and Canada Pension Plan credits using a supplied schedule of rates and other data (paragraphs 6-116 through 6-122).

13. Recall the types and amounts of tax credits that can be transferred to a spouse or common-law partner (paragraphs 6-123 and 6-124).

14. Calculate the political contributions tax credit using a supplied schedule of rates and other data (paragraphs 6-128 through 6-130).

15. Calculate the labour sponsored funds tax credit using a supplied schedule of rates and other data (paragraphs 6-131 and 6-132).

16. Calculate the new Canada Employment credit and public transit passes credit using a supplied schedule of rates and other data (paragraphs 6-133 through 6-136).

17. Be aware of the new children's fitness credit and apprenticeship job creation credit (paragraphs 6-137 through 6-140).

18. Explain the basic provisions of the refundable GST credit and the child tax benefit system (paragraphs 6-141 through 6-150).

19. Calculate the OAS and EI clawbacks using a supplied schedule of rates and other data (paragraphs 6-151 through 6-159).

20. Complete a simple personal tax return using the ProFile T1 tax preparation software program (pages S-54 through S-67 in this Study Guide).

CHAPTER SEVEN

How To Work Through Chapter Seven

We recommend the following approach in dealing with the material in this chapter:

Tax And Accounting Procedures Compared And General Rules
☐ Read the text pages 221 (from paragraph 7-1) through 226 (through paragraph 7-29).

☐ Complete Exercise Seven-1 on page 226 of the text. The solution is on page S-87.

Capital Cost Allowances - General Overview
☐ Read the text pages 227 (from paragraph 7-30) through 229 (through paragraph 7-32).

Half-Year (a.k.a First Year) Rules
☐ Read the text page 229 (from paragraph 7-33) and 230 (through paragraph 7-37).

☐ Complete Exercises Seven-2 through Seven-4 on page 230 of the text. The solutions are on page S-87.

Short Fiscal Periods
☐ Read the text pages 230 (from paragraph 7-38) and 231 (through paragraph 7-42).

☐ Complete Exercise Seven-5 on page 231 of the text. The solution is on page S-87.

Tax Planning Considerations
☐ Read the text pages 231 (from paragraph 7-43) and 232 (through paragraph 7-47).

☐ Complete Exercise Seven-6 on page 232 of the text. The solution is on pages S-87 and S-88.

Dispositions Of Depreciable Assets
☐ Read the text pages 232 (from paragraph 7-48) and 233 (through paragraph 7-56).

☐ Complete Exercise Seven-7 on page 234 of the text. The solution is on page S-88.

Recapture Of Capital Cost Allowance
☐ Read the text pages 234 (from paragraph 7-57) and 232 (through paragraph 7-60).

☐ Complete Exercise Seven-8 on page 234 of the text. The solution is on page S-88.

Terminal Losses
☐ Read the text page 234 (from paragraph 7-61) and 235 (through paragraph 7-64).

☐ Complete Exercise Seven-9 on page 235 of the text. The solution is on page S-88.

CCA Schedule - Example
☐ Read the text page 235 (paragraph 7-65).

Separate Class Election
☐ Read the text pages 236 (from paragraph 7-66) and 237 (through paragraph 7-73).

☐ Complete Exercise Seven-10 on page 237 of your text. The solution is on page S-88.

Special Rules For Buildings

☐ Read the text pages 237 (from paragraph 7-74) and 238 (through paragraph 7-78).

☐ Complete Exercise Seven-11 on page 238 of the text. The solution is on pages S-88 and S-89 .

☐ Complete Self Study Problems Seven-1, Seven-2, and Seven-3 on pages 252 and 253 of the text. The solutions are on pages S-90 through S-93.

Deferral Provisions On Replacement Property

☐ Read the text pages 238 (from paragraph 7-79) through 240 (through paragraph 7-89).

☐ Complete Exercise Seven-12 on page 240 of the text. The solution is on page S-89.

☐ Read the text page 240 (paragraph 7-90).

☐ Complete Self Study Problem Seven-4 on pages 253 and 254 of the text. The solution is on pages S-93 and S-94.

Change In Use

☐ Read the text pages 240 (from paragraph 7-91) through 242 (through paragraph 7-99).

☐ Complete Exercise Seven-13 on pages 242 and 243 of the text. The solution is on page S-89.

☐ Read the text page 243 (from paragraph 7-100 through paragraph 7-102).

☐ Complete Self Study Problem Seven-5 on page 254 of the text. The solution is on pages S-94 and S-95 .

Cumulative Eligible Capital

☐ Read the text pages 243 (from paragraph 7-103) through 246 (through paragraph 7-119).

☐ Complete Exercise Seven-14 on page 246 of the text. The solution is on page S-89.

CEC Disposal Election

☐ Read the text pages 246 (from paragraph 7-120) and 247 (through paragraph 7-122).

☐ Complete Exercise Seven-15 on page 247 of the text. The solution is on pages S-89 and S-90.

☐ Complete Self Study Problems Seven-6 and Seven-7 on pages 254 and 255 of the text. The solutions are on pages S-95 through S-97.

Effects on CEC of Business Terminations, Death And Replacement Properties

☐ Read the text page 248 (from paragraph 7-123 through paragraph 7-126).

To Complete This Chapter

☐ Review the Key Terms Used In This Chapter on page 248 of the text. Consult the Glossary for the meaning of any key terms you do not know.

☐ Review the Glossary Flashcards and complete the Key Terms Self-Test for the Chapter. These features can be found in two places, on your Student CD-ROM under the heading "Key Term Practice" and on the web site.

☐ Review the Learning Objectives of the Chapter found on page S-98 of this Study Guide.

☐ As a review, we recommend that you view the PowerPoint Slides for Chapter Seven that are on your Student CD-ROM. The PowerPoint Viewer program can be installed from the Student CD-ROM.

Solution to Chapter Seven Exercises

Exercise Seven - 1 Solution

The correct classes for each of the assets would be as follows:

Asset	Class
Taxicab	16
Manufacturing and processing equipment	43
Franchise with a limited life	14
Passenger vehicle with a cost of $120,000*	10.1
Water storage tank	6
Photocopy machine	8
Leasehold improvements	13
Rental building*	1

*These two assets would have to be allocated to separate classes. In addition, the taxpayer could elect to include the photocopy machine in a separate class.

Exercise Seven - 2 Solution

CCA should have been $48,900 [($326,000)(1/2)(30%)]. The amount recorded was $6,520 [($326,000)(1/2)(4%)]. This error understated deductions and overstated income by $42,380 ($48,900 - $6,520).

Exercise Seven - 3 Solution

The CCA for 2006 on the 2001 capital costs would be $3,467 [($52,000 ÷ 15)]. The CCA on the 2006 capital costs, after taking into consideration the half-year rules, would be $1,550 [($31,000 ÷ 10)(1/2)]. The total for the year would be $5,017 ($3,467 + $1,550).

Exercise Seven - 4 Solution

The required information would be calculated as follows:

January 1, 2006 UCC Balance		$212,000
Add: Additions	$37,400	
Deduct: Dispositions	(18,300)	19,100
Deduct: One-Half Net Additions [(1/2)($19,100)]		(9,550)
CCA Base		$221,550
2006 CCA At 20 Percent		(44,310)
Add: One-Half Net Additions		9,550
January 1, 2007 UCC Balance		$186,790

Exercise Seven - 5 Solution

The maximum CCA for the year is $4,821 [(20%)($115,000)(1/2)(153/365)].

Exercise Seven - 6 Solution

Following the rule that, when less than the maximum CCA is to be deducted, the amounts deducted should be taken from the class(es) with the lowest rates, the required calculations would be as follows:

Required Total		$45,000
Maximum CCA - Class 1 [(4%)($426,000)]	($17,040)	
Maximum CCA - Class 8 [(20%)($126,000)]	(25,200)	(42,240)
Required Balance		$ 2,760

As they are both 30 percent declining balance classes, the remaining $2,760 could be taken from either Class 10 or Class 10.1. It would be advisable to use Class 10.1, as recapture is not recorded for this class. In addition, if the Class 10.1 vehicle is going to be disposed of in the near future, it could be better tax planning to take the maximum CCA for Class 10.1 of $6,300 [(30%)($21,000)] and reduce the Class 8 CCA to $21,660 ($45,000 - $6,300 - $17,040). Since there is no recapture for Class 10.1, this could increase future deductions of the other classes. Whether this would be advantageous depends on the anticipated proceeds of disposition.

Exercise Seven - 7 Solution

For accounting purposes, there would be a gain of $82,500 ($126,000 - $43,500), the full amount of which would be included in accounting Net Income. For tax purposes, there would be a capital gain of $29,000 ($126,000 - $97,000), of which one-half, or $14,500, would be included in income. The capital cost of $97,000 would be subtracted from the UCC, leaving a balance of $2,365,000. While this disposition would reduce the maximum CCA for the current and subsequent years, there would be no recapture (the balance in Class 8 is still positive) or terminal loss (there are still assets in Class 8).

Exercise Seven - 8 Solution

The effect would be an addition of $2,117 ($24,883 - $27,000) in recaptured CCA. While there would also be a taxable capital gain of $750 [($28,500 - $27,000)(1/2)], this would not be included in Subdivision b's net business income.

Exercise Seven - 9 Solution

As there is a positive balance in Class 8 at the end of the year, but no remaining assets, there would be a terminal loss of $6,883 ($24,883 - $18,000). This loss is fully deductible against other income.

Exercise Seven - 10 Solution

Photocopiers would be included in Class 8, a 20 percent declining balance class. If no election is made, there will be a deduction for CCA of $23,800 {[(10)($20,000) - (2)($3,000) + (2)($22,000)][1/2][20%]}. Alternatively, if each machine is allocated to a separate class, there will be a deduction for CCA of $20,400 {[(8)($20,000) + (2)($22,000)][1/2][20%]}. In addition, there will be a terminal loss of $34,000 [($20,000 - $3,000)(2)]. The use of the election increases the total deductible amount by $30,600 ($20,400 + $34,000 - $23,800).

Exercise Seven - 11 Solution

In the absence of the special rules, there would be a capital gain of $325,000 ($750,000 - $425,000) on the land. The $162,500 [(1/2)($325,000)] taxable amount would be reduced by the $115,000 ($615,000 - $500,000) terminal loss on the building, resulting in a net income inclusion of $47,500 ($162,500 - $115,000). ITA 13(21.1)(a) modifies the results in such situations by deeming the proceeds of disposition for the building to be:

The Lesser Of:
- The FMV of the land and building $1,250,000
  Reduced By The Lesser Of:
    - The ACB of the land = $425,000
    - The FMV of the land = $750,000   (425,000) $825,000
- The Greater Of:
    - The FMV of the building = $500,000
    - The Lesser Of:
      The cost of the building = $930,000
      The UCC of the building = $615,000 $615,000

With the building proceeds at $615,000, the terminal loss is eliminated. The deemed proceeds for the land are $635,000 ($1,250,000 - $615,000), resulting in a capital gain of $210,000 ($635,000 - $425,000). In effect, this eliminates the terminal loss of $115,000 by reducing the capital gain by the same amount, from $325,000 to $210,000. The net income inclusion would be $105,000 [(1/2)($210,000)], an increase of $57,500 ($105,000 - $47,500) from the unadjusted result.

Exercise Seven - 12 Solution

The Company would have to record recapture of $750,000 ($650,000 - $1,400,000) for 2005. This is reversed during 2006 by electing under ITA 13(4). The result is that the UCC of the new building would be limited to $1,600,000 ($2,350,000 - $750,000).

Exercise Seven - 13 Solution

The amount that will be added to the UCC balance is $147,000 [$111,000 + (1/2)($183,000 - $111,000)]. The maximum CCA of $7,400 [(15%)($147,000)(1/2)(245/365)] involves both the half-year rule and the short fiscal period procedures.

Exercise Seven - 14 Solution

The required income inclusion can be calculated as follows:

	CEC Balance	CEC Deductions
2004 CEC Addition [(3/4)($85,600)]	$64,200	
2004 CEC Amount At 7 Percent	(4,494)	$4,494
Balance January 1, 2005	$59,706	
2005 CEC Amount At 7 Percent	(4,179)	4,179
Balance January 1, 2006	$55,527	
Proceeds From Sale [(3/4)($93,400)]	(70,050)	
Balance After Sale	($14,523)	$8,673

The negative balance in the CEC account after the sale is more than the total of the CEC deductions in the past two years ($8,673). Given this, the income inclusion will be as follows:

- $8,673 (the CEC deducted), plus
- $3,900 [(2/3)($14,523 - $8,673)].

As a result, $12,573 ($8,673 + $3,900) will be included in income in 2006. Note that the $3,900 income inclusion could also be calculated by taking one-half of the gain (similar to capital gains treatment) on the disposition [$3,900 = (1/2)($93,400 - $85,600)].

Exercise Seven - 15 Solution

The following table compares the balance in the CEC account assuming the election is not made with the balance assuming the election is made:

	No Election	With Election
2005 Addition [(3/4)($514,000)]	$385,500	$385,500
2005 CEC Amount [($385,500)(7%)]	(26,985)	(26,985)
January 1, 2006 CEC Balance	$358,515	$358,515
Proceeds Of Sale [(3/4)($296,000)]	(222,000)	Nil
Deemed Proceeds Of Sale [(3/4)($223,000)]	Nil	(167,250)
Balance After Sale	$136,515	$191,265
Taxable Capital Gain	N/A	$ 36,500

If no election is made, there will be no income inclusion and the only tax consequence of the disposition is a reduction in the current and future CEC amounts.

If an election is made, there would be a capital gain of $73,000 ($296,000 - $223,000), resulting in an income inclusion of $36,500 [(1/2)($73,000)] and a balance in the CEC account that is $54,750 ($191,265 - $136,515) higher.

Solution to Self Study Problem Seven - 1

The maximum 2006 deduction for CCA and the January 1, 2007 UCC can be calculated as follows:

	Class 8	Class 10	Class 1
Opening Balance	$ 96,000	$ 6,700	$115,000
Additions	52,000	8,000	-0-
Dispositions	(35,000)	(20,000)	(110,000)
One-Half Net Additions	(8,500)	N/A	N/A
CCA Base	$104,500	($ 5,300)	$ 5,000
CCA	(20,900)		
One-Half Net Additions	8,500		
Recapture		5,300	
Terminal Loss			(5,000)
January 1, 2007 UCC Balance	$ 92,100	Nil	Nil

Class 8 The CCA for Class 8 is $20,900 [(20%)($104,500)].

Class 10 As the cost of the used car is less than $30,000, its cost is added to Class 10. With respect to the retirement, only the capital cost of the truck sold is deducted from Class 10. The excess of the $25,000 proceeds over the capital cost of $20,000 is a $5,000 capital gain, one-half of which would be taxable. The $12,000 net deduction creates a negative balance in the class and, as a consequence, no CCA will be taken for 2006. However, the negative balance of $5,300 will have to be taken into income as recapture.

Class 1 In Class 1, since the building sold is the last asset in the class, there is a terminal loss of $5,000. Since the land that the building was situated on was leased, the special rules on dispositions of buildings at a loss do not apply.

Summary Results The preceding results can be summarized as follows:

CCA - Class 8	($20,900)
Recapture - Class 10	5,300
Terminal Loss - Class 1	(5,000)
Subtotal	($20,600)
Taxable Capital Gain - Class 10 [(1/2)($25,000 - $20,000)]	2,500
Decrease In Net Income For Tax Purposes	($18,100)

Solution to Self Study Problem Seven - 2

2001 Solution   The required calculations are as follows:

Additions To Class [(20 Cars)($12,000)]	$240,000
One-Half Net Additions [(1/2)($240,000)]	(120,000)
CCA Base	$120,000
CCA [($120,000)(30%)(122/365)]	(12,033)
One-Half Net Additions	120,000
January 1, 2002 UCC Balance	$227,967

Note that one-half of the net additions for the year is deducted to provide the basis for calculating the 2001 CCA, and then added back to establish the opening UCC base for the next period. The other point that is illustrated in this first year is application of the short fiscal period rules. As the business was established on September 1, 2001, its operations were carried out for only 122 of the 365 days in that year. This means that only a proportionate share of the annual CCA charge may be taken. Note that it is the length of the taxation year, not the period of ownership of the assets, that establishes the fraction of the year for which CCA is to be recorded.

2002 Solution   The required calculations are as follows:

Opening Balance For The Class	$227,967
Additions [(5 Cars)($12,500)]	62,500
Dispositions (Proceeds)	(27,500)
One-Half Net Additions [(1/2)($62,500 - $27,500)]	(17,500)
CCA Base	$245,467
CCA At 30 Percent	(73,640)
One-Half Net Additions	17,500
January 1, 2003 UCC Balance	$189,327

Here again, one-half of the net additions for the year are deducted in establishing the base for calculating CCA, with the same amount being added back to determine the opening UCC for the next period.

2003 Solution   The required calculations are as follows:

Opening Balance For The Class	$189,327
Dispositions (Proceeds)	(38,000)
CCA Base	$151,327
CCA At 30 Percent	(45,398)
January 1, 2004 UCC Balance	$105,929

The calculations are simplified by the absence of additions to the delivery car fleet. To establish the CCA base, it is only necessary to deduct the proceeds of the dispositions. The new UCC is the CCA base, less the CCA for the period.

2004 Solution The required calculations are as follows:

Opening Balance For The Class	$105,929
Dispositions (Proceeds)	(128,000)
Negative Balance	($ 22,071)
Recapture	22,071
January 1, 2005 UCC Balance	Nil

The inability to replace the fleet cars in a timely fashion was a costly mistake in that the $22,071 in recapture will be included in the 2004 Net Income. In a more realistic situation, it is likely that actions would have been taken to delay the retirement of the older cars and, thereby, avoid the tax implications of recapture. There is no election available to defer the recapture as the election would only apply if the voluntarily replaced property was real property. Note also that when recapture occurs, the balance in the class for the next period is reduced to zero.

2005 Solution The required calculations are as follows:

Opening Balance For The Class	Nil
Acquisitions [(25 Cars)($16,000)]	$400,000
One-Half Net Additions [(1/2)($400,000)]	(200,000)
CCA Base	$200,000
CCA At 30 Percent	(60,000)
One-Half Net Additions	200,000
January 1, 2006 UCC Balance	$340,000

As was the case in 2001 and 2002, one-half of the net additions must be deducted in establishing the base for CCA and then added back to determine the opening UCC balance for the next period.

2006 Solution The required calculations are as follows:

Opening Balance For The Class	$340,000
Dispositions (Proceeds)	(268,000)
Terminal Loss	$ 72,000

At this point, all of the assets in Class 10 have been retired and there is still a $72,000 UCC balance. This results in a terminal loss that will be deducted in full from the Net Income of Golden Dragon Ltd.

Solution to Self Study Problem Seven - 3

Part A The required calculation of the maximum CCA is as follows:

	Class 1	Class 8	Class 10
Opening Balance	$876,000	$220,000	$163,000
Additions	-0-	-0-	122,000
Proceeds Of Disposition	-0-	-0-	(87,000)
One-Half Net Additions	-0-	-0-	(17,500)
CCA Base	$876,000	$220,000	$180,500
CCA Rate	4%	20%	30%
Maximum CCA	$ 35,040	$ 44,000	$ 54,150

This gives a maximum amount for CCA of $133,190 for the taxation year.

Part B   Since Marion Enterprises only has 2006 Net and Taxable Income before CCA of $53,000, the business may wish to deduct less than the maximum CCA that is available to them. However, there is no question that the business will wish to deduct the $53,000 that is required to reduce the current year's Taxable Income to nil.

Assuming the 2006 CCA deduction is limited to $53,000, it would normally be deducted in the class or classes with the lowest rates. This would leave the unused amounts in classes with higher rates which, in turn, would maximize the amount that could be deducted in the first profitable years. Taking this approach, the $53,000 would be deducted as follows:

Class 1 (Maximum Available)	$35,040
Class 8 (Required Balance)	17,960
Total CCA	$53,000

This CCA deduction would reduce 2006 Taxable Income to nil.

Part C   It would be advisable to deduct an additional $46,000. This would create a business loss in 2006 of $46,000, which could then be carried back to claim refunds of taxes paid in the three preceding years.

Beyond the deduction of $99,000 ($53,000 + $46,000), the solution to the problem becomes less clear cut. If additional CCA is taken, it will serve to create a business loss that can only be deducted as a carry forward over the next 10 years. If there is not sufficient Taxable Income in the next 10 years to absorb this carry over, the benefit of the loss will not be realized. Given the uncertainty expressed about profits for the next 11 to 13 years, the prudent course of action may be to only deduct 2006 CCA of $99,000. However, the alternatives here should be explained and discussed with management.

Assuming the 2006 CCA deduction is limited to $99,000, it would normally be deducted in the class or classes with the lowest rates. This would leave the unused amounts in classes with higher rates which, in turn, would maximize the amount that could be deducted in the first profitable years. Taking this approach, the $99,000 would be deducted as follows:

Class 1 (Maximum Available)	$35,040
Class 8 (Maximum Available)	44,000
Class 10 (Required Balance)	19,960
Total CCA	$99,000

This CCA deduction would reduce 2006 Taxable Income to nil and would create an unused business loss carry back of $46,000.

Solution to Self Study Problem Seven - 4

2005   For 2005, the insurance proceeds would be subtracted from the class, leaving a negative balance of $122,000. This $122,000 would have to be taken into 2005 income as recapture. It will be added back to the UCC on January 1, 2006 to create a UCC balance of nil.

2006   Using ITA 13(4), Trail Resources Ltd. would file an amended return for the 2005 taxation year. The $122,000 of recapture that was recognized in that year would be reversed, with the overall result that this amount would be subtracted from the UCC applicable to the new asset. This would provide for the following calculation of 2006 maximum CCA and January 1, 2007 UCC:

Opening UCC - Class 1		Nil
Add: Cost Of New Building	$650,000	
Deduct: Deemed Proceeds of Disposition (122,000)		$528,000
Deduct: One-Half Net Additions		(264,000)
Base For CCA		$264,000
Maximum CCA [($264,000)(4%)]		(10,560)
Add: One-Half Net Additions		(264,000)
UCC Balance, January 1, 2007		$517,440

The reasonableness of the answer can be verified by noting that the $528,000 is equal to the initial UCC of $368,000, less the insurance proceeds of $490,000, plus the cost of the new building of $650,000. The half year rule is applied to the net addition to Class 1.

Solution to Self Study Problem Seven - 5

As the 2004 change in use is from personal to business, the deemed disposition will take place at a value, for CCA purposes, of cost plus one-half of the excess of fair market value over cost [ITA 13(7)(b)]. Although Miss Coos previously owned this building, the half-year rule applies to this change in use because a personal residence is not a depreciable property. Given this, the maximum CCA that can be deducted in the three years can be calculated as follows:

Maximum CCA For 2004

Cost	$ 90,000
Bump Up On Transfer [(1/2)($120,000 - $90,000)]	15,000
Transfer Value	$105,000
Rental Portion	30%
UCC At Transfer	$ 31,500
One-Half Net Additions	(15,750)
CCA Base	$ 15,750
Maximum Class 1 CCA At 4 Percent	(630)
One-Half Net Additions	15,750
January 1, 2005 UCC	$ 30,870

Note While this information is not required by the problem, this deemed disposition would result in a taxable capital gain of $4,500 [(1/2)(30%)($120,000 - $90,000)]. It is likely that Ms. Coos would designate this property as her principal residence for 2002 and 2003, thereby eliminating this gain from her income (this is discussed in more detail in Chapter 10).

Maximum CCA For 2005

2005 Opening UCC	$ 30,870
Maximum CCA At 4 Percent	(1,235)
January 1, 2006 UCC	$ 29,635

Maximum CCA For 2006

2006 Opening UCC	$ 29,635
Dispositions (Note)	(10,500)
CCA Base	$ 19,135
Maximum CCA At 4 Percent	(765)
January 1, 2007 UCC	$ 18,370

Note The deemed proceeds would be 10 percent of $140,000, or $14,000. However, this is greater than the $10,500 [(10%)($105,000)] cost associated with the disposition. As the lower of these figures must be used, the deduction is $10,500. While this information is not required by the problem, there would also be a taxable capital gain of $1,000 [(1/2)(10%)($140,000 - $120,000)]. Note that the $120,000 adjusted cost base used in the calculation of the taxable capital gain is not the same as the $105,000 capital cost used in the calculation of CCA. This is due to the fact that there is no limit on the adjusted cost base to be recognized in the new value, as is the case for the capital cost for CCA purposes. In all cases, the adjusted cost base of the reacquisition will be equal to the fair market value of the asset.

Solution to Self Study Problem Seven - 6

Class 1 - Building   There were no additions or dispositions in this class. As a consequence, the maximum CCA would be $25,000 [(4%)($625,000)]. The January 1, 2007 UCC of Class 1 would be $600,000.

Class 8 - Office Furniture And Equipment   The required calculations for this class would be as follows:

Opening Balance	$155,000
Additions During Fiscal Year	27,000
Dispositions During Fiscal Year	(22,000)
One-Half Net Additions	(2,500)
CCA Base	$157,500
Capital Cost Allowance (20%)	(31,500)
One-Half Net Additions	2,500
January 1, 2007 UCC Balance	$128,500

With respect to the disposition during the year, there would be a capital gain of $13,000 ($35,000 - $22,000), one-half of which is taxable. Only the capital cost of $22,000 is deducted from the UCC of the class.

Class 10 - Vehicles   The required calculations for this class would be as follows:

Opening Balance	$118,000
Additions During Fiscal Year	33,000
Dispositions During Fiscal Year ($8,500 + $8,000)	(16,500)
One-Half Net Additions	(8,250)
CCA Base	$126,250
Capital Cost Allowance (30%)	(37,875)
One-Half Net Additions	8,250
January 1, 2007 UCC Balance	$ 96,625

Note that the amount received from the insurance company on the destroyed vehicle is treated as proceeds from a disposition.

Class 12 - Tools   The tools are eligible for a write-off rate of 100 percent, and they are not subject to the half-year rules on net additions. As a consequence, the entire $34,000 can be deducted as CCA for the current year, leaving no January 1, 2007 balance in the account.

Class 13 - Leasehold Improvements   In general, leasehold improvements will be written off over the term of the lease on a straight line basis. For purposes of applying this calculation, the term of the lease would include the first renewal option, beginning in a period after the improvements were made. In the case of the original improvements, the period to be used is 12 years. With respect to the improvements during the current year, the write-off period will be 9 years. Also note that Class 13 assets are subject to the half-year rules on net additions. The required calculations are as follows:

Opening Balance	$ 61,750
Additions	45,000
CCA Base	$106,750
Capital Cost Allowance:	
First Improvements ($78,000 ÷ 12)	(6,500)
Current Improvements [($45,000 ÷ 9)(1/2)]	(2,500)
January 1, 2007 UCC Balance	$ 97,750

Class 43 - Manufacturing Equipment   The required calculations are as follows:

Opening Balance	$217,000
Dispositions (Proceeds)	(188,000)
Terminal Loss	$ 29,000

At this point, all of the assets in Class 43 have been retired and there is still a $29,000 UCC balance. This results in a terminal loss that will be deducted in full from the Net Income of Atlantic Manufacturing Company.

Class 45 - Computers   The rate for Class 45 is 45 percent and the class is subject to the first year rules. The required calculations for this class would be as follows:

Opening Balance	$10,000
Additions During Fiscal Year	28,000
One-Half Net Additions	(14,000)
CCA Base	$24,000
Capital Cost Allowance (45%)	(10,800)
One-Half Net Additions	14,000
January 1, 2007 UCC Balance	$27,200

Cumulative Eligible Capital   The required calculations for the sale of the licence would be as follows:

Opening Balance	Nil
Proceeds Of Disposition [($87,000)(3/4)]	($65,250)
Negative Balance	($65,250)
Addition To Balance	65,250
January 1, 2007 Balance	Nil

The proceeds are based on 75 percent of the amount received. Therefore, 75 percent of the proceeds of $87,000 would be deducted, thereby creating a negative balance for cumulative eligible capital in the amount of $65,250. As no CEC has been deducted in previous years, the entire negative balance in the cumulative eligible capital account would be multiplied by two-thirds (1/2 ÷ 3/4), resulting in an income inclusion of $43,500. In effect, the entire $87,000 proceeds is being given capital gains treatment, with only one-half of this amount being included in income. The $65,250 will also be added back to the CEC balance, restoring the balance to nil.

Summary Of The Results   The maximum CCA for the year and the January 1, 2007 UCC balances can be summarized as follows:

	Maximum CCA	UCC
Class 1	$ 25,000	$600,000
Class 8	31,500	128,500
Class 10	37,875	96,625
Class 12	34,000	Nil
Class 13	9,000	97,750
Class 43	Nil	Nil
Class 45	10,800	27,200

In addition, the following income effects resulted from the information provided in the problem:

Taxable Capital Gain On Class 8 Assets [(1/2)($13,000)]	$ 6,500
Terminal Loss On Class 43 Assets	(29,000)
Income From License Sale [(2/3)($65,250)]	43,500
Total Inclusion	$21,000

Solution to Self Study Problem Seven - 7

The required schedule showing the relevant balances in the cumulative eligible capital account would be as follows:

	CEC Balance	CEC Deductions
2003 Addition [(3/4)($500,000)]	$375,000	
2003 CEC Amount At 7 Percent	(26,250)	$26,250
CEC Balance, January 1, 2004	$348,750	
2004 CEC Amount At 7 Percent	(24,413)	24,413
CEC Balance, January 1, 2005	$324,337	
2005 CEC Amount At 7 Percent	(22,704)	22,704
CEC Balance, January 1, 2006	$301,633	
Proceeds From Sale [(3/4)($780,000)]	(585,000)	
Balance After Sale	($283,367)	$73,367

As can be seen in the preceding table, $73,367 of the negative balance reflects CEC deductions that have been made in previous years. This full amount will have to be included in 2006 income. The remaining $210,000 ($283,367 - $73,367) reflects three-quarters of the $280,000 ($780,000 - $500,000) gain on the disposition. This will have to be converted to the one-half capital gains inclusion rate by multiplying by two-thirds, which will result in a further income inclusion in 2006 of $140,000 [(2/3)($210,000)]. This gives a total 2006 income inclusion of $213,367 ($73,367 + $140,000).

Chapter Seven Learning Objectives

After completing Chapter 7, you should be able to:

1. Describe the differences between the accounting procedures used for depreciable assets and the tax procedures used for these assets (paragraphs 7-1 through 7-10).

2. Determine the types of costs that are included in the amounts that are added to depreciable asset classes (paragraphs 7-11 through 7-22).

3. Demonstrate an understanding of the available for use rules (paragraphs 7-23 through 7-25).

4. Recall the general rules for segregating depreciable assets into classes (paragraphs 7-26 through 7-28).

5. Recall the types of assets that must be allocated to separate classes (paragraph 7-29).

6. Demonstrate an understanding of the basic elements of the CCA system (paragraphs 7-30 and 7-31).

7. Recall the rates and methods that are applicable to common CCA classes in order to determine the maximum CCA for the period (paragraph 7-32).

8. Apply the first year rules in the determination of maximum CCA for the period (paragraphs 7-33 through 7-37).

9. Apply the short fiscal period rules in the determination of maximum CCA for the period (paragraphs 7-38 through 7-42).

10. Explain the tax planning considerations that are involved when a business takes less than maximum CCA (paragraphs 7-43 through 7-47).

11. Determine the tax consequences associated with dispositions of depreciable assets, including recapture, terminal losses, and capital gains (paragraphs 7-48 through 7-65).

12. Apply the provisions relating to separate class elections (paragraphs 7-66 through 7-73).

13. Apply the replacement property rules associated with voluntary and involuntary dispositions of depreciable assets (paragraphs 7-74 through 7-90).

14. Determine the tax consequences of changing the use of a depreciable asset (paragraphs 7-91 through 7-102).

15. Apply the provisions relating to eligible capital expenditures (paragraphs 7-103 through 7-126).

CHAPTER EIGHT

How To Work Through Chapter Eight

We recommend the following approach in dealing with the material in this chapter:

Defining Business Income
☐ Read the text pages 261 (from paragraph 8-1) and 262 (through paragraph 8-4).

Business Income Vs. Capital Gains
☐ Read the text pages 262 (from paragraph 8-5) and 263 (through paragraph 8-10).

☐ Complete Exercise Eight-1 on page 263 of the text. The solution is on page S-102.

Business Income And GAAP
☐ Read the text pages 264 (from paragraph 8-11) and 265 (through paragraph 8-13).

Inclusions - Amounts Received And Receivable
☐ Read the text page 265 (from paragraph 8-14 through paragraph 8-18).

Reserves For Bad Debts
☐ Read the text pages 266 (from paragraph 8-19) and 267 (through paragraph 8-26).

☐ Complete Exercise Eight-2 on page 267 of the text. The solution is on page S-102.

Reserves For Undelivered Goods And Services
☐ Read the text page 267 (paragraph 8-27).

☐ Complete Exercise Eight-3 on page 267 of the text. The solution is on page S-102.

Reserves For Unpaid Amounts
☐ Read the text page 268 (paragraph 8-28).

☐ Complete Exercise Eight-4 on page 268 of the text. The solution is on page S-102.

Other Inclusions
☐ Read the text page 268 (paragraph 8-29).

General Restrictions On Deductions From Business And Property Income
☐ Read the text pages 269 (from paragraph 8-30) through 273 (through paragraph 8-56).

☐ Complete Exercise Eight-5 on page 273 of the text. The solution is on page S-102.

☐ Read the text pages 273 (from paragraph 8-57) through 275 (through paragraph 8-70).

Restrictions On Deductions From Business Income
(Reasonableness, Meals And Entertainment And Automobile Costs)
☐ Read the text pages 275 (from paragraph 8-71) through 277 (through paragraph 8-83)

☐ Complete Exercise Eight-6 on page 278 of the text. The solution is on page S-102.

☐ Read the text pages 278 (from paragraph 8-84) and 279 (through paragraph 8-88).

☐ Complete Exercise Eight-7 on page 280 of the text. The solution is on page S-103.

Leasing Property

☐ Read the text page 280 (from paragraph 8-89 through paragraph 8-92).

☐ Complete Exercise Eight-8 on page 280 of the text. The solution is on page S-103.

Restrictions On Claiming Input Tax Credits

☐ Read the text page 281 (paragraph 8-93).

Specific Deductions From Business Income

☐ Read the text pages 281 (from paragraph 8-94) and 279 (through paragraph 8-100).

☐ Complete Exercise Eight-9 on page 282 of the text. The solution is on page S-103.

☐ Read the text pages 282 through 284 (paragraph 8-101).

Reconciliation Of Accounting Net Income And Net Income For Tax Purposes

☐ Read the text pages 284 (from paragraph 8-102) through 287 (through paragraph 8-107).

Taxation Year

☐ Read the text pages 287 (from paragraph 8-108) and 288 (through paragraph 8-114).

☐ Complete Exercise Eight-10 on page 288 of the text. The solution is on page S-103.

Income For Farmers

☐ Read the text pages 288 (from paragraph 8-115) and 289 (through paragraph 8-120).

☐ Complete Exercise Eight-11 on page 289 of the text. The solution is on page S-103.

☐ Read the text pages 289 (from paragraph 8-121) and 290 (through paragraph 8-124).

Income For Professionals

☐ Read the text page 290 (paragraphs 8-125 and 8-126).

☐ Complete Exercise Eight-12 on page 290 of the text. The solution is on page S-103.

Scientific Research And Experimental Development

☐ Read the text page 291 (paragraphs 8-127 through 8-130).

Ceasing To Carry On A Business

☐ Read the text pages 291 (from paragraph 8-131) and 292 (through paragraph 8-136).

☐ Complete Exercise Eight-13 on page 292 of the text. The solution is on page S-103.

☐ Complete Self Study Problems Eight-1 through Eight-6 on pages 301 through 307 of the text. The solutions are on pages S-103 through S-111.

If The Appendix To Chapter 8 (Overview Of Corporate Tax) Has Been Assigned

☐ Read the Appendix - Taxable Income And Tax Payable For Corporations on pages 295 (from paragraph 8A-1) through 300 (through paragraph 8A-37).

To Complete This Chapter

☐   Review the Key Terms Used In This Chapter on page 293 of the text. Consult the Glossary for the meaning of any key terms you do not know.

☐   Review the Glossary Flashcards and complete the Key Terms Self-Test for the Chapter. These features can be found in two places, on your Student CD-ROM under the heading "Key Term Practice" and on the web site.

☐   Review the Learning Objectives of the Chapter found on page S-112 of this Study Guide.

☐   As a review, we recommend that you view the PowerPoint Slides for Chapter Eight that are on your Student CD-ROM. The PowerPoint Viewer program can be installed from the Student CD-ROM.

Solution to Chapter Eight Exercises

Exercise Eight - 1 Solution

Provided that she can demonstrate that her intent was to operate the building as a rental property, the gain should qualify as a capital gain.

Exercise Eight - 2 Solution

The net decrease for the year will be $19,600 ($16,000 - $17,200 - $18,400).

Exercise Eight - 3 Solution

The amount to be included in net business income would be calculated as follows:

Cash Sales	$53,400
Accounts Receivable	26,300
Reserve For Undelivered Services	(5,600)
Reserve For Bad Debts	(425)
Net Business Income	$73,675

Exercise Eight - 4 Solution

As some of the proceeds are not receivable for more than two years, a reserve can be deducted under ITA 20(1)(n). The maximum reserve, based on the gross profit of $65,000, for each of the five years would be as follows:

2006 [(100%)($65,000)]	$65,000
2007 [(75%)($65,000)]	48,750
2008 [(50%)($65,000)]	32,500
2009	Nil
2010	Nil

As December 31, 2009 is more than 36 months after the sale was made, no reserve can be deducted for 2009 or 2010.

Exercise Eight - 5 Solution

As Ms. Johnson owns 30 percent of the common shares, she is clearly a specified shareholder. Her relevant equity balance would be $1,620,000 [(30%)($2,400,000) + (100%)($900,000)]. Given this, the disallowed interest would be calculated as follows:

Total Interest Paid To Ms. Johnson [(9%)($4,500,000)]	$405,000
Maximum Deductible Interest [(9%)(2)($1,620,000)]	(291,600)
Disallowed Interest	$113,400

Exercise Eight - 6 Solution

With respect to the amount of CCA, since the business commenced operations on September 15, 2006, the CCA is limited to the proportion of the year the business was in operation (108/365) and the first year rules would apply. The base amount for the CCA calculation is limited to the Class 10.1 maximum of $30,000. With respect to the interest, the car was financed for a total of 108 days with a limit of $10 per day. As a result, the amounts that can be deducted are as follows:

CCA [(1/2)(108/365)(30%)($30,000)]	$1,332
Interest Costs [($10)(108 Days)]	1,080
Total Deduction	$2,412

Exercise Eight - 7 Solution

The amount he can deduct is limited to $2,229, the least of:

- $4,925 [($985)(5)];
- $4,080 [($800)(153/30)]; and
- $2,229 {[$4,925][$30,000 ÷ (85%)($78,000)]}.

Exercise Eight - 8 Solution

For tax purposes, the lease would be treated as an operating lease, with the deduction being based only on the lease payments. Under GAAP, the lease would have to be treated as a purchase (capitalized). This is because the lease term is more than 75 percent of the asset's expected useful life. This means that the accounting deductions would be for amortization on the capitalized asset and interest costs on the associated liability.

Exercise Eight - 9 Solution

The required adjustment will be an addition of $2,300 ($13,500 - $11,200) to cost of sales, with a corresponding reduction in net business income.

Exercise Eight - 10 Solution

Mr. Gelato's additional business income for 2006 will be $15,088 [($12,300)(184 Days ÷ 150 Days)]. The 184 days is for the period July 1 through December 31, while the 150 days is for the period February 1 through June 30. The total business income that Mr. Gelato will have to report for 2006 is $27,388 ($12,300 + $15,088).

Exercise Eight - 11 Solution

Ms. Morph appears to be a part-time farmer and, as a consequence, her farm losses will be restricted. Since her loss is greater than $15,000, the amount she can deduct for 2006 will be limited to $8,750 [$2,500 + (1/2)($15,000 maximum - $2,500)]. The remaining $9,950 ($18,700 - $8,750) restricted farm loss is available for carry over.

Exercise Eight - 12 Solution

Mr. Winters' income for the current year under the three alternatives would be as follows:

Cash Basis The cash basis income would be $252,000 ($35,000 + $57,000 + $160,000).

Billed Basis The billed basis income would be $220,000 ($35,000 + $185,000).

Accrual Basis The accrual basis income would be $245,000.

Exercise Eight - 13 Solution

The tax effect for Mr. Donato would be a net deduction in the determination of business income of $1,450 [$3,800 - ($53,450 - $48,200)]. Mr. Labelle would have to include the $5,250 ($53,450 - $48,200) difference between the face value and the price paid in income. Subsequent to the sale, 100 percent of any difference between the $53,450 face value of the receivables and amounts actually collected will be included in Mr. Labelle's Net Income For Tax Purposes.

Solution to Self Study Problem Eight - 1

Part A In Part A(i), Ms. Wise is an employee and, because her income includes commissions, she can deduct expenses related to the production of employment income under ITA 8(1)(f), provided no deduction is made under ITA 8(1)(h) or ITA 8(1)(h.1).

Deductions under ITA 8(1)(f) are limited to the amount of commissions earned. Alternatively, traveling costs and motor vehicle costs other than capital costs can be deducted under ITA 8(1)(h) and ITA 8(1)(h.1). Deductions under these provisions are not limited to commission income.

The deduction of dues and other expenses under ITA 8(1)(i) and automobile capital costs (CCA and financing costs) under ITA 8(1)(j) is permitted without regard to other provisions used.

	ITA 8(1)(f) (Limited To $15,000)	ITA 8(1) (h) and (h.1)	ITA 8(1) (i) and (j)	Part A(ii)
Professional Dues	Nil	Nil	$ 600	$ 600
Automobile Costs:				
Operating Costs [(35,000/50,000)($6,000)]	$4,200	4,200	Nil	4,200
Financing Costs [(35,000/50,000)($2,500)]	Nil	Nil	1,750	1,750
CCA (Note One)	Nil	Nil	5,355	5,355
Home Office Costs:				
Utilities [(40%)($3,550)]	Nil	Nil	1,420	1,420
Maintenance [(40%)($1,500)]	Nil	Nil	600	600
Insurance [(40%)($950)]	380	Nil	Nil	380
Property Taxes [(40%)($4,700)]	1,880	Nil	Nil	1,880
Interest [(40%)($13,500)]	Nil	Nil	Nil	5,400
CCA [($48,000)(4%)]	Nil	Nil	Nil	1,920
Travel Costs	23,000	23,000	Nil	23,000
Non-Deductible Meals [(50%)($8,000)]	(4,000)	(4,000)	Nil	(4,000)
Entertainment Expenses	12,000	Nil	Nil	12,000
Non-Deductible (Note Two)	(7,250)	Nil	Nil	(7,250)
Total	$33,210	$23,200	$9,725	$47,255

The deduction for home office costs has been split between ITA 8(1)(i) and (f). Since the maintenance portion can be deducted under ITA 8(1)(i), it is not limited by the commission income. The insurance and property tax components are limited as they are deducted under ITA 8(1)(f). A limitation, which is not illustrated in this problem, prevents the deduction of home office costs from creating an employment loss.

As the ITA 8(1)(f) amount is limited to the $15,000 in commission income, the total deduction using ITA 8(1)(f), (i) and (j), is $24,725 ($15,000 + $9,725).

The total deduction using ITA 8(1)(h), (h.1), (i) and (j), is $32,925 ($23,200 + $9,725). Note that when this approach is used, home office costs are limited to utilities and maintenance. Further, there is no deduction for entertainment costs. However, this approach results in deductions totalling $8,200 ($32,925 - $24,725) more than the amount available using ITA 8(1)(f), (i), and (j) due to the effect of the commission income limit.

Comparing Parts A (i) and A (ii), there is a difference of $14,330 ($47,255 - $32,925) between the maximum employee and self-employed calculations, illustrating the importance of the difference between being an employee and being self-employed. This problem is, of course, somewhat unrealistic in that, if Ms. Wise was an employee, it is likely that she would be compensated or reimbursed for at least part of her employment related expenses.

Note One   The car will be allocated to Class 10.1 at a value of $30,000, the 2005 limit. The excess of $23,000 will not be deductible. Maximum CCA for 2005 would have been $4,500 [(30%)(1/2)($30,000)]. The deductible amount for 2005 would have been this amount, multiplied by the portion of her total usage that was related to income producing activity.

The January 1, 2006 UCC would be $25,500 ($30,000 - $4,500) and maximum CCA for 2006 would have been $7,650 [(30%)($25,500)]. Note that, in determining the relevant UCC value, the full amount of maximum 2005 CCA was deducted, not just the portion that was actually deducted in that year. The deductible amount for 2006 equals $5,355 [(70%)($7,650)].

Note Two   The non-deductible costs charged by the local country club are as follows:

Membership Dues	$2,500
Entertainment Costs [(50%)($9,500)]	4,750
Total Non-Deductible	$7,250

Part B   As will be discussed in Chapter 10, capital gains on an individual's principal residence are, in general, not subject to income taxes. While a strict application of the relevant rules would remove from principal residence status the portion of Doreen's home that was used for income producing activities, the administrative procedures of the CRA do not follow this approach. It appears that, as long as no CCA is taken on the work space portion of the home, 100 percent of the property will qualify as a principal residence. Given this, and the assumption that real estate prices are increasing, it would not be wise for Ms. Wise to take CCA on her office space.

Solution to Self Study Problem Eight - 2

The required calculations would be as follows:

Accounting Net Income	$298,000
Additions:	
Item 1 - LIFO Excess ($296,000 - $271,000)	25,000
Item 2 - Increase In Warranty Reserve	14,500
Item 3 - Income Tax Expense	158,000
Item 5 - Depreciation Expense	53,750
Item 7 - Contributions To Registered Charity	4,300
Item 10 - Life Insurance Premium	3,100
Item 12 - Golf Club Membership	1,400
Item 12 - 50% Of Business Meals (50% of $3,400)	1,700
Item 13 - Cost Of Amending Articles (Note One)	14,300
Item 14 - Appraisal Costs (Note Two)	7,400
Item 15 - Stock Issue Costs (Note Three)	12,480
Subtotal	$593,930
Deduction:	
Item 11 - Bond Premium Amortization	(5,900)
Net Income For Tax Purposes	$588,030

Note One   The cost of amending the Company's articles would be considered an eligible capital expenditure, three-quarters of which would be added to cumulative eligible capital.

Note Two   The fees paid to appraise certain Company assets for sale would be added to the adjusted cost base of these assets.

Note Three   ITA 20(1)(e) requires the deduction of stock issue costs over a five year period at a rate of 20 percent per year. For the current year, 80% of the total stock issue costs of $15,600 are non-deductible and added to accounting Net Income.

Other Items   Further explanation related to the items not included in the preceding calculation of Net Income For Tax Purposes are as follows:

Item 4   As the landscaping costs have already been deducted in accounting Net Income, they do not require adjustment for tax purposes.

Item 6   While interest on late income tax instalments is clearly not deductible, there does not appear to be a similar prohibition against interest on late property taxes. We would note here that the 2004 budget proposals proposes the elimination of deductibility for all fines and penalties. This would not appear to include interest for late payment of municipal taxes.

Item 8   The tax treatment of such payments would be the same as the accounting treatment.

Item 9   The tax treatment of volume discounts would be the same as the accounting treatment.

Solution to Self Study Problem Eight - 3

The required calculations would be as follows:

Accounting Income Before Taxes	$426,000
Additions:	
Item 2 - Contributions To Charities	2,500
Item 2 - Contributions To Political Parties	1,000
Item 3 - LIFO/FIFO Adjustment (Note One)	4,000
Item 4 - Amortization Expense	241,000
Item 5 - Amount Paid To Cousin (Note Two)	10,000
Item 8 - Warranty Reserve (Note Three)	9,000
Item 12 - Non-Deductible Meals And Entertainment (50% Of $13,500)	6,750
Item 13 - Amortization Of Bond Discount	1,800
Item 14 - Non-Deductible Lease Payments (Note Four)	13,037
Subtotal	$715,087
Deductions:	
Item 6 - Capital Cost Allowance	(389,000)
Item 10 - Issue Costs (Note Five)	(1,600)
Item 11 - Landscaping Costs	(11,000)
Net Income For Tax Purposes	$313,487

Note One   As LIFO cannot be used for tax purposes, the tax figures will have to be adjusted to a FIFO basis. This will require a $20,000 ($366,000 - $346,000) increase in the opening inventory and a $24,000 ($447,000 -$423,000) increase in the closing inventory. This will reduce cost of goods sold by $4,000 and increase Taxable Income by a corresponding amount.

Note Two Under ITA 67, this amount would be disallowed as not being reasonable in the circumstances.

Note Three For tax purposes, warranty costs can only be deducted as incurred. Therefore, the $9,000 ($27,000 - $18,000) increase in the warranty reserve must be added back to accounting income.

Note Four Under ITA 67.3, the deductible amount of the lease payments is limited to the least of:

- $18,000
- [($800)(365/30)] = $9,733
- {[$18,000][$30,000 ÷ (85%)($128,000)]} = $4,963

The non-deductible portion of the lease payments is $13,037 ($18,000 - $4,963).

Note Five Under ITA 20(1)(e), issue costs must be amortized at the rate of 20 percent per year. As the full amount was treated as an asset in the accounting records, the required adjustment is a deduction of $1,600 [(20%)($8,000)].

Several of the items described in the problem did not require any adjustment. The explanations for these omissions are as follows:

Item 1 As the accounting income figure is before taxes, no adjustment is required for the estimate of income tax expense.

Item 7 As the advertising was not directed at the Canadian market, it can be deducted for tax purposes and no adjustment is required.

Item 9 As the same bad debt estimates were used for tax purposes and accounting purposes, no adjustment is required with respect to bad debts.

Solution to Self Study Problem Eight - 4

The required calculations would be as follows:

Accounting Income (Loss) Before Taxes	($113,000)
Additions:	
Item 2 - Property Taxes On Recreational Facility	1,100
Item 3 - Donations (Note One)	13,700
Item 6 - Lease Cancellation Payment (Note Two)	17,000
Item 8 - Insurance Premium (Note Three)	9,500
Item 9 - Excess Of FIFO Inventory Value Over LIFO Value	37,200
Item 13 - Renovation Costs (Note Four)	153,000
Item 14 - Wife's Convention Expenses	1,900
Item 15 - Bond Discount Amortization	950
Item 16 - Cost Of Amending Articles (Note Five)	3,600
Item 17 - Non-Deductible Portion Of	
Meals And Entertainment [(50%)($12,500)]	6,250
Net Income For Tax Purposes	$131,200

Note One   The contributions to registered charities will be deductible in the computation of Taxable Income, but not in the computation of income from a business. Charitable contributions are still a deduction for corporations, although they are eligible for tax credit treatment for individuals. The political contributions are not deductible at any stage, but will generate a credit in determining the amount of Tax Payable.

Note Two   ITA 20(1)(z) requires that lease cancellation payments be amortized over the term of the lease remaining immediately before cancellation. The amount to be deducted is a pro rata calculation based on the number of days remaining subsequent to the cancellation. As the cancellation occurred on December 31, 2006, none of the amount would be deductible during the current year. The $17,000 would be deducted over the seven years that would have remained of the lease term, at the rate of $2,429 per year.

Note Three   Life insurance premiums where the employer is the beneficiary are not considered to be incurred for the purpose of earning income and are therefore not deductible except where they are required by a creditor in relation to financing.

Note Four   These amounts serve to extend the life of the relevant asset and should be treated as capital expenditures.

Note Five   The payment to amend the articles of incorporation would be an eligible capital expenditure and three-quarters of the $3,600 would be added to the cumulative eligible capital amount. The Company would be able to deduct amortization of this amount. However, you have been instructed to ignore such deductions in this problem.

Other Items   Further explanation related to the items not included in the preceding calculation of Net Income For Tax Purposes are as follows:

Item 1   If the damages relate to a transaction that produces business income, they are considered a business expense.

Item 4   Landscaping costs are fully deductible under ITA 20(1)(aa).

Item 5   Losses of this type, unless they result from the activity of senior officers or shareholders, are considered to be deductible as a normal cost of doing business.

Item 7   The bonus to the president would be deductible in 2006.

Item 10   Such appraisal costs are considered to be deductible as a normal cost of doing business.

Item 11   The $51,000 in management bonuses would be deductible in 2006. The forfeited bonuses would be given the same treatment for tax purposes as they were in the accounting records. The $34,000 of unpaid bonuses that were forfeited would result in a denial of the expenses in 2005. As a result, 2005 Taxable Income would increase by $34,000 since the unpaid bonuses were not paid within the 6 month ITA 78(4) deadline.

Item 12   The bad debts would be fully deductible.

Item 14   The $3,300 in costs associated with the president attending the convention would be deductible.

Item 16   Both the costs of defending against the breach of contract action, as well as the costs related to the income tax reassessment, would be fully deductible.

Solution to Self Study Problem Eight - 5

The current year Net Income For Tax Purposes of Darlington Inc. would be calculated as follows:

Accounting Income	$ 596,000
Additions:	
Item 1 - Income Tax Expense	55,000
Item 2 - LIFO Inventory Adjustment	5,000
Item 5 - Depreciation Expense	623,000
Item 5 - Taxable Capital Gain On Class 8 Disposition	
[($550,000 - $400,000)(1/2)]	75,000
Item 6 - Non-Deductible Meals And Entertainment	
[(50%)($41,400)]	20,700
Item 7 - Club Fees	2,500
Item 8 - Property Taxes On Vacant Land	15,000
Subtotal	$1,392,200
Deductions:	
Item 3 - Landscaping Costs	(95,000)
CCA (see CCA Calculations)	(930,500)
Terminal Loss (See Class 10 CCA Calculation)	(113,000)
Item 5 - Gain On Class 8 Disposition	(225,000)
Net Income For Tax Purposes	$ 28,700

CCA Calculations

Class 1 - Building   The new building acquired is a Class 1 property. The half-year rule applies and this gives a maximum CCA amount of $10,500 [($650,000 - $125,000)(1/2)(4%)]. This leaves a January 1, 2007 UCC balance of $514,500 ($650,000 - $125,000 - $10,500).

Class 3 - Building   There were no additions or dispositions in this class. As a consequence, the maximum CCA would be $50,000 [(5%)($1,000,000)]. The January 1, 2007 UCC balance is $950,000 ($1,000,000 - $50,000).

Class 8 - Office Furniture And Equipment   The required calculations for this class would be as follows:

January 1, 2006 UCC Balance	$4,200,000
Additions	700,000
Dispositions (Cost)	(400,000)
One-Half Net Additions	(150,000)
CCA Base	$4,350,000
CCA At 20 Percent	(870,000)
One-Half Net Additions	150,000
January 1, 2007 UCC Balance	$3,630,000

With respect to the sale that occurred during the year, there would be a capital gain of $150,000 ($550,000 - $400,000). One-half, or $75,000, is included in the Company's Net Income For Tax Purposes, and the accounting gain of $225,000 is deducted.

Class 10 - Vehicles   All of the cars were sold during the year for proceeds that totalled less than their capital cost and the UCC of the class. The remaining balance in the class of $113,000 ($800,000 - $687,000) is a terminal loss that is fully deductible.

Summary Of The Results The maximum CCA and January 1, 2007 UCC balances can be summarized as follows:

	Maximum CCA	UCC
Class 1	$ 10,500	$ 514,500
Class 3	50,000	950,000
Class 8	870,000	3,630,000
Total	$930,500	

In addition, there was a taxable capital gain on the sale of the Class 8 assets of $75,000 and a terminal loss in Class 10 of $113,000.

Other Notes

- The cost of goods sold for the year under the LIFO inventory valuation assumption was $5,000 ($20,000 - $15,000) higher than it would have been using FIFO. As a result, this difference must be added to Net Income For Tax Purposes.

- ITA 19.01 provides for the full deduction of advertising costs in foreign periodicals directed at the Canadian market, provided 80 percent or more of their non-advertising content is original editorial content. If the original editorial content is less than 80 percent, the deduction is equal to 50 percent of the costs. Note that this applies only to periodicals and not other print or broadcast media.

- Landscaping costs are fully deductible.

- The property taxes on the vacant land are not deductible. They can be added to the cost of the land if the land was acquired for the purpose of earning either business or property income and may be deducted to the extent of any net income earned on the land.

Solution to Self Study Problem Eight - 6

Christine's business income for the period ending December 31, 2006 can be calculated as follows:

Design Power
Statement of Income and Expenses
For the seven month period ended December 31, 2006

Revenue collected	$22,000
Revenue billed	4,000
Work-In-Progress	1,500
Total revenue	$27,500
Capital cost allowance (Note 1)	$ 2,237
Home office expenses [(20%)($6,400)]	1,280
Legal and business license fees	1,000
Meals and entertainment [(50%)($500)]	250
Automobile expenses (Note 2)	1,960
Office and computer supplies	650
Printing sub-contract fees	1,800
Total expenses	$ 9,177
Net Income For Tax Purposes	$18,323

Note 1   CCA amounts are calculated as follows:

	Class 8 Furniture	Class 10 Car	Class 45 Computer	Class 12 Software
Additions	$2,000	$18,000	$5,000	$1,200
One-Half Net Additions	(1,000)	(9,000)	(2,500)	(600)
CCA Base	$1,000	$ 9,000	2,500	$ 600
CCA Rate	20%	30%	45%	100%
CCA For Full Year	$ 200	$ 2,700	$1,125	$ 600

As the car is only used 70 percent for business, only $1,890 [(70%)($2,700)] of the CCA on the car can be deducted. As Christine's business operated only from June 1, for a total of 214 days in 2006, her CCA must be calculated on a pro rata basis. The total maximum CCA for 2006 is $2,237 [($200 + $1,890 + $1,125 + $600)(214/365)]. Note that the CCA is available for the portion of the year since the inception of the business, not the portion of the year since the assets were acquired.

Note 2   The business portion of the automobile operating expenses is 70 percent of gasoline and oil ($1,100), licence and registration ($200), insurance ($800), and interest on car loan ($700), for a deduction of $1,960. No portion of the down payment is deductible.

Chapter Eight Learning Objectives

After completing Chapter 8, you should be able to:

1. Distinguish between business income and capital gains, including the criteria used by the courts in making this distinction (paragraphs 8-1 through 8-10).

2. Describe the major differences between net business income and Net Income as determined under GAAP (paragraphs 8-11 through 8-13).

3. Recall the various items that are included in net business income (paragraphs 8-14 through 8-18 and paragraph 8-29).

4. Apply the system of reserves that can be used in determining net business income (paragraphs 8-19 through 8-28).

5. Apply the restrictions on deductions that apply to business or property income (paragraphs 8-30 through 8-70).

6. Apply the restrictions on deductions that apply to business income (paragraphs 8-71 through 8-92).

7. Recall the restrictions on claiming input tax credits (paragraph 8-93).

8. Apply the inventory valuation procedures that are used for determining net business income (paragraphs 8-94 through 8-100).

9. Recall the deductions that are specified in the *Income Tax Act* for calculating net business income (paragraph 8-101).

10. Be able to reconcile accounting Net Income with net business income (paragraphs 8-102 through 8-107).

11. Recall the rules for determining taxation years (paragraphs 8-108 through 8-114).

12. Apply the special provisions related to farming activities (paragraphs 8-115 through 8-124).

13. Apply the special rules for the income of professionals (paragraphs 8-125 and 8-126).

14. Apply the special rules that apply to scientific research and experimental development expenditures (paragraphs 8-127 through 8-130).

15. Apply the provisions related to the disposition of inventories and accounts receivable in situations where a business is being sold (paragraphs 8-131 through 8-136).

If The Appendix To Chapter 8 (Overview Of Corporate Tax) Has Been Assigned

16. Demonstrate a basic understanding of Taxable Income and Tax Payable for corporations (paragraphs 8A-1 through 8A-37).

CHAPTER NINE

How To Work Through Chapter Nine

We recommend the following approach in dealing with the material in this chapter:

Property Income - General Concept
☐   Read the text pages 321 (from paragraph 9-1) and 322 (through paragraph 9-4).

Interest As A Deduction (Including IT-533)
☐   Read the text pages 322 (from paragraph 9-5) through 327 (through paragraph 9-33).

Discount And Premium On Long-Term Issued Debt
☐   Read the text page 327 (from paragraph 9-34 through paragraph 9-37).

☐   Complete Exercise Nine-1 on page 328 of the text. The solution is on page S-115.

☐   Read the text page 328 (paragraphs 9-38 and 9-39).

☐   Complete Exercise Nine-2 on page 329 of the text. The solution is on page S-115.

Interest Income - General Provisions
☐   Read the text pages 329 (from paragraph 9-40) and 330 (through paragraph 9-46).

☐   Complete Exercise Nine-3 on page 330 of the text. The solution is on page S-115.

Discount And Premium On Long-Term Debt Holdings
☐   Read the text pages 330 (from paragraph 9-47) and 331 (through paragraph 9-48).

Prescribed Debt Obligations
☐   Read the text page 331 (from paragraph 9-49 through paragraph 9-51).

☐   Complete Exercise Nine-4 on page 332 of the text. The solution is on page S-116.

Indexed Debt Obligations
☐   Read the text page 332 (from paragraph 9-52 and 9-53).

Accrued Interest At Transfer
☐   Read the text pages 332 (from paragraph 9-54) and 333 (through paragraph 9-55).

☐   Complete Exercise Nine-5 on page 333 of the text. The solution is on page S-116.

Payments Based On Production Or Use (Royalties)
☐   Read the text page 333 (from paragraph 9-56 through paragraph 9-59).

Rental Income
☐   Read the text pages 334 (from paragraph 9-60) through 336 (through paragraph 9-69).

☐   Complete Exercise Nine-6 on page 336 of the text. The solution is on page S-116.

☐   Complete Self Study Problem Nine-1 on page 354 of the text. The solution is on pages S-118 and S-119.

Cash Dividends From Taxable Canadian Corporations

☐ Read the text pages 336 (from paragraph 9-70) through 332 (through paragraph 9-82).

☐ Complete Exercise Nine-7 on page 339 of the text. The solution is on page S-116.

☐ Read the text pages 339 (from paragraph 9-83) through 342 (through paragraph 9-96).

☐ Complete Exercise Nine-8 on page 342 of the text. The solution is on pages S-116 and S-117.

Comparison Of Investment Returns

☐ Read the text page 343 (from paragraph 9-97 through paragraph 9-99).

☐ Complete Self Study Problems Nine-2 through Nine-4 on pages 354 and 355 of the text. The solutions are on pages S-119 through S-121.

Stock Dividends And Capital Dividends

☐ Read the text pages 343 (from paragraph 9-100)and 344 (through paragraph 9-102).

Mutual Funds

☐ Read the text pages 344 (from paragraph 9-103) through 345 (through paragraph 9-113).

☐ Complete Exercise Nine-9 on page 346 of the text. The solution is on page S-117.

Income Trusts

☐ Read the text pages 346 (from paragraph 9-114) and 347 (through paragraph 9-121).

Foreign Source Income

☐ Read the text pages 347 (from paragraph 9-122) and 348 (through paragraph 9-125).

☐ Complete Exercise Nine-10 on page 348 of the text. The solution is on page S-117.

Shareholder Benefits

☐ Read the text pages 348 (from paragraph 9-126) through 351 (through paragraph 9-139).

☐ Complete Exercises Nine-11 through Nine-13 on pages 351 and 352 of the text. The solutions are on pages S-117 and S-118.

☐ Complete Self Study Problem Nine-5 on page 355 of the text. The solution is on page S-122.

Tax Credits Revisited

☐ Read the text page 352 (from paragraph 9-140 through paragraph 9-142).

To Complete This Chapter

☐ Review the Key Terms Used In This Chapter on page 353 of the text. Consult the Glossary for the meaning of any key terms you do not know.

☐ Review the Glossary Flashcards and complete the Key Terms Self-Test for the Chapter. These features can be found in two places, on your Student CD-ROM under the heading "Key Term Practice" and on the web site.

☐ Review the Learning Objectives of the Chapter found on page S-123 of this Study Guide.

☐ As a review, we recommend that you view the PowerPoint Slides for Chapter Nine that are on your Student CD-ROM. The PowerPoint Viewer program can be installed from the Student CD-ROM.

Solution to Chapter Nine Exercises

Exercise Nine - 1 Solution

In each of the years 2006, 2007, and 2008, Moreau would have a deduction for interest of $40,000 [(4%)($1,000,000)]. When the bonds are retired in 2008, there would be a loss of $15,000 ($1,000,000 - $985,000). The bonds are sold for more than 97 percent of their maturity amount. In addition, the four-thirds test is met since the effective interest rate of 4.6 percent is less than four-thirds of the coupon rate [(4%)(4/3) = 5.3%]. As a result, it would appear that this loss would be fully deductible. This gives a total deduction of $135,000 over the three year period [(3)($40,000) + $15,000].

For accounting purposes, interest expense would be $45,000 in each of the three years. This is made up of the annual payment of $40,000, plus amortization of the discount of $5,000 [(1/3)($1,000,000 - $985,000)]. Note that the total for the three year period would be the same $135,000 [(3)($45,000)] that was deducted for tax purposes.

Exercise Nine - 2 Solution

The tax consequences under each of the three assumptions would be as follows:

Money Lender In this case, there would be an income inclusion of $400,000 ($1,400,000 - $1,000,000) in the current year. The interest deduction for the year would be $180,000 [(18%)($1,000,000)].

No Deliberate Premium In this case, the premium would have no immediate tax consequences and there would be no tax consequences when the bonds mature. The interest deduction for the year would be $180,000 [(18%)($1,000,000)]. Given that the bonds are paid off for less than the proceeds from their issuance, this result provides the issuer of the bonds with an untaxed gain of $400,000.

Deliberate Premium In this case, the premium would be amortized at the rate of $40,000 per year ($400,000 ÷ 10). This means the interest deduction for the year would be $140,000 ($180,000 - $40,000).

Exercise Nine - 3 Solution

The total interest to be recorded on the investment is $28,800 [($60,000)(8%)(6 years)]. It will be allocated as follows: 2006 - nil, 2007 - $4,800, 2008 - $4,800, 2009 - $6,000, 2010 - $3,600, 2011 - $4,800, and 2012 - $4,800.

As no anniversary date occurred and no interest was received during 2006, no interest will have to be included in Ms. Dumont's 2006 tax return.

In 2007, the first anniversary date occurs on September 30 and this requires the recognition of $4,800 [(8%)($60,000)] of interest.

In 2008, the second anniversary date occurs and this requires the recognition of an additional $4,800 of interest.

In 2009, the third anniversary date requires the recognition of $4,800 and, in addition, a $15,600 [(8%)($60,000)(3.25 Years)] payment is received. As $14,400 [(3)($4,800)] of this amount has been accrued on the three anniversary dates, only $1,200 of this amount will be added to income. This gives a total for the year 2009 of $6,000 ($4,800 + $1,200).

In 2010, the anniversary date will require recognition of $4,800. However, only $3,600 of this amount will be included as $1,200 was recognized in 2009.

In 2011, $4,800 will be recognized on the anniversary date.

In 2012, a payment of $13,200 [(2.75)($4,800)] will be received. As $8,400 ($3,600 + $4,800) of the amount received has been recorded on the 2010 and 2011 anniversary dates, the total for 2012 will be $4,800 ($13,200 - $8,400).

Exercise Nine - 4 Solution

With respect to the maturity amount, the interest to be included in the purchaser's tax return would be calculated as follows:

Year	Initial Balance	Interest At 7%	Closing Balance
2006	$204,075	$14,285	$218,360
2007	218,360	15,285	233,645
2008	233,645	16,355	250,000

Calculations of interest income with respect to the coupon payments are as follows:

Year	Initial Balance	Interest At 7%	Cash Received	Closing Balance
2006	$45,925	$3,215	($17,500)	$31,640
2007	31,640	2,215	(17,500)	16,355
2008	16,355	1,145	(17,500)	Nil

Exercise Nine - 5 Solution

Mr. Lay will have to include the full $6,000 received. However, under ITA 20(14) he is eligible for a deduction of $2,000 [($3,000)(4/6)], reflecting the interest that was accrued on the bonds at the time of purchase. The net amount of $4,000 will be included in his tax return.

Exercise Nine - 6 Solution

As the improvements will have to be added to her CCA base, her maximum available CCA on the rental property is $3,560 [(4%)(1/2)($185,000 - $42,000 + $35,000)]. However, the maximum CCA that she can deduct will be limited by her net rental income before CCA. This amount is $2,100 ($7,200 - $5,100).

Exercise Nine - 7 Solution

The Tax Payable by Mr. Johns would be calculated as follows:

Dividends Received	$17,000
Gross Up At 25 Percent	4,250
Taxable Dividends [(1.25)($17,000)]	$21,250
Taxes At 41 Percent (29% + 12%)	$8,713
Dividend Tax Credit [(2/3 + 30%)($4,250)]	(4,108)
Federal And Provincial Tax Payable	$ 4,605

The after tax retention is $12,395 ($17,000 - $4,605). Note that to calculate this amount, the taxes are deducted from the dividends received and not the grossed up taxable dividends.

Exercise Nine - 8 Solution

The Tax Payable by Ms. Holt would be calculated as follows:

Dividends Received	$15,000
Gross Up At 45 Percent	6,750
Taxable Dividends [(1.45)($15,000)]	$21,750
Taxes At 43.5 Percent (29% + 14.5%)	$ 9,461
Dividend Tax Credit [(11/18 + 40%)($6,750)]	(6,825)
Federal And Provincial Tax Payable	$ 2,636

The after tax retention is $12,364 ($15,000 - $2,636). Note that to calculate this amount, the taxes are deducted from the dividends received and not the grossed up taxable dividends.

Exercise Nine - 9 Solution

Given the purchase price per unit is $13, the reinvestment will result in Ms. Tiompkins receiving 80.77 ($1,050 ÷ $13) additional units. This will leave her holding 3,580.77 units with an adjusted cost base of $40,425 ($39,375 + $1,050). Her adjusted cost base per unit after the reinvestment is $11.29 ($40,425 ÷ 3,580.77).

Exercise Nine - 10 Solution

Part A   If the foreign source income is non-business income, the withholding in excess of 15 percent is a deduction rather than a tax credit. This means that the total withholding of $7,500 will be divided into a credit of $4,500 [($30,000)(15%)] and a deduction of $3,000 [($30,000)(25% - 15%)]. Norah's incremental Taxable Income will be $27,000 ($30,000 - $3,000) and her incremental Tax Payable will be $3,330 [($27,000)(29%) - $4,500].

Part B   If the foreign source income is business income, all of the $7,500 withholding will be treated as a tax credit. This means that Norah's incremental Taxable Income will be $30,000 and her incremental Tax Payable will be $1,200 [($30,000)(29%) - $7,500]. Note the significant reduction in Tax Payable when the full amount of withholding is treated as a credit, as opposed to part of it being treated as a deduction.

Exercise Nine - 11 Solution

It is likely that Ms. Rourke will have to include the $50,000 principal amount of the loan in her Net Income For Tax Purposes for the current year. She owns more than 10 percent of the shares, making her a specified employee. While she is an employee, it is unlikely that this type of loan would be generally available to all employees and, as a consequence, it is likely that she received the loan because of her shareholder status as opposed to her employee status. In the unlikely event that the loan is not included in income, she will have to include imputed interest at the prescribed rate for the period of the loan. For the current year, the rate is 4 percent and her shareholder benefit for the year is $1,000 [(4%)($50,000)(6/12)]. The imputed interest rate and benefit will vary as the prescribed rate changes. Note, however, if imputed interest is assessed, some portion of the amount may be deductible as it relates to the acquisition of an automobile to be used in employment duties.

Exercise Nine - 12 Solution

Part A   If the loan is repaid on January 1, 2007, it will not be included in two consecutive Generic Inc. Balance Sheets. As a consequence, the principal amount will not have to be included in Ms. Fisk's income. However, as it is a low interest loan, she will be assessed with a taxable benefit on the loan. The amount would be $2,835 [($162,000)(5% - 2%)(7/12)].

Part B   If the loan is not repaid until December 31, 2007, it will appear in two consecutive Generic Inc. Balance Sheets. This means the $162,000 in principal will have to be included in Ms. Fisk's income for the taxation year ending December 31, 2006. However, there will be no imputed interest benefit based on the loan's low rate of interest. In addition, when the loan is repaid, the payment can be deducted from Net Income For Tax Purposes.

Exercise Nine - 13 Solution

It was assumed that this loan did not qualify as a home relocation loan.

Provided Mr. Hasid receives the loan in his capacity as an employee of Hasid Ltd., the loan is one of the exceptions listed under ITA 15(2). This means that the principal amount will not have to be included in income. However, as the loan is interest free, a taxable benefit will arise. It will be calculated by applying the prescribed rate of 5 percent to the principal of the loan for all periods that it is outstanding. The amounts would be $1,025 [($123,000)(5%)(2/12)] for 2006 and $6,150 [($123,000)(5%)] for 2007.

If Mr. Hasid cannot claim that he received the loan in his capacity as an employee of Hasid Ltd., the $123,000 principal amount will have to be included in income in 2006. However, no taxable benefit will be assessed for the fact that it is an interest free loan. When the loan is repaid in 2008, Mr. Hasid will be able to deduct $123,000 from his Net Income For Tax Purposes.

Solution to Self Study Problem Nine - 1

CCA On Properties A And B   Properties A and B cost less than $50,000 and, as a consequence, can be included in a single Class 1 account. Maximum CCA on these properties would be calculated as follows:

Balance, January 1 ($21,500 + $43,000)	$64,500
Disposition (At Capital Cost)	(36,000)
Balance At End Of Year	$28,500
CCA Rate	4%
Maximum CCA For The Year	$ 1,140

Note the proceeds of disposition for CCA purposes are not the actual proceeds of $72,000, but only the capital cost of $36,000. The extra $36,000 would be a capital gain, resulting in a taxable capital gain of $18,000 [(1/2)($36,000)].

CCA On Other Class 1 Properties   The other properties will be allocated to separate Class 1 balances. The recapture and maximum CCA for the year on these properties will be calculated as follows:

	Property C	Property D	Property E
Balance, January 1	$46,000	$64,000	Nil
Additions (Dispositions)	(61,000)	-0-	$192,000
Recapture	($15,000)		
Transfer To Income	15,000		
Balance Before Adjustments	$ -0-	$64,000	$192,000
One-Half Net Additions		-0-	(96,000)
CCA Base		$64,000	$ 96,000
Maximum CCA At 4 Percent		(2,560)	(3,840)
One-Half Net Additions		-0-	96,000
Balance, December 31 (If Maximum Is Taken)		$61,440	$188,160

Total Maximum CCA   This gives a total maximum CCA for Class 1 of $7,540 ($1,140 + $2,560 + $3,840).

Property Income   In calculating the net property income (loss) for Mr. Drake, the rules that restrict CCA deductions on rental properties must be taken into consideration. These rules are discussed in IT-195R4, "Rental Property - Capital Cost Restrictions". This Interpretation Bulletin makes it clear that in determining the maximum CCA deduction, net rental income, before CCA for all classes of rental properties, must first be determined. The maximum CCA deduction that can then be taken is limited to the amount that will reduce this balance to nil. Using this approach, net property income is calculated as follows:

	Rental Revenues	Cash Expenses
Property A	$ 5,200	$ 3,450
Property B	6,700	3,350
Property C	12,200	12,250
Property D	15,300	21,150
Property E	2,000	2,900
Totals	$41,400	$43,100

Income (Loss) Before CCA And Recapture ($41,400 - $43,100)	($ 1,700)
Recapture From Sale Of Property C	15,000
Rental Income Before CCA	$13,300)
Maximum CCA	(7,540)
Net Property Income	$ 5,760

In addition to the net property income calculated above, there is also the taxable capital gain of $18,000 resulting from the sale of Property A.

Solution to Self Study Problem Nine - 2

After Tax Return On The Bonds   This amount would be calculated as follows:

Interest Received [(7.75%)($20,000)]	$1,550
Taxes At 38% (26% + 12%)	(589)
After Tax Return	$ 961

After Tax Return On Preferred Shares   This amount would be calculated as follows:

Dividends Received [(5%)($20,000)]	$1,000
Gross Up Of 45 Percent	450
Taxable Dividends	$1,450

Taxes At 38% (26% + 12%)	$551
Dividend Tax Credit [(11/18 + 30%)($450)]	(410)
Tax Payable	$141

Dividends Received	$1,000
Tax Payable	(141)
After Tax Return	$ 859

Conclusion   Based on after tax returns, the investment in bonds is the better alternative.

Solution to Self Study Problem Nine - 3

Guaranteed Investment Certificate   The required calculations for this investment are as follows:

Interest Received [($600,000)(4.5%)]	$27,000
Federal/Provincial Tax Payable [($27,000)(29% + 12%)]	(11,070)
After Tax Return	$15,930

Preferred Shares   The required calculations for this investment are as follows:

Dividends Received [($600,000)(5.25%)]	$31,500
Gross Up of 45 Percent	14,175
Taxable Income	$45,675

Federal/Provincial Tax Payable [($45,675)(29% + 12%)]	$18,727
Federal/Provincial Dividend Tax Credit [($14,175)(11/18 + 31%)]	(13,057)
Total Tax Payable	$ 5,670

After Tax Return ($31,500 - $5,670)	$25,830

High Tech Shares   The required calculations for this investment are as follows:

Capital Gain ($675,000 - $600,000)	$75,000
Non-Taxable One-Half	(37,500)
Taxable Capital Gain	$37,500

Federal/Provincial Tax Payable [($37,500)(29% + 12%)]	$15,375

After Tax Return ($75,000 - $15,375)	$59,625

Solution to Self Study Problem Nine - 4

The after tax cash flows associated with the alternative investments would be as follows:

Guaranteed Investment Certificate   The before tax return here would be $5,500 and this would result in an after tax return calculated as follows:

Interest [($100,000)(5.5%)]	$5,500
Federal/Provincial Tax Payable [($5,500)(29% + 15%)]	(2,420)
After Tax Cash Flow	$3,080

Rental Property   The net rental income from the property would be calculated as follows:

Gross Rents	$13,200
Expenses	(9,600)
CCA (Property Sold Prior To Year End)	Nil
Net Rental Income	$ 3,600

In addition to this net rental income, Ms. Holmes anticipates a capital gain of $10,000 ($175,000 - $165,000), of which one-half, or $5,000, would be included in her income. The total after tax cash flow would be as follows:

Net Rental Income	$ 3,600
Capital Gain	10,000
Tax Payable [($3,600 + $5,000)(29% + 15%)]	(3,784)
After Tax Cash Flow	$ 9,816

Norton Ltd. Shares   The calculations here would be as follows:

Dividends Received	$5,000	
Gross Up of 45 Percent	2,250	
Taxable Dividends		$7,250
Capital Gain	$6,000	
Inclusion Rate	1/2	
Taxable Capital Gain		3,000
Net Income For Tax Purposes		$10,250

Tax At 44% (29% + $15%)	$4,510
Dividend Tax Credit [($2,250)(11/18 + 35%)] ⊃5%	(2,163)
Tax Payable	$2,347

Before Tax Cash Flow ($5,000 + $6,000)	$11,000
Tax Payable	(2,347)
After Tax Cash Flow	$ 8,653

Based on cash flow considerations only, it would appear that Ms. Holmes should acquire the rental property. However, this alternative probably involves the highest degree of risk and can require significant personal involvement if there are problems with the tenant or repairs become necessary. In addition, the real estate investment is the least liquid of the three alternatives and Ms. Holmes might encounter difficulties in the disposition of this investment. While you were not asked to consider transaction costs, we would also point out that they would be much higher on this investment than on either of the other two.

In choosing between the guaranteed investment certificate and the shares of Norton Ltd., the after tax cash flows from the shares are considerably higher. However, the return on the shares is made up of dividends and a potential capital gain, both of which are more uncertain than the interest on the guaranteed investment certificate. Given this, the possibility of greater than anticipated dividends and/or capital gains must be weighed against the additional risk of lower than anticipated returns.

Solution to Self Study Problem Nine - 5

Mr. Blaine is an employee and shareholder of Blaine Enterprises. As a result, if the loan is outstanding on two successive Balance Sheet dates for the corporation, the entire principal amount will have to be included in Mr. Blaine's personal income for tax purposes in the year the loan was received. Note, however, if the principal amount of the loan is included in Mr. Blaine's income, no taxable benefit will be assessed with respect to imputed interest.

It does not appear that Blaine Enterprises is offering other employees loans to acquire houses. If this was the case, and Mr. Blaine was granted the loan in his capacity as an employee, he would not have to include the loan in income. However, he would be assessed a taxable benefit in the amount of imputed interest on the outstanding loan balance. The interest rate to be used is established on a quarterly basis in ITR 4301. This loan would not qualify for a home relocation loan deduction as it can be assumed that the property that he is acquiring is not 40 kilometers closer to his work since he bicycles to work.

Given the fact that Mr. Blaine is a shareholder as well as an employee, the proposal does not offer any fundamental advantage over paying himself additional salary and, as a consequence, Mr. Blaine should be advised that his interest free loan plan will not work as smoothly as he has anticipated. The one advantage would be that, unlike salary that cannot be removed from income at a later point in time, repayment of the loan will allow Mr. Blaine to deduct the amount repaid under ITA 20(1)(j).

An additional consideration is that if his salary of $57,000 is his earned income for RRSP purposes, he is not creating the maximum RRSP deduction room possible. (RRSP contributions are covered in Chapter 13.) If he pays himself additional salary, he will be able to contribute more to his RRSP.

Chapter Nine Learning Objectives

After completing Chapter 9, you should be able to:

1. Explain the nature of property income (paragraphs 9-1 through 9-4).

2. Describe the rules applicable to the deductibility of interest payments and be able to apply these rules to various types of borrowing (paragraphs 9-5 through 9-33).

3. Apply the provisions relating to the treatment of discount and premium on long-term issued debt (paragraphs 9-34 through 9-39).

4. Calculate the taxable amount of interest income for both individuals and corporations (paragraphs 9-40 through 9-46).

5. Explain the tax treatment of discounts and premiums on long-term debt holdings (paragraphs 9-47 and 9-48).

6. Explain the tax treatment of prescribed debt obligations and indexed debt obligations (paragraphs 9-49 through 9-51).

7. Apply the provisions related to accrued interest at the time of transfer of debt obligations (paragraphs 9-52 and 9-55).

8. Demonstrate a basic understanding of the tax procedures for royalties and payments based on production or use (paragraphs 9-56 through 9-59).

9. Calculate net rental income (paragraphs 9-60 through 9-69).

10. Apply the gross up and tax credit mechanism to determine the tax consequences of receiving eligible and non-eligible dividend income (paragraphs 9-70 through 9-96).

11. Compare the after-tax returns from various types of investments (paragraphs 9-97 through 9-99).

12. Explain the general treatment of stock dividends and capital dividends (paragraphs 9-100 through 9-102).

13. Demonstrate an understanding of the provisions relating to mutual funds (paragraphs 9-104 through 9-113).

14. Demonstrate an understanding of the provisions relating to income trusts (paragraphs 9-114 through 9-121).

15. Calculate the tax consequences of receiving foreign source income (paragraphs 9-122 through 9-125).

16. Determine the tax consequences of various shareholder benefits (paragraphs 9-126 through 9-139).

CHAPTER TEN

How To Work Through Chapter Ten

We recommend the following approach in dealing with the material in this chapter:

Economic Background And General Rules
☐ Read the text pages 365 (from paragraph 10-1) through 369 (through paragraph 10-23).

☐ Complete Exercises Ten-1 and Ten-2 on page 369 of the text. The solutions are on page S-128.

☐ Read the text pages 369 (from paragraph 10-24) and 370 (through paragraph 10-28).

Assets Acquired Before 1972
☐ Read the text pages 370 (from paragraph 10-29) and 371 (through paragraph 10-33).

Identical Properties
☐ Read the text page 371 (from paragraph 10-34 through paragraph 10-35).

☐ Complete Exercise Ten-3 on page 372 of the text. The solution is on page S-128.

☐ Complete Self Study Problem Ten-1 on page 400 of the text. The solution is on page S-132.

☐ Read the text page 372 (paragraphs 10-36 through 10-39).

Partial Dispositions
☐ Read the text page 372 (paragraph 10-40).

Warranties
☐ Read the text pages 372 and 373 (paragraph 10-41).

☐ Complete Exercise Ten-4 on page 373 of the text. The solution is on page S-128.

Bad Debts On Sales Of Capital Property
☐ Read the text page 373 (paragraphs 10-42 and 10-43).

☐ Complete Exercise Ten-5 on page 373 of the text. The solution is on page S-128.

Capital Gains Reserves
☐ Read the text pages 373 (from paragraph 10-44) through 375 (through paragraph 10-59).

☐ Complete Exercise Ten-6 on page 375 of the text. The solution is on page S-129.

☐ Complete Self Study Problem Ten-2 on page 400 of the text. The solution is on pages S-133 and S-134.

Deferral Provisions On Replacement Property
☐ Read the text pages 375 (from paragraph 10-60) through 379 (through paragraph 10-77).

☐ Complete Exercise Ten-7 on page 379 of the text. The solution is on page S-129.

☐ Complete Self Study Problems Ten-3 and Ten-4 on pages 400 through 402 of the text. The solutions are on pages S-134 through S-138.

Deferral Provisions On Small Business Investments

☐ Read the text pages 379 (from paragraph 10-78) through 380 (through paragraph 10-80).

☐ Complete Exercise Ten-8 on page 380 of the text. The solution is on page S-129.

Changes In Use

☐ Read the text pages 380 (from paragraph 10-81) and 381 (through paragraph 10-84).

☐ Complete Exercise Ten-9 on page 381 of the text. The solution is on page S-129.

☐ Complete Self Study Problem Ten-5 on page 402 of the text. The solution is on pages S-138 and S-139.

Principal Residence

☐ Read the text pages 381 (from paragraph 10-85) through 383 (through paragraph 10-91).

☐ Complete Exercises Ten-10 and Ten-11 on page 383 of the text. The solutions are on pages S-129 and S-130.

☐ Read the text pages 383 (from paragraph 10-92) and 384 (through paragraph 10-96).

☐ Complete Exercise Ten-12 on page 384 of the text. The solution is on page S-130.

☐ Complete Self Study Problem Ten-6 on page 402 of the text. The solution is on pages S-139 and S-140.

☐ Read the text page 384 (paragraphs 10-97 and 10-98).

☐ Complete Exercise Ten-13 on page 385 of the text. The solution is on page S-130.

☐ Read the text page 385 (from paragraph 10-99) through 387 (through paragraph 10-106).

Personal Use Property

☐ Read the text pages 387 (from paragraph 10-107) and 388 (through paragraph 10-114).

☐ Complete Exercise Ten-14 on page 388 of the text. The solution is on page S-131.

Gains And Losses On Foreign Currency

☐ Read the text pages 388 (from paragraph 10-115) through 390 (through paragraph 10-125).

☐ Complete Exercise Ten-15 on page 390 of the text. The solution is on page S-131.

Options

☐ Read the text page 391 (from paragraph 10-126 through paragraph 10-129).

Capital Gains And Tax Planning

☐ Read the text pages 391 (from paragraph 10-130) and 392 (through paragraph 10-131).

Capital Property And The GST

☐ Read the text pages 392 (from paragraph 10-132) through 395 (through paragraph 10-155).

☐ Complete Self Study Problem Ten-7 on page 403 of the text. The solution is on page S-141.

Residential Property And The New Housing Rebate

☐ Read the text page 395 (paragraph 10-156 through paragraph 10-163).

☐ Complete Self Study Problem Ten-8 on page 403 of the text. The solution is on page S-141.

If The Appendix - Disposition Of Shares Acquired With Stock Options Has Been Assigned

☐ Read the Appendix on pages 397 (from paragraph 10A-1) through 399 (through paragraph 10A-5).

☐ Complete Exercise Ten-16 on page 399 of the text. The solution is on pages S-131 and S-132.

To Complete This Chapter

☐ Review the Key Terms Used In This Chapter on page 396 of the text. Consult the Glossary for the meaning of any key terms you do not know.

☐ Review the Glossary Flashcards and complete the Key Terms Self-Test for the Chapter. These features can be found in two places, on your Student CD-ROM under the heading "Key Term Practice" and on the web site.

☐ Review the Learning Objectives of the Chapter found on pages S-142 and S-143 of this Study Guide.

☐ As a review, we recommend that you view the PowerPoint Slides for Chapter Ten that are on your Student CD-ROM. The PowerPoint Viewer program can be installed from the Student CD-ROM.

Solution to Chapter Ten Exercises

Exercise Ten - 1 Solution

The capital cost of this Class 1 asset would be $3,500,000 ($5,600,000 - $600,000 - $1,500,000). Given this, the maximum CCA in this first year would $70,000 [(1/2)($3,500,000)(4%)].

Exercise Ten - 2 Solution

The total loss on the sale of 1,000 shares would be $8,500 [(1,000)($14.50 - $23.00)]. As she acquires 600 shares of identical property within 30 days of the sale, 60 percent (600/1,000) of the loss would be disallowed. This $5,100 [(60%)($8,500)] disallowed loss would be added to the adjusted cost base of the new shares. This gives a total adjusted cost base for the new shares of $13,350 [(600)($13.75) + $5,100], or $22.25 per share. The remaining capital loss of $3,400 will create an allowable capital loss of $1,700 [(1/2)($3,400)].

Exercise Ten - 3 Solution

The average cost of the shares purchased in 2005 is $23.76 {[(650)($23.50) + (345)($24.25)] ÷ 995}. Given this, Ms. Montrose's taxable capital gain for 2005 is calculated as follows:

Proceeds Of Disposition [($25.50)(210)]	$5,355
Adjusted Cost Base [($23.76)(210)]	(4,990)
Capital Gain	$ 365
Inclusion Rate	1/2
Taxable Capital Gain	$ 183

When her 2006 purchase is added to the remaining balance, her average cost becomes $25.34 {[(785)($23.76) + (875)($26.75)] ÷ 1,660}. Given this, Ms. Montrose's taxable capital gain for 2006 is calculated as follows:

Proceeds Of Disposition [($29.50)(340)]	$10,030
Adjusted Cost Base [($25.34)(340)]	(8,616)
Capital Gain	$ 1,414
Inclusion Rate	1/2
Taxable Capital Gain	$ 707

Exercise Ten - 4 Solution

For 2005, there will be a taxable capital gain of $27,500 [(1/2)($292,000 - $237,000)]. During 2006, there will be an allowable capital loss of $2,400 [(1/2)($4,800)]. This allowable capital loss will only be deductible in 2006 against 2006 taxable capital gains. However, it can be carried back and deducted against the 2005 capital gain in the determination of an amended 2005 Taxable Income.

Exercise Ten - 5 Solution

For 2005, there will be an allowable capital loss of $7,500 [(1/2)($110,000 - $125,000)]. For 2006, there will be an allowable capital loss of $17,500 [(1/2)(Nil - $35,000)]. The total allowable capital loss of $25,000 ($7,500 + $17,500) over the two years is equivalent to the allowable capital loss that would have resulted if the property had been sold for cash of $75,000. The capital loss would equal $50,000 ($125,000 - $75,000) and the allowable capital loss would be $25,000 [(1/2)($50,000)].

These allowable capital losses will only be deductible against taxable capital gains. However, they can be carried over to other years in which the taxpayer has taxable capital gains and deducted in the determination of Taxable Income.

Exercise Ten - 6 Solution

Mr. Goodson's capital gain on this transaction is $71,800 ($382,000 - $293,000 - $17,200). The maximum reserve for 2005 is $56,387, the lesser of:

- $56,387 [($71,800)($300,000 ÷ $382,000)]
- $57,440 [($71,800)(20%)(4 - 0)]

For 2006, the maximum reserve is $43,080, the lesser of :

- $45,110 [($71,800)($240,000 ÷ $382,000)]
- $43,080 [($71,800)(20%)(4 - 1)]

Exercise Ten - 7 Solution

As the replacement did not occur until 2006, Hadfeld's 2005 tax return will include a taxable capital gain of $112,500 [(1/2)($950,000 - $725,000)], and recapture of $101,850 ($725,000 - $623,150). In 2006, these amounts can be removed from income and asset values through an amended return. The capital cost of the new building will be $755,000 [$980,000 - ($950,000 - $725,000)]. Its UCC will be $653,150 ($755,000 - $101,850).

Each of these amounts are $30,000 more than the old capital cost and UCC. This reflects the $30,000 ($980,000 - $950,000) over and above the insurance proceeds that the Company spent on replacing the building.

Exercise Ten - 8 Solution

The capital gain is $600,000 ($1,350,000 - $750,000) and the lesser of the proceeds of disposition and the cost of the replacement shares is the $1,200,000 cost of the replacement shares. Given this, the permitted deferral would be $533,333 [($600,000)($1,200,000 ÷ $1,350,000)]. This means that the adjusted cost base of the JH Inc. shares is $666,667 ($1,200,000 - $533,333).

Exercise Ten - 9 Solution

This change in use will be a deemed disposition and re-acquisition of the property. For capital gains purposes, the transaction will take place at the fair market value of $111,000, resulting in a taxable capital gain for Ms. Larson of $44,000 [(1/2)($111,000 - $23,000)]. The new capital cost for the property will be $111,000.

As the change is from personal to business use and the fair market value is greater than the cost, the new UCC for the property will be its cost, plus one-half of the difference between the fair market value and the cost. This amount is $67,000 [$23,000 + (1/2)($111,000 - $23,000)]. Maximum CCA on this amount would be $1,340 [($67,000)(4%)(1/2)].

Exercise Ten - 10 Solution

There would be no tax consequences due to the sales. There would be a capital gain on the first sale of $20,500 ($109,500 - $89,000). This gain could be eliminated by designating the first property as his principal residence for the six years 1997 through 2002. The gain reduction would be calculated as follows:

$$\left(\$20,500 \times \frac{6}{6} \right) = \underline{\underline{\$20,500}}$$

The $26,000 ($178,000 - $152,000) capital gain on the second home could be eliminated by designating the second property as his principal residence for the years 2003 through 2006 and adding the plus one in the numerator. The gain reduction would be calculated as follows:

$$\left(\$26,000 \times \frac{(4+1)}{5} \right) = \underline{\underline{\$26,000}}$$

Exercise Ten - 11 Solution

The annual gain on the house is $6,000 [($198,000 - $126,000) ÷ 12 Years], while the annual gain on the cottage is $6,500 [($143,500 - $85,000) ÷ 9 Years]. Given this, the years 1999 through 2006 should be allocated to the cottage. When these eight years are combined with the plus one in the numerator of the reduction formula, the $58,500 gain on the cottage will be completely eliminated. This leaves the years 1995 through 1998 for the Ottawa house, resulting in the following gain reduction:

$$\left(\$72,000 \times \frac{(4+1)}{12} \right) = \underline{\underline{\$30,000}}$$

This will leave a total capital gain on the sale of the two properties of $42,000 ($72,000 + $58,500 - $58,500 - $30,000).

Exercise Ten - 12 Solution

The 2007 change in use would be treated as a deemed disposition/re-acquisition at the fair market value of $210,000. As the home was personal use property, the loss would not be deductible.

If she does not elect under ITA 45(2), she would likely take CCA for 2007. The maximum amount would be $4,200 [($210,000)(4%)(1/2)]. This would result in a net rental income for 2007 of $4,800 ($21,600 - $12,600 - $4,200).

When the property is sold in 2008, she would have a taxable capital gain of $67,500 [($345,000 - $210,000)(1/2)]. In addition, there would be recapture of CCA of $4,200, the amount of CCA taken in 2007.

If she did not take CCA in 2007, her net rental income would be $9,000. However, she could then elect under ITA 45(2) and this means that the property could continue to be designated as her principal residence in 2007. Given this, the capital gain could be eliminated by the principal residence deduction. In addition, there would be no recapture. This is clearly a better alternative.

Exercise Ten - 13 Solution

The maximum CCA for 2005 would be $7,500 [($375,000)(4%)(1/2)]. Deducting this amount would result in a 2005 net rental income of $2,300 ($9,800 - $7,500).

Because he has deducted CCA for this year, he cannot treat the property as his principal residence and, when he moves in on January 1, 2006, the change in use will create a deemed disposition/re-acquisition at the fair market value of $450,000. This will result in a taxable capital gain of $37,500 [($450,000 - $375,000)(1/2)]. There would also be recapture of the $7,500 of CCA taken in 2005.

When he sells the property at the end of the year for $510,000, there will be an additional taxable capital gain of $30,000 [($510,000 - $450,000)(1/2)]. The total 2006 income inclusion will be $75,000 ($37,500 + $7,500 + $30,000)

If he does not take CCA in 2005, his net rental income will be $9,800. However, if he makes the ITA 45(3) election, the unit can be designated as his principal residence for both 2005 and 2006. This means that there will be no additional income in 2006. This is clearly a better alternative.

Exercise Ten - 14 Solution

The results would be as follows:

	Personal Use Property	Listed Personal Property
Gain On Sailboat ($68,000 - $43,000)	$25,000	
Gain On Oil Painting ($25,000 - $1,000)		$24,000
Loss On Personal Automobile	Nil	
Loss On Necklace ($23,000 - $46,000)		(23,000)
Capital Gain	$25,000	$ 1,000
Inclusion Rate	1/2	1/2
Net Taxable Capital Gain	$12,500	$ 500

The total taxable capital gain on the dispositions is equal to $13,000 ($12,500 + $500). While the loss on the automobile is not deductible as it is personal use property, the loss on the diamond necklace can be deducted against the gain on the oil painting because it is listed personal property. The adjusted cost base of the oil painting is deemed to be $1,000 using the $1,000 floor rule.

Exercise Ten - 15 Solution

In 2005, as a result of his share purchase, Mr. Pratt will have an exchange gain of $612 [(450)(TT$68)(C$0.20 - C$0.18)]]. As this qualifies as an ITA 39(2) foreign currency capital gain, he will only include $206 [(1/2)($612 - $200)] of this in his Net Income For Tax Purposes.

In 2006, there will be a capital gain on the sale of $2,952 {[(450)(TT$96)(C$0.21)] - [(450)(TT$68)(C$0.20)]}. None of this gain qualifies under ITA 39(2), so there would be no $200 exclusion. Mr. Pratt's 2006 Net Income For Tax Purposes will include $1,476, or one-half, of this gain.

Exercise Ten - 16 Solution

The total specified value of the shares acquired through options during 2006 is $10,000 [(500 Shares)($20)]. This means he can defer all of the employment income, a total of $11,250 [(250)($35 - $20) + (250)($50 - $20)]. There is no effect on 2006 income.

The 700 shares sold during 2007 would be made up of his original holding of 500 non-deferral shares, plus 200 of the option shares acquired on January 15. The tax consequences would be as follows:

Taxable Capital Gains:	
[(500 Shares)($55.00 - $23.50)(1/2)]	$ 7,875
[(200 Shares)($55.00 - $35.00)(1/2)]	2,000
Employment Income [(200 Shares)($35.00 - $20.00)]	3,000
ITA 110(1)(d) Deduction [(1/2)($3,000)]	(1,500)
2007 Increase In Taxable Income	$11,375

The 300 shares sold during 2008 would be made up of the 50 remaining shares acquired on January 15, 2006, along with the 250 acquired on October 3, 2006. The tax consequences would be as follows:

Employment Income:	
[(50)($35.00 - $20.00)]	$ 750
[(250)($50.00 - $20.00)]	7,500
ITA 110(1)(d) Deduction [(1/2)($7,500 + $750)]	(4,125)
2008 Increase In Taxable Income	$4,125

Taxable Capital Gains (Losses):	
[(50)($30.00 - $35.00)(1/2)]	($ 125)
[(250)($30.00 - $50.00)(1/2)]	(2,500)
2008 Allowable Capital Loss	($2,625)

Note that these two amounts cannot be netted, as allowable capital losses are not deductible against employment income. Unless Jean has taxable capital gains on other 2008 dispositions, he will not be able to deduct the $2,625 allowable capital loss in the current year.

Solution to Self Study Problem Ten - 1

Acquisition Or Sale Date	Shares Purchased (Sold)	Cost Per Share	Total Cost	Average Cost/Share
October 15, 1999	5,500	$40.00	$220,000	
November 8, 1999	(1,500)	(40.00)	(60,000)	
December 12, 2002	3,200	79.00	252,800	
Subtotal	7,200		$412,800	$ 57.33
February 3, 2003	(2,600)	(57.33)	(149,058)	
Subtotal	4,600		$263,742	
January 15, 2004 Stock Dividend	460	99.00	45,540	
June 15, 2004	3,800	104.00	395,200	
Subtotal	8,860		$704,482	
December 23, 2005 Stock Dividend	886	125.00	110,750	
March 15, 2006 Balances	9,746		$815,232	

The taxable capital gain resulting from the November 8, 1999 sale of shares would be calculated as follows:

Proceeds Of Disposition [(1,500)($52)]	$78,000
Adjusted Cost Base [(1,500)($40)]	(60,000)
Capital Gain	$18,000
1999 Inclusion Rate	3/4
Taxable Capital Gain	$13,500

The taxable capital gain resulting from the February 3, 2003 sale of shares would be as follows:

Proceeds Of Disposition [(2,600)($94)]	$244,400
Adjusted Cost Base [(2,600)($57.33)]	
(See preceding table for per share adjusted cost base)	(149,058)
Capital Gain	$ 95,342
Inclusion Rate	1/2
Taxable Capital Gain	$ 47,671

The taxable capital gain resulting from the March 15, 2006 sale of shares would be as follows:

Proceeds Of Disposition [(9,746)($174)]	$1,695,804
Adjusted Cost Base (Remainder)	(815,232)
Capital Gain	$ 880,572
Inclusion Rate	1/2
Taxable Capital Gain	$ 440,286

Solution to Self Study Problem Ten - 2

Total Gain The total amount of the taxable capital gain can be calculated as follows:

Proceeds Of Disposition		$500,000
Less:		
Adjusted Cost Base	$230,000	
Disposition Costs	20,000	250,000
Total Capital Gain		$250,000
Inclusion Rate		1/2
Total Taxable Capital Gain		$125,000

Reserve Limits As Miss Stevens has not received the entire proceeds in the year of sale, she is entitled under ITA 40(1) to establish a reserve. The reserve that would be available at the end of each year would be the lesser of:

- [(Capital Gain)(Proceeds Not Yet Due ÷ Total Proceeds)]
- [(Capital Gain)(20%)(4 - Number Of Preceding Years Ending After Disposition)]

2006 Gain As the cash proceeds during 2006 are well in excess of 20 percent of the total proceeds, the maximum reserve at the end of 2006 would be calculated as follows:

[($250,000)($300,000 ÷ $500,000)] = $150,000

With a reserve of $150,000, the capital gain to be recognized for 2006 would be $100,000 ($250,000 - $150,000). This would result in a taxable capital gain of $50,000.

2007 Gain At the end of 2007, the two calculations provide equal results as follows:

- [($250,000)($300,000 ÷ $500,000)] = $150,000
- [($250,000)(20%)(Four Years - One Year)] = $150,000

This means the 2007 taxable capital gain would be calculated as follows:

Addition Of The 2006 Reserve	$ 150,000
Deduction Of The 2007 Reserve	(150,000)
2007 Capital Gain	Nil

2008, 2009, And 2010 Gains In these three years no further proceeds are receivable and, as a consequence, the reserve calculation based on proceeds not receivable until after December 31 would remain unchanged at $150,000. However, the alternative calculations would decline to:

- $100,000 at the end of 2008 ($250,000)[(20%)(Four Years - Two Years)],
- $50,000 at the end of 2009 [($250,000)[(20%)(Four Years - Three Years)],
- nil at the end of 2010 [($250,000)[(20%)(Four Years - Four Years)].

This means that a gain of $50,000 would be recognized in each of the three years and would require the inclusion of a taxable capital gain of $25,000 in each year's Net Income For Tax Purposes. At this point, the entire taxable capital gain of $125,000 would have been taken into income as per the following schedule:

Year	Capital Gain	Taxable Capital Gain
2006	$100,000	$50,000
2007	-0-	-0-
2008	50,000	25,000
2009	50,000	25,000
2010	50,000	25,000
Total	$250,000	$125,000

2011 And 2012 Gains   As the entire taxable capital gain was taken into Net Income For Tax Purposes by the end of 2010, no further gains will be recognized in either 2011 or 2012.

Solution to Self Study Problem Ten - 3

Part A - With respect to Net Income For Tax Purposes, the 2006 tax effects related to the involuntary dispositions would be as follows:

Land   In the absence of the ITA 44(1) election, the taxable capital gain on the land would be as follows:

Proceeds Of Disposition	$723,000
Adjusted Cost Base	(256,000)
Capital Gain	$467,000
Inclusion Rate	1/2
Taxable Capital Gain	$233,500

Building   In the absence of the ITA 44(1) election, the taxable capital gain on the building would be as follows:

Proceeds Of Disposition	$4,800,000
Adjusted Cost Base	(3,700,000)
Capital Gain	$1,100,000
Inclusion Rate	1/2
Taxable Capital Gain	$ 550,000

If the ITA 13(4) election is not used, the disposition of the building would result in recapture as per the following calculation:

Capital Cost	$3,700,000
UCC	(1,856,000)
Recaptured CCA	$1,844,000

Building Contents   In the absence of the ITA 44(1) election, the taxable capital gain on the building contents would be as follows:

Proceeds Of Disposition	$1,256,000
Adjusted Cost Base	(972,000)
Capital Gain	$ 284,000
Inclusion Rate	1/2
Taxable Capital Gain	$ 142,000

If the ITA 13(4) election is not used, the disposition of the building contents would result in recapture as per the following calculation:

Capital Cost	$972,000
UCC	(72,000)
Recaptured CCA	$900,000

Part B The effects of using the ITA 13(4) and ITA 44(1) elections can be calculated as follows:

Land The taxable capital gain can be reduced to the following under the ITA 44(1) election:

Proceeds Of Disposition	$723,000
Cost Of Replacement Property	(500,000)
Capital Gain	$223,000
Inclusion Rate	1/2
Taxable Capital Gain	$111,500

If the election is used, the adjusted cost base of the replacement property (which is equal to the adjusted cost base of the expropriated land) would be calculated as follows:

Actual Cost	$500,000
Capital Gain Deferred By Election ($467,000 - $223,000)	(244,000)
Deemed Cost	$256,000

Building The taxable capital gain can be reduced to the following under the ITA 44(1) election:

Proceeds Of Disposition	$4,800,000
Cost Of Replacement Property	(5,700,000)
Capital Gain	$ -0-

The adjusted cost base of the replacement property (which is equal to the adjusted cost base of the old building plus the $900,000 excess of the cost of the new building over the insurance proceeds) would be calculated as follows:

Actual Cost	$5,700,000
Capital Gain Deferred By Election ($1,100,000 - Nil)	(1,100,000)
Deemed Cost	$4,600,000

Use of the ITA 13(4) election would eliminate the recapture and leave the following UCC for the new property:

Capital Cost	$4,600,000
Recapture Deferred By Election ($1,844,000 - Nil)	(1,844,000)
UCC	$2,756,000

Building Contents If this were a voluntary disposition, the building contents would not be "former business property" and would not qualify for either the ITA 13(4) election or the ITA 44(1) election. However, as this is an involuntary disposition, both elections are available. Use of the ITA 44(1) election would reduce the capital gain on the building contents to the amount shown in the following calculation:

Proceeds Of Disposition	$1,256,000
Cost Of Replacement Property	(1,233,000)
Capital Gain	$ 23,000
Inclusion Rate	1/2
Taxable Capital Gain	$ 11,500

The capital cost of the new building contents would be as follows:

Actual Cost	$1,233,000
Capital Gain Deferred By Election ($284,000 - $23,000)	(261,000)
Deemed Cost	$ 972,000

Use of the ITA 13(4) election would eliminate the recapture and leave the following UCC for the new property:

Capital Cost	$972,000
Recapture Deferred By Election ($900,000 - Nil)	(900,000)
UCC	$ 72,000

Part C   As there was a $223,000 capital gain remaining on the land and no gain remaining on the building, a reduction of Net Income For Tax Purposes can be achieved under the ITA 44(6) election. In fact, the excess of replacement cost over the old cost for the building is sufficient that all of the gain can be eliminated on the land without creating a gain on the building. This is accomplished by electing under ITA 44(6) to transfer $223,000 of the land proceeds to the building proceeds. This will completely eliminate the $223,000 capital gain on the land and will increase the capital gain removed by elections on the building by $223,000. In turn, the deemed cost of the building will now be $4,377,000 ($4,600,000 - $223,000) and the UCC will be $2,533,000 ($4,600,000 - $223,000 - $1,844,000). The adjusted cost base of the land will remain at $256,000.

Note that this election is not made without a cost. Had the $223,000 been left as a capital gain, tax would have applied on only one-half of the total. While we have eliminated this $111,500 in income, we have given up future CCA for the full amount of the $223,000. In other words, we have given up $223,000 in future deductions in return for eliminating $111,500 of income in 2006. This makes the use of this election somewhat questionable. Factors that should be considered include whether capital gains are taxed at different rates than business income (corporations) and the anticipated future tax rates and timing of Taxable Income.

Solution to Self Study Problem Ten - 4

Part A   With respect to Net Income For Tax Purposes, the sale of the Toronto property would have the following tax effects:

Land   In the absence of the ITA 44(1) election, the capital gain on the land would be as follows:

Proceeds Of Disposition	$772,000
Adjusted Cost Base	(137,000)
Capital Gain - No ITA 44(1) Election	$635,000

However, this can be reduced under the ITA 44(1) election as follows:

Proceeds Of Disposition	$772,000
Cost Of Replacement Property	(253,000)
Capital Gain Using ITA 44(1) Election	$519,000

This will result in a $259,500 [(1/2)($519,000)] taxable capital gain being included in 2006 Net Income For Tax Purposes. The adjusted cost base of the replacement property, which is equal to the adjusted cost base of the land sold, would be calculated as follows:

Actual Cost	$253,000
Capital Gain Deferred By Election ($635,000 - $519,000)	(116,000)
Deemed Cost	$137,000

Building In the absence of the ITA 44(1) election, the capital gain on the building would be as follows:

Proceeds Of Disposition	$989,000
Adjusted Cost Base	(605,000)
Capital Gain - No ITA 44(1) Election	$384,000

This gain can be eliminated by using the ITA 44(1) election as follows:

Proceeds Of Disposition	$ 989,000
Cost Of Replacement Property	(1,042,000)
Capital Gain Using ITA 44(1) Election	$ -0-

No capital gain would be included in 2006 Net Income For Tax Purposes and the adjusted cost base of the new building, which is equal to the adjusted cost base of the building that was sold, plus the $53,000 excess of the cost of the new building over the proceeds from the old building, would be calculated as follows:

Actual Cost	$1,042,000
Capital Gain Deferred By Election	(384,000)
Deemed Cost	$ 658,000

If the ITA 13(4) election is not used, the disposition of the building results in recapture as follows:

Capital Cost	$605,000
UCC	(342,000)
Recapture - No ITA 13(4) Election	$263,000

Use of the ITA 13(4) election would eliminate the recapture and leave the following UCC for the new property:

Capital Cost	$658,000
Recapture Deferred By Election	(263,000)
UCC	$395,000

Note that the UCC for the new building is equal to the UCC of the old building ($342,000), plus the additional $53,000 in funds required for its acquisition.

Equipment   As this is a voluntary disposition, the equipment does not qualify as "former business property" and, as a consequence, neither the ITA 44(1) nor the ITA 13(4) election can be used. However, as there were no other assets in the class at the end of 2006, there will be a terminal loss of $13,000 ($127,000 - $114,000). The new equipment has a capital cost equal to its actual cost of $205,000. This is also equal to the UCC.

Part B   As calculated in Part A, there was a $519,000 capital gain on the land and no gain on the building. Some reduction of Net Income For Tax Purposes can be achieved under the ITA 44(6) election. However, the reduction is limited to the $53,000 difference between the $989,000 fair market value of the old building and the $1,042,000 cost of the replacement building. This would reduce the capital gain on the land by $53,000. The adjusted cost base of the replacement land would remain at $137,000. This would still leave the capital gain on the building at nil. This can be shown as follows:

Deemed Proceeds Of Disposition ($989,000 + $53,000)	$1,042,000
Less: Cost Of Replacement Property	1,042,000
Capital Gain	$ -0-

Using this election, Net Income For Tax Purposes would be reduced by $26,500 [(1/2)($53,000)]. It would be possible to further reduce the gain on the land by transferring more of the proceeds to the building. The result, however, would be a new gain on the building that would be equal to the gain reduction on the land.

Also note that there is a cost involved with this election. While the Company has reduced its 2006 Net Income For Tax Purposes by one-half of the $53,000 capital gain, it has forgone future CCA for the full amount of $53,000.

With the use of this election, the deemed cost of the new building would be $605,000 [$1,042,000 - ($989,000 + $53,000 - $605,000)] and the UCC would be reduced to $342,000 ($605,000 - $263,000).

Solution to Self Study Problem Ten - 5

2005 Solution   As the property is being transferred from personal to business use and its fair market value is greater than its cost, ITA 13(7)(b) requires that, for the purposes of calculating CCA, the property be recorded at an amount equal to its cost, plus one-half of the excess of its fair market value over cost. The half-year rule is applicable as a personal residence is not a depreciable property. The UCC would be calculated as follows:

Cost ($176,000 - $83,000)	$ 93,000
Bump-Up On Transfer -	
{[1/2][($253,000 - $106,000) - ($176,000 - $83,000)]}	27,000
Capital Cost For CCA Purposes	$120,000
Rental Share	32%
Opening UCC	$ 38,400
One-Half Net Additions	(19,200)
CCA Base	$ 19,200
CCA [($19,200)(4%)]	(768)
One-Half Net Additions	19,200
January 1, 2006 UCC	$ 37,632

Based on the preceding information, the 2005 net rental income would be calculated as follows:

Rents [(12)($850)]	$10,200
Expenses [(32%)($5,600)]	(1,792)
CCA	(768)
Net Rental Income	**$ 7,640**

There would also be a taxable capital gain in 2005, on the deemed disposition of the property, in the amount of $12,320 [(1/2)(32%)($253,000 - $176,000)]. Note that the capital gain calculation is based on the full fair market value at the time of the change in use. The value for the building calculated in the preceding schedule is used only for purposes of determining maximum CCA. It is likely that this taxable capital gain will be eliminated by designating the property as Mr. Blake's principal residence for the years 1987 through 2005.

2006 Solution   In this year, the transfer is from business to personal use and, as a consequence, the disposition will result in a deduction from UCC in an amount equal to the lesser of 11 percent of the capital cost for CCA purposes ($120,000) and 11 percent of the fair market value of $168,000 ($278,000 - $110,000). The calculations are as follows:

Opening UCC	$37,632
Additions (Improvements)	12,350
Dispositions [(11%)($120,000)]	(13,200)
One-Half Net Additions	Nil
CCA Base	**$36,782**
CCA [($36,782)(4%)]	(1,471)
January 1, 2007 UCC	**$35,311**

Based on the preceding information, the 2006 net rental income would be calculated as follows:

Rents [(6)($850) + (6)($750)]	$9,600
Expenses {[(32%)($2,900)] + [(21%)($3,200)]}	(1,600)
CCA	(1,471)
Net Rental Income	**$6,529**

In addition to the net rental income calculated in the preceding table, there would be a taxable capital gain on the property in the amount of $1,375 [(1/2)(11%)($278,000 - $253,000)]. Since the improvements were made after the change in use, their cost is not included in the capital gain calculation.

Solution to Self Study Problem Ten - 6

Part A - Use Of ITA 40(2)(b)   The calculations here begin with the calculation of the gain per year of ownership for the entire period 1972 through 2006. The amounts would be as follows:

English Bay = [($515,000 - $125,000) ÷ 35] = $11,143

Cottage = [($320,000 - $40,000) ÷ 30] = $9,333

As the annual gain is greater on the English Bay property, this should be the designated principal residence for most of the years. The gain on this property can be completely eliminated by designating 34 years to the property, and adding the one additional year that is available in the exemption formula. This will leave one year to be used on the cottage, and the exemption here would be calculated as follows:

$$\{[(1 + 1) \div 30](\$280,000)\} = \underline{\$18,667}$$

Under this approach, the total capital gain to be recognized in 2006 would be as follows:

Gain On English Bay	$390,000
Exemption On English Bay	(390,000)
Gain On Cottage	280,000
Exemption On Cottage	(18,667)
Total Capital Gain Using ITA 40(2)(b)	$261,333

Part B - Use Of ITA 40(6)   Under this approach, there would be separate calculations of the annual gains on the two properties for both the pre-1982 period and the post-1981 period. These calculations are as follows:

Annual Gains, 1972 Through 1981

English Bay = [($335,000 - $125,000) ÷ 10] = $21,000

Cottage = [($205,000 - $40,000) ÷ 5] = $33,000

Total Gains, 1982 Through 2006

English Bay = ($515,000 - $335,000) = $180,000

Cottage = ($320,000 - $205,000) = $115,000

Under this alternative approach, it would be appropriate to maximize the exemption for the cottage during the ten year period 1972 through 1981, as the per year amount for the cottage is $33,000, vs. $21,000 for the English Bay property. As this property was only owned for five years during this period, the complete elimination of the gain on the cottage would require the use of four designated years, plus the one additional year. This would leave six years for the English Bay property, and the exemption would be calculated as follows:

[(6 + 1) ÷ 10][$335,000 - $125,000] = $147,000

For the period 1982 through 2006, the larger gain would be on the English Bay property and, as a consequence, the exemption on this property should be maximized. As the plus one rule does not apply in this period, the entire 25 years will be required to eliminate the gain on this property, and no years can be allocated to the cottage. Summarizing the results under this dual approach, we would use the following calculations:

Cottage Gain - 1972-1981	$165,000
Exemption	(165,000)
English Bay Gain - 1972-1981	210,000
Exemption	(147,000)
English Bay Gain - 1982-2006	180,000
Exemption	(180,000)
Cottage Gain - 1982-2006	115,000
Exemption	(-0-)
Total Capital Gain Using ITA 40(6) Election	$178,000

Note that the use of ITA 40(6) results in a significantly lower gain than was the case using ITA 40(2)(b). The difference is $83,333 ($261,333 - $178,000).

Solution to Self Study Problem Ten - 7

A. The purchase of the commercial property will be taxable at 6 percent. Therefore, GST of $600,000 [($10,000,000)(6%)] will be payable by Tiffany.

B. As Tiffany is a GST registrant, the Company is responsible for remitting the GST on the purchase. No election is required. When Tiffany's GST return is filed for the period including the purchase date, the required remittance of $600,000 should be reported. At the same time, Tiffany can also claim any available input tax credit. The input tax credit is $408,000 {[($600,000)(60%)] + [($600,000)(40%)(20%)]}.

Therefore, the required GST remittance will be $600,000, for the GST on the purchase, from which a $408,000 input tax credit can be deducted, for a net cash outlay of $192,000. In the calculation of the input tax credit, we assume that the 20 percent general administrative expense allocation is also a reasonable allocation for Tiffany's commercial use of the space.

C. The lease to commercial tenants is a commercial activity, so Tiffany will have to charge GST on the lease.

Solution to Self Study Problem Ten - 8

The GST and total cost of each purchase would be:

Shuswap Cedar A-Frame

GST = Nil
Total Cost = $120,000

Millcreek Bi-Level

GST = [($90,000+$14,000)(6%)] - [($90,000+$14,000)(6%)(36%)] + [($10,000)(6%)]
= $6,240 - $2,246 + $600
= $4,594

Total Cost = $90,000 + $14,000 + $10,000 + $4,594 = $118,594

Sunset Beach Cottage

The renovations are considered substantial. Since the renovations would be done by the vendor prior to the sale, the purchase would be deemed to be that of a "new" home. Therefore, the purchase price would be subject to the full GST and a new housing rebate could be claimed on the total, as follows:

GST = [($116,000)(6%)] - [($116,000)(6%)(36%)]
= $6,960 - $2,506
= $4,454

Total Cost = $116,000 + $4,454 = $120,454

Chapter Ten Learning Objectives

After completing Chapter 10, you should be able to:

1. Explain the economic basis for treating capital gains more favourably than other types of income (paragraphs 10-1 through 10-10).

2. Apply the general rules for the determination of gains and losses on the disposition of capital assets (paragraphs 10-11 through 10-28).

3. Demonstrate an understanding of why capital gains and losses on assets acquired prior to December 31, 1971 are determined using alternative rules (paragraphs 10-29 through 10-33).

4. Calculate capital gains and losses on dispositions of identical properties (paragraphs 10-34 through 10-39).

5. Calculate capital gains and losses on partial dispositions of capital property and on properties that are sold with warranties (paragraphs 10-40 and 10-41).

6. Determine the tax consequence of a bad debt arising on debts acquired through the sale of capital assets (paragraphs 10-42 and 10-43).

7. Apply the rules related to capital gains reserves (paragraphs 10-44 through 10-59).

8. Apply the deferral provisions for capital gains arising on voluntary and involuntary dispositions of property that is subsequently replaced (paragraphs 10-60 through 10-77).

9. Apply the deferral provisions available on the disposition of small business investments (paragraphs 10-78 through 10-80).

10. Determine the amount of capital gain or loss resulting from a change in the use of a capital asset (paragraphs 10-81 through 10-84).

11. Apply the basic rules related to the reduction of taxation of capital gains arising from the disposition of a principal residence (paragraphs 10-85 through 10-91).

12. Describe the principal residence elections that are available under ITA 45(1), 45(3), and 40(6) (paragraphs 10-92 through 10-104).

13. Demonstrate a basic understanding of the procedures associated with the disposition of farm property that is also a principal residence (paragraphs 10-105 and 10-106).

14. Determine the tax consequences that result from dispositions of personal use property (paragraphs 10-107 through 10-111)

15. Determine the tax consequences that result from dispositions of listed personal property (paragraphs 10-112 through 10-114).

16. Determine the tax consequences that result from foreign currency transactions (paragraphs 10-115 through 10-125).

17. Determine the tax consequences that result from dispositions of options (paragraphs 10-126 through 10-129).

18. Explain the role of capital gains and losses in tax planning (paragraphs 10-130 and 10-131).

19. Calculate the effects of GST on the acquisition and disposition of capital property (paragraphs 10-132 through 10-163).

If The Appendix - Disposition Of Shares Acquired With Stock Options Has Been Assigned

20. Demonstrate an understanding of the provisions associated with the dispositions of shares acquired with stock options (paragraphs 10-A1 through 10-A5).

CHAPTER ELEVEN

How To Work Through Chapter Eleven

We recommend the following approach in dealing with the material in this Chapter:

Other Income And Deductions - Introduction
☐   Read the text page 415 (paragraphs 11-1 through 11-4).

Other Sources Of Income - Subdivision d
☐   Read the text pages 416 (from paragraph 11-5) and 417 (through paragraph 11-14).

Spousal Support And Child Support Received
☐   Read the text pages 417 (from paragraph 11-15) through 419 (through paragraph 11-31).

☐   Complete Exercise Eleven-1 on page 419 of the text. The solution is on page S-147.

☐   Complete Self Study Problem Eleven-1 on page 438 of the text. The solution is on page S-148.

Income Inclusions From Deferred Income Plans And Annuities
☐   Read the text pages 419 (from paragraph 11-32) through 421 (through paragraph 11-39).

☐   Complete Exercise Eleven-2 on page 421 of the text. The solution is on page S-147.

Education And Social Assistance Payments
☐   Read the text pages 421 (from paragraph 11-40) and 422 (through paragraph 11-43).

Lump-Sum Payments
☐   Read the text pages 422 (from paragraph 11-44) and 423 (through paragraph 11-49).

Registered Education Savings Plans (RESPs), Canada Education Savings Grants And Canada Learning Bonds
☐   Read the text pages 423 (from paragraph 11-50) and 424 (through paragraph 11-55).

☐   Complete Exercise Eleven-3 on page 424 of the text. The solution is on page S-147.

☐   Read the text pages 425 (from paragraph 11-56) through 428 (through paragraph 11-76).

Other Deductions - Subdivision e
☐   Read the text page 428 (from paragraph 11-77 through paragraph 11-80).

Moving Expenses
☐   Read the text pages 429 (from paragraph 11-81) through 430 (through paragraph 11-90).

☐   Complete Exercise Eleven-4 on page 431 of the text. The solution is on page S-147.

☐   Complete Self Study Problem Eleven-2 on pages 438 and 439 of the text. The solution is on pages S-148 and S-149.

Child Care Expenses

☐ Read the text pages 431 (from paragraph 11-91) through 434 (through paragraph 11-101).

☐ Complete Exercise Eleven-5 on page 434 of the text. The solution is on page S-147.

☐ Complete Self Study Problem Eleven-3 on page 439 of the text. The solution is on page S-149.

Disability Supports Deduction

☐ Read the text pages 434 (from paragraph 11-102) and 435 (through paragraph 11-109).

☐ Complete Exercise Eleven-6 on page 436 of the text. The solution is on page S-147.

To Complete This Chapter

☐ Review the Key Terms Used In This Chapter on page 437 of the text. Consult the Glossary for the meaning of any key terms you do not know.

☐ Review the Glossary Flashcards and complete the Key Terms Self-Test for the Chapter. These features can be found in two places, on your Student CD-ROM under the heading "Key Term Practice" and on the web site.

☐ Review the Learning Objectives of the Chapter found on page S-150 of this Study Guide.

☐ As a review, we recommend that you view the PowerPoint Slides for Chapter Eleven that are on your Student CD-ROM. The PowerPoint Viewer program can be installed from the Student CD-ROM.

Solution to Chapter Eleven Exercises

Exercise Eleven - 1 Solution

The total required child support is $9,000 [(6 Months)($1,500)] and Sandra's payments will be allocated to this requirement first. This means that $9,000 of her payment will not be deductible to her or taxable to Jerry. The remaining $2,000 ($11,000 - $9,000) will be considered a payment towards spousal support and will be deductible to Sandra and taxable to Jerry.

Exercise Eleven - 2 Solution

A total of $63,492 [(4)($15,873)] in payments will be received from this annuity. The $15,873 will be included in his annual tax return. However, the net taxable amount is $2,123 ($15,873 - $13,750) because the annuity was purchased with after tax funds and he is eligible for a deduction equal to:

$$\left(\frac{\$55,000}{\$63,492}\right)(\$15,873) = \$13,750$$

Exercise Eleven - 3 Solution

For 2006, the contributions to Jeanine's RESP total $1,700. This is within the annual limit of $4,000, as well as the $2,000 limit for contributions eligible for CESGs. This means that the 2006 CESG would be $440 {[(40%)($500)] + [(20%)($1,700 - $500)]}.

For 2007, the contributions to Jeanine's RESP total $3,900. This is within the annual limit of $4,000 and, as a consequence, there will be no tax on excess contributions. However, Jeanine's plan has accumulated only $4,000 in room for contributions eligible for CESGs. As $1,700 of this was used in 2006, only $2,300 remains for use in 2007. This means that the 2007 CESG would be $560 {[(40%)($500)] + [(20%)($2,300 - $500)]} and $1,600 ($1,700 + $3,900 - $4,000) of the total contributions will not be eligible for CESGs. If it is expected that annual contributions to Jeanine's RESP will be less than $2,000 in the future, this would suggest that Jeanine's grandfather should limit his 2007 contribution to $800 and defer the extra $1,600 to the following year. In that year, it would eligible for a grant.

Exercise Eleven - 4 Solution

Her potentially deductible costs are $7,600 ($6,400 + $1,200). While she cannot personally deduct the $1,300 related to the visit to Regina her employer can pay for these costs without creating a taxable benefit. This leaves $4,700 ($6,000 - $1,300) of her employer's contribution that must be applied to her deductible costs. In turn, this leaves $2,900 ($7,600 - $4,700) that she can potentially deduct in 2006. However, the 2006 deduction is limited to the $2,000 that she earned at the new work location, leaving $900 to be carried forward and deducted in 2007.

Exercise Eleven - 5 Solution

The deduction will have to be made by the lower income spouse, Mr. Sampras. The deduction will be the least of the following amounts:

- The actual costs of $10,500.
- Annual Child Care Expense Amount of $15,000 [(1)($7,000) + (2)($4,000)].
- 2/3 of Mr. Sampras' earned income, an amount of $13,000 [(2/3)($14,000 + $5,500)].

The least of these three amounts is $10,500.

Exercise Eleven - 6 Solution

As Jose is not eligible for the ITA 118.3 disability tax credit, he will deduct the cost of full time attendant care under ITA 64. When combined with the other disability support costs, the qualifying costs total $36,000 ($23,000 + $18,000 - $5,000). As this is less than his income from employment, he will be able to deduct the full amount of these costs.

Solution to Self Study Problem Eleven - 1

The minimum Net Income For Tax Purposes for the Madison brothers would be calculated as follows:

	Arthur	Jules	Stanley
Net Employment Income	$ 6,000	$18,000	$23,000
Net Business Income	-0-	5,000	-0-
Net Property Income	8,000	-0-	11,000
Employment Insurance Received	3,000	-0-	-0-
Pension Benefits Received	-0-	3,000	-0-
Income Under ITA 3(a)	$17,000	$26,000	$34,000
Net Taxable Capital Gains - ITA 3(b)	2,813	-0-	-0-
Total Under ITA 3(a) And 3(b)	$19,813	$26,000	$34,000
Spousal Support Payments - ITA 3(c)	-0-	-0-	(4,800)
Total Under ITA 3(a), 3(b), 3(c)	$19,813	$26,000	$29,200
Business And Property Loss - ITA 3(d)	-0-	(4,000)	(12,000)
Net Income For Tax Purposes	$19,813	$22,000	$17,200

One-half of Arthur's capital gain is included in income. Jules Madison has an unused capital loss of $3,000 ($17,000 - $14,000) and Stanley Madison has an unused capital loss of $10,000 that can be carried over to other years.

While the charitable donations and tuition fees will generate credits against Tax Payable, they are not deductible in the computation of Net Income For Tax Purposes.

Solution to Self Study Problem Eleven - 2

The allowable moving expenses can be calculated as follows:

First Trip Hotel And Food After Acquiring New Residence (4 Days At $150)		$ 600
Selling Costs Of Old Residence ($9,500 + $1,400)		10,900
Acquisition Cost Of New Residence ($1,850 + $600)		2,450
Halifax Hotel And Food (3 days At $140)		420
Expenses Of Travel To Regina:		
Gasoline	$350	
Hotel (7 Days At $95)	665	
Food (7 Days At $45)	315	1,330
Moving Company Fees		3,800
Hotel And Food In Regina (8 Days At $140)		1,120
Total Allowable Expenses		$20,620
Employment Income In New Location		(10,500)
Carry Over To Next Year		$10,120

Notes:

1. With respect to the first trip, only the cost of meals and lodging that occurred after the acquisition of the new residence would be allowed. The airfare, the cost of car rentals, and the cost of meals and lodging prior to the acquisition of the new residence would not be deductible.

2. The taxes on the old home to the date of sale would not be an allowable moving expense.

3. Food and lodging costs near the old or new residences are limited to 15 days in total. For Ms. Fox, this would include 4 days on her first trip to Regina, the 3 days in Halifax, but only 8 of the 16 days during which she lived in a hotel on arriving in Regina. Note that the 7 days spent travelling to Regina are not included in the 15 day total.

4. The storage costs are deductible.

5. The unused moving cost balance of $10,120 can be carried over and applied against employment income in the following year only.

To use the simplified method to calculate milage, Ms. Fox would need to know how many kilometers she drove related to the move, as well as the appropriate rate for Nova Scotia.

Solution to Self Study Problem Eleven - 3

Generally, the spouse with the lower income must claim the deduction for child care expenses. However, under certain circumstances, for example if this spouse is hospitalized, the spouse with the higher income can claim the deduction for the period of hospitalization. Thus, Mr. Pleasant can claim the least of the following:

Actual Payments (48 weeks at $100)	$ 4,800
Annual Amount [(3)($4,000)]	12,000
2/3 Of Earned Income [(2/3)($33,000)]	22,000
Periodic Amount [($100)(3)(6 weeks)]	1,800

There does not appear to be any requirement that actual child care costs claimed by the higher income spouse need to be limited to the specific amounts paid during the six week period of eligibility. This means that the lowest of the preceding figures would be $100 per child for six weeks, which would result in a deduction of $1,800 for Mr. Pleasant.

Mrs. Pleasant's deduction will be based on the least of:

Actual Payments	$ 4,800
Annual Amount	12,000
2/3 Of Earned Income [(2/3)($18,000)]	12,000

Here the lowest figure is the actual costs of $4,800. This amount will be reduced by the $1,800 that was deducted by Mr. Pleasant. This results in a $3,000 deduction for Mrs. Pleasant.

Chapter Eleven Learning Objectives

1. Identify the major other sources of income that are listed under Subdivision d of the *Income Tax Act* (paragraphs 11-1 through 11-14).

2. Demonstrate an understanding of the tax treatment of child support and spousal support payments (paragraphs 11-15 through 11-31).

3. Identify the income inclusions from deferred income plans and annuity payments (paragraphs 11-32 and 11-39).

4. Apply the rules related to education assistance payments, social assistance, and workers' compensation payments (paragraphs 11-40 through 11-43).

5. Apply the rules related to lump-sum payments (paragraphs 11-44 through 11-49).

6. Demonstrate an understanding of the provisions associated with Registered Education Savings Plans (RESPs), Canada Education Savings Grants and Canada Learning Bonds (paragraphs 11-50 through 11-76).

7. Identify the other deductions under Subdivision e for annuity payments, support payments and CPP contributions (paragraphs 11-77 through 11-80).

8. Determine the deductible amount of moving expenses for an individual (paragraphs 11-81 through 11-90).

9. Determine the deductible amount of child care expenses (paragraphs 11-91 through 11-101).

10. Apply the provisions related to the disability supports deduction (paragraphs 11-102 through 11-109).

CHAPTER TWELVE

How To Work Through Chapter Twelve

We recommend the following approach in dealing with the material in this Chapter:

Non-Arm's Length Transfers Of Property
☐ Read the text pages 447 (from paragraph 12-1) through 449 (through paragraph 12-8).

☐ Complete Exercises Twelve-1 and Twelve-2 on page 449 of the text. The solutions are on page S-153.

☐ Complete Self Study Problem Twelve-1 on page 474 of the text. The solution is on pages S-155 and S-156.

Applicability Of ITA 69
☐ Read the text pages 449 (from paragraph 12-9) and 450 (through paragraph 12-12).

☐ Complete Exercise Twelve-3 on page 450 of the text. The solution is on page S-153.

Inter Vivos Transfers To A Spouse And Others
☐ Read the text pages 450 (from paragraph 12-13) through 452 (through paragraph 12-21).

☐ Complete Exercise Twelve-4 on page 452 of the text. The solution is on page S-153.

Transfer Of Farm Property To A Child
☐ Read the text pages 452 (from paragraph 12-22) and 453 (through paragraph 12-25).

☐ Complete Exercise Twelve-5 on page 453 of the text. The solution is on page S-153.

Income Attribution
☐ Read the text pages 453 (from paragraph 12-26) through 456 (through paragraph 12-40).

☐ Complete Exercises Twelve-6 through Twelve-8 on pages 456 and 457 of the text. The solutions are on pages S-153 and S-154.

☐ Complete Self Study Problems Twelve-2 through Twelve-4 on pages 474 though 476 of the text. The solutions are on pages S-156 through S-161.

Anti-Avoidance Provisions And Tax Planning
☐ Read the text pages 457 (from paragraph 12-41) through 459 (through paragraph 12-46).

Leaving Or Entering Canada
☐ Read the text pages 459 (from paragraph 12-47) and 460 (through paragraph 12-53).

☐ Complete Exercises Twelve-9 and Twelve-10. The Exercises are on page 460 of the text. The solutions are on page S-154.

☐ Read the text pages 460 (from paragraph 12-54) and 461 (through paragraph 12-56).

Elective Dispositions
☐ Read the text page 461 (paragraphs 12-57 and 12-58).

☐ Complete Exercise Twelve-11 on page 461 of the text. The solution is on page S-154.

Emigration - Security For Departure Tax, Unwinding A Deemed Disposition And Short-Term Residents
☐ Read the text pages 462 (from paragraph 12-59) and 463 (through paragraph 12-70).

☐ Complete Exercise Twelve-12 on page 463 of the text. The solution is on page S-154.

Emigration And Stock Options
☐ Read the text pages 463 (from paragraph 12-71) and 464 (through paragraph 12-76).

Death Of A Taxpayer - Representation And Deemed Dispositions
☐ Read the text pages 465 (from paragraph 12-77) and 466 (through paragraph 12-82).

Rollover To A Spouse, A Common-Law Partner, Or A Spousal Trust
☐ Read the text page 466 (paragraphs 12-83 through 12-86).

☐ Complete Exercise Twelve-13 on page 466 of the text. The solution is on page S-155.

Tax Free Transfers Other Than To A Spouse Or Common-Law Partner
☐ Read the text pages 466 and 467 (paragraphs 12-87 and 12-88).

☐ Complete Self Study Problem Twelve-5 on page 476 of the text. The solution is on pages S-161 through S-162.

Filing Returns And Payment Of Taxes
☐ Read the text pages 467 (from paragraph 12-89) through 470 (through paragraph 12-107).

Allowable Capital Losses - Special Rules At Death
☐ Read the text pages 470 (from paragraph 12-108) and 471 (through paragraph 12-111).

☐ Complete Exercise Twelve-14 on page 471 of the text. The solution is on page S-155.

Charitable Donations, Medical Expenses And Deferred Income Plans - Special Rules At Death,
☐ Read the text pages 471 (from paragraph 12-112) and 472 (through paragraph 12-114).

To Complete This Chapter
☐ Review the Key Terms Used In This Chapter on page 472 of the text. Consult the Glossary for the meaning of any key terms you do not know.

☐ Review the Learning Objectives of the Chapter found on pages S-163 and S-164 of this Study Guide.

☐ Review the Glossary Flashcards and complete the Key Terms Self-Test for the Chapter. These features can be found in two places, on your Student CD-ROM under the heading "Key Term Practice" and on the web site.

☐ As a review, we recommend that you view the PowerPoint Slides for Chapter Twelve that are on your Student CD-ROM. The PowerPoint Viewer program can be installed from the Student CD-ROM.

Solution to Chapter Twelve Exercises

Exercise Twelve - 1 Solution

Mr. Lipky's proceeds of disposition will be the amount received of $95,000, resulting in a capital loss of $5,000 ($95,000 - $100,000). His brother's adjusted cost base will be the fair market value of the land, or $75,000, and he will have no gain or loss on his sale at $75,000. As a result, the $20,000 capital loss that has been realized cannot be claimed by either Cal or his brother.

Exercise Twelve - 2 Solution

As the transfer was to a related party for an amount less than the fair market value of the asset, Ms. Lee will be deemed to have received the fair market value of $56,600. This will result in a taxable capital gain of $1,800 [(1/2)($56,600 - $53,000)] and recapture of CCA of $15,800 ($53,000 - $37,200). The capital cost of the property to her father will be $37,200, the amount paid for the asset. He will have a taxable capital gain of $9,700 [(1/2)($56,600 - $37,200)]. As a result, there has been double taxation of the difference between $56,600 and $37,200.

Exercise Twelve - 3 Solution

Under ITA 69(1.2), the proceeds of disposition in this case will be the greater of the $33,000 actual proceeds and the $211,000 fair market value of the property without considering the lease. The greater amount would be $211,000, resulting in a taxable capital gain for Mr. Bates of $89,000 [(1/2)($211,000 - $33,000)]. The adjusted cost base to the corporation would be the actual transfer price of $33,000. This would lead to double taxation on a subsequent sale of the property on the difference between $211,000 and $33,000.

Exercise Twelve - 4 Solution

If Ms. Sharp does not elect out of ITA 73(1), the property will be transferred at the UCC of $110,000. There would be no tax consequences at the time of transfer. While the spouse would receive the property with a UCC of $110,000, the capital cost of $175,000 would be retained, with the difference being considered deemed CCA. The $300,000 proceeds of disposition do not affect these results.

If she elects out of ITA 73(1), the transfer will be made at $300,000, resulting in a capital gain of $125,000 ($300,000 - $175,000). In addition, she will have recapture of $65,000 ($175,000 - $110,000). With Ms. Sharp electing out of ITA 73(1), ITA 69 becomes applicable. Because the transfer was made for consideration in excess of the fair market value of the property, the capital cost to her spouse will be limited to the fair market value of $225,000, raising the possibility of double taxation on any subsequent sale.

Exercise Twelve - 5 Solution

With respect to the land, the $280,000 paid is between the $250,000 adjusted cost base floor and the $325,000 fair market value ceiling. Therefore, the proceeds of disposition would be $280,000, resulting in a capital gain for Mr. Nobel of $30,000 ($280,000 - $250,000). The $280,000 would also be the adjusted cost base for his daughter.

With respect to the barn, as there was no consideration given, the transfer would take place at the UCC floor of $85,000. There would be no tax consequences for Mr. Nobel. With respect to his daughter, she would assume a UCC value of $85,000. However, the old capital cost of $115,000 would be retained by the daughter, with the $30,000 difference being treated as deemed CCA.

Exercise Twelve - 6 Solution

As ITA 73(1) provides for a tax free rollover of capital property to a spouse, there would be no tax consequences for either Mr. or Mrs. Moreau in 2005. For 2006, both the dividends and the capital gain would be attributed to Mrs. Moreau. There would be no tax consequences for

Mr. Moreau in 2006. The taxable amount of the dividends of $3,625 and the taxable capital gain of $9,500 [(1/2)($42,000 - $23,000)] would be included in Mrs. Moreau's Net Income For Tax Purposes.

Exercise Twelve - 7 Solution
As there is no provision for a tax free transfer of shares to a child, Mrs. Moreau will have a taxable capital gain in 2005 of $7,000 [(1/2)($37,000 - $23,000)]. For 2006, the taxable amount of the dividends of $3,625 would be attributed to Mrs. Moreau and would be included in Mrs. Moreau's Net Income For Tax Purposes. However, the 2006 taxable capital gain of $2,500 [(1/2)($42,000 - $37,000)] would be taxed in Nicki's hands.

Exercise Twelve - 8 Solution
Unless Mr. Bronski elects out of ITA 73(1) by including a gain in his 2005 tax return, there will be no tax consequences to either Mr. or Mrs. Bronski in 2005. In addition, because the transfer is a tax free rollover, the adjusted cost base of the bonds to Mrs. Bronski will be $115,000.

If Mr. Bronski does not elect out of ITA 73(1), the income attribution rules will apply. Even if he did elect out of ITA 73(1), the rules would still apply as the loan does not bear interest at the prescribed rate.

All of the 2006 interest income on the bonds will be attributed to Mr. Bronski. In addition to the interest of $6,100, there would be a taxable capital gain of $7,000 [(1/2)($129,000 - $115,000)], which would also be attributed to Mr. Bronski. The total addition to Mr. Bronski's income for 2006 is $13,100 ($6,100 + $7,000).

Exercise Twelve - 9 Solution
There would be a deemed disposition on her departure, leaving her liable for the taxes on a $10,500 [(1/2)($49,000 - $28,000)] taxable capital gain.

Exercise Twelve - 10 Solution
As real property is exempt from the deemed disposition provision contained in ITA 128.1(4)(b), there would be no tax consequences with respect to the rental property at the time of Mr. Chrysler's departure. However, real property is Taxable Canadian Property and, as a consequence, he would be liable for Canadian taxes on both recapture and capital gains resulting from a subsequent sale of the property, even after he becomes a non-resident.

Exercise Twelve - 11 Solution
With respect to the shares of the Canadian private company, there would be a required deemed disposition, resulting in a taxable capital gain of $57,500 [(1/2)($235,000 - $120,000)]. In the absence of an election on the rental property, this would be the only tax consequence resulting from her departure. However, if Ms. Lopez elects under ITA 128.1(4)(d) to have a deemed disposition on her rental property, the result will be a terminal loss on the building of $42,000 ($142,000 - $100,000) and an allowable capital loss on the land of $15,000 [(1/2)($60,000 - $30,000)]. These amounts can be used to eliminate income tax on all but $500 of the $57,500 taxable capital gain on the securities.

Exercise Twelve - 12 Solution
In the absence of ITA 128.1(4)(b)(iv), there would be a deemed disposition of both the U.K. shares and the Canadian shares at the time of Mr. Brookings' departure from Canada. As it appears that he has been in Canada for less than 60 months in the last 10 years, there will be no deemed disposition of the U.K. shares that he owned prior to his arrival in Canada. There will, however, be a deemed disposition of the Canadian shares acquired during his stay in Canada. This will result in a taxable capital gain of $8,500 [(1/2)($92,000 - $75,000)].

There will be no deemed disposition of the vacant Canadian land as it is taxable Canadian property. The fact that the land was inherited is not relevant to its exclusion from a deemed disposition as it was inherited prior to his emigration.

Exercise Twelve - 13 Solution

With respect to truck A, it would be transferred to her husband at its UCC value of $25,500 [($51,000)($33,000/$66,000)]. No income would be included in Ms. Lardner's final tax return and, while the UCC value for the truck in Michel's hands would be the $25,500 transfer value, it would retain its original capital cost of $42,000 with the difference between the two values being treated as deemed CCA. Truck B would be transferred to Melinda at its fair market value of $33,000. This would result in $7,500 ($33,000 - $25,500) in recapture being included in Ms. Lardner's final tax return. The $33,000 transfer price would be the UCC value to Melinda. Since Ms. Lardner's original capital cost exceeds the $33,000 fair market value, Melinda would retain Ms. Lardner's $42,000 capital cost with the difference between the two values being treated as deemed CCA.

Exercise Twelve - 14 Solution

The carry forward must be applied on an adjusted basis to eliminate the 2006 taxable capital gain. To implement this, the $7,500 amount (three-quarter basis) must be adjusted to $5,000 (one-half basis). The $2,000 taxable capital gain will use $2,000 of the adjusted 1990 carry forward, leaving $3,000. This amount must be adjusted back to the 3/4 inclusion rate. The resulting $4,500 [(3/2)($3,000)] can be applied against any other type of income in 2006 or, if there is not sufficient other income in that year, against any other type of income in 2005 (amended return). This can be verified using the 100 percent figures, which give the same $4,500 [(3/4)($10,000 - $4,000)] amount.

Solution to Self Study Problem Twelve - 1

Case A In this Case, the shares were transferred at a price that was below market value. However, John Bolton will have deemed proceeds under ITA 69(1)(b) equal to the fair market value of $525,000 [(5,000)($105)]. With his cost base at $225,000 [(5,000)($45)], this will result in a capital gain of $300,000, one-half of which would be included in John's Net Income For Tax Purposes. From the point of view of Alex Bolton, his cost base for the shares will be the actual price paid of $375,000 [(5,000)($75)]. This means that, if Alex Bolton sells these shares at some later point in time for a price in excess of $75, the difference between his proceeds of disposition and the price per share he paid of $75 would be taxed in his hands. In effect, any gain arising from a sales price of up to $105 will be subject to double taxation.

Case B In this situation, the gain to be recorded by John Bolton would be based on $625,000 [(5,000)($125)], the actual amount received. This would result in a capital gain of $400,000 ($625,000 - $225,000), one-half of which would be included in John's Net Income For Tax Purposes. From the point of view of Alex Bolton, ITA 69(1)(a) would limit his adjusted cost base to $525,000, the fair market value of the shares at the time of purchase. In a manner similar to Case A, there is the likelihood of double taxation being assessed on the difference between the $625,000 price paid and the $525,000 fair market value at the time of the sale.

Case C In this Case, both the proceeds to John Bolton and the adjusted cost base to Alex Bolton will be equal to the amount paid for the shares. This will result in John recording a capital gain of $300,000 as calculated in Case A, one-half of which would be included in John's Net Income For Tax Purposes. However, in this Case, the adjusted cost base to Alex Bolton will be $525,000 and no double taxation will arise.

Case D In this Case, Mr. John Bolton will be deemed to have received proceeds equal to the fair market value of $525,000. This will result in the same $300,000 capital gain that was calculated in Cases A and C, one-half of which will be included in John's Net Income For Tax Purposes. As in Case C, the adjusted cost base to Alex Bolton will be $525,000 and no double taxation will arise.

Solution to Self Study Problem Twelve - 2

Mr. Langdon would be assessed for income attribution of $10,500 ($5,000 + $5,500). As Heather did not use the funds to produce income, there would be no tax consequences of making the loan to her.

Solution to Self Study Problem Twelve - 3

The results can be summarized as follows:

	Net Income For Tax Purposes		
	2006	2007	2008
Case A			
Dr. Bolt	Nil	$26,825	$37,500
Mr. Bolt	Nil	Nil	Nil
Case B			
Dr. Bolt	Nil	$26,825	$37,500
Mr. Bolt	Nil	Nil	Nil
Case C			
Dr. Bolt	$20,000	Nil	Nil
Mr. Bolt	Nil	$26,825	$17,500
Case D			
Dr. Bolt	Nil	$26,825	$37,500
Mr. Bolt	Nil	Nil	Nil
Case E			
Dr. Bolt	$20,000	$26,825	$60,000
Mr. Bolt	Nil	Nil	Nil
Case F			
Dr. Bolt	$20,000	$26,825	Nil
Dolly Bolt	Nil	Nil	$17,500
Case G			
Dr. Bolt	$20,000	Nil	Nil
Dolly Bolt	Nil	$26,825	$17,500
Case H			
Dr. Bolt	$20,000	$26,825	Nil
Dirk Bolt	Nil	Nil	$17,500

The details of each Case are as follows:

Case A   With ITA 73(1) in effect, the December 31, 2006 transfer would be a deemed disposition at the adjusted cost base of $185,000. This means that Dr. Bolt would not record a capital gain at the time of the transfer and the adjusted cost base of the securities to Mr. Bolt would be $185,000. In 2007, the $26,825 in taxable dividends would be attributed back to Dr. Bolt and included in her Net Income For Tax Purposes for that year. When Mr. Bolt sells the securities, the 2008 taxable capital gain of $37,500 [(1/2)($260,000 - $185,000)] would also be attributed back to Dr. Bolt. This transfer would not affect Mr. Bolt's Net Income For Tax Purposes in any of the three years under consideration.

Case B   With ITA 73(1) in effect, the December 31, 2006 transfer would still take place at the adjusted cost base of $185,000, and the resulting 2006, 2007, and 2008 results for both Dr. Bolt and Mr. Bolt would be identical to Case A.

Case C   With the decision to elect out of ITA 73(1) and payment of consideration equal to fair market value, the transfer will be recorded as a disposition at fair market value. This will result in a 2006 taxable capital gain for Dr. Bolt of $20,000 [(1/2)($225,000 - $185,000)] and an adjusted cost base to Mr. Bolt of $225,000. Given that the transfer was at fair market value and Dr. Bolt chose to elect out of ITA 73(1), there would be no attribution of either income or capital gains. The taxable dividends of $26,825 will be included in Mr. Bolt's 2007 Net Income For Tax Purposes, and the 2008 taxable capital gain of $17,500 [(1/2)($260,000 - $225,000)] will be included in his 2008 Net Income For Tax Purposes. The transfer would not affect Dr. Bolt's Net Income For Tax Purposes in either 2007 or 2008.

Case D   As ITA 73(1) continues to be applicable in this Case, the transfer would take place at the adjusted cost base of $185,000, and both eligible dividends and capital gains would be attributed back to Dr. Bolt. For both Dr. and Mr. Bolt, the results for all three years would be identical to those described in Case A.

Case E   When a taxpayer elects out of ITA 73(1) and a transfer is made for consideration that is less than fair market value, the provisions of ITA 69(1) are applicable to the transferor. Under these provisions, if a taxpayer disposes of a property for less than its fair market value, the proceeds of disposition are deemed to be the fair market value amount. This will result in Dr. Bolt recording a 2006 taxable capital gain of $20,000 [(1/2)($225,000 - $185,000)]. As the transfer is for consideration that is less than the fair market value of the securities, the income attribution rules will be applicable, resulting in the 2007 taxable dividends of $26,825 being included in Dr. Bolt's 2007 Net Income For Tax Purposes. In addition, the 2008 taxable capital gain of $60,000 [(1/2)($260,000 - $140,000)] would also be attributed back to her and included in her 2008 Net Income For Tax Purposes.

Note that the adjusted cost base for the securities is based on the actual price paid by Mr. Bolt, subjecting the $40,000 ($225,000 - $185,000) difference between the transfer price and Dr. Bolt's adjusted cost base to double taxation if the shares are sold at a price between $185,000 and $225,000. In addition, Dr. Bolt's $45,000 ($185,000 - $140,000) loss on the sale would not be deductible. Since Mr. Bolt's adjusted cost base is $140,000, if the shares are sold at a price between $140,000 and $185,000, he will be taxed on the capital gain, despite the fact that Dr. Bolt's loss was disallowed.

Dr. Bolt's total taxable capital gain on these shares is $80,000 ($20,000 + $60,000). This is $42,500 more than the taxable capital gain in Case A and represents [(1/2)($225,000 - $140,000)]. The transfer would not affect Mr. Bolt's Net Income For Tax Purposes in any of the three years under consideration.

Case F   Under ITA 69, a non-arm's length gift is deemed to be a disposition and acquisition to be recorded by both parties at fair market value. This means that Dr. Bolt would have to record a 2006 taxable capital gain of $20,000 [(1/2)($225,000 - $185,000)]. As a gift to a minor was involved, income attribution rules will apply and the 2007 taxable dividends of $26,825 will have to be included in the 2007 Net Income For Tax Purposes of Dr. Bolt.

However, the attribution rules do not apply to capital gains when the attribution results from a transfer to someone under 18 years of age. As a consequence, Dolly Bolt will include a taxable capital gain of $17,500 [(1/2)($260,000 - $225,000)] in her 2008 Net Income For Tax Purposes. The transfer will have no effect on the 2006 and 2007 Net Income For Tax Purposes of Dolly Bolt, nor on the 2008 Net Income For Tax Purposes of Dr. Bolt.

Case G   The transfer at fair market value will result in Dr. Bolt recording a taxable capital gain of $20,000 [(1/2)($225,000 - $185,000)] in 2006. As the transfer is at fair market and the related loan requires interest at commercial rates, the income attribution rules are not applicable. This means that Dolly will include taxable dividends of $26,825 in her 2007 Net Income For Tax Purposes and a taxable capital gain of $17,500 [(1/2)($260,000 - $225,000)] in her 2008 Net Income For Tax Purposes. The transaction will have no effect on the 2007 and 2008 Net Income For Tax Purposes of Dr. Bolt, nor on the 2006 Net Income For Tax Purposes of Dolly Bolt.

Case H   As the transfer is at fair market value, Dr. Bolt will have a taxable capital gain of $20,000 [(1/2)($225,000 - $185,000)] included in her 2006 Net Income For Tax Purposes. Dirk's adjusted cost base for the securities will be $225,000, and the transfer will not affect his 2006 Net Income For Tax Purposes. As Dirk is not under 18 years of age, the attribution rules found in ITA 74.1(2) do not apply. However, ITA 56(4.1) indicates that income attribution applies in situations where an interest free or low interest loan has been given to a non-arm's length individual, and one of the main purposes of the loan is to reduce or avoid taxes. As Dirk has only limited income and would be in a lower tax bracket than Dr. Bolt, it is likely that this condition would apply in this Case. As a result, the 2007 taxable dividends of $26,825 would be included in the 2007 Net Income For Tax Purposes of Dr. Bolt, rather than in the Net Income For Tax Purposes of her son. However, the 2008 taxable capital gain of $17,500 [(1/2)($260,000 - $225,000)] would not be attributed back to Dr. Bolt. Rather, it would be included in the 2008 Net Income For Tax Purposes of Dirk Bolt.

Solution to Self Study Problem Twelve - 4

Note   As the farm would be considered qualified farm property, any capital gains arising from a transfer would be eligible for the $500,000 lifetime capital gains deduction. If Long Consulting Ltd. is a qualified small business corporation, capital gains on the disposition of these shares would also be eligible for the $500,000 deduction.

Long Consulting Ltd. - Gift To Spouse   ITA 73(1) permits transfers of a capital property to a spouse at its tax value (adjusted cost base or UCC). This means that the shares in Long Consulting Ltd. could be gifted to Mr. Long with no immediate tax consequences. However, the tax basis for these shares would remain at the adjusted cost base of $210,000 and income attribution would apply.

Any dividends paid on the shares would be attributed to Mrs. Long. In addition, should Mr. Long subsequently sell these shares for $475,000, the resulting taxable capital gain of $132,500, as calculated below, would also be attributed to Mrs. Long.

Proceeds (Fair Market Value)	$475,000
Adjusted Cost Base	(210,000)
Capital Gain	$265,000
Inclusion Rate	1/2
Taxable Capital Gain	$132,500

As an alternative, Mrs. Long could elect out of the provisions of ITA 73(1). Under ITA 69, the gift would be recorded as a disposition at the $475,000 fair market value. Mrs. Long would have an immediate taxable capital gain of $132,500 (as calculated in the preceding paragraph) and Mr. Long's adjusted cost base would be $475,000. However, if the transfer is a gift, and Mr. Long does not use his own funds to purchase the shares, income attribution would apply to any dividends received by Mr. Long and to any capital gain arising from a later sale at an amount in excess of $475,000.

Long Consulting Ltd. - Gift To Children   Under ITA 69, a gift to a related party is deemed to be a transfer at fair market value. Given this, a taxable capital gain of $132,500 (as calculated for Mr. Long) would result from a transfer to either child.

The adjusted cost base to the children would be the fair market value of $475,000. The effect of the gift on Mrs. Long's immediate tax situation would be the same, regardless of which child receives the gift.

As Mary is under 18 years of age, a transfer to her would result in all dividend income received by Mary prior to her reaching age 18 being attributed back to Mrs. Long. However, if Mary sells the shares for more or less than her adjusted cost base of $475,000, the resulting capital gain or loss would not be attributed back to Mrs. Long. This would be the case whether or not Mary was 18 or older at the time of the sale. As Barry is over 18, the gift would not result in attribution of either dividends or capital gains.

Rental Property - Gift To Spouse   Here again, ITA 73(1) would permit a transfer to Mr. Long at tax values with no immediate tax consequences. The tax basis of the property would not be changed. However, as the transfer is a gift, income attribution rules would apply. This means that any net rental income would be attributed to Mrs. Long. In addition, if Mr. Long were to later sell the property for its current fair market value of $275,000, the following amounts would be attributed to Mrs. Long:

Capital Cost	$190,000
UCC	(125,000)
Recaptured CCA	$ 65,000
Proceeds Of Disposition	$275,000
Adjusted Cost Base	(190,000)
Capital Gain	$ 85,000
Inclusion Rate	1/2
Taxable Capital Gain	$ 42,500

Mrs. Long could also elect out of the provisions of ITA 73(1) and transfer the rental property at its fair market value. However, if she does, she would immediately be taxed on the recapture as well as the taxable capital gain. Electing out of ITA 73(1) would not change the fact that the transfer is a gift to a spouse and, as a consequence, future rental income, capital gains, and recapture would be attributed to Mrs. Long.

Rental Property - Gift To Children   There is no exemption from the general rules of ITA 69 for transfers of depreciable property to children. As a consequence, Mrs. Long would be subject to taxation based on a disposition of the property at its fair market value of $275,000. This would result in immediate taxation on a $42,500 taxable capital gain and recapture in the amount of $65,000 (see preceding calculations).

The tax base to either of the children would be $275,000 and a sale at this price would have no tax consequences for either Mrs. Long or the children. Here again, however, if this property were given to Mary, the income attribution rules of ITA 74.1 would apply to any amount of property income subsequently earned. This would mean that until Mary reached 18 years of age, all property income would be attributed to Mrs. Long. Alternatively, if the property were gifted to her son, Barry, all subsequent income would be taxed in his hands. There would be no attribution of further capital gains on a gift to either child.

Dynamics Inc. - Gift To Spouse   As with the other properties, these shares could be given to Mr. Long and, under the provisions of ITA 73(1), no immediate tax consequences would arise. However, any dividend income on the shares would be attributed to Mrs. Long and, if Mr. Long were to sell them for their fair market value of $384,000, the income attribution rules of ITA 74.1 would require that the following taxable capital gain be attributed to the income of Mrs. Long:

Proceeds Of Disposition	$384,000
Adjusted Cost Base	(212,000)
Capital Gain	$172,000
Inclusion Rate	1/2
Taxable Capital Gain	$ 86,000

Mrs. Long could elect out of ITA 73(1) by recording the $86,000 taxable capital gain at the time of the transfer to her spouse. However, as long as the property was transferred as a gift, attribution would apply to both dividend income received by Mr. Long and to any further capital gains realized on a subsequent sale.

Dynamics Inc. - Gift To Children   In the case of a transfer to either of her children, ITA 69 would require that the gift be treated as a deemed disposition with the proceeds at the fair market value of $384,000. This would result in an immediate taxable capital gain of $86,000, as was calculated in the preceding paragraph. However, the tax base to the children would be the fair market value of $384,000 and there would be no tax consequences for any of the parties if a sale took place at that price.

As was the case with the other properties considered, a transfer to Mary would result in the application of the income attribution rules of ITA 74.1. This would mean that subsequent dividend income on these shares would be allocated to Mrs. Long until Mary reaches 18 years of age. If Mary were to sell the property for more than $384,000, there would be no attribution of the capital gain. If the shares were transferred to Barry, there would be no attribution of either dividends or capital gains.

Farm Land - Gift To Spouse   As with all of the other properties, Mrs. Long could make a tax free transfer of the farm land to her husband under ITA 73(1). The transfer would take place at the adjusted cost base of $80,000 and, in the event of a subsequent sale, the following taxable capital gain would be attributed to Mrs. Long under ITA 74.1:

Proceeds Of Disposition	$175,000
Adjusted Cost Base	(80,000)
Capital Gain	$ 95,000
Inclusion Rate	1/2
Taxable Capital Gain	$ 47,500

Alternatively, Mrs. Long could elect out of ITA 73(1) and transfer the property at its fair market value of $175,000, resulting in the taxable capital gain of $47,500 being recognized at the time of transfer.

As farm income is considered to be business income rather than property income, there would be no attribution of any farm income that arises while Mr. Long is holding the property.

Farm Land - Gift To Children   ITA 73(3) permits the inter vivos transfer of farm property used by the taxpayer or her family to a child on a tax free basis. The deemed proceeds would be Mrs. Long's adjusted cost base, which means that Mrs. Long would incur no taxation at the time of the gift to either child. The adjusted cost base to either child would be the same $80,000 that was deemed to be the proceeds of the disposition.

As noted in our discussion of the transfer of this property to Mr. Long, because farm income is business income rather than property income, there will be no attribution of farm income in the case of a transfer to either child.

On most transfers to related minors, there is no attribution of capital gains. This is a reflection of the fact that, unlike the rules for transfers to a spouse, there is no general rollover provision for transfers to related minors on a tax free basis. However, when a transfer is made to a related minor under the provisions of ITA 73(3) and the transfer value is below fair market value, ITA 75.1 requires that any subsequent gain resulting from a disposition by the transferee before they reach age 18 be attributed back to the transferor.

This means that, if the farm property is transferred to Mary and she sells the property for $175,000 before she reaches age 18, a taxable capital gain of $47,500 (see preceding calculations for Mr. Long) will be attributed to Mrs. Long.

Solution to Self Study Problem Twelve - 5

Note As the farm would be considered qualified farm property, any capital gains would be eligible for the $500,000 lifetime capital gains deduction. Further, if Caswell Enterprises is a qualified small business corporation, capital gains on the disposition of these shares would also be eligible for the $500,000 deduction.

Case A Whenever a taxpayer dies, there is a deemed disposition of all of his property. If the transfer is to a spouse, the disposition is deemed to have taken place at the adjusted cost base of capital property other than depreciable property, or at the UCC of depreciable property. This would mean that there would be no immediate tax consequences associated with Mr. Caswell's death in this Case, where all of the property is transferred to his spouse. Note, however, that on a subsequent disposition by Mr. Caswell's spouse, her tax base would be the same as Mr. Caswell's. These values would be as follows:

Rental Property - UCC	$ 67,000
Rental Property - Capital Cost	95,000
General Industries Ltd. - Adjusted Cost Base	200,000
Farm Land - Adjusted Cost Base	325,000
Caswell Enterprises - Adjusted Cost Base	275,000

It is possible, after Mr. Caswell's death, for his legal representative to elect to have assets transferred to his spouse at fair market values. This would result in taxable capital gains and other income being included in his final tax return. However, this would not be a reasonable alternative unless Mr. Caswell has unused loss carry forwards at the time of his death, or the lifetime capital gains deduction can be utilized on his final return.

Case B This Case is more complex and would follow the general rules applicable to transfers made at death to anyone other than a spouse. For both depreciable and non-depreciable property, other than farm property, the transfer will be deemed to have taken place at fair market value.

In the case of farm land that is being used by the taxpayer or a member of his family, ITA 70(9) permits a tax free transfer of such property to a child, at the time of death. The deemed proceeds would be Mr. Caswell's adjusted cost base, resulting in no tax consequences for his estate. As you would expect, the adjusted cost base to Mr. Caswell's son, John, would be the same $325,000 that was deemed to be the proceeds of the disposition on Mr. Caswell's death.

In the case of the rental property, the deemed proceeds would be $133,000, resulting in Taxable Income of $47,000 for Mr. Caswell's estate. This would be calculated as follows:

Deemed Proceeds Of Disposition	$133,000
Adjusted Cost Base	(95,000)
Capital Gain	$ 38,000
Inclusion Rate	1/2
Taxable Capital Gain	$ 19,000

Capital Cost	$ 95,000
UCC	(67,000)
Recaptured CCA	$ 28,000

The capital cost and UCC for his son, John, is the fair market value of $133,000.

In the case of the General Industries shares and the shares of a Canadian controlled private corporation, the deemed proceeds would be the fair market value and the tax consequences to Mr. Caswell's estate would be as follows:

	General Industries	Caswell Enterprises
Deemed Proceeds	$350,000	$426,000
Adjusted Cost Base	(200,000)	(275,000)
Capital Gain	$150,000	$151,000
Inclusion Rate	1/2	1/2
Taxable Capital Gain	$ 75,000	$ 75,500

This gives a total increase in Net Income of $197,500 ($19,000 + $28,000 + $75,000 + $75,500).

Case C   With respect to the departure from Canada, ITA 128.1(4)(b) requires a deemed disposition of all property except real property, property used in a Canadian business, and excluded personal property [i.e., a variety of items specified under ITA 128.1(9)]. This means there would be a deemed disposition for Mr. Caswell of both the General Industries Ltd. shares and the Caswell Enterprises shares. The tax consequences of the two dispositions would be as follows:

	General Industries	Caswell Enterprises
Deemed Proceeds	$350,000	$426,000
Adjusted Cost Base	(200,000)	(275,000)
Capital Gain	$150,000	$151,000
Inclusion Rate	1/2	1/2
Taxable Capital Gain	$ 75,000	$ 75,500

This gives a total increase in Net Income of $150,500 ($75,000 + $75,500).

Two additional facts might be noted here. First, Mr. Caswell could elect under ITA 128.1(4)(d) to have a deemed disposition of the other properties at the time of his departure. Given the amounts already added to his income, this would not appear to be a desirable alternative unless he can utilize the lifetime capital gains deduction on the farm land. Also of importance is the fact that Mr. Caswell can defer the taxation on these amounts. Provided adequate security is provided, ITA 220(4.5) allows an emigrant to defer the taxation on deemed dispositions created by ITA 128.1(4)(b) until such time as the assets are sold. This would likely be an attractive alternative to Mr. Caswell.

Chapter Twelve Learning Objectives

After completing Chapter 12, you should be able to:

1. Determine the tax consequences of non-arm's length transfers of property to related individuals at values other than fair market value (paragraphs 12-1 through 12-12).

2. Describe the special rollover provisions applicable to inter vivos transfers of property to a spouse and inter vivos transfers of farm property to a child (paragraphs 12-13 through 12-25).

3. Apply the income attribution rules to inter vivos transfers of property to a spouse and to related individuals who are under the age of 18 (paragraphs 12-26 through 12-40).

4. Describe some of the anti-avoidance provisions that relate to the income attribution rules (paragraphs 12-41 and 12-42).

5. Be able to describe some of the tax planning techniques that are available to mitigate the income attribution rules (paragraph 12-43).

6. Describe the income attribution rules applicable to transfers to other related parties (paragraphs 12-44 through 12-46).

7. List the types of assets that are subject to the deemed disposition rules on entering or leaving Canada (paragraphs 12-47 through 12-49).

8. Demonstrate an understanding of the tax provisions related to immigration to Canada (paragraphs 12-50 and 12-51).

9. Demonstrate an understanding of the tax provisions related to emigration from Canada (paragraphs 12-52 through 12-56).

10. Describe the availability and use of elective dispositions on departures from Canada (paragraphs 12-57 and 12-58).

11. Explain the security for departure tax and its application (paragraphs 12-59 through 12-63).

12. Describe the provisions available for unwinding a deemed disposition on departure from Canada (paragraphs 12-64 through 12-68).

13. Explain the rules applicable to short-term residents of Canada (paragraphs 12-69 and 12-70).

14. Calculate the tax consequences of the deemed disposition on departure from Canada of shares acquired through the exercise of stock options (paragraphs 12-71 through 12-76).

15. Calculate the tax consequences resulting from the deemed disposition of all capital property at the time of an individual's death (paragraphs 12-77 through 12-82).

16. Apply the rollover provisions that are available at the time of an individual's death (paragraphs 12-83 through 12-88).

17. List the different tax returns that can be filed by the representatives of a deceased person and their due dates (paragraphs 12-89 through 12-91).

---

18. Explain the reasons for filing multiple tax returns for a deceased person in the year of death (paragraphs 12-92 through 12-95).

19. Demonstrate an understanding that certain credits and deductions can be claimed on any return in the year of death, while there are restrictions for other returns (paragraphs 12-96 though 12-98).

20. Explain the concept of a rights or things return and the treatment of unpaid wages at death (paragraphs 12-99 through 12-103).

21. Demonstrate an understanding of the procedures for the payment of taxes arising on the death of a taxpayer (paragraphs 12-104 and 12-105).

22. Demonstrate an understanding of the treatment of allowable capital losses in relation to a deceased taxpayer (paragraphs 12-106 through 12-109).

23. Demonstrate a basic understanding of the treatment of charitable donations and medical expenses in the year of death (paragraphs 12-110 and 12-111).

24. Be aware that RRSPs and RRIFs have special rules at time of death that will be covered in Chapter 13 (paragraph 12-112).

CHAPTER THIRTEEN

How To Work Through Chapter Thirteen

We recommend the following approach in dealing with the material in this Chapter:

Planning For Retirement
☐   Read the text pages 485 (from paragraph 13-1) through 488 (through paragraph 13-14).

Registered Retirement Savings Plans (RRSPs)
☐   Read the text pages 488 (from paragraph 13-15) through 492 (through paragraph 13-38).

☐   Complete Exercise Thirteen-1 on page 492 of the text. The solution is on page S-168.

Earned Income
☐   Read the text pages 492 (from paragraph 13-39) and 493 (through paragraph 13-41).

☐   Complete Exercises Thirteen-2 and Thirteen-3 on page 493 of the text. The solutions are on page S-168.

Pension Adjustments (PAs)
☐   Read the text page 493 (from paragraph 13-42 through paragraph 13-44).

☐   Complete Exercise Thirteen-4 The Exercise is on page 494 of the text. The solution is on page S-168.

Money Purchase RPPs And DPSPs
☐   Read the text pages 494 (from paragraph 13-45) and 495 (through paragraph 13-51).

☐   Complete Exercise Thirteen-5 on page 495 of the text. The solution is on page S-168.

☐   Complete Self Study Problem Thirteen-1 on page 519 of the text. The solution is on pages S-169 and S-170.

Past Service Pension Adjustments (PSPAs)
☐   Read the text pages 495 (from paragraphs 13-52) and 496 (through paragraph 13-58).

Pension Adjustment Reversals (PARs)
☐   Read the text pages 496 (from paragraph 13-59) and 497(through paragraph 13-61).

Examples Of RRSP Deduction Calculations
☐   Read the text pages 497 and 498 (paragraph 13-62) .

☐   Complete Exercise Thirteen-6 on page 498 of the text. The solution is on page S-168.

Undeducted And Excess RRSP Contributions
☐   Read the text pages 498 (from paragraph 13-63) and 499 (through paragraph 13-68).

☐   Complete Exercise Thirteen-7 on page 499 of the text. The solution is on pages S-168 and S-169.

Tax Planning - Excess RRSP Contributions

☐ Read the text page 500 (from paragraph 13-69 through paragraph 13-72).

☐ Complete Self Study Problems Thirteen-2 and Thirteen-3 on pages 519 and 520 of the text. The solutions are on pages S-170 and S-171.

RRSP And RRIF Administration Fees

☐ Read the text page 500 (paragraph 13-73).

RRSP Withdrawals And Voluntary Conversions

☐ Read the text pages 500 (from paragraph 13-74) and 501 (through paragraph 13-79).

Involuntary Termination Due To Age Limitation

☐ Read the text page 501(from paragraph 13-80 through paragraph 13-82).

Departure From Canada And Death Of The Registrant

☐ Read the text pages 501 (from paragraph 13-83) through 503 (through paragraph 13-94).

Spousal RRSP

☐ Read the text pages 503 (from paragraph 13-95) and 504 (through paragraph 13-103).

☐ Complete Exercise Thirteen-8 on page 504 of the text. The solution is on page S-169.

Home Buyers' Plan (HBP)

☐ Read the text pages 504 (from paragraph 13-104) through 506 (through paragraph 13-115).

☐ Complete Exercise Thirteen-9 on page 507 of the text. The solution is on page S-169.

Lifelong Learning Plan (LLP)

☐ Read the text pages 507 (from paragraph 13-116) and 508 (through paragraph 13-126).

☐ Complete Exercise Thirteen-10 on page 508 of the text. The solution is on page S-169.

Registered Pension Plans (RPPs)

☐ Read the text pages 508 (from paragraph 13-127) through 510 (through paragraph 13-138).

Registered Retirement Income Funds (RRIFs)

☐ Read the text pages 510 (from paragraph 13-139) through 511 (through paragraph 13-147).

☐ Complete Exercise Thirteen-11 on page 511 of the text. The solution is on page S-169.

Death Of The Annuitant

☐ Read the text pages 511 (from paragraph 13-148) and 512 (through paragraph 13-155).

Deferred Profit Sharing Plans (DPSPs) And Profit Sharing Plans

☐ Read the text pages 512 (from paragraph 13-156) and 513 (through paragraph 13-163).

Transfers Between Plans

☐ Read the text pages 513 (from paragraph 13-164) and 514 (through paragraph 13-165).

Retiring Allowances

☐ Read the text page 514 (paragraphs 13-166 and 13-167).

☐ Complete Exercise Thirteen-12 on page 514 of the text. The solution is on page S-169.

☐ Complete Self Study Problems Thirteen-4 and Thirteen-5 on page 521 of the text. The solutions are on pages S-172 through S-174.

Retirement Compensation Arrangements

☐ Read the text pages 515 (from paragraph 13-168) and 516 (through paragraph 13-176).

Salary Deferral Arrangements

☐ Read the text pages 516 (from paragraph 13-177) and 517 (through paragraph 13-182).

Individual Pension Plans (IPPs)

☐ Read the text page 517 (paragraphs 13-183 and 13-184).

To Complete This Chapter

☐ Review the Key Terms Used In This Chapter on page 517 of the text. Consult the Glossary for the meaning of any key terms you do not know.

☐ Review the Glossary Flashcards and complete the Key Terms Self-Test for the Chapter. These features can be found in two places, on your Student CD-ROM under the heading "Key Term Practice" and on the web site.

☐ Review the Learning Objectives of the Chapter found on pages S-175 and S-176 of this Study Guide.

☐ As a review, we recommend that you view the PowerPoint Slides for Chapter Thirteen that are on your Student CD-ROM. The PowerPoint Viewer program can be installed from the Student CD-ROM.

Solution to Chapter Thirteen Exercises

Exercise Thirteen - 1 Solution

The addition to the RRSP deduction room for 2005 is $6,840 [(18%)($38,000)]. At the end of the year, his Unused RRSP Deduction Room would be $7,140 ($4,800 + $6,840 - $4,500) and he has undeducted RRSP contributions of $1,500 ($6,000 - $4,500).

Exercise Thirteen - 2 Solution

His Earned Income for RRSP purposes would be $70,500 ($56,000 + $2,500 + $12,000).

Exercise Thirteen - 3 Solution

Her Earned Income for RRSP purposes would be $54,500 ($82,000 + $3,000 - $12,500 - $18,000).

Exercise Thirteen - 4 Solution

The basic mechanism here is the Pension Adjustment (PA). Individuals who belong to an RPP or a DPSP have their RRSP Deduction Limit reduced by the amount of their PA for the previous year. PAs are designed to reflect the amount of contributions or benefits that have been accumulated in employer sponsored RPPs and DPSPs.

Exercise Thirteen - 5 Solution

The Pension Adjustment will be $6,400 ($2,300 + $1,800 + $2,300).

Exercise Thirteen - 6 Solution

The required calculations would be as follows:

Unused Deduction Room - End Of 2005	$10,750
Lesser Of:	
• 2006 RRSP Dollar Limit = $18,000	
• 18% Of 2005 Earned Income Of $66,530* = $11,975	11,975
Less 2005 PA	(4,800)
2006 RRSP Deduction Limit	$17,925
Lesser Of:	
• RRSP Deduction Limit = $17,925	
• Available Contributions = $19,760 ($6,560 + $13,200)	(17,925)
Unused Deduction Room - End Of 2006	$ Nil

*Earned Income = $6,530 - $18,000 + $75,600 + $2,400

While he has no Unused RRSP Deduction Room, he has $1,835 ($19,760 - $17,925) in undeducted contributions that can be carried forward and deducted in a subsequent year in which there is sufficient RRSP deduction room.

Exercise Thirteen - 7 Solution

Ms. Brownell will have a $16,500 addition to her deduction room in 2005, and a $18,000 addition in 2006. These are the RRSP Dollar Limits for these years, as both of these figures are less than 18 percent of her Earned Income for 2004 and 2005. (The Earned Income effect has a one year lag.) Her 2006 Earned Income will affect her 2007 RRSP deduction room and is not relevant to this Exercise. As her 2005 contribution is $17,500, she will only be in excess of her deduction room by $1,000 and no penalty will be assessed. However, when she makes the May 1, 2006 contribution, she will be over her deduction room by $3,000 [$17,500 +

$20,000 - ($16,500 + $18,000)]. A 1 percent per month penalty is applicable to amounts above $2,000. As a consequence, there will be a 2006 penalty of $80 [(1%)($3,000 - $2,000)(8)].

Exercise Thirteen - 8 Solution

As the withdrawal occurs before January 1, 2007, Mrs. Garveau will be responsible for the taxes on $5,000 of the withdrawal, the amount of her contribution. The remaining $4,000 will be taxed in the hands of her husband.

Exercise Thirteen - 9 Solution

Ms. DeBoo will have to repay $867 [(1/15)($18,000 - $5,000)] during 2006. Note that the voluntary payment that was made during 2005 did not reduce the fraction of the remaining balance that must be paid in 2006.

Exercise Thirteen - 10 Solution

There are no tax consequences associated with the withdrawal of $5,000. As he will have no education tax credit in either 2007 or 2008, his repayment period begins in 2008. As he makes the required payments of $500 ($5,000 ÷ 10) within 60 days of the end of each of the years 2008 through 2017, there are no tax consequences associated with his repayments.

Exercise Thirteen - 11 Solution

He has no required minimum withdrawal for 2006, the year the RRIF is established. His minimum withdrawal for 2007 will be $27,500 [$660,000 ÷ (90 - 66)].

Exercise Thirteen - 12 Solution

It would appear that Mr. Bartoli began working for his employer in 1976. Given this, he can rollover a total of $59,500 [($2,000)(20 Years Before 1996) + ($1,500)(13 Years Before 1989)] to his RRSP. The remainder of the retiring allowance will be taxed in 2006.

Solution to Self Study Problem Thirteen - 1

Mr. Barnes' 2005 Earned Income for RRSP purposes would be calculated as follows:

Salary	$55,000
Taxable Benefits	1,150
Union Dues	(175)
Net Employment Income	$55,975
Business Income	4,150
Rental Loss	(11,875)
Spousal Support Received	2,400
Earned Income	$50,650

Part A - Not A Member Of RPP Or DPSP Under the assumption that Mr. Barnes is not a member of a Registered Pension Plan or a Deferred Profit Sharing Plan, the increase in his RRSP Deduction Limit for 2006 is the lesser of $18,000 and $9,117 (18 percent of 2005 Earned Income). In this case, $9,117 would be the smaller amount.

Also note that Canada Pension Plan contributions do not reduce Earned Income for RRSP purposes.

Based on the preceding, Mr. Barnes' maximum deductible RRSP contribution for 2006 is calculated as follows:

2005 Unused RRSP Deduction Room	$ 700
2006 Earned Income Limit (18% Of $50,650)	9,117
RRSP Deduction Limit	$9,817

Part B - Member Of RPP   In this case, the maximum 2006 deduction would be the amount calculated in Part A, reduced by his 2005 Pension Adjustment of $4,200. This would leave a maximum deductible RRSP contribution of only $5,617 ($9,817 - $4,200). Note that while Mr. Barnes' actual net employment income for 2005 would be reduced by any RPP contributions made for that year, the employment income amount used in the calculation of Earned Income for RRSP purposes does not reflect this reduction.

Solution to Self Study Problem Thirteen - 2

Part A   Mr. Beasley's net employment income for 2005 would be $22,700, his gross salary of $24,000, reduced by his RPP contributions of $1,300.

Part B   Mr. Beasley's maximum deductible 2006 RRSP contribution would be equal to the lesser of $18,000 and 18 percent of his 2005 Earned Income, reduced by his 2005 Pension Adjustment. His Earned Income would be calculated as follows:

Net Employment Income	$22,700
RPP Contributions	1,300
Spousal Support	9,000
Net Rental Loss	(5,000)
Earned Income	$28,000

Eighteen percent of this amount is $5,040, which is less than the limit of $18,000. Therefore, his maximum deductible 2006 RRSP contribution would be $2,440, $5,040 less the 2005 Pension Adjustment of $2,600. Note that the damage award, royalties, interest, dividends, and gift are not included in Earned Income.

Part C   As Mr. Beasley has made no contributions prior to 2006, he has no undeducted contributions. In addition, he has interest income and dividends that are subject to current Tax Payable. This would suggest that Mr. Beasley should contribute the maximum deductible amount of $2,440 in 2006. In addition, he should make a further 2006 contribution of $2,000, the maximum over contribution that would not subject him to the 1 percent per month penalty on such amounts. While he could not currently deduct this over contribution, it will enjoy the benefit of having any income earned while in the plan compounded on a tax free basis. Further, this amount can be deducted in any future year, subject to the usual RRSP deduction limits.

Note that this $4,440 contribution should be made, as soon as possible, whether or not Mr. Beasley decides to make the maximum deduction of $2,440 in 2006. Since he will not be in the maximum federal tax bracket until 2007, it could be advantageous to defer taking the $2,440 available deduction until 2007.

Solution to Self Study Problem Thirteen - 3

Part A Ms. Stratton's net employment income would be calculated as follows:

Gross Salary	$120,000
Additions:	
Employer's Contribution To Provincial Health Insurance Plan	482
Employer's Contributions For Life Insurance	96
Trip To Bermuda	4,500
Deductions:	
RPP Contributions	(2,390)
Professional Dues	(225)
Net Employment Income	$122,463

The reasons for not including the other items given in the problem in the preceding calculation are as follows:

1. Income taxes withheld cannot be deducted in the calculation of Net Income For Tax Purposes or Taxable Income.

2. Contributions to registered charities create a credit against Tax Payable, but cannot be deducted in the calculation of net employment income.

3. Employer payments to employee dental plans and private health care plans are not a taxable benefit.

4. Employer payments to employee group income protection plans are not a taxable benefit.

5. The EI and CPP contributions are eligible for tax credit treatment.

6. Employer payments for membership fees in social or recreational clubs are generally not a taxable benefit to the employee, provided the facilities are used for business purposes.

7. As the travel allowance is based on actual milage and costs, it would be a non-taxable allowance.

8. Contributions to the Registered Retirement Savings Plan can be deducted under Subdivision e, but not in the calculation of net employment income.

Part B Ms. Stratton's maximum deductible 2006 RRSP contribution is calculated as follows:

Unused Deduction Room - End of 2005	Nil
Lesser Of:	
• 2006 RRSP Dollar Limit = $18,000	
• [(18%)($122,463 + $2,390)] = $22,474	$18,000
Less 2005 PA	(5,560)
Maximum Deductible RRSP Contribution	$12,440

This means that $1,560 ($14,000 - $12,440) of the contribution will not be deductible in 2006.

However, the $14,000 contribution is still a good idea. Funds invested in an RRSP accumulate earnings on a tax free basis and, unless non-deductible contributions accumulate to more than $2,000, no penalty is applied. Further, contributions that are not deducted can be carried forward and are available for deduction in any subsequent year. This means that Ms. Stratton will enjoy the benefits of tax free compounding without experiencing any unfavourable tax consequences.

Solution to Self Study Problem Thirteen - 4

Part A   With respect to the retiring allowance, ITA 56(1)(a)(ii) requires that the entire $125,000 must be included in income. Then, to the extent that such amounts are transferred or contributed to an RRSP for which the taxpayer is the annuitant, the taxpayer is entitled to a deduction under ITA 60(j.1), equal to $2,000 for each year of service prior to 1996 with the employer, plus an additional $1,500 for each year of service before 1989, for which the employee was not a member of an RPP or a DPSP. This provides for the following maximum deduction under ITA 60(j.1):

19 Years At $2,000 Per Year	$38,000
12 Years At $1,500 Per Year	18,000
Allowable Rollover	$56,000

Given this calculation, the maximum RRSP deduction that Mr. Colt would be allowed for 2006 would be calculated as follows:

Retiring Allowance Rollover (See Preceding)	$56,000
Opening RRSP Deduction Room	32,000
Addition For Year [(18%)($46,000)]	8,280
Pension Adjustment	(8,000)
Maximum Deduction	$88,280

Part B   Mr. Colt will be able to deduct the full $50,000 of the retiring allowance that was transferred to his own RRSP. While another $38,280 could have been deducted under ITA 60(j.1), the amounts transferred to a spousal RRSP are not eligible for this deduction. However, contributions to the spousal RRSP can be deducted under ITA 60(i). Using the assumed maximum ITA 60(i) deduction calculated in the preceding paragraph, we can calculate the following amount of non-deductible contributions:

Total Contributions	$125,000
Maximum Deduction Under ITA 60(j.1)	(50,000)
Maximum Regular Deduction ($88,280 - $56,000)	(32,280)
Non-Deductible Contributions	$ 42,720

To the extent that non-deductible contributions exceed $2,000, they are subject to a heavy penalty of 1 percent per month. As a consequence, Mr. Colt should immediately withdraw $40,720 ($42,720 - $2,000) from the spousal RRSP. If this occurs before March 2, 2007, he can contribute and deduct an additional $6,000 ($56,000 - $50,000) to his own RRSP.

Unless he is in need of the funds, he should leave the $2,000 non-deductible contribution in the spousal plan in order to enjoy the advantages of tax free accumulation of earnings on the $2,000 cushion that is available.

Solution to Self Study Problem Thirteen - 5

The most desirable solution would be to find benefits that would be fully deductible to the Company and free of taxation for Mr. Jones. The only items that fall into this category would be payments for private health care plans and discounts on company merchandise. Discounts on industrial engines are not likely to be of any value to Mr. Jones. However, Mr. Jones should arrange to have the Company provide private health care coverage, including a dental plan. The Company could also pay the premiums on a disability insurance plan without it becoming a taxable benefit to Mr. Jones at the time of payment. Any benefits received under such a plan would have to be taken into income when received.

In terms of tax deferral, Mr. Jones should be included in the Company's Registered Pension Plan (RPP). Once he is admitted to the plan, both he and the Company should make the maximum contributions that are permitted under the terms of the plan. The limiting factor here is that these contributions cannot result in a Pension Adjustment that is in excess of the lesser of 18 percent of Mr. Jones' compensation for the year or the money purchase limit for the year under consideration ($19,000 for 2006).

While there is no indication that the Company has such an arrangement, a Deferred Profit Sharing Plan (DPSP) might also be useful. Whether or not Mr. Jones would be able to use such an arrangement would depend on the total employee/employer contributions to the Company's RPP. Contributions to a DPSP are included in the calculation of Mr. Jones' Pension Adjustment and, when combined with the RPP contributions, the total is subject to the limitation described in the preceding paragraph.

It would also be advisable for Mr. Jones to arrange for some of the compensation to be received in the form of a retiring allowance to be paid to a Registered Retirement Savings Plan (RRSP) at the end of the three years. As he will have been employed a total of 14 years by Martin, 11 of them prior to 1996, a total of $22,000 ($2,000 per year of pre-1996 service) could be rolled over in this form. In addition, an amount of $1,500 per year of pre-1989 service while not a member of the RPP could also be rolled over on a tax free basis to this RRSP.

The Company could provide a loan to Mr. Jones to purchase his new residence. As Mr. Jones is moving, he is eligible for a deduction of the benefit associated with a $25,000 interest free "home relocation" loan. Any additional low interest or interest free loan will result in imputed interest being added to Mr. Jones' Taxable Income without an offsetting deduction.

Whether or not this will be beneficial will depend on a number of factors including whether he is able to raise the funds at a rate lower than that specified under Regulation 4301 for assessing imputed interest. As the Regulation 4301 rate changes on a quarterly basis, some attention would also have to be given to expected future movements of this rate. However, Mr. Jones can use the rate in effect at the time the loan is made for the first five years.

The Company could provide Mr. Jones with an automobile. In this case, Mr. Jones will be assessed for a personal benefit of a standby charge (24 percent per year of the capital cost or two-thirds of the lease payments, if he is not eligible for a reduction) and for operating costs (one-half of the standby charge or $0.22 per kilometer of personal use).

Whether or not this will be desirable depends on an analysis of how Mr. Jones would actually use the car. In some cases, especially if the car has a list price of more than $30,000, the taxable benefit may exceed the actual benefit, making this an undesirable form of compensation.

The Company could pay the dues for any recreational facilities that Mr. Jones might wish to use. While these amounts will not be treated as a taxable benefit to Mr. Jones, the payments will not be deductible to the Company. Given that both the Company and Mr. Jones will be subject to similar marginal tax rates, there would appear to be no significant advantage to this type of arrangement.

The Company could provide assistance with the costs that will be incurred by Mr. Jones in moving to Hamilton. With respect to costs that Mr. Jones would be permitted to deduct, it makes little difference whether the Company pays the costs, or simply pays an equivalent amount in salary and lets Mr. Jones pay the costs and deduct them. However, certain types of moving costs that would not be deductible by Mr. Jones can be paid by the Company without creating a taxable benefit. An example of this would be compensation for a loss on a personal residence owned by Mr. Jones in Vancouver. (See Chapter 11)

If Martin Manufacturing has a year end after July 6, it can declare a bonus in the third year, but not pay it until the following calendar year. This will defer Mr. Jones' taxation of the bonus by one year without deferring Martin's deduction.

Since Mr. Jones has been operating as a consultant for the last 12 years, it may be possible to structure the project so that he will be considered an independent contractor rather than an employee. This would considerably increase the amount and type of expenditures that would be deductible by him and also create an opportunity to income split with his wife, if she could assist him in the project in some way. In considering this alternative it should be kept in mind that, if Mr. Jones is not an employee, some of the possibilities that have been previously discussed would no longer be feasible. For example, unless Mr. Jones is an employee, it would not be possible for him to be a member of the Company's RPP.

Another possibility would be for Mr. Jones to provide his services through a corporation. However, this would probably not be helpful. Given his relationship with Martin Manufacturing Company, any corporation would likely be viewed as a personal services business and taxed at full corporate rates.

As an incentive, the Company could grant Mr. Jones options to purchase its stock. This would have no tax cost to the Company. The timing of the tax cost of the options for Mr. Jones could be delayed until after retirement.

Chapter Thirteen Learning Objectives

After completing Chapter 13, you should be able to:

1. Explain the general procedures used to provide tax deferral on retirement saving (paragraphs 13-1 through 13-12).

2. Describe the difference between a defined benefit pension plan and a defined contribution (a.k.a. money purchase) pension plan (paragraphs 13-13 and 13-14).

3. Describe the basic operation of RRSPs (paragraphs 13-15 through 13-30).

4. Calculate the RRSP Deduction Limit for an individual (paragraphs 13-31 through 13-34).

5. Calculate an individual's Unused RRSP Deduction Room (paragraphs 13-35 through 13-38).

6. Calculate Earned Income for RRSP purposes (paragraphs 13-39 through 13-41).

7. Demonstrate an understanding of the concepts underlying Pension Adjustments (PAs) (paragraphs 13-42 through 13-52).

8. Demonstrate an understanding of the concepts underlying Past Service Pension Adjustments (PSPAs) (paragraphs 13-53 through 13-58).

9. Demonstrate an understanding of the concepts underlying Pension Adjustment Reversals (PARs) (paragraphs 13-59 through 13-62).

10. Apply the tax treatment of undeducted RRSP contributions (paragraph 13-63 and 13-64).

11. Determine whether an individual has made "excess" contributions to an RRSP and identify associated tax planning issues (paragraphs 13-65 through 13-72).

12. Recall the tax treatment of RRSP and RRIF administration fees (paragraph 13-73).

13. Apply the provisions relating to voluntary withdrawals and conversions of RRSPs (paragraphs 13-74 through 13-79).

14. Apply the provisions relating to RRSP terminations due to age limitation (paragraphs 13-80 through 13-82).

15. Apply the provisions relating to departure from Canada and death of the registrant (paragraphs 13-83 through 13-94).

16. Apply the provisions associated with spousal RRSPs and identify associated tax planning issues (paragraphs 13-95 through 13-103).

17. Describe and apply the provisions of the Home Buyers' Plan (paragraphs 13-104 through 13-115).

18. Describe and apply the provisions of the Lifelong Learning Plan (paragraphs 13-116 through 13-126).

19. Demonstrate an understanding of the provisions associated with Registered Pension Plans (RPPs) (paragraphs 13-127 through 13-138).

20. Describe the role that RRIFs play in tax planning related to retirement, as well as the basic operation of these plans (paragraphs 13-139 through 13-155).

21. Demonstrate an understanding of the provisions related to Deferred Profit Sharing Plans (DPSPs) (paragraphs 13-156 through 13-161).

22. Demonstrate a basic understanding of Profit Sharing Plans (PSPs) (paragraphs 13-162 and 13-163).

23. Recall the tax free transfers that can be made between various types of plans (paragraphs 13-164 and 13-165).

24. Apply the special rules associated with retiring allowances (paragraphs 13-166 and 13-167).

25. Demonstrate a basic understanding of the provisions related to Retirement Compensation Arrangements (paragraphs 13-168 through 13-176).

26. Demonstrate a basic understanding of Salary Deferral Arrangements (paragraphs 13-177 through 13-182).

27. Be aware that Individual Pension Plans (IPPs) exist (paragraphs 13-183 and 13-184).

CHAPTER FOURTEEN

How To Work Through Chapter Fourteen

On-Line Survey

We would appreciate your feedback on this text. Your comments will help us to improve it. In addition, students who complete the survey will have their name entered in a draw for a $100 cash prize.

To complete a brief, on-line survey, visit the "Student And General Resources" web page on our web site at:

www.pearsoned.ca/byrdchen/ctp2007/

We recommend the following approach in dealing with the material in this Chapter:

Taxable Income Introduction And Overview
☐ Read the text pages 533 (from paragraph 14-1) and 534 (through paragraph 14-6).

Revoked Stock Option Election
☐ Read the text pages 534 (from paragraph 14-7) and 535 (through paragraph 14-9).

☐ Complete Exercise Fourteen-1 on page 535 of the text. The solution is on page S-193.

Treatment Of Losses
☐ Read the text pages 536 (from paragraph 14-10) through 538 (through paragraph 14-30).

☐ Complete Exercise Fourteen-2 on pages 538 and 539 of the text. The solution is on page S-193.

Non-Capital Losses
☐ Read the text page 539 (from paragraph 14-31 through paragraph 14-33).

☐ Complete Exercise Fourteen-3 on page 539 of the text. The solution is on page S-193.

☐ Read the text page 540 (from paragraph 14-34 through paragraph 14-35).

Net Capital Losses
☐ Read the text pages 540 (from paragraph 14-36) through 542 (through paragraph 14-44).

☐ Complete Exercise Fourteen-4 on page 542 of the text. The solution is on pages S-193 and S-194.

Allowable Business Investment Losses (ABILs)
☐ Read the text pages 542 (from paragraph 14-45) through 544 (through paragraph 14-54).

☐ Complete Exercise Fourteen-5 on page 544 of the text. The solution is on page S-194.

Farm Losses
☐ Read the text page 544 (paragraphs 14-55 through 14-58).

☐ Complete Exercise Fourteen-6 on page 545 of the text. The solution is on page S-194.

☐ Complete Self Study Problem Fourteen-1 on page 568 of the text. The solution is on pages S-198 through S-200.

Lifetime Capital Gains Deduction
☐ Read the text pages 545 (from paragraph 14-59) through 548 (through paragraph 14-80).

☐ Complete Exercise Fourteen-7 on pages 548 and 549 of the text. The solution is on page S-194.

☐ Read the text pages 549 (from paragraph 14-81) through 550 (through paragraph 14-88).

☐ Complete Exercise Fourteen-8 on page 551 of the text. The solution is on page S-195.

☐ Complete Self Study Problem Fourteen-2 on page 568 of the text. The solution is on page S-201.

Ordering Of Deductions And Losses
☐ Read the text pages 551 (from paragraph 14-89) through 553 (through paragraph 14-98).

☐ Complete Exercise Fourteen-9 on page 553 of the text. The solution is on page S-195.

Tax Payable Overview
☐ Read the text pages 553 (from paragraph 14-99) and 554 (through paragraph 14-104).

Tax On Split Income
☐ Read the text pages 554 (from paragraph 14-105) through 555 (through paragraph 14-113).

☐ Complete Exercise Fourteen-10 on page 556 of the text. The solution is on pages S-195 and S-196.

Transfer Of Dividends To A Spouse Or Common-Law Partner
☐ Read the text page 556 (paragraph 14-114).

☐ Complete Exercise Fourteen-11 on page 556 of the text. The solution is on page S-196.

☐ Complete Self Study Problem Fourteen-3 on pages 568 and 569 of the text. The solution is on pages S-201 and S-202.

Charitable Donations Credit Revisited
☐ Read the text pages 557 (from paragraph 14-115) through 560 (through paragraph 14-135).

☐ Complete Exercise Fourteen-12 on page 560 of the text. The solution is on page S-196.

☐ Complete Self Study Problem Fourteen-4 on pages 569 and 570 of the text. The solution is on pages S-203 through S-205.

☐ Read the text pages 560 (from paragraph 14-136) and 561 (through paragraph 14-141).

☐ Complete Exercise Fourteen-13 on page 561 of the text. The solution is on pages S-196 and S-197.

☐ Read the text pages 561 (from paragraph 14-142)and 562 (through paragraph 14-145).

Foreign Tax Credits Revisited
☐ Read the text pages 562 (from paragraph 14-146) and 563 (through paragraph 14-157).

☐ Complete Exercise Fourteen-14 on page 564 of the text. The solution is on page S-197.

☐ Complete Self Study Problem Fourteen-5 on pages 570 and 571 of the text. The solution is on pages S-205 through S-207.

Alternative Minimum Tax (AMT)

☐ Read the text pages 564 (from paragraph 14-158) through 566 (through paragraph 14-171).

☐ Complete Exercise Fourteen-15 on page 566 of the text. The solution is on page S-197 and S-198.

☐ Complete Self Study Problem Fourteen-6 on pages 571 and 572 of the text. The solution is on pages S-207 and S-208.

Comprehensive Tax Payable

☐ Complete Self Study Problem Fourteen-7 on pages 572 through 574 of the text. The solution is on pages S-208 through S-211.

Sample Personal Tax Return For Chapter 14

☐ Read the Sample Personal Tax Return For Chapter 14 found on pages S-180 through S-192 of this Study Guide. The complete sample tax return is available on the Student CD-ROM included with the text in two formats, a T1 ProFile return file and a .PDF file. To view the files, access your Student CD-ROM (not the ProFile Tax Suite CD-ROM) and under the heading "Textbook Support Files", select the option "Tax Return Files".

☐ When the updated Intuit ProFile software is available in January, 2007, updated sample tax returns and updated Cases that use ProFile software, as well as instructions on how to install the updated software program, will be available at:

www.pearsoned.ca/byrdchen/ctp2007

Tax Return Software

☐ You may wish to review the Suggestions For Working With Profile Software found on pages S-65 through S-67 of this Study Guide.

☐ Complete Self Study Case Fourteen-1 using the ProFile T1 Software. The Self Study Case is on pages 574 through 577 of the text. (As this Self Study Case is a continuation of Self Study Case 6-1, referring to the Chapter 6 version may be of assistance.) The condensed solution is on pages S-211 through S-215 of this Study Guide. The complete sample tax return is available on the Student CD-ROM included with the text in two formats, a T1 ProFile return file and a .PDF file.

This Self Study Case is extended in Self Study Problem Fourteen-7, using 2006 rates.

To Complete This Chapter

☐ Review the Key Terms Used In This Chapter on page 567 of the text. Consult the Glossary for the meaning of any key terms you do not know.

☐ Review the Glossary Flashcards and complete the Key Terms Self-Test for the Chapter. These features can be found in two places, on your Student CD-ROM under the heading "Key Term Practice" and on the web site.

☐ Review the Learning Objectives of the Chapter found on page S-216 of this Study Guide.

☐ As a review, we recommend that you view the PowerPoint Slides for Chapter Fourteen that are on your Student CD-ROM. The PowerPoint Viewer program can be installed from the Student CD-ROM.

Sample Personal Tax Return For Chapter 14

The following example contains a T1 individual income tax return completed using the ProFile T1 Personal Income Tax Program for 2005 tax returns from Intuit Canada. As software for 2006 is not yet available, this example contains 2005 rates and credits.

When the updated Intuit ProFile software is available in January, 2007, the updated 2006 version of this sample return, as well as instructions on how to install the updated software program, will be available on the web site at:

www.pearsoned.ca/byrdchen/ctp2007

This example was introduced in Chapter 6 and is expanded in this Chapter to contain other components of Taxable Income and Tax Payable. For comparison purposes, you might find it useful to review the Chapter 6 version of this example. The Chapter 6 version also contains more information on how to view the files.

Sample Files On Student CD-ROM

The complete sample tax return is available on the Student CD-ROM included with this book in two versions, a T1 ProFile return file and a .PDF file.

To View The Tax Return Files

Under the heading "Textbook Support Files", is the option to view "Tax Return Files ". Select this option and you will see two drop-down lists. To view the ProFile file, select the file "Sample - Chapter 14" from the ProFile drop-down list. To view the .PDF file, select the file "PDF Sample - Chapter 14" from the PDF drop-down list.

Sample Problem Data

George Kercher (SIN 527-000-145) is a divorced, semi-retired air force pilot living in Banff, Alberta. George was born on February 24, 1954.

He has been your client for many years. Besides doing his 2005 tax return, he would like you to present any tax planning points that he should consider.

After some discussion with George, you confirm that he has never owned any foreign property. As he has for many years, George authorizes the CRA to provide information to Elections Canada and he authorizes you to e-file his return. He is currently living at 69 Beaver Street in Banff, Alberta T0L 0C0. His home phone number is (111) 111-1111.

He informs you that on February 12, 2005, he received $2 million from his mother's estate. Using some of these funds, George bought a house in Banff. The remainder of the funds were invested with his stockbroker, Bull & Bear Inc.

George supports his two daughters:

- Janice (SIN 527-000-269), born June 6, 1992, is in high school and she had no earnings during the year.
- Willa (SIN 527-000-228) was born on January 22, 1986 and is attending university in Edmonton. Willa had Net Income of $3,300 during 2005.

George loves flying, so for the last two summers he has been flying fire bombers June 1 to September 30 for the provincial forest service fire control squad located in Banff.

He brings you the following receipts and documents:

1. A T4 (included in this example).

2. A T2202A "Tuition And Education Amounts Certificate" for himself from Athabasca University. It showed he was a part time student for 6 months and paid $575 in tuition for 2005.

3. A receipt for $1,000 from the Canadian Wildlife Federation dated December 3, 2005.

4. A statement from the Banff Dental Clinic that he paid a total of $1,200 during 2005. This consisted of $850 for himself on November 24, and $150 for Willa and $200 for Janice on December 15.

5. An instalment statement for 2005 that showed that George had paid the CRA instalments of $1,500 on September 15 and December 15 ($3,000 in total). These were the instalments requested by the CRA for the year due to his self-employed income in the previous year.

6. His 2004 Notice of Assessment that shows that his 2005 RRSP Deduction Limit is $13,979. He has no undeducted RRSP contributions from previous years.

7. An RRSP contribution receipt for $2,000 from Bull & Bear Inc. dated February 20, 2006.

8. A receipt for $2,000 from George's 40 year old sister, Shirley Burns (SIN 527-000-582) for child care. She took care of Janice after school during 2005.

9. A receipt for Janice from the Peak Rock Climbing Camp in Whistler, B.C. The receipt for two weeks at the camp was $1,600.

10. An agreement of purchase and sale for the purchase of a house at 69 Beaver St. in Banff. The deal closed March 31, 2005. His new home is 5 kilometers from the Alberta Fire Control offices.

11. A receipt for $2,148 from the Mountain Moving Company dated April 1, 2005. The invoice showed that the fee was charged to pack and move George's household effects from his rented townhouse in Calgary, to Banff, a total of 125 kilometers. George and his daughters made the move in his truck. Since he has no other receipts he tells you to use the simplified method to calculate his moving costs.

12. A T2202A "Tuition And Education Amounts Certificate" for Willa from the University of Alberta. It showed she was a full time student for 4 months and paid $2,100 in tuition for 2005. She had signed the certificate authorizing the transfer of all tuition and education amounts to her father.

Other Information

During your discussion with George, you note the following information:

1. He had forgotten to include his T4A and T5. He will be dropping those off to you this week. (These are included in this example.)

2. On January 8, 2005, George sold his 1971 Ford Mustang for $50,000. The car was driven only on sunny Sunday afternoons. Its original price in 1990 was $6,000, and George reconditioned it over the years at a cost of $12,000.

3. At the beginning of 2005, George has a net capital loss carry forward of $2,580 [(1/2)($5,160)] from 2003.

4. During 2005, he paid $6,000 in spousal support to his ex-wife, Marilyn (SIN 527-000-103), pursuant to a written agreement.

5. In the winter months, George gives private flying lessons. His statement of income of this unincorporated business, Kercher's Flying School, for the fiscal year ended December 31, 2005 is as follows:

Kercher's Flying School

Lesson fees	$30,200
Plane rentals	$ 9,600
Business meals and entertainment	3,250
Licenses and fees	1,650
Office expenses	550
Accounting fees	300
Total expenses	$ 15,350
Net Income	$ 14,850

6. George owns a commercial property at 9700 Jasper Avenue, Edmonton, Alberta T5J 4C8. The property had been purchased on February 15, 2003 for $600,000 of which $160,000 was allocated to the land. Shortly after George purchased the building, the major tenant went bankrupt and he had rental losses for 2003 and 2004. No capital additions were made since the building's acquisition. The financial information for the property, for the year ended December 31, 2005, is as follows:

Rental income	$46,700
Mortgage interest	$19,500
Property taxes	11,750
Maintenance and repairs	5,100
Management and administration fees	8,200
Accounting fees	1,000
Total expenses	$45,550
Net Income	$ 1,150

Notes To The Chapter 14 Return

1. All GST implications have been ignored in this example.

2. Janice has been claimed as the eligible dependant (See "Dependant" form). This information also appears on Schedule 5. Since Willa is over 17 years of age, she cannot be claimed for the eligible dependant credit.

3. Since Willa is over 17 years of age, her medical expenses are reduced by 3 percent of her Net Income For Tax Purposes. Willa should file a return in order to receive the GST credit. Since Willa did not pay her own dental bill, she cannot claim the refundable medical expense supplement herself.

4. Inheritances are not taxable.

5. On the T2032, Statement of Professional Activities, the non-deductible portion of business meals and entertainment of $1,625 (50% of $3,250) has been excluded.

6. George has claimed his net capital loss carry forward of $2,580 as his taxable capital gains were well in excess of this amount.

7. The deduction for child care costs is limited to $100 per week for overnight camp fees. The $2,000 paid to Shirley Burns is totally deductible.

8. Form T1M, Claim For Moving Expenses should be filled out to calculate the deductible moving expenses. George cannot deduct the costs of purchasing his new home because he had been living in a rented townhouse in Calgary. On Form T1M, since the "Simplified Method" box is checked, the program calculates the allowable deduction for milage using the 2005 Alberta rate.

9. Since the rental property has been showing a loss since its acquisition, no CCA could have been taken prior to 2005. As a result, the beginning of the year UCC of the building will be George's original allocation of $440,000 ($600,000 - $160,000 land cost). The CCA for 2005 is limited to $1,150, the amount that reduces his rental income to nil.

10. George is not eligible for the refundable medical expense supplement in this version of the example as his income is too high. Note that although his income is too high to claim the medical expenses for himself and Janice, he can still claim the allowable amount of Willa's medical expenses. One tax planning point that should be considered since the medical expenses occurred late in the year is whether he should save them for the following year. He may be able to claim them by using the 12 month period ending in the year rule if he has other medical expenses.

11. Given the funds from his mother's estate, George should contribute to his RRSP the maximum deductible in 2006 as soon as possible, as well as the allowable $2,000 overcontribution. He should also consider opening an RESP for Janice if he has not already done so and contribute the maximum allowable. She can still benefit from the Canada Education Savings Grant program.

Printed Return

On the following pages you will find George's T4, T4A, T5, his T1 Summary, his T1 jacket and his Schedule 1. The complete return can be found on the Student CD-ROM.

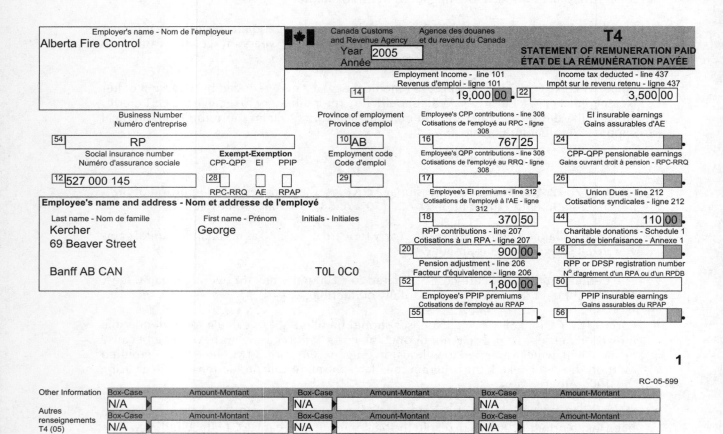

1

RC-05-599

Other Information	Box-Case	Amount-Montant	Box-Case	Amount-Montant	Box-Case	Amount-Montant
Autres renseignements T4 (05)	N/A		N/A		N/A	
	N/A		N/A		N/A	

Complete Return Available On Student CD-ROM

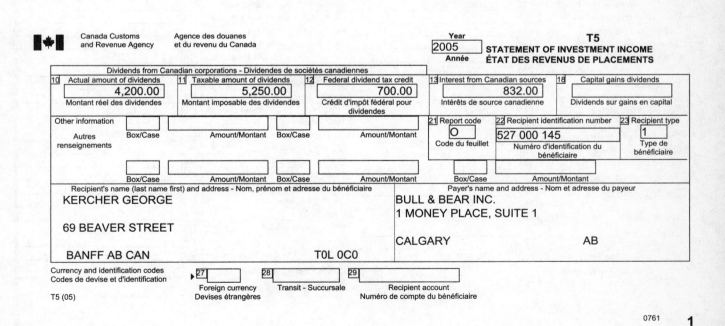

Kercher, George Chapter 14 Example   SIN: 527 000 145
Summary

2005 Tax Summary

Total income		George Chapter 14 Example
Employment *	101	19,000
Old Age Security	113	
CPP/QPP benefits	114	
Other pensions	115	27,000
Employment Insurance	119	
Taxable dividends	120	5,250
Interest	121	832
Limited partnership	122	
Rental	126	
Taxable capital gains	127	16,000
Support payments	128	
RRSP	129	
Other	130	
Self-employment *	135	16,475
Workers' compensation and social assistance	147	
Total income	**150**	**84,557**

Net income		
RPP	207	900
RRSP *	208	2,000
Union and professional dues	212	110
Child care expenses	214	2,200
Disability supports deduction	215	
Business investment loss	217	
Moving expenses	219	2,205
Support payments	220	6,000
Carrying charges and interest	221	
CPP/QPP on self-employment	222	816
Exploration and development	224	
Employment expenses	229	
Social benefits repayment	235	
Other deductions *	231	
Net income	**236**	**70,327**

Taxable income		
Canadian Forces personnel	244	
Home relocation loan	248	
Security options deductions	249	
Other payments deduction	250	
Losses of other years *	251	2,580
Capital gains deduction	254	
Northern residents deductions	255	
Additional deductions	256	
Taxable income	**260**	**67,747**

2006 Estimated	George Chapter 14 Example	
GST/HST credit		
Child Tax Benefit	693	00
RRSP contribution limit	15,464	00

* More than one line is considered

Non-refundable tax credits		George Chapter 14 Example
Basic personal amount	300	8,648
Age amount	301	
Spouse / eligible dependant *	303	7,344
Infirm dependants	306	
CPP/QPP	308	1,583
Employment Insurance	312	371
Adoption expenses	313	
Pension income amount	314	1,000
Caregiver amount	315	
Disability amount	316	
Interest on student loans	319	
Tuition / education	323	1,295
Transfers *	318	3,700
Medical expenses	332	51
Subtotal	**335**	**23,991**
Credit at 15%	338	3,599
Donations and gifts	349	262
Non-refundable tax credits	**350**	**3,861**

Total payable		
Federal tax	11	12,412
Non-refundable tax credits	350	3,861
Dividend tax credit	425	700
Minimum tax carry-over/other *	426	
Basic federal tax	**13**	**7,852**
Non resident surtax *	14	
Foreign tax credits / other		
Federal tax	**406**	**7,852**
Political/investment tax credit *	410	
Labour-sponsored tax credit	414	
Alternative minimum tax		
Additional tax on RESP	418	
Net federal tax	**260**	**7,852**
CPP contributions payable	421	1,631
Social benefits repayment	422	
Provincial/territorial tax	428	2,571
Total payable	**435**	**12,053**

Total credits		
Income tax deducted *	437	8,500
QC or YT abatement *	440	
CPP overpayment	448	
EI overpayment	450	
Medical expense supplement	452	
GST/HST rebate	457	
Instalments	476	3,000
Provincial tax credits	479	
Other credits	454	
Total credits	**482**	**11,500**
Balance owing (refund)		553
Combined balance (refund)		553

Complete Return Available On Student CD-ROM

Page 1 of 1

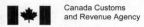 Canada Customs and Revenue Agency   Agence des douanes et du revenu du Canada

T1 GENERAL 2005

Income Tax and Benefit Return

Identification

7

Information about you

First name and initial
George Chapter 14 Example

Last name
Kercher

Care of

Mailing address: Apt. No. – Street No. Street name
69 Beaver Street

P.O. Box   **R.R.**

City
Banff

Prov./Terr.
AB

Postal Code
T0L 0C0

Information about you

Enter your social insurance number (SIN)   527 000 145

Enter your date of birth: Year/Month/Day
1954-02-24

Your language of correspondence: English [X]   Français [ ]
Votre langue de correspondance :

Your marital status on December 31, 2005:
(see the "Marital status" section in the guide for details)

1 [ ] Married   2 [ ] Living common law   3 [ ] Widowed
4 [X] Divorced   5 [ ] Separated   6 [ ] Single

Information about your residence

Enter your province or territory of
residence on **December 31, 2005:**   Alberta

Enter the province or territory where you **currently** reside if
it is not the same as that shown
above for your mailing address:

If you were self-employed in 2005,
enter the province or territory of
self-employment: Alberta

If you **became** or **ceased** to be a **resident of Canada in 2005**, give the
date of:

Month/Day   Month/Day
entry _____   or   departure _____

Information about your spouse or common-law partner (if you checked box 1 or 2 above)

Enter his or her social insurance number:

Enter his or her first name:

Enter his or her net income for 2005 to claim
certain credits: (see the guide for details)

Check this box if he or she was self-employed in 2005: 1 [ ]

If this return is for a deceased
person, enter the date of death: Year/Month/Day

Do not use this area

Elections Canada

THIS SECTION APPLIES <u>ONLY</u> TO CANADIAN CITIZENS.
DO <u>NOT</u> ANSWER THIS QUESTION IF YOU ARE NOT A CANADIAN CITIZEN.

As a Canadian citizen, I authorize the Canada Revenue Agency to provide my name, address,
and date of birth to Elections Canada for the National Register of Electors.
Your authorization is required each year. This information will be used only for purposes permitted
under the *Canada Elections Act*.   Yes [X] 1   No [ ] 2

Goods and services tax/harmonized sales tax (GST/HST) credit application
See the guide for details.
Are you applying for the GST/HST credit?   Yes [ ] 1   No [X] 2

Your guide contains valuable information to help you complete your return.

When you come to a line on the return that applies to you, look up the line number in the guide for more information.

Do not use this area	172				171				

S - 187

Kercher, George Chapter 14 Example   SIN: 527 000 145

2

Please answer the following question

Did you own or hold foreign property at any time in 2005 with a total cost of more than CAN$100,000? (read the "Foreign income" section in the guide for details)   **266**   Yes ☐ 1   No ☒ 2

If *yes*, attach a completed Form T1135.

If you had dealings with a non-resident trust or corporation in 2005, see the "Foreign income" section in the guide.

As a Canadian resident, you have to report your income from all sources both inside and outside Canada.

Total income

Employment income (box 14 on all T4 slips)		**101**	19,000 00
Commissions included on line 101 (box 42 on all T4 slips)	**102**		
Other employment income		**104**	
Old Age Security pension (box 18 on the T4A(OAS) slip)		**113**	
CPP or QPP benefits (box 20 on the T4A(P) slip)		**114**	
Disability benefits included on line 114 (box 16 on the T4A(P) slip)	**152**		
Other pensions or superannuation		**115**	27,000 00
Employment Insurance and other benefits (box 14 on the T4E slip)		**119**	
Taxable amount of dividends from taxable Canadian corporations (see the guide)		**120**	5,250 00
Interest and other investment income (**attach** Schedule 4)		**121**	832 00
Net partnership income: limited or non-active partners only (**attach** Schedule 4)		**122**	
Rental income Gross **160** 46,700 00 Net		**126**	
Taxable capital gains (**attach** Schedule 3)		**127**	16,000 00
Support payments received Total **156** Taxable amount		**128**	
RRSP income (from all T4RSP slips)		**129**	
Other income Specify:		**130**	

Self-employment income (see lines 135 to 143 in the guide)

Business income	Gross **162**	Net **135**	
Professional income	Gross **164** 30,200 00	Net **137**	16,475 00
Commission income	Gross **166**	Net **139**	
Farming income	Gross **168**	Net **141**	
Fishing income	Gross **170**	Net **143**	

Workers' compensation benefits (box 10 on the T5007 slip)	**144**		
Social assistance payments	**145**		
Net federal supplements (box 21 on the T4A(OAS) slip)	**146**		

Add lines 144, 145, and 146 (see line 250 in the guide) ▶ 147

Add lines 101, 104 to 143, and 147
This is your **total income.**   **150**   84,557 00

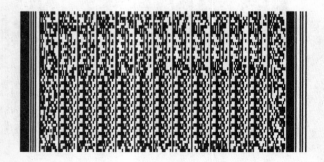
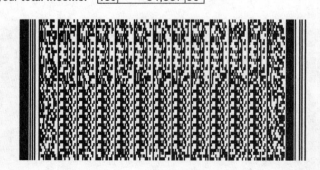

Kercher, George Chapter 14 Example   SIN: 527 000 145

Attach your Schedule 1 (federal tax) and Form 428 (provincial or territorial tax) here. Also attach here any other schedules, information slips, forms, receipts, and documents that you need to include with your return.

Net income

Enter your **total income** from line 150			150	84,557 00

Pension adjustment (box 52 on all T4 slips and box 34 on all T4A slips)	**206**	1,800 00	

Registered pension plan deduction (box 20 on all T4 slips and box 32 on all T4A slips)	**207**	900 00	
RRSP deduction (see Schedule 7 and **attach** receipts)	**208**	2,000 00	
Saskatchewan Pension Plan deduction (maximum $600)	**209**		
Annual union, professional, or like dues (box 44 on all T4 slips, or from receipts)	**212**	110 00	
Child care expenses (**attach** Form T778)	**214**	2,200 00	
Disability supports deduction	**215**		
Business investment loss Gross **228** Allowable deduction	**217**		
Moving expenses	**219**	2,204 88	
Support payments made Total **230** 6,000 00 Allowable deduction	**220**	6,000 00	
Carrying charges and interest expenses (**attach** Schedule 4)	**221**		
Deduction for CPP or QPP contributions on self-employment and other earnings (**attach** Schedule 8)	**222**	815 52 •	
Exploration and development expenses (**attach** Form T1229)	**224**		
Other employment expenses	**229**		
Clergy residence deduction	**231**		
Other deductions Specify:	**232**		
Add lines 207 to 224, 229, 231, and 232. 233		14,230 40 ▶	14,230 40
Line 150 minus line 233 (if negative, enter "0"). This is your **net income before adjustments.** 234			70,326 60

Social benefits repayment (if you reported income on line 113, 119, or 146, see line 235 in the guide)	**235**		•
Line 234 minus line 235 (if negative, enter "0"). If you have a spouse or common-law partner, see line 236 in the guide. This is your **net income.** 236			70,326 60

Taxable income

Canadian Forces personnel and police deduction (box 43 on all T4 slips)	**244**		
Employee home relocation loan deduction (box 37 on all T4 slips)	**248**		
Security options deductions	**249**		
Other payments deduction (if you reported income on line 147, see line 250 in the guide)	**250**		
Limited partnership losses of other years	**251**		
Non-capital losses of other years	**252**		
Net capital losses of other years	**253**	2,580 00	
Capital gains deduction	**254**		
Northern residents deductions (**attach** Form T2222)	**255**		
Additional deductions Specify:	**256**		
Add lines 244 to 256. 257		2,580 00 ▶	2,580 00
Line 236 minus line 257 (if negative, enter "0") This is your **taxable income.** 260			67,746 60

Use your taxable income to calculate your federal tax on Schedule 1 and your provincial or territorial tax on Form 428.

Kercher, George Chapter 14 Example   SIN: 527 000 145

Refund or Balance owing   4

Net federal tax: enter the amount from line 19 of Schedule 1 (**attach** Schedule 1, even if the result is "0")	420	7,851 66
CPP contributions payable on self-employment and other earnings (**attach** Schedule 8)	421	1,631 03
Social benefits repayment (enter the amount from line 235)	422	
Provincial or territorial tax (**attach** Form 428, even if the result is "0")	428	2,570 53

Add lines 420 to 428
This is your **total payable.** | **435** | 12,053 22 •

Total income tax deducted (from all information slips)	**437**	8,500 00 •
Refundable Québec abatement	**440**	•
CPP overpayment (enter your excess contributions)	**448**	•
Employment Insurance overpayment (enter your excess contributions)	**450**	•
Refundable medical expense supplement	**452**	•
Refund of investment tax credit (**attach** Form T2038(IND))	**454**	•
Part XII.2 trust tax credit (box 38 on all T3 slips)	**456**	•
Employee and partner GST/HST rebate (**attach** Form GST370)	**457**	•
Tax **paid** by instalments	**476**	3,000 00 •
Provincial or territorial credits (**attach** Form 479 if it applies)	**479**	•

Add lines 437 to 479
These are your **total credits.** 482   11,500 00 ▶   11,500 00

Line 435 minus line 482   553 22

If the result is negative, you have a **refund**.
If the result is positive, you have a **balance owing**.
Enter the amount below on whichever line applies.

Generally, we do not charge or refund a difference of $2 or less.

Refund **484**   •   Balance owing **485**   553 22 •

Amount enclosed **486**   •

Direct deposit - Start or change (see line 484 in the guide)

You do not have to complete this area every year. Do not complete it this year if your direct deposit information for your refund has not changed.

Refund and GST/HST credit - To start direct deposit or to change account information only, **attach** a "void" cheque or complete lines 460, 461, and 462.

Note: To deposit your **CCTB** payments (including certain related provincial or territorial payments) into the **same** account, also check box 463.

Branch number	Institution number	Account number	CCTB
460	**461**	**462**	**463**
(5 digits)	(3 digits)	(maximum 12 digits)	

Attach to page 1 a **cheque** or **money order** payable to the Receiver General. Your payment is due no later than April 30, 2006.

I certify that the information given on this return and in any documents attached is correct, complete, and fully discloses all my income.

Sign here _____

It is a serious offence to make a false return.

Telephone (111) 111-1111   Date 2006-05-19

490 X
Name   **For professional tax preparers only**
      Clarence Byrd Inc.
Address   139 Musie Loop Road
      Chelsea, Quebec J9B 1Y6
Telephone   (819) 827-3000

Do not use this area	**487**	**488**					

RC-05-148

Kercher, George Chapter 14 Example   SIN: 527 000 145

T1-2005   **Federal Tax**   **Schedule 1**

Complete this schedule to claim your federal non-refundable tax credits and to calculate your net federal tax.

You must attach a copy of this schedule to your return.

Enter your **taxable income** from line 260 of your return   67,746|60 **1**

Use the amount on line 1 to determine which **ONE** of the following columns you have to complete.

If the amount on line 1 is:	$35,595 or less	more than $35,595 but not more than $71,190	more than $71,190 but not more than $115,739	more than $115,739
Enter the amount from line 1 above	**2**	67,746|60 **2**	**2**	**2**
Base amount	**3**	35,595|00 **3**	71,190|00 **3**	115,739|00 **3**
Line 2 minus line 3 (this amount cannot be negative)	0|00 **4**	32,151|60 **4**	**4**	**4**
Rate	x 15.00 % **5**	x 22.00 % **5**	x 26.00 % **5**	x 29.00 % **5**
Multiply the amount on line 4 by the rate on line 5	**6**	7,073|35 **6**	**6**	**6**
Tax on base amount	0|00 **7**	5,339|00 **7**	13,170|00 **7**	24,753|00 **7**
Add lines 6 and 7	**8**	12,412|35 **8**	**8**	**8**

Federal non-refundable tax credits

Basic personal amount	claim $8,648 **300**	8,648	00
Age amount (if you were born in 1940 or earlier)	(maximum $3,979) **301**	
Spouse or common-law partner amount:		
Base amount 8,079	00		
Minus: his or her net income (from page 1 of your return) 0	00		
Result: (if negative, enter "0")	(maximum $7,344) ▶ **303**	
Amount for an eligible dependant (**attach** Schedule 5)	(maximum $7,344) **305**	7,344	00
Amount for infirm dependants age 18 or older (**attach** Schedule 5)	**306**	
CPP or QPP contributions:		
through employment from box 16 and box 17 on all T4 slips	(maximum $1,861.20) **308**	767	25 •
on self-employment and other earnings (**attach** Schedule 8)	**310**	815	52 •
Employment Insurance premiums from box 18 on all T4 slips	(maximum $760.50) **312**	370	50 •
Adoption expenses	**313**	
Pension income amount	(maximum $1,000) **314**	1,000	00
Caregiver amount (**attach** Schedule 5)	**315**	
Disability amount	**316**	
Disability amount transferred from a dependant	**318**	
Interest paid on your student loans	**319**	
Tuition and education amounts (**attach** Schedule 11)	**323**	1,295	00
Tuition and education amounts transferred from a child	**324**	3,700	00
Amounts transferred from your spouse or common-law partner (**attach** Schedule 2)	**326**	

Medical expenses for **self, spouse or common-law partner, and your dependent children born in 1988 or later** (see the guide) **330**   1,050|00

Minus: $1,844 or 3% of line 236, whichever is **less**   1,844|00

                                           Subtotal (if negative, enter "0")   (A)

Allowable amount of medical expenses for **other dependants**
(see the calculation at line 331 in the guide and **attach** Schedule 5) **331**   51|00 (B)

                        Add lines (A) and (B).   51|00 ▶ **332**   51|00

                        Add lines 300 to 326, and 332. **335**   23,991|27

                        Multiply the amount on line 335 by 15% = **338**   3,598|69

Donations and gifts (**attach** Schedule 9)   **349**   262|00

                Total federal non-refundable tax credits: Add lines 338 and 349. **350**   3,860|69

                                                                      continue

Kercher, George Chapter 14 Example SIN: 527 000 145

Net federal tax

Enter the amount from line 8			12,412	35 **9**
Federal tax on split income (from line 4 of Form T1206)	**424**		• **10**	
Add lines 9 and 10		12,412|35 ▶	12,412|35 **11**

Enter the amount from line 350	350	3,860|69	
Federal dividend tax credit (13.3333% of the amount on line 120 of your return)	**425**	700|00 •	
Overseas employment tax credit (**attach** Form T626)	426		
Minimum tax carry-over (**attach** Form T691)	**427**	•	
Add lines 350, 425, 426, and 427		4,560|69 ▶	4,560|69 **12**

Basic federal tax: Line 11 minus line 12 (if negative, enter "0") 429   7,851|66 **13**

Federal foreign tax credit:
Where you **only** have foreign non-business income, calculate your federal foreign tax credit below. Otherwise, use Form T2209, *Federal Foreign Tax Credits*, if you have foreign business income. **Enter on this line the amount you calculated**   **14**

Federal logging tax credit

Federal tax: Line 13 minus line 14 (if negative, enter "0") 406   7,851|66 **15**

Total federal political contributions (**attach** receipts)	**409**		
Federal political contribution tax credit (see the guide)	**410**	•	
Investment tax credit (**attach** Form T2038(IND))	**412**		
Labour-sponsored funds tax credit			
Net cost **413** Allowable credit **414**		•	
Add lines 410, 412, and 414. **416**		▶	**16**

Line 15 minus line 16 (if negative, enter "0")
(if you have an amount on line 424 above, see Form T1206) 417   7,851|66 **17**

Additional tax on RESP accumulated income payments (**attach** Form T1172) 418   **18**

Net federal tax: Add lines 17 and 18
Enter this amount on line 420 of your return. 420   7,851|66 **19**

Federal foreign tax credit: (see lines 431 and 433 in the guide)

Make a separate calculation for each foreign country. Enter on line 14 above the result from line (i) or line (ii), whichever is **less**.

Non-business income tax paid to a foreign country   **431**   • **(i)**

Net foreign non-business income *   **433**   X   Basic federal tax ***   =   **(ii)**

Net income **

* Reduce this amount by any income from that foreign country for which you claimed a capital gains deduction, and by any income from that country that was, under a tax treaty, either exempt from tax in that country or deductible as exempt income in Canada (included on line 256). Also reduce this amount by the lesser of lines E and F on Form T626.
** Line 236 plus the amount on line 3 of Form T1206, minus the total of the amounts on lines 244, 248, 249, 250, 253, 254, and minus any amount included on line 256 for foreign income deductible as exempt income under a tax treaty, income deductible as net employment income from a prescribed international organization, or non-taxable tuition assistance from box 21 of the T4E slip. If the result is less than the amount on line 433, enter your **Basic federal tax***** on line (ii).
*** Line 429 plus the amount on lines 425 and 426, and minus any refundable Québec abatement (line 440) and any federal refundable First Nations abatement (line 441 on the return for residents of Yukon).

Solution to Chapter Fourteen Exercises

Exercise Fourteen - 1 Solution

The specified value of the $20 options is $80,000 [(4,000)($20)]. Her election on these options defers employment income of $30 ($50 - $20) per option, or a total of $120,000 [(4,000)($30)].

The specified value of the $25 options is $200,000 [(8,000)($25)]. As a result, her maximum deferral would be on $100,000, or one-half, of the $25 options. The maximum potential deferral here is $115 ($140 - $25) per share, or a total of $460,000 [(1/2)(8,000)($115)]. If Ms. Flux does not revoke her election on the $20 options, she will only be able to elect on a specified value of $20,000 on these $25 options. This would result in an additional deferral of $92,000 [(10%)(8,000)($115)], resulting in a total 2006 deferral of $212,000 ($120,000 + $92,000).

Alternatively, if she revokes the election on the $20 options, she will be able to elect on the maximum $100,000 specified value of the $25 options, resulting in a deferral of $460,000. This is clearly the better alternative.

Exercise Fourteen - 2 Solution

Mr. Smothers will have a net capital loss carry forward on listed personal property from 2005 of $5,500 [(1/2)($89,000 - $100,000)]. This can only be applied against the 2006 taxable gain of $2,000 [(1/2)($5,000 - $1,000)]. As this is a listed personal property loss carry forward, it will be deducted in the calculation of Net Income For Tax Purposes, leaving this balance at the amount of his employment income, $62,000. This will also be his 2006 Taxable Income. In addition, he will have a net capital loss carry forward of $3,500 ($5,500 - $2,000) that can only be applied against taxable capital gains on listed personal property.

If the sale had been of shares, Mr. Smothers would have had a regular net capital loss carry forward of $5,500 from 2005. His 2006 Net Income For Tax Purposes would have been $64,000 ($62,000 + $2,000) and his Taxable Income would have been $62,000 ($64,000 - $2,000), the same as under the original assumption. The $3,500 net capital loss carry forward would be available to be applied against any taxable capital gains.

Exercise Fourteen - 3 Solution

In this Exercise, the E in the ITA 111(8) formula would be equal to $60,200 ($58,000 + $2,200), F [income under ITA 3(c)] would be equal to $48,000 ($35,000 + $13,000), and D would be equal to $2,200. This leaves a non-capital loss balance of $10,000 ($60,200 - $48,000 - $2,200). Note that this is the excess of the business loss of $58,000, over the $48,000 in positive sources of income for the year. The additional farm loss of $2,200 would be allocated to a separate loss balance. It is included in the E component and then deducted in the D component. Since it is less than $2,500, the farm loss is fully deductible, whether it is restricted or not.

Exercise Fourteen - 4 Solution

Her minimum 2006 Net Income For Tax Purposes will be $10,000 ($40,000 - $30,000). Since she does not anticipate future capital gains, she will want to use as much of her net capital loss carry forward as she can. As the amount of this net capital loss carry forward is less than the current year's taxable capital gain, she can apply all of it in 2006. To do so, she will convert $5,000 of her non-capital loss to a non-capital loss carry over. This is calculated as follows:

Amount E ($30,000 + $15,000)	$45,000
Amount F [ITA 3(c) Income]	(40,000)
Non-Capital Loss Carry Over	$ 5,000

Her minimum Taxable Income will be nil after deducting the $15,000 net capital loss carry forward. The only loss carry over available at the end of the year is a $5,000 non-capital loss carry over.

Exercise Fourteen - 5 Solution

The Allowable Business Investment Loss for the year would be calculated as follows:

Loss On Disposition	$50,000
Reduction For Capital Gains Deduction [(2/1)($13,000)]	(26,000)
Business Investment Loss	$24,000
Inclusion Rate	1/2
Allowable Business Investment Loss	$12,000

All of the $12,000 can be deducted against Mr. Latvik's employment income. With respect to the disallowed $26,000, it becomes an ordinary capital loss, of which $18,000 can be deducted against the current year's capital gains on the publicly traded securities. This leaves a net capital loss carry over of $4,000 [(1/2)($26,000 - $18,000)].

Exercise Fourteen - 6 Solution

During 2005, her farm loss was limited to $8,750 [$2,500 + (1/2)($12,500)]. The remaining restricted farm loss of $7,250 ($16,000 - $8,750) can be carried forward to 2006. In 2006, $3,500 of this carry forward can be deducted against the 2006 farm income. The remaining restricted farm loss of $3,750 ($7,250 - $3,500) will be carried forward to future years. Ms. Bodkin's 2006 Net Income For Tax Purposes is $88,500 ($85,000 + $3,500) and her 2006 Taxable Income is $85,000 ($85,000 + $3,500 - $3,500).

Exercise Fourteen - 7 Solution

The annual gains limit is **$26,000** ($42,000 - $16,000). This is calculated using the ITA 110.6 formula as follows:

The A component of the formula would be equal to **$42,000**, the lesser of:

- $74,000 ($114,000 - $82,000 + $42,000); and
- $42,000.

The B component would be **$16,000**, the sum of:

- $13,000*; and
- $3,000.

  *The amount by which $45,000, exceeds $32,000 ($114,000 - $82,000 + $42,000 - $42,000).

Note that the net taxable capital gain on non-qualifying property was $32,000 ($114,000 - $82,000). The mechanics of the B component of the formula are such that the first $32,000 of the $45,000 net capital loss deduction was charged against these gains and did not erode the annual gains limit. Only the remaining $13,000 ($45,000 - $32,000) served to reduce the annual gains limit.

It would be advisable for Ms. Slovena to deduct only $32,000 of the net capital loss carry forward. If she did this, her annual gains limit would increase to $39,000 ($42,000 - Nil - $3,000). Although she would have used $13,000 ($39,000 - $26,000) more of her lifetime capital gains deduction, her tax liability for 2006 would not change and she would have a net capital loss carry forward of $13,000 ($45,000 - $32,000) that could be applied against any type of capital gain for an unlimited period of time.

Exercise Fourteen - 8 Solution

For 2006, his maximum lifetime capital gains deduction is $223,500, the least of the following three items:

Available Deduction His remaining deduction would be $232,000 [$250,000 - $5,000 - (1/2)($26,000)].

Annual Gains Limit In the absence of capital gains on non-qualifying property in any of the years under consideration, the simplified version of this calculation can be used. The annual gains limit for 2006 would be the qualifying taxable capital gain of $255,000 [(1/2)($510,000)], reduced by the net capital loss carry forward deducted of $31,500 [(1/2)($63,000)]. This leaves a net amount of $223,500 ($255,000 - $31,500).

Cumulative Gains Limit In the absence of capital gains on non-qualifying property in 1986 and 1989, the annual gains limits for 1986 and 1989 would simply be the amount of the taxable capital gains on qualifying property in those years. Given this, the required calculation would be as follows:

Sum Of Annual Gains Limits	
($5,000 + $17,333 + $223,500)	$245,833
Previous Years' Capital Gains Deduction ($5,000 + $17,333)	(22,333)
Cumulative Gains Limit	$223,500

Note that if he had deducted only $23,000 of his net capital loss carry forward, his annual gains limit would have been $232,000 ($255,000 - $23,000). This would have allowed Mr. Loussier to use all of his remaining lifetime capital gains deduction.

Exercise Fourteen - 9 Solution

Alan's Net Income For Tax Purposes would be calculated as follows:

Income Under ITA 3(a):		
Business Income	$12,000	
Employment Income	56,000	
Farming Income	3,500	$71,500
Income Under ITA 3(b):		
Taxable Capital Gains		9,000
Net Income For Tax Purposes		$80,500

Alan's Taxable Income is as follows:

Net Income For Tax Purposes	$80,500
Loss Carry Forwards:	
Restricted Farm Losses (Limited to farming income)	(3,500)
Net Capital Losses (Limited to taxable capital gains)	(9,000)
Non-Capital Losses (All)	(36,000)
Taxable Income	$32,000

The restricted farm loss carry forward would be $4,500 ($8,000 - $3,500). The capital loss carry forward on a 100 percent basis would be $22,000 ($40,000 - $18,000). The 1990 net capital loss balance would be $16,500 [(3/4)($22,000)]. There would be no non-capital loss carry forward.

Exercise Fourteen - 10 Solution

The required calculations are as follows:

	Tax Otherwise Determined	Tax Per ITA 120.4(3)
Tax On Split Income [(125%)($15,000)(29%)]	$5,438	$5,438
Tax On Taxable Income [($12,200)(15.25%)]	1,861	N/A
Dividend Tax Credit [(2/3)(25%)($15,000)]	(2,500)	(2,500)
Basic Personal Tax Credit	(1,348)	N/A
Alternative Tax Payable Amounts	$3,451	$2,938

Norton's federal Tax Payable would be $3,451, the greater of these two amounts.

Exercise Fourteen - 11 Solution

Without the transfer, Mr. Ho's wife would have income of $8,990 [(145%)($6,200)] and, as her income is greater than $8,256, he would have no spousal tax credit. With the transfer, he would be eligible for the full $1,145. Given this, the analysis of his position at the federal level is as follows:

Additional Taxes On Dividends [(145%)($6,200)(29%)]	$2,607
Spousal Tax Credit	(1,145)
Dividend Tax Credit [(11/18)(45%)($6,200)]	(1,705)
Tax Increase (Decrease)	($ 243)

As there is an decrease in federal Tax Payable, the election would be desirable.

Exercise Fourteen - 12 Solution

With the gift being made at $85,000, Ms. Felder will have a taxable capital gain of $11,500 [(1/2)($85,000 - $62,000)], plus recapture of $34,000 ($62,000 - $28,000), for a total Net Income For Tax Purposes of $45,500. Given this, her maximum credit base would be calculated as follows:

75 Percent Of Net Income For Tax Purposes [(75%)($45,500)]	$34,125
25 Percent Of Taxable Capital Gain [(25%)($11,500)]	2,875
25 Percent Of Recaptured CCA [(25%)($34,000)]	8,500
Total Limit And Net Income For Tax Purposes	$45,500

Using this base, the maximum credit would be $13,168 [(15.25%)($200) + (29%)($45,500 - $200)]. However, she does not need all of this credit to reduce her Tax Payable to nil:

Tax On First $36,378	$5,548
Tax At 22 Percent On Remaining $9,122	2,007
Tax Before Credits	$7,555
Basic Personal Credit	(1,348)
Tax Payable Before Donations Credit	$6,207

Given this amount of Tax Payable, the use of $21,497 of her donation will produce the $6,207 [(15.25%)($200) + (29%)($21,497 - $200)] credit that will reduce her federal Tax Payable to nil. This leaves a carry forward of $63,503 ($85,000 - $21,497).

Exercise Fourteen - 13 Solution

As the donation was made after May 1, 2006, none of the capital gain will be included in Mr. Radeem's income. This means that his Taxable Income for 2006 will consist of his employment income of $90,000. Based on the fair market value of the donated shares, Mr. Radeem's maximum base for his charitable donations tax credit would be $67,500 [(75%)($90,000)]. If he were to use this amount, his 2006 charitable donations tax credit would be $19,548

[(15.25%)($200) + (29%)($67,500 - $200)]. However, he does not need this amount to reduce his Tax Payable to nil:

Tax On First $72,756	$13,551
Tax At 26 Percent On Remaining $17,244 ($90,000 - $72,756)	4,483
Tax Before Credits	$18,034
Tax Credits (Given)	(4,000)
Tax Payable Before Donations Credit	$14,034

Given this amount of Tax Payable, the use of $48,486 of his donation will produce the $14,034 [(15.25%)($200) + (29%)($48,486 - $200)] credit that will reduce his federal Tax Payable to nil. This leaves a carry forward of $61,514 ($110,000 - $48,486).

Exercise Fourteen - 14 Solution

Ms. Cheung's credit for foreign tax paid would be the lesser of $420 [(12%)($3,500)] and an amount determined by the following formula:

$$\left[\frac{\text{Foreign Non} - \text{Business Income}}{\text{Adjusted Division B Income}} \right] [\text{Tax Otherwise Payable}]$$

In this formula, the Adjusted Division B Income would be $47,500 ($50,000 - $2,500). Tax Otherwise Payable would be $5,767 [$5,548 + (22%)($43,500 - $36,378) - $1,348]. Using these figures, the calculation would be $425 [($3,500 ÷ $47,500)($5,767)].

As the foreign tax paid would be the lesser of the two figures, her tax credit for 2006 would be $420.

Exercise Fourteen - 15 Solution

Mr. Blouson's regular Tax Payable would be calculated as follows:

Tax On First $72,756	$13,551
Tax At 26 Percent On $12,244 ($85,000 - $72,756)	3,183
Total	$16,734
Basic Personal Credit	(1,348)
Dividend Tax Credit [(11/18)(45%)($20,000)]	(5,500)
Regular Federal Tax Payable	$9,886

For alternative minimum tax purposes, his adjusted taxable income would be calculated as follows:

Regular Taxable Income	$85,000
30 Percent Of Capital Gains [(30%)(2)($22,500)]	13,500
Dividend Gross Up [(45%)($20,000)]	(9,000)
Adjusted Taxable Income	$89,500

Calculation of the alternative minimum tax would be as follows:

Adjusted Taxable Income	$89,500
Basic Exemption	(40,000)
Amount Subject To Tax	$49,500
Rate	15.25%
Minimum Tax Before Credit	$ 7,549
Basic Personal Credit	(1,348)
Alternative Minimum Tax	$ 6,201

Mr. Blouson would not pay the alternative minimum tax as $6,201 is less than the regular Tax Payable of $9,886. Note that the $50,000 RRSP deduction does not affect the alternative minimum tax calculation.

Solution to Self Study Problem Fourteen - 1

2003 Analysis   Mr. Fox's Net Income For Tax Purposes and Taxable Income would be calculated as follows:

ITA 3(a)		
Employment Income	$18,000	
Business Income	14,500	
Taxable (Grossed Up) Dividends	6,250	$38,750
ITA 3(b)		
Taxable Capital Gains	$ Nil	
Allowable Capital Losses [(1/2)($3,600)]	(1,800)	Nil
ITA 3(c)		$38,750
ITA 3(d)		
Farm Loss (See Note)		(4,250)
Net Income For Tax Purposes And Taxable Income		$34,500

Note   Given that Mr. Fox is only a part time farmer, his deductible farm loss would be restricted as follows:

Total Farm Loss		$6,000
Deductible Amount:		
First $2,500	($2,500)	
One-Half Of $3,500 ($6,000 - $2,500)	(1,750)	(4,250)
Restricted Farm Loss Carry Forward		$1,750

As noted in the problem, none of the losses can be carried back before 2003. This would leave the following carry forward balances at the end of 2003:

- 2003 Restricted Farm Loss Carry Forward — $1,750
- 2003 Net Capital Loss Carry Forward [(1/2)($3,600)] — $1,800

2004 Analysis   Mr. Fox's Net Income For Tax Purposes and Taxable Income would be calculated as follows:

ITA 3(a)		
Employment Income	$16,000	
Taxable (Grossed Up) Dividends	8,156	$24,156
ITA 3(b)		
Taxable Capital Gains [(1/2)($7,400)]	$ 3,700	
Allowable Capital Losses	Nil	3,700
ITA 3(c)		$27,856
ITA 3(d)		
Business Loss		(39,000)
Net Income For Tax Purposes		$ Nil
2003 Net Capital Loss Carry Forward (Less Than $3,700)		(1,800)
Taxable Income		$ Nil

Since there are taxable capital gains this year, and the problem states that Mr. Fox would like to deduct the maximum amount of his net capital loss carry forwards, the net capital loss carry forward of $1,800 is added to the balance of the non-capital loss. The non-capital loss for the year would be calculated as follows:

Business Loss	$39,000
2003 Net Capital Loss Deducted	1,800
ITA 3(c) Income	(27,856)
Non-Capital Loss Carry Over For 2004	$12,944

This non-capital loss will be carried back to 2003, resulting in the following amended Taxable Income for that year:

2003 Taxable Income (As Reported)	$34,500
Non-Capital Loss Carry Back From 2004	(12,944)
2003 Amended Taxable Income	$21,556

This carry back leaves Mr. Fox with more than his required $10,000 in Taxable Income. There would be the following carry forward balances at the end of 2004:

- 2003 Restricted Farm Loss Carry Forward $1,750

2005 Analysis   Mr. Fox's Net Income For Tax Purposes and Taxable Income would be calculated as follows:

ITA 3(a)		
Employment Income	$19,000	
Business Income	34,000	
Farming Income	8,000	
Taxable (Grossed Up) Dividends	10,000	$71,000
ITA 3(b)		
Taxable Capital Gains [(1/2)($6,300)]	$ 3,150	
Allowable Capital Losses	Nil	3,150
ITA 3(c)		$74,150
ITA 3(d)		Nil
Net Income For Tax Purposes		$74,150
Farm Loss Carry Forward (Less Than $8,000)		(1,750)
Taxable Income		$72,400

Given the deduction of the farm loss carry forward, there are no loss carry overs remaining at the end of 2005.

2006 Analysis Mr. Fox's Net Income For Tax Purposes and Taxable Income would be calculated as follows:

ITA 3(a)		
Employment Income	$12,000	
Taxable (Grossed Up) Dividends	12,656	$24,656
ITA 3(b)		
Taxable Capital Gains	$ Nil	
Allowable Capital Losses [(1/2)($6,000)]	(3,000)	Nil
ITA 3(c)		$24,656
ITA 3(d)		
Business Loss	($52,000)	
Farm Loss	(2,000)	(54,000)
Net Income For Tax Purposes And Taxable Income		$ Nil

The non-capital loss carry over for the year would be calculated as follows:

Business Loss	$52,000
Farm Loss (Unrestricted)	2,000
ITA 3(c) Income	(24,656)
Non-Capital Loss Carry Over For 2006	$29,344

The farm loss is less than $2,500 and so is part of the unrestricted portion of the farm loss. The entire non-capital loss carry over could be carried back to 2005, but the problem requires that losses be carried back to the earliest possible year. As a result, some of this loss must be carried back to 2003. Since Mr. Fox requires $10,000 in Taxable Income to fully utilize his personal tax credits, the maximum carry back to 2003 is $11,556, calculated as follows:

2003 Taxable Income (As Amended)	$21,556
Non-Capital Loss Carry Back From 2006	(11,556)
2003 Amended Taxable Income (Minimum)	$10,000

This carry back leaves Mr. Fox with his required $10,000 in Taxable Income. The remaining non-capital loss carry over of $17,788 ($29,344 - $11,556) can be carried back to 2005.

There would be a $3,000 net capital loss carry over for 2006. The entire net capital loss carry over can be carried back to 2005, since the carry back is less than the $3,150 taxable capital gains recorded in 2005.

This will result in the following amended Taxable Income for that year:

2005 Taxable Income (As Reported)	$72,400
Non-Capital Loss Carry Back From 2006	(17,788)
Net Capital Loss Carry Back From 2006	(3,000)
2005 Amended Taxable Income	$51,612

There are no loss carry forwards remaining at the end of 2006.

Solution to Self Study Problem Fourteen - 2

Mr. Borgen's minimum Taxable Income would be calculated as follows:

Net Employment Income	$36,000
Net Taxable Capital Gains ($37,500 - $9,000)	28,500
Interest Expense	(17,000)
Net Income For Tax Purposes	$47,500
Net Capital Loss Carry Forward	Nil
Lifetime Capital Gains Deduction (See Note)	(11,500)
Taxable Income	$36,000

Note The lifetime capital gains deduction is the least of:

Capital Gains Deduction Available	$250,000
Annual Gains Limit	$ 28,500
Cumulative Net Taxable Capital Gains	$ 28,500
Cumulative Net Investment Loss	(17,000)
Cumulative Gains Limit	$ 11,500

It would have been possible for Mr. Borgen to deduct the $9,900 net capital loss carry forward instead of $9,900 of the lifetime capital gains deduction. The carry forward period on net capital losses is unlimited and it can be applied against any type of capital gain. In contrast, the lifetime capital gains deduction can only be used for certain types of capital gains that are not common. As a result, use of the lifetime capital gains deduction is probably the better alternative.

Solution to Self Study Problem Fourteen - 3

Mr. and Mrs. Bahry's Taxable Income would be calculated as follows:

	Mr. Bahry	Mrs. Bahry
Old Age Security Benefits (See Note)	$ 5,800	$ 5,800
Registered Pension Plan Receipts	12,340	820
Registered Retirement Income Fund Receipts	N/A	700
Canada Pension Plan Receipts	3,690	830
Dividends Received	1,600	336
Gross Up On Dividends (45 Percent)	720	151
Interest On Savings Accounts	1,239	443
Net Taxable Capital Gain:		
Mr. Bahry	Nil	
Mrs. Bahry		Nil
Taxable Income	$25,389	$ 9,080

Note Neither Mr. nor Mrs. Bahry would have to repay any OAS benefits as both Net Income figures are well below the threshold income of $62,144.

Mr. Bahry cannot take the spousal credit because Mrs. Bahry's Net Income is more than $8,256 ($7,505 + $751). Mrs. Bahry cannot transfer her dividends under ITA 82(3) as the transfer would give her Net Income of $8,593 ($9,080 - $336 - $151) and this would not increase or create a spousal credit.

Mrs. Bahry must include the $151 gross up on her dividends in her Taxable Income, which decreases the amount of tax credits she can transfer. She must decrease the amount of the age and pension credits she can transfer by the excess of her Taxable Income (including the dividends) over the basic personal amount. As a result, she cannot claim the dividend tax credit. Since Mr. Bahry is not eligible for the ITA 82(3) election, her dividend tax credit will be lost. The total credit base that can be transferred is calculated as follows:

Age	$4,066
Pension (On $820 + $700 Only)	1,520
Less Excess Of Taxable Income Over Basic Personal Amount ($9,080 - $8,839)	(241)
Credit Base Transferred To Spouse	$5,345

Mr. Bahry's maximum tax credits would be as follows:

Base Amount	$ 8,839
Age (No Reduction Required)	4,066
Pension	2,000
Transfers From Mrs. Bahry (See Preceding)	5,345
Credit Base	$20,250
Rate	15.25%
Total	$ 3,088
Dividend Tax Credit [(11/18)($720)]	440
Charitable Donations [(15.25%)($200) + (29%)($1,210 + $300 - $200)]	411
Total Credits	$ 3,939

Charitable donations can be claimed by either spouse, as long as the total donations are less than 75 percent of the claiming spouse's Net Income For Tax Purposes. As Mrs. Bahry has no Tax Payable, Mr. Bahry will claim her charitable donations. It is usually advantageous for one spouse to claim all the charitable donations if they total more than $200, as the low rate of credit is only applied once.

Neither Mr. Bahry's allowable capital loss of $1,988 [(50%)($3,975)] nor Mrs. Bahry's allowable capital loss of $160 [(50%)($820 - $500)] can be deducted in 2006. They can be carried back three years and carried forward indefinitely to be applied against taxable capital gains.

Solution to Self Study Problem Fourteen - 4

Taxable Income   Ms. Worthmore's minimum Taxable Income is calculated as follows:

Employment Income		
Gross Salary - Intra Graphics	$72,476	
Gross Salary - Lindworth Inc.	2,500	
RPP Contributions	(1,233)	
Premium For Provincial Health Care	1056	$74,799
Income From Property		
Dividend Attribution (Note One)	$ 264	
Dividends From Lindworth (Note Two)	5,406	
Loan Principal (Note Two)	5,000	10,670
Taxable Capital Gains		
Attribution From Husband (Note Three)	$ 1,144	
Transfer To Jayne (Note Four)	122	
Lackmere Shares (Note Five)	394	
Agricultural Land (Note Six)	9,000	10,660
Other Income And Deductions		
Spousal Support Payments	($ 2,700)	
RRSP Deduction (Note Seven)	(7,039)	(9,739)
Net Income For Tax Purposes And Taxable Income		**$86,390**

Note One   There would be income attribution for the dividends received by Mr. Dalton on the shares received as a gift. The grossed up dividend of $264 [(145%)($3.50)(52)] would be taxed in Ms. Worthmore's hands and she would claim the related dividend tax credit of $50 [(11/18)(45%)($3.50)(52)].

Note Two   The grossed up non-eligible dividends from Lindworth Inc. would be included in the amount of $5,406 [(125%)($4,325)]. She would claim the related dividend tax credit of $721 [(2/3)(25%)($4,325)]. With respect to the loan principal, it will be outstanding on more than two consecutive corporate year ends and, as a consequence, it must be included in Ms. Worthmore's Net Income For Tax Purposes. However, there will be no imputed interest on the loan and, when it is repaid, it can be deducted by Ms. Worthmore.

Note Three   In the case of transfers to a spouse, unless an election is made not to have Section 73 apply, the property is transferred at the adjusted cost base of the transferor. There is no recognition of capital gains at the time of transfer. However, when Mr. Dalton sells the shares on August 31, 2006, there would be attribution of taxable capital gains in the amount of $1,144 [($56 - $12)(52)(1/2)].

Note Four   In the case of a gift to a minor child, it is treated as a deemed disposition at fair market value. This results in a taxable capital gain at the time of transfer in the amount of $122 [($27 - $18)(27)(1/2)].

Note Five   The taxable capital gain on the Lackmere Ltd. shares would be computed using the average value for the shares. The average value would be calculated as follows:

122 Shares At $92	$11,224
178 Shares At $71	12,638
Total Cost	$23,862
Average Cost ($23,862 ÷ 300 Shares)	$ 79.54

This results in a taxable capital gain of $394 [($86 - $79.54)(122)(1/2)].

Note Six   When there is a non-arms' length transfer of property for consideration of less than fair market value, ITA 69 deems that, for the transferor, the transfer takes place at fair market value.   This will result in a taxable capital gain of $9,000 [($28,000 - $10,000)(1/2)]. Note that for her brother, his adjusted cost base will only be the transfer price of $10,000. This will result in a capital gain for him if he subsequently sells the land for more than $10,000.

Note Seven   Ms. Worthmore's 2005 Earned Income (assumed to be equal to the 2006 figure) is as follows:

Gross Salary - Intra	$72,476
Gross Salary - Lindworth	2,500
Employment Benefit - Provincial Health Care	1,056
Spousal Support Paid And Deducted	(2,700)
Earned Income	$73,332

Ms. Worthmore's maximum deductible 2006 RRSP contribution is calculated as follows:

Unused Deduction Room - End of 2005	Nil
Lesser Of:	
• 2006 RRSP Dollar Limit = $18,000	
• [(18%)($73,332)] = $13,200	$13,200
Less 2005 PA	(6,161)
Maximum Deductible RRSP Contribution	$ 7,039

This means the excess contribution of $461 ($7,500 - $7,039) can be carried forward and deducted in future years.

Tax Payable   Ms. Worthmore's Tax Payable can be calculated as follows:

Tax On First $72,756		$13,551
Tax On Next $13,634 ($86,390 - $72,756) At 26 Percent		3,545
Gross Federal Tax Payable		$17,096
Basic Personal Amount	($ 8,839)	
Spousal [$7,505- ($750 + $2,475 - $751)]	(5,031)	
CPP	(1,911)	
EI	(729)	
Canada Employment	(250)	
Transfer Of Spouse's Tuition, Education and		
Textbook - Lesser of:		
• $5,000		
• [$2,300 + (4)($400) + (4)($65)] = $4,160	(4,160)	
Medical Expenses (Note Eight)	(11,222)	
Credit Base	($32,142)	
Rate	15.25%	(4,902)
Eligible Dividend Tax Credit (Note One)		(50)
Non-Eligible Dividend Tax Credit (Note Two)		(721)
Charitable Donations [(15.25%)($200) + (29%)($342 - $200)]		(72)
Political Contributions [(3/4)($100)]		(75)
Federal Tax Payable		$11,276

Note Eight   Ms. Worthmore can claim all of the medical expenses of her daughters, Joyce and June without taking into consideration June's income, as she is under 18 years of age.

Allowable medical expenses are as follows:

Health Care Premium, Joyce And June Medical Expenses	
($1,056 + $2,200 + $9,850)	$13,106
Threshold - Lesser Of: [(3%)($86,390)] And $1,884	(1,884)
Allowable Medical Expenses	$11,222

Solution to Self Study Problem Fourteen - 5

Taxable Income   Mr. Slater's Net Income For Tax Purposes And Taxable Income would be calculated as follows:

Employment Income - Salary		$ 35,000
Proprietorship Income (Note One)		26,000
Income From Investments:		
Interest On Savings Account	$ 4,600	
Interest On Loans To Friends	12,000	
Eligible Canadian Dividends [($44,000)(145%)]	63,800	
Dividends From U.S Corporations		
(Before Withholding, No Gross Up)	10,000	
	$90,400	
Safety Deposit Box Rental	(150)	90,250
Taxable Capital Gain [(1/2)($111,500 - $23,000)]		44,250
Restricted Farm Loss (Note Three):		
Revenues	$36,000	
Expenses	(45,000)	
Total Loss	($ 9,000)	
Non-Deductible Portion [(1/2)($9,000 - $2,500)]	3,250	(5,750)
CPP Benefits		5,100
Old Age Security Benefits		5,800
Net Income Before OAS Repayment		$200,650
OAS Repayment - Lesser Of:		
• $5,800		
• $20,776 [(15%)($200,650 - $62,144)]		(5,800)
Net Income For Tax Purposes And Taxable Income		$194,850

Note One   The drawings from the proprietorship have no effect on the Taxable Income of Mr. Slater. Funds invested are capital and not deductible. The proprietorship income of $28,300 is reduced by the interest of $2,300 on the proprietorship bank loan.

Note Two   Since Mr. Slater is not a full time farmer, his farm loss would be restricted to $2,500, plus 50 percent of the next $6,500 ($9,000 - $2,500), a total of $5,750. The $3,250 balance could be carried back to the preceding three years and forward for 20 years, to be deducted against farming income.

Tax Payable   Mr. Slater's Tax Payable would be calculated as follows:

Tax On First $118,285		$25,389
Tax On Next $76,565 ($194,850 - $118,285) At 29 Percent		22,204
Gross Federal Tax		$47,593
Tax Credits:		
Basic Personal Amount	($ 8,839)	
Mr. Slater's Age ($4,066 - $4,066)	Nil	
Spousal	(7,505)	
Spouse's Disability	(6,741)	
Canada Employment	(250)	
Credit Base	($23,335)	
Rate	15.25%	(3,559)
Charitable Donations		
[(15.25%)($200) + (29%)($2,700 - $200)]		(756)
Dividend Tax Credit [(11/18)(45%)($44,000)]		(12,100)
Basic Federal Tax Payable		$31,178
Foreign Tax Credit (Note Three)		(1,500)
Federal Political Contributions Tax Credit (Note Four)		(350)
Federal Tax Payable		$29,328
Credits:		
Employer Withholding	($9,000)	
Instalments	(2,500)	(11,500)
Balance Before Interest And Penalties		$17,828
Late Filing Penalty (Note Five)		1,070
Interest (Note Six)		256
Amount Owing On June 30		$19,154

Note Three   The federal foreign tax credit will be the lesser of the foreign tax actually paid of $1,500 and an amount determined by the following formula:

[(Foreign Non-Business Income ÷ Adjusted Net Income)(Taxes Otherwise Payable*)]

*Basic Federal Tax before the dividend tax credit is deducted.

This amount would be ($10,000 ÷ $194,850) multiplied by ($31,178 + $12,100). This equals $2,221, leaving the actual taxes of $1,500 as the lesser amount.

Note Four   The political contributions tax credit can be calculated as follows:

3/4 Of First $400	$300
1/2 Of The Next $100	50
Total Credit	$350

Note Five   The due date for Mr. Slater's return is June 15, as he has business income. The penalty for the late filing of a return is 5 percent plus 1 percent per month for each complete month after the filing deadline. By filing on July 15, 2006, Mr. Slater's penalty will be 6 percent of $17,828, or $1,070.

Note Six   Although interest calculations are based on daily compounding, this is difficult to compute. As such, the use of simple interest is commonly used in problems. Simple interest on late taxes at a rate of 7 percent from May 1, 2007 is calculated as follows:

[($17,828)(7%)(75/365)] = $256

Other Notes   Other points that should be noted are as follows:

- The gambling income would not be taxable unless Mr. Slater's activity was extensive enough to be considered a business.
- Inheritances are capital receipts and do not constitute Taxable Income.
- The life insurance premiums are not deductible.
- The mortgage payments on his personal residence are not deductible.

Solution to Self Study Problem Fourteen - 6

Regular Tax Payable   The minimum regular Taxable Income and Tax Payable calculations would be as follows:

	Cheryl	Alma	Irene
Employment And Business Income	$ 60,800	$42,000	$ 22,900
Dividends Received	26,300	Nil	29,400
Non-Eligible Dividend Gross Up (25%)	6,575	Nil	7,350
Taxable Capital Gains	9,100	Nil	300,000
Retiring Allowance	Nil	58,000	Nil
RRSP Deductions (Note 1)	(2,344)	(58,000)	Nil
Net Income For Tax Purposes	$100,431	$42,000	$359,650
Lifetime Capital Gains Deduction	(9,100)	Nil	(250,000)
Taxable Income	$ 91,331	$42,000	$109,650
Federal Tax (Note 2)	$ 18,381	$ 6,785	$ 23,143
Basic Personal Credit	(1,348)	(1,348)	(1,348)
Dividend Tax Credit (2/3 of Gross Up)	(4,383)	Nil	(4,900)
Regular Federal Tax Payable	$ 12,650	$ 5,437	$ 16,895

Note 1   Cheryl's 2006 RRSP Deduction Room is calculated as follows:

Lesser Of:
- 2006 RRSP Dollar Limit = $18,000
- 18% Of 2005 Earned Income Of $60,800 = $10,944 $10,944

Less 2005 PA	(8,600)
2006 RRSP Deduction Limit	$ 2,344

Although she contributed $3,500, her RRSP deduction is limited to $2,344 and she has $1,156 ($3,500 - $2,344) in undeducted contributions that can be carried forward and deducted in a subsequent year in which there is sufficient RRSP deduction room.

Note 2   The federal Tax Payable, before the dividend tax credit, was calculated as follows:

	Taxable Income	Federal Tax Calculations	Federal Tax
Cheryl	$ 91,331	$13,551 + (26%)($18,575)	$18,381
Alma	$ 42,000	$ 5,548 + (22%)($ 5,622)	$ 6,785
Irene	$109,650	$13,551 + (26%)($36,894)	$23,143

Alternative Minimum Tax Payable   The alternative minimum tax (AMT) calculations would be as follows:

	Cheryl	Alma	Irene
Regular Taxable Income	$91,331	$42,000	$109,650
30% Of Capital Gains (Note)	5,460	Nil	180,000
Dividend Gross Up	(6,575)	Nil	(7,350)
Adjusted Taxable Income	$90,216	$42,000	$282,300
AMT Exemption	(40,000)	(40,000)	(40,000)
AMT Base	$50,216	$ 2,000	$242,300
Rate	15.25%	15.25%	15.25%
Federal AMT Before Credit	$ 7,658	$ 305	$ 36,951
Basic Personal Credit	(1,348)	(1,348)	(1,348)
Federal AMT	$ 6,310	$ Nil	$ 35,603
Regular Federal Tax Payable	(12,650)		(16,895)
Additional Tax Required	$ Nil		$ 18,708

Note The 30 percent capital gain inclusion can be calculated by taking 30 percent of double the taxable capital gain.

The excess of AMT over regular tax payable for Irene can be carried forward for seven years and applied against any future excess of regular Tax Payable over the alternative minimum tax.

Solution to Self Study Problem Fourteen - 7

This is an extension of Self Study Case 14-1 (tax return preparation case). It has been updated for 2006 rates.

Part A
Rental Income Since Eleanor is currently renting out her house, but plans to move back into it, no CCA is taken on the Class 1 building to preserve her principal residence status. Since the cost is equal to the UCC, no CCA has been taken on the building in the previous year. Her CCA on the appliances would not affect her principal residence election and should be taken. The payments on principal are not deductible.

If she chose to take CCA on the building, the maximum potential CCA for the year would be $6,756 [(4%)($168,900)] since the first year one-half rule does not apply to her second year of rental. The maximum deductible CCA on the building would be limited to the net rental income after the CCA on the appliances of $5,553 ($5,887 - $334). This would reduce her Tax Payable for 2006, but she would no longer be eligible for the principal residence gain reduction on the property. In addition, the CCA would be recaptured on a subsequent sale if the proceeds were greater than the UCC.

Ms. Trubey's net rental income can be calculated as follows:

Gross Rental Income		$15,600
Less Expenses:		
Property Taxes	$2,190	
Insurance	1,093	
Interest	5,378	
Maintenance And Repairs ($291 + $300)	591	
Legal Fees	173	
Utilities	288	(9,713)
Rental Income Before CCA		$ 5,887
CCA On Class 8 Assets [(20%)($921 + $1,500 - $750)]		(334)
Net Rental Income		$ 5,553

The required calculations for Ms. Trubey's balance owing (refund) would be as follows:

Employment Income	$ 60,202	
RPP Deduction	(2,406)	
Union Dues	(749)	$57,047
CPP Benefits		4,823
Pension Income		22,249
Taxable Amount Of Eligible Dividends		2,324
Interest Income ($509 + $311)		820
Rental Income		5,553
Taxable Capital Gains [(1/2)($982)]		491
RRSP Deduction - Least Of:		
• ($18,000 - $4,376) = $13,624		
• [(18%)($38,873) - $4,376] = $2,621		
• ($1,665 + $2,620) = $4,285		(2,621)
Child Care Expenses [(2)($100) + $400]		(600)
Net And Taxable Income		**$90,086**

Federal Tax On First $72,756		$13,551
Federal Tax On Next $17,330 At 26 Percent		4,506
Gross Federal Tax		$18,057
Basic Personal Amount	($ 8,839)	
Eligible Dependant - Amy	(7,505)	
Caregiver - Marjorie	(3,933)	
EI Premiums	(729)	
CPP Contributions	(1,911)	
Canada Employment	(250)	
Transfer Of Tuition, Education And Textbook - Lesser Of:		
• $5,000		
• [$7,000 + (8)($400) + (8)($65) + (2)($120)		
+ (2)($20)] = $11,000	(5,000)	
Pension	(2,000)	
Medical Expenses (Note One)	(1,459)	
Credit Base	($31,626)	
Rate	15.25%	(4,823)
Charitable Donations [(15.25%)($200) +		
(29%)($175 + $375 + $50 - $200)]		(147)
Dividend Tax Credit [(18.9655%)($2,324)]		(441)
Net Federal Tax		$12,646
Provincial Tax (Given)		6,105
Income Tax Deducted ($19,408 + $3,511)		(22,919)
Instalments Paid (Given)		(2,528)
Balance Owing (Refund)		**($ 6,696)**

Note One Allowable medical expenses are as follows:

Eleanor And Minor Child (Amy) Medical Expenses	
($392 + $1,350 + $450 + $1,120)	$3,312
Threshold - Lesser Of: [(3%)($90,086)] And $1,884	(1,884)
Subtotal	$1,428
Marjorie's Medical Expenses - Lesser Of:	
• [($50 + $75) - (3%)($5,800)] = Nil	
• Absolute Limit = $10,000	Nil
Diane's Medical Expense - Lesser Of:	
• [$100 - (3%)($2,300)] = $31	
• Absolute Limit = $10,000	31
Allowable Medical Expenses	$1,459

Notes To Eleanor's Tax Return

• Diane transfers the $5,000 maximum education related credits to Eleanor and carries forward the remaining $6,000 [$7,000 + (8)($400) + (8)(65) + (2)($120) + (2)($20) - $5,000].

• Eleanor cannot claim the charitable donation made by Diane, but Diane can carry it forward for up to five years.

• Her daughter, Diane, should file a tax return to make her education related tax credits and charitable donation tax credit available for carry forward. If she does not file, she will not be eligible for the GST credit and she will not benefit from the RRSP deduction room created during the year.

• Her mother, Marjorie, should file a tax return in order to receive the GST credit.

• Eleanor is eligible for the caregiver tax credit for her mother as her income is well below the threshold.

• Since Diane and Marjorie are over 17 years of age, their medical expenses are reduced by 3 percent of their Net Income For Tax Purposes. This means that none of Marjorie's medical expenses can be claimed by Eleanor.

• Eleanor paid too much in instalments. It should be determined why this happened, to try and prevent overpaying instalments again.

• The child care costs for overnight camps are limited to $100 per week, but the Y Day Camp cost is not limited as it is not an overnight camp.

Part B

Eleanor 2006 Earned Income is calculated as follows:

Employment Income	$ 60,202	
Union Dues	(749)	$59,453
Rental Income (See Part A)		5,553
Earned Income		$65,006

The maximum deductible RRSP contribution that Eleanor can make for 2007 is calculated as follows:

The Lesser Of:
* $18,000
* [(18%)($65,006)] = $11,701 $11,701
Less Her 2006 PA   (7,829)

Maximum 2007 RRSP Deduction $ 3,872
Undeducted RRSP Contributions From 2006 ($4,285 - $2,621) (1,664)

Maximum Deductible RRSP Contribution For 2007 $ 2,208

Note that if Eleanor chooses to deduct CCA on her rental building and reduces her net rental income to nil, her maximum deductible RRSP contribution will be reduced by $1,000 [(18%)($5,553)].

Eleanor should contribute at least the maximum deductible contribution as early in 2007 as possible. She can overcontribute up to $2,000 without penalty. Since she is holding Bank of Montreal shares outside of her RRSP (her T5 shows dividends), if she does not have the funds available, she could consider transferring some of those shares into her RRSP. However, if there is a gain on the shares, she will create a tax liability for the capital gain. If there is a loss, it will be denied.

Solution to Self Study Case Fourteen - 1

This solution includes selected schedules and worksheets from the ProFile T1 return. Note that the program can only be used to calculate 2005 (not 2006) tax returns, and the problem and solution reflect this fact. The complete tax return is available on the Student CD-ROM (not the ProFile Tax Suite CD-ROM).

Under the heading "Textbook Support Files", is the option to view "Tax Return Files". Select this option and you will see two drop-down lists.

* To view the ProFile file, select the file "Self Study Case 14-1" from the ProFile drop-down list.

* To view the .PDF file, select the file "PDF Self Study Case 14-1" from the PDF drop-down list.

For more information on how to use your Student CD-ROM and the ProFile tax program, refer to the sample tax returns in this Study Guide.

Notes to tax return

* Her daughter, Diane, transfers the $5,000 maximum tuition and education credit to Eleanor and carries forward the remaining $5,400 [$7,000 + (2)($120) + (8)($400) - $5,000].

* Eleanor cannot claim the charitable donation made by Diane, but Diane can carry it forward for up to five years.

* Diane should file a tax return to make her education related tax credits and charitable donation tax credit available for carry forward. If she does not file, she will not be eligible for the GST credit and she will not benefit from the RRSP deduction room created during the year.

* Her mother, Marjorie, should file a tax return in order to receive the GST credit. However, she will need to obtain a Social Insurance Number to do so.

- Eleanor is eligible for the caregiver tax credit for her mother as her income is well below the threshold.

- Since Diane and Marjorie are over 17 years of age, their medical expenses are reduced by 3 percent of their Net Income For Tax Purposes. This means that none of Marjorie's medical expenses can be claimed by Eleanor.

- Eleanor paid too much in instalments. It should be determined why this happened, to try and prevent overpaying instalments again.

- The child care costs for overnight camps are limited to $100 per week, but the Y Day Camp cost is not limited as it is not an overnight camp.

- Since Eleanor is currently renting out her house, but plans to move back into it, no CCA is taken on the Class 1 building to preserve her principal residence status. Since the cost is equal to the UCC, no CCA has been taken on the building in the previous year. Her CCA on the appliances would not affect her principal residence election and should be taken. The payments on principal are not deductible. If she chose to take CCA on the building, the maximum potential CCA for the year would be $6,756 [(4%)($168,900)] since the first year one-half rule does not apply to the second year of rental. The maximum deductible CCA on the building would be limited to the net rental income after the CCA on the appliances of $5,553 ($5,887 - $334). This would reduce her Tax Payable for 2005, but she would no longer be eligible for the principal residence gain reduction on the property. In addition, the CCA would be recaptured on a subsequent sale if the proceeds were greater than the UCC.

Part B

The maximum deductible RRSP contribution that Eleanor can make for 2006 is calculated as $2,208 by the program on the form "RRSPLimit". To access the form, press <F4> and type "RRSPlimit" in the form box.

Note that if Eleanor chooses to deduct CCA on her rental building and reduces her net rental income to nil, her maximum deductible RRSP contribution will be reduced by $1,000 [(18%)($5,553)].

Eleanor should contribute at least the maximum deductible contribution as early in 2006 as possible. She can overcontribute up to $2,000 without penalty. Since she is holding Bank of Montreal shares outside of her RRSP (her T5 shows dividends), if she does not have the funds available, she could consider transferring some of those shares into her RRSP. However, if there is a gain on the shares, she will create a tax liability for the capital gain. If there is a loss, it will be denied.

Trubey, Eleanor Chap 14 Prob   SIN: 527 000 087
Summary

2005 Tax Summary

Total income		Eleanor Chap 14 Prob	
Employment *	101	60,202	
Old Age Security	113		
CPP/QPP benefits	114	4,823	
Other pensions	115	22,249	
Employment Insurance	119		
Taxable dividends	120	2,324	
Interest	121	820	
Limited partnership	122		
Rental	126	5,552	
Taxable capital gains	127	491	
Support payments	128		
RRSP	129		
Other	130		
Self-employment *	135		
Workers' compensation and social assistance	147		
Total income	**150**	**96,463**	

Net income			
RPP	207	2,406	
RRSP *	208	2,621	
Union and professional dues	212	749	
Child care expenses	214	600	
Disability supports deduction	215		
Business investment loss	217		
Moving expenses	219		
Support payments	220		
Carrying charges and interest	221		
CPP/QPP on self-employment	222		
Exploration and development	224		
Employment expenses	229		
Social benefits repayment	235		
Other deductions *	231		
Net income	**236**	**90,087**	

Taxable income			
Canadian Forces personnel	244		
Home relocation loan	248		
Security options deductions	249		
Other payments deduction	250		
Losses of other years *	251		
Capital gains deduction	254		
Northern residents deductions	255		
Additional deductions	256		
Taxable income	**260**	**90,087**	

2006 Estimated	Eleanor Chap 14 Prob	
GST/HST credit		
Child Tax Benefit	181	00
RRSP contribution limit	2,208	00

* More than one line is considered

Non-refundable tax credits		Eleanor Chap 14 Prob	
Basic personal amount	300	8,648	
Age amount	301		
Spouse / eligible dependant *	303	7,344	
Infirm dependants	306		
CPP/QPP	308	1,861	
Employment Insurance	312	761	
Adoption expenses	313		
Pension income amount	314	1,000	
Caregiver amount	315	3,848	
Disability amount	316		
Interest on student loans	319		
Tuition / education	323		
Transfers *	318	5,000	
Medical expenses	332	1,499	
Subtotal	335	29,961	
Credit at 15%	338	4,494	
Donations and gifts	349	146	
Non-refundable tax credits	**350**	**4,640**	

Total payable			
Federal tax	11	18,083	
Non-refundable tax credits	350	4,640	
Dividend tax credit	425	310	
Minimum tax carry-over/other *	426		
Basic federal tax	**13**	**13,133**	
Non resident surtax *	14		
Foreign tax credits / other			
Federal tax	**406**	**13,133**	
Political/investment tax credit *	410		
Labour-sponsored tax credit	414		
Alternative minimum tax			
Additional tax on RESP	418		
Net federal tax	**260**	**13,133**	
CPP contributions payable	421		
Social benefits repayment	422		
Provincial/territorial tax	428	6,104	
Total payable	**435**	**19,237**	

Total credits			
Income tax deducted *	437	22,919	
QC or YT abatement *	440		
CPP overpayment	448		
EI overpayment	450		
Medical expense supplement	452		
GST/HST rebate	457		
Instalments	476	2,528	
Provincial tax credits	479		
Other credits	454		
Total credits	**482**	**25,447**	

Balance owing (refund)	(6,209)
Combined balance (refund)	(6,209)

Complete Return Available On Student CD-ROM

Page 1 of 1

S - 213

Trubey, Eleanor Chap 14 Prob   SIN: 527 000 087

T1-2005   **Federal Tax**   **Schedule 1**

Complete this schedule to claim your federal non-refundable tax credits and to calculate your net federal tax.

You must attach a copy of this schedule to your return.

Enter your **taxable income** from line 260 of your return 90,086 82 **1**

Use the amount on line 1 to determine which **ONE**
of the following columns you have to complete.

If the amount on line 1 is:	$35,595 or less	more than $35,595 but not more than $71,190	more than $71,190 but not more than $115,739	more than $115,739
Enter the amount from line 1 above	**2**	**2**	90,086 82 **2**	**2**
Base amount	**3**	35,595 00 **3**	71,190 00 **3**	115,739 00 **3**
Line 2 minus line 3 (this amount cannot be negative)	0 00 **4**	**4**	18,896 82 **4**	**4**
Rate	x 15.00 % **5**	x 22.00 % **5**	x 26.00 % **5**	x 29.00 % **5**
Multiply the amount on line 4 by the rate on line 5	**6**	**6**	4,913 17 **6**	**6**
Tax on base amount	0 00 **7**	5,339 00 **7**	13,170 00 **7**	24,753 00 **7**
Add lines 6 and 7	**8**	**8**	18,083 17 **8**	**8**

Federal non-refundable tax credits

Basic personal amount	**claim $8,648**	**300**	8,648 00
Age amount (if you were born in 1940 or earlier)	**(maximum $3,979)**	**301**	

Spouse or common-law partner amount:

Base amount	8,079 00		
Minus: his or her net income (from page 1 of your return)	0 00		
Result: (if negative, enter "0")	**(maximum $7,344)** ▶	**303**	
Amount for an eligible dependant (**attach** Schedule 5)	**(maximum $7,344)**	**305**	7,344 00
Amount for infirm dependants age 18 or older (**attach** Schedule 5)		**306**	
CPP or QPP contributions:			
through employment from box 16 and box 17 on all T4 slips	**(maximum $1,861.20)**	**308**	1,861 00 •
on self-employment and other earnings (**attach** Schedule 8)		**310**	•
Employment Insurance premiums from box 18 on all T4 slips	**(maximum $760.50)**	**312**	760 50 •
Adoption expenses		**313**	
Pension income amount	**(maximum $1,000)**	**314**	1,000 00
Caregiver amount (**attach** Schedule 5)		**315**	3,848 00
Disability amount		**316**	
Disability amount transferred from a dependant		**318**	
Interest paid on your student loans		**319**	
Tuition and education amounts (**attach** Schedule 11)		**323**	
Tuition and education amounts transferred from a child		**324**	5,000 00
Amounts transferred from your spouse or common-law partner (**attach** Schedule 2)		**326**	

Medical expenses for **self, spouse or common-law partner, and your dependent children born in 1988 or later** (see the guide)	**330**	3,312 00	
Minus: $1,844 or 3% of line 236, whichever is **less**		1,844 00	
Subtotal (if negative, enter "0")		1,468 00 (A)	
Allowable amount of medical expenses for **other dependants** (see the calculation at line 331 in the guide and **attach** Schedule 5)	**331**	31 00 (B)	
Add lines (A) and (B).		1,499 00 ▶	**332**	1,499 00

Add lines 300 to 326, and 332.	**335**	29,960 50

Multiply the amount on line 335 by 15% =	**338**	4,494 08
Donations and gifts (**attach** Schedule 9)	**349**	146 00
Total federal non-refundable tax credits: Add lines 338 and 349.	**350**	4,640 08

continue

Page 1 of 2

Trubey, Eleanor Chap 14 Prob SIN: 527 000 087

Net federal tax

Enter the amount from line 8				18,083 17	9
Federal tax on split income (from line 4 of Form T1206)	424				• 10
	Add lines 9 and 10	18,083 17 ▶		18,083 17	11

Enter the amount from line 350		350	4,640 08		
Federal dividend tax credit (13.3333% of the amount on line 120 of your return)	425		309 89 •		
Overseas employment tax credit (**attach** Form T626)	426				
Minimum tax carry-over (**attach** Form T691)	427		•		
Add lines 350, 425, 426, and 427			4,949 97 ▶	4,949 97	12

Basic federal tax: Line 11 minus line 12 (if negative, enter "0") 429   13,133 20   **13**

Federal foreign tax credit:
Where you **only** have foreign non-business income, calculate your federal foreign tax credit below. Otherwise, use Form T2209, *Federal Foreign Tax Credits*, if you have foreign business income. **Enter on this line the amount you calculated**   **14**

Federal logging tax credit

Federal tax: Line 13 minus line 14 (if negative, enter "0") 406   13,133 20   **15**

Total federal political contributions (**attach** receipts)	409			
Federal political contribution tax credit (see the guide)	410		•	
Investment tax credit (**attach** Form T2038(IND))	412		•	
Labour-sponsored funds tax credit				
Net cost 413	Allowable credit 414		•	
Add lines 410, 412, and 414. 416		▶		16

Line 15 minus line 16 (if negative, enter "0")
(if you have an amount on line 424 above, see Form T1206) 417   13,133 20   **17**

Additional tax on RESP accumulated income payments (**attach** Form T1172) 418   **18**

Net federal tax: Add lines 17 and 18
Enter this amount on line 420 of your return. 420   13,133 20   **19**

Federal foreign tax credit: (see lines 431 and 433 in the guide)

Make a separate calculation for each foreign country. Enter on line 14 above the result from line (i) or line (ii), whichever is **less**.

Non-business income tax paid to a foreign country		431		• (i)

Net foreign non-business income *	433	310 94	X	Basic federal tax ***	13,443 09	=	46 40 (ii)
Net income **		90,086 82					

  *   Reduce this amount by any income from that foreign country for which you claimed a capital gains deduction, and by any income from that country that was, under a tax treaty, either exempt from tax in that country or deductible as exempt income in Canada (included on line 256). Also reduce this amount by the lesser of lines E and F on Form T626.
 **   Line 236 plus the amount on line 3 of Form T1206, minus the total of the amounts on lines 244, 248, 249, 250, 253, 254, and minus any amount included on line 256 for foreign income deductible as exempt income under a tax treaty, income deductible as net employment income from a prescribed international organization, or non-taxable tuition assistance from box 21 of the T4E slip. If the result is less than the amount on line 433, enter your   **Basic federal tax*** on line (ii).
***   Line 429 plus the amount on lines 425 and 426, and minus any refundable Québec abatement (line 440) and any federal refundable First Nations abatement (line 441 on the return for residents of Yukon).

Chapter Fourteen Learning Objectives

After completing Chapter 14, you should be able to:

1. Recall the specified deductions from Net Income For Tax Purposes in the calculation of Taxable Income (paragraphs 14-1 through 14-6).

2. Apply the provision for revoking the election to defer the employment income benefit associated with stock options (paragraphs 14-7 through 14-9).

3. Recall the general rules for the treatment of losses (paragraphs 14-10 through 14-25).

4. Explain the treatment of losses on personal use property (paragraph 14-26).

5. Apply the loss carry over provisions applicable to losses on listed personal property (paragraphs 14-27 through 14-30).

6. Apply the loss carry over provisions applicable to non-capital losses (paragraphs 14-31 through 14-33).

7. Apply the loss carry over provisions applicable to net capital losses (paragraphs 14-34 through 14-35).

8. Apply the rules for the conversion of a net capital loss carry over to a non-capital loss carry over (paragraphs 14-36 through 14-44).

9. Explain the special features associated with Allowable Business Investment Losses (paragraphs 14-45 through 14-54).

10. Apply the loss carry over provisions applicable to regular and restricted farm losses (paragraphs 14-55 through 14-58).

11. Apply the provisions of the lifetime capital gains deduction (paragraphs 14-59 through 14-88).

12. Demonstrate an understanding of the importance of ordering of deductions and losses in computing Net Income For Tax Purposes and Taxable Income (paragraphs 14-89 through 14-98).

13. Recall the basic calculations involved in determining Tax Payable (paragraphs 14-99 through 14-104).

14. Calculate the amount of federal Tax Payable on split income (paragraphs 14-105 through 14-113).

15. Apply the provisions for the transfer of dividends to a spouse or common-law partner (paragraph 14-114).

16. Calculate the charitable donations tax credit for donations of various types of property (paragraphs 14-115 through 14-145).

17. Calculate foreign business and non-business income tax credits (paragraphs 14-146 through 14-157).

18. Apply the provisions associated with the alternative minimum tax (paragraphs 14-158 through 14-171).

19. Complete a personal tax return using the ProFile T1 tax preparation software program (pages S-180 through S-192 in this Study Guide).

CHAPTER FIFTEEN

Web Site

As a reminder, the web site for this book can be found at:

www.pearsoned.ca/byrdchen/ctp2007/

Here you will find:

- Glossary Flashcards and Key Terms Self-Tests
- Updates and corrections to the textbook and Study Guide
- PowerPoint slides for Chapters 15 to 19
- Links to other relevant web sites
- A short on-line survey ($100 cash prize available)
- Instructions on how to install the 2006 ProFile program and download updated sample tax returns and Cases when the updated ProFile software is available in January, 2007
- A "Guide to Using Your Student CD-ROM"

How To Work Through Chapter Fifteen

We recommend the following approach in dealing with the material in this Chapter:

Computation Of Net Income For Corporations
☐ Read the text pages 593 and 594 (paragraph 15-1 through Figure 15-1).

☐ Complete Exercise Fifteen-1 on page 594 of the text. The solution is on page S-221 of this Study Guide. All solutions to Exercises and Self Study Problems can be found in this Study Guide and the page numbers all start with the prefix S-.

Deductions Available For Corporations In The Computation Of Taxable Income
☐ Read the text pages 595 and 596 (paragraph 15-5 through Figure 15-2).

☐ Complete Self Study Problem Fifteen-1 on page 646 of the text. The solution is on page S-227.

Dividends Received From Other Corporations
☐ Read the text page 596 (paragraph 15-10 through 15-12).

☐ Complete Exercise Fifteen-2 on page 597 of the text. The solution is on page S-221.

Dividends - Other Situations
☐ Read the text pages 597 and 598 (paragraph 15-13 through 15-23).

☐ Complete Exercise Fifteen-3 on page 598 of the text. The solution is on page S-221.

☐ Complete Self Study Problem Fifteen-2 on page 647 of the text. The solution is on page S-228.

Foreign Source Dividends Received
☐ Read the text pages 598 and 599 (paragraph 15-24).

Loss Carry Forwards And Acquisition Of Control

☐ Read the text pages 599 through 601 (paragraph 15-25 through 15-41).

☐ Complete Exercise Fifteen-4 on page 601 of the text. The solution is on pages S-221 and S-222.

☐ Read the text pages 601 through 603 (paragraph 15-42 through 15-53).

☐ Complete Exercise Fifteen-5 on page 603 of the text. The solution is on page S-222.

☐ Complete Self Study Problem Fifteen-3 on page 648 of the text. The solution is on pages S-228 through S-231.

Non-Capital Loss Carry Over For A Corporation

☐ Read the text pages 603 through 605 (paragraph 15-54 through 15-60).

☐ Complete Exercises Fifteen-6 and Fifteen-7 on page 605 of the text. The solutions are on page S-222.

Ordering Of Deductions

☐ Read the text page 606 (paragraph 15-61 through 15-66).

☐ Complete Self Study Problem Fifteen-4 on page 648 of the text. The solution is on pages S-231 and S-232.

Geographical Allocation Of Income

☐ Read the text pages 606 and 607 (paragraph 15-67 through 15-76).

☐ Complete Self Study Problem Fifteen-5 on page 649 of the text. The solution is on pages S-232 and S-233.

Federal Tax Payable For Corporations

☐ Read the text pages 607 through 609 (paragraph 15-77 through 15-87).

☐ Complete Exercise Fifteen-8 on page 609 of the text. The solution is on page S-223.

2006 Budget Proposals - Corporate Tax Rates

☐ Read the text page 609 (paragraph 15-88 and 15-89).

Provincial Tax Payable For Corporations

☐ Read the text pages 609 through 611 (paragraph 15-90 through 15-101).

Other Goals Of The Corporate Tax System

☐ Read the text pages 611 and 612 (paragraph 15-102 through 15-103).

Large Corporations Tax Phase Out

☐ Read the text page 612 (paragraph 15-104 through 15-106).

Introduction To The Small Business Deduction

☐ Read the text pages 612 through 616 (paragraph 15-107 through 15-131).

Associated Companies

☐ Read the text pages 616 through 620 (paragraph 15-132 through 15-147).

☐ Complete Exercise Fifteen-9 on page 620 of the text. The solution is on page S-223.

☐ Complete Self Study Problem Fifteen-6 on page 649 of the text. The solution is on page S-233.

Calculating The Small Business Deduction
☐ Read the text pages 620 through 622 (paragraph 15-148 through 15-158).

☐ Complete Exercise Fifteen-10 on page 622 of the text. The solution is on page S-223.

Elimination Of The Small Business Deduction For Large CCPCs
☐ Read the text pages 622 through 624 (paragraph 15-159 through 15-170).

☐ Complete Exercise Fifteen-11 on page 624 of the text. The solution is on page S-224.

Personal Services Corporations
☐ Read the text pages 624 and 625 (paragraph 15-171 through 15-176).

Professional Corporations And Management Companies
☐ Read the text pages 625 and 626 (paragraph 15-177 through 15-178).

Manufacturing And Processing Profits Deduction
☐ Read the text pages 626 through 628 (paragraph 15-179 through 15-193).

☐ Complete Exercise Fifteen-12 on page 628 of the text. The solution is on page S-224.

☐ Read the text pages 628 through 631 (paragraph 15-194 through 15-215).

☐ Complete Exercise Fifteen-13 on page 631 of the text. The solution is on page S-225.

☐ Complete Self Study Problem Fifteen-7 on page 650 of the text. The solution is on pages S-233 and S-234.

General Rate Reduction
☐ Read the text pages 632 and 633 (paragraph 15-216 through 15-224).

☐ Complete Exercise Fifteen-14 on page 633 of the text. The solution is on page S-225.

☐ Read the text pages 633 and 634 (paragraph 15-225 through 15-230).

☐ Complete Exercise Fifteen-15 on page 634 of the text. The solution is on pages S-225 and S-226.

☐ Complete Self Study Problems Fifteen-8, Fifteen-9, and Fifteen-10 on pages 650 through 652 of the text. The solutions are on pages S-234 through S-238.

Foreign Tax Credits For Corporations - Introduction
☐ Read the text page 634 (paragraph 15-231).

Foreign Non-Business (Property) Income Tax Credit
☐ Read the text page 635 (paragraph 15-232 through 15-237).

Foreign Business Income Tax Credit
☐ Read page 636 (paragraph 15-238 through 15-241).

☐ Complete Exercise Fifteen-16 on page 636 of the text. The solution is on page S-226.

Investment Tax Credits
☐ Read the text pages 636 through 639 (paragraph 15-242 through 15-261).

☐ Complete Exercise Fifteen-17 on page 639 of the text. The solution is on pages S-226 and S-227.

☐ Read the text page 640 (paragraph 15-262 through15-265).

Special Incentives For SR&ED Expenditures

☐ Read the text pages 640 through 643 (paragraph 15-266 through 15-289).

To Complete This Chapter

☐ Review the Key Terms Used In This Chapter on page 644 of the text. Consult the Glossary for the meaning of any key terms you do not know.

☐ Review the Glossary Flashcards and complete the Key Terms Self-Test for the Chapter. These features can be found in two places, on your Student CD-ROM under the heading "Key Term Practice" and on the web site.

☐ Review the Learning Objectives of the Chapter found on pages S-239 and S-240 of this Study Guide.

☐ As a review, we recommend that you view the PowerPoint Slides for Chapter Fifteen that are available on the web site. If you do not have access to the Microsoft PowerPoint program, the PowerPoint Viewer program can be installed from the Student CD-ROM.

Solution to Chapter Fifteen Exercises

Exercise Fifteen - 1 Solution

Item 1 You would add the accounting loss of $5,600 ($48,300 - $53,900). You would also add the recapture of CCA of $13,700 ($34,600 - $48,300), for a total addition of $19,300.

Item 2 As goodwill is not amortized for accounting purposes and there was no impairment during the year, no adjustment of the accounting figures is required. However, when the goodwill is added to the CEC balance, it would be subject to amortization at a rate of 7 percent per year. This means that you would subtract CEC amortization of $9,450 [($180,000)(3/4)(7%)].

Item 3 You would add the charitable donations of $15,000.

Item 4 You would deduct the premium amortization of $4,500.

Exercise Fifteen - 2 Solution

Net Income For Tax Purposes	$263,000
Dividends Received	(14,200)
Charitable Donations	(8,600)
Non-Capital Loss Carry Forward	(82,000)
Net Capital Loss Carry Forward*	(14,250)
Taxable Income	$143,950

*At the current year's inclusion rate, the potential deduction for the 1998 net capital loss is $18,000 [(1/2)($36,000)]. However, the actual deduction is limited to the current year's taxable capital gains of $14,250. The remaining net capital loss carry forward is $5,625 {[3/4][$36,000 - (2)($14,250)]}.

The political contributions are not deductible in determining Taxable income, but are eligible for a tax credit.

Exercise Fifteen - 3 Solution

As Loren has not held the shares for 365 days, this transaction would be subject to the stop loss rules. The deductible loss would be calculated as follows:

Proceeds Of Disposition [($21.15)(1,000)]	$21,150
Adjusted Cost Base [($25.30)(1,000)]	(25,300)
Total Loss	($ 4,150)
Disallowed Portion [($2.16)(1,000)]	2,160
Capital Loss	($ 1,990)
Inclusion Rate	1/2
Allowable Capital Loss	($ 995)

Exercise Fifteen - 4 Solution

No Acquisition Of Control   Taxable Income for 2005 would be nil, with a non-capital loss carry over of $135,000 ($57,000 - $192,000). Net Income For Tax Purposes for 2006 would be $289,000 ($42,000 + $247,000) and, if there was no acquisition of control, the total $135,000 non-capital loss carry forward could be deducted, resulting in a 2006 Taxable Income of $154,000 ($289,000 - $135,000).

Acquisition Of Control   The results for 2005 would be the same — a Taxable Income of nil, with a non-capital loss carry over of $135,000. However, if there was an acquisition of control on January 1, 2006, the non-capital loss carry forward could only be used to the extent of the pen business income of $42,000. This means that Taxable Income would be $247,000 ($289,000 - $42,000), with a non-capital loss carry forward of $93,000 ($135,000 - $42,000).

Exercise Fifteen - 5 Solution

It would clearly be desirable to elect to have a deemed disposition of the non-depreciable assets. This could be achieved by electing to have a deemed disposition of the non-depreciable assets for $650,000.   This would result in a $75,000 taxable capital gain [(1/2)($650,000 - $500,000)] on the deemed disposition. This will leave $35,000 ($110,000 - $75,000) of the net capital loss carry forward.

This $35,000 could be eliminated by electing to have a deemed disposition of the depreciable property at an elected value of $470,000. This election would produce the required taxable capital gain of $35,000 [(1/2)($470,000 - $400,000)].

The election would also produce recapture of $50,000 ($400,000 - $350,000). As this is $5,000 ($50,000 - $45,000) greater than the operating loss, this would result in Taxable Income and Tax Payable. However, the ability to use the remaining $35,000 net capital loss carry forward is probably worth the cost of the Tax Payable on the extra $5,000 of income.

Exercise Fifteen - 6 Solution

The non-capital loss balance at the end of the year would be calculated as follows:

Amount E	
ABIL	$ 5,250
Dividends Received	48,000
Business Loss	273,000
Net Capital Loss Carry Forward Deducted*	13,500
Total	$339,750
Amount F - ITA 3(c) Income	
[$48,000 + $27,200 + (1/2)($111,000 - $84,000)]	(88,700)
Non-Capital Loss At End Of Year	$251,050

*Limited to net taxable capital gains of $13,500 [(1/2)($111,000 - $84,000)]. There is a 1997 net capital loss carry forward of $8,250 [$28,500 - ($13,500)(3/4 ÷ 1/2)] at the end of the year.

Exercise Fifteen - 7 Solution

Hacker's Net Income For Tax Purposes for 2006 would be nil, the business and property income of $63,500, less the allowable business investment loss of $75,750 [(1/2)($151,500)].

The net capital loss carry over balance at the end of the year would be $7,650 [(1/2)($23,100 - $38,400)].

As only $63,500 of allowable business investment loss can be deducted against current income, the remainder would be a non-capital loss carry over of $12,250 ($75,750 - $63,500).

Exercise Fifteen - 8 Solution

The percentage of Taxable Income earned in each province would be calculated as follows:

	Gross Revenues		Wages And Salaries	
	Amount	Percent	Amount	Percent
Ontario	$1,303,000	44.6%	$ 52,000	31.5%
Manitoba	896,000	30.7%	94,000	57.0%
Not Related To A Province	724,000	24.7%	19,000	11.5%
Total	$2,923,000	100.0%	$165,000	100.0%

The average of the two percentages applicable for income not related to a province is 18.1%, leaving an average for income related to a province of 81.9%. Given this, federal Tax Payable can be calculated as follows:

Base Amount Of Part I Tax [(38%)($226,000)]	$85,880
Surtax [(4%)(28%)($226,000)]	2,531
Federal Tax Abatement [(10%)(81.9%)($226,000)]	(18,509)
General Rate Reduction [(7%)($226,000)]	(15,820)
Federal Tax Payable	$54,082

Exercise Fifteen - 9 Solution

Top And Middle   Top and Middle are associated under ITA 256(1)(a) as Top controls Middle.

Top And Bottom   Top and Bottom are associated under ITA 256(1)(b) as they are both controlled by the same person, Mr. Top. He controls Top directly. In addition, he controls Bottom through a combination of indirect ownership (Middle's 22 percent) and direct ownership {his own 5 percent, his minor son's 15 percent [deemed his by ITA 256(1.3)], and a further 10 percent through options [deemed his by ITA 256(1.4)]}.

Middle And Bottom   Middle and Bottom are associated under ITA 256(1)(b) as they are both controlled by the same person, Mr. Top. Mr. Top controls Middle indirectly through Top. He controls Bottom through a combination of direct and indirect control, as described in the discussion of Top and Bottom.

Exercise Fifteen - 10 Solution

As a CCPC throughout the year and with no associated companies, Kartoom is eligible for the full amount of the $300,000 annual business limit. Further, its active business income is greater than $300,000. However, the amount eligible for the small business deduction will be limited by the adjusted Taxable Income of $195,000. This amount is calculated as follows:

Net Income For Tax Purposes	$470,000
Dividends	(85,000)
Non-Capital Loss Carry Forward	(160,000)
Taxable Income	$225,000
10/3 Times Foreign Non-Business Tax Credit [(10/3)(15%)($60,000)]	(30,000)
Adjusted Taxable Income	$195,000

Exercise Fifteen - 11 Solution

The B component of the ITA 125(5.1) reduction formula is $2,925 [(.00225)($11,300,000 - $10,000,000)]. Given this, the required reduction would be calculated as follows:

$$[(\$300,000)(\$2,925 \div \$11,250)] = \underline{\$78,000}$$

This reduction leaves the annual business limit at $222,000 ($300,000 - $78,000).

The foreign non-business income tax credit is equal to $5,400 [(15%)($36,000)]. The small business deduction for Largely Small Inc. is equal to 16 percent of the least of:

• Active Business Income ($1,233,000 - $36,000)		$1,197,000
• Taxable Income ($1,233,000 - $914,000)	$319,000	
Less 10/3 Times Non-Business Income FTC		
Of $5,400	(18,000)	$ 301,000
• Reduced Annual Business Limit ($300,000 - $78,000)		$ 222,000

The small business deduction is equal to $35,520 [(16%)($222,000)].

Exercise Fifteen - 12 Solution

The small business deduction for Marion Manufacturing would be equal to 16 percent of the least of:

• Active Business Income		$311,000
• Taxable Income ($362,000 - $210,000)	$152,000	
Less 3 Times Business Income FTC Of $3,150	(9,450)	$142,550
• Annual Business Limit		$300,000

Based on this, the small business deduction would be $22,808 [(16%)($142,550)].

The M&P deduction would be equal to 7 percent of the lesser of:

• M&P Profits	$311,000	
Less Amount Eligible For Small Business Deduction	(142,550)	$168,450
• Taxable Income	$152,000	
Less:		
Amount Eligible For Small Business Deduction	(142,550)	
3 Times Business Income FTC Of $3,150	(9,450)	
Aggregate Investment Income	(30,000)	$ Nil

The M&P profits deduction would be equal to nil.

It would have been possible to increase the small business deduction to the annual maximum of $300,000 by increasing Taxable Income to $309,450. This could be done by deducting only $52,550 ($362,000 - $300,000 - $9,450) of the charitable donations. The remaining unclaimed donations of $157,450 ($210,000 - $52,550) could be carried forward for up to five years.

Although this increases Taxable Income and the total Tax Payable for the year, there could still be an ultimate tax savings with this approach, as the small business deduction cannot be carried over, while charitable donations can be. As the Exercise states that Marion expects large increases in income in the future, this approach could be advantageous.

Exercise Fifteen - 13 Solution

The components of the M&P formula would be as follows:

• Adjusted Active Business Income		$ 333,000
• Cost Of Capital:		
Owned Assets [(10%)($1,432,000)]	$143,200	
Leased Assets	26,000	$ 169,200
• Cost Of M&P Capital		
Total Capital	$169,200	
Non-Qualifying:		
Storing Finished Goods [(12%)($143,200)]	(17,184)	
Purchasing Operations [(10%)($143,200)]	(14,320)	
Employee Facilities [(10%)($143,200)]	(14,320)	$ 123,376
Fraction		100/85
Total		$ 145,148
• Cost Of Labour ($987,000 + $45,000)		$1,032,000
• Cost Of M&P Labour		
Cost Before Adjustment		$ 987,000
Fraction		100/75
Total		$1,316,000

As $1,316,000 is larger than the cost of labour figure, we will use the $1,032,000 cost of labour figure.

Using these numbers, the M&P formula provides the following M&P profits:

$$(\$333,000)\left(\frac{\$145,148 + \$1,032,000}{\$169,200 + \$1,032,000}\right) = \$326,332$$

Exercise Fifteen - 14 Solution

The federal Tax Payable for Marchand Inc. would be calculated as follows:

Base Amount Of Part I Tax [(38%)($320,000)]	$121,600
Corporate Surtax [(4%)(28%)($320,000)]	3,584
Federal Tax Abatement [(10%)($320,000)]	(32,000)
M&P Deduction [(7%)($180,000)]	(12,600)
General Rate Reduction [(7%)($320,000 - $180,000)]	(9,800)
Federal Tax Payable	$ 70,784

Exercise Fifteen - 15 Solution

The federal Tax Payable for Redux Ltd. would be calculated as follows:

Base Amount Of Part I Tax [(38%)($200,000)]	$76,000
Federal Surtax [(4%)(28%)($200,000)]	2,240
Federal Tax Abatement [(10%)($200,000)]	(20,000)
Small Business Deduction (Note One)	(16,800)
M&P Deduction (Note Two)	(2,800)
General Rate Reduction (Note Three)	(3,850)
Federal Tax Payable	$34,790

Note One The small business deduction would be equal to 16 percent of the least of active business income ($200,000), Taxable Income ($200,000), and the Company's business limit ($105,000). The deduction is $16,800 [(16%)($105,000)].

Note Two The M&P deduction would be equal to 7 percent of the lesser of $40,000 (M&P profits of $145,000, reduced by the $105,000 that is eligible for the small business deduction), and $95,000 (Taxable Income, reduced by the $105,000 that is eligible for the small business deduction). The M&P deduction would be $2,800 [(7%)($40,000)].

Note Three The general rate reduction would be calculated as follows:

Taxable Income		$200,000
Less:		
Amount Eligible For The SBD	($105,000)	
Amount Eligible For The M&P Deduction	(40,000)	(145,000)
Base For General Rate Reduction		$ 55,000
Rate		7%
ITA 123.4(2) General Rate Reduction		$ 3,850

Exercise Fifteen - 16 Solution

The Taxable Income figure would be $16,000 ($146,000 - $30,000 - $75,000 - $25,000). Based on this figure, the required calculation of Part I Tax Payable would be as follows:

Base Amount Of Part I Tax [(38%)($16,000)]	$6,080
Corporate Surtax [(4%)(28%)($16,000)]	179
Subtotal	$6,259
Federal Tax Abatement [(85%)(10%)($16,000)]	(1,360)
General Rate Reduction [(7%)($16,000)]	(1,120)
Foreign Business Income Tax Credit (See Note)	(1,129)
Part I Tax Payable	$2,650

Note The foreign business income tax credit would be the least of:

- The amount withheld $3,000

- $\left[\dfrac{\$20,000}{\$146,000 - \$30,000 - \$25,000} \right]$ [$6,259 − $1,120] $1,129

- $6,259 $6,259

The unused foreign tax amount of $1,871 ($3,000 - $1,129) can be carried back three years and forward for seven years.

Exercise Fifteen - 17 Solution

The total amount of investment tax credits available can be calculated as follows:

Qualified Property [(10%)($123,000)]		$ 12,300
SR&ED Current Expenditures [(35%)($1,200,000)]		420,000
SR&ED Capital Expenditures:		
1st $800,000 [(35%)($2,000,000 - $1,200,000)]	$280,000	
Remaining $700,000 [(20%)($1,500,000 - $800,000)]	140,000	420,000
Total Available Amount		$852,300

The refund available would be as follows:

Qualified Property [(40%)($12,300)]	$ 4,920
SR&ED Current Expenditures [(100%)($420,000)]	420,000
SR&ED Capital Expenditures [(40%)($420,000)]	168,000
Total Refund Available	$592,920

The non-refunded investment tax credit of $259,380 ($852,300 - $592,920) can be carried back three years and forward 20 years to be applied against Tax Payable.

The deductible R&D expenditures for the following year will be reduced by the refundable investment tax credit of $588,000 ($420,000 + $168,000) and the cost of the qualified property will be similarly reduced in the following year by $4,920.

Solution to Self Study Problem Fifteen - 1

1. The required adjustments would be:

   - Add: Amortization expense of $254,000.
   - Deduct: CCA of $223,000.

2. The required adjustment would be:

   - Deduct: Premium amortization of $2,000.

3. The maximum capital gains reserve, based on the receipt of one-half of the proceeds, is equal to $10,000 [(1/2)(1/2)($120,000 - $80,000)]. The required adjustments would be:

   - Deduct: Accounting gain of $67,000 ($120,000 - $53,000).
   - Add: Taxable capital gain, net of the maximum capital gains reserve, of $10,000 [(1/2)($120,000 - $80,000) - $10,000].

   There is no recapture on this disposition as the Company still owns Class 43 assets, and there is a positive balance in the class at the end of the year.

4. The required adjustments would be:

   - Add: Membership fees of $8,000.
   - Add: Non-deductible entertainment expenses of $6,000 [(50%)($12,000)].

5. The required adjustment would be:

   - Add: Charitable donations of $11,000.

6. The required adjustments would be:

   - Add: Accounting loss of $16,000 ($23,000 - $39,000).
   - Add: Recapture of $23,000 (Nil - $23,000).

Solution to Self Study Problem Fifteen - 2

The minimum Net Income For Tax Purposes and Taxable Income of Margo Ltd. would be calculated as follows:

Pre-Tax Accounting Income		$ 31,940
Additions:		
Inventory Reserve	$15,000	
Property Taxes On Vacant Land	1,200	
Depreciation Expense	35,600	
Write-Down Of Goodwill (Impairment Loss)	1,700	
Charitable Donations	19,800	
Taxable Capital Gain [(1/2)($30,500 - $21,000)]	4,750	
Warranty Provision	5,500	
Social Club Membership Fees	7,210	
Interest On Late Income Tax Instalments	1,020	
Foreign Taxes Withheld	270	
Premium On Share Redemption	480	92,530
Deductions:		
CCA	($78,000)	
Amortization Of Cumulative		
Eligible Capital (Note)	(1,785)	
Accounting Gain On Sale Of Investments	(9,500)	(89,285)
Net Income For Tax Purposes		$ 35,185
Deductions:		
Charitable Donations	($19,800)	
Dividends	(3,000)	(22,800)
Taxable Income		$ 12,385

Note   The cumulative eligible capital account has an addition of $25,500 [(3/4)($34,000)] for the goodwill acquired.   Amortization for the year is $1,785 [(7%)($25,500)].

Solution to Self Study Problem Fifteen - 3

Deemed Year End   As a result of the acquisition of control, LF will have a deemed taxation year end on April 30, 2006. This results in a short January 1, 2006 through April 30, 2006 taxation year for LF. The effects of this include:

- An additional year will be counted towards the expiry of the non-capital losses.
- If CCA is to be taken, it will have to be calculated for a portion of the year.
- Any net capital loss balance that can't be used will expire.
- All of the usual year end procedures (timing of bonuses, inclusion of reserves, etc.) will have to be carried out.

For the first year after the acquisition of control, LF can choose a new fiscal year end, on any date up to 53 weeks after the deemed year end.

Non-Capital Loss Balance   The non-capital loss balance at April 30, 2006 is calculated as follows:

2004 And 2005 Non-Capital Losses ($180,000 + $140,000)		$320,000
Short Fiscal Period Loss:		
Operating Loss To April 30, 2006	$55,000	
Class 43 - Excess Of UCC Over FMV		
[Required Write-Down To FMV Under ITA 111(5.1)]	90,000	145,000
Non-Capital Loss Balance		$465,000

If the non-capital loss cannot be used in the year ending April 30, 2006, it will be carried forward and can be deducted against income earned in the same or a similar line of business in future years. However, if there is doubt about LF's ability to use the non-capital loss carry forward balance before it expires, an election can be made to have one or more deemed dispositions [ITA 111(4)(e)] in order to trigger capital gains or recapture, either of which can be used to absorb the non-capital loss.

Net Capital Loss Balance   If the net capital loss balance of $75,000 cannot be used in the year ending April 30, 2006, it will expire on the acquisition of control. However, as noted in the preceding paragraph, LF can make an election to have one or more deemed dispositions in order to trigger taxable capital gains against which the net capital loss balance can be applied.

Possible Elections   Assets with potential capital gains or recapture are as follows:

Asset	Cost	UCC	FMV
Land	$450,000	N/A	$925,000
Class 3	675,000	$515,000	650,000
Class 8	25,000	10,000	15,000

Asset	Maximum Recapture	Maximum Capital Gain
Land	N/A	$475,000
Class 3	$135,000	Nil
Class 8	5,000	Nil
Total Income	$140,000	$475,000

Note that when the fair market value of the asset exceeds its adjusted cost base, the election can be made at any value between these two values. This means that, in the case of LF's Land, all or part of the accrued capital gain can be recognized.

If the election is made on the Land, its adjusted cost base will be increased to the elected value. If the election is made on the depreciable assets, their UCC will be increased to the elected value. However, for purposes of determining future recapture or capital gains, the cost of the depreciable assets will be unchanged. The difference between their original cost to LF and their new UCC is deemed to have been claimed as CCA.

Recommendation - Uncertainty As To Future Income   At a minimum, elections should be made to ensure use of the net capital loss carry forward, as it will not survive the acquisition of control. Further, if there is uncertainty with respect to the ability of OLC and LF to generate income in the same or similar line of business, in amounts sufficient to absorb the non-capital loss carry forward, additional elections should be made to absorb as much of this balance as possible. This would require elections on all of the assets listed in the preceding table. The resulting Taxable Income would be calculated as follows:

Land - Taxable Capital Gain [(1/2)($475,000)]	$237,500
Class 3 - Recaptured CCA	135,000
Class 8 - Recaptured CCA	5,000
Total Income From ITA 111(4)(e) Elections	$377,500
Short Fiscal Period Loss	(145,000)
Net Income For Tax Purposes	$232,500
Net Capital Loss Carry Forward (All)	(75,000)
Subtotal	$157,500
Non-Capital Loss Carry Forward (Maximum Needed)	(157,500)
Taxable Income	Nil

This leaves a non-capital loss carry forward of $162,500 ($320,000 - $157,500).

Recommendation - Expected Future Income   If the Companies believe that they will be able to generate sufficient income to use the non-capital loss carry forward in future periods, they will not want to make elections that will result in maximum pre-acquisition income. If the elections are made, the losses will increase the adjusted cost base or UCC balance of the assets the elections are made on. In the case of the Land, the increased cost will not be of benefit until the land is sold. In the case of the depreciable assets, the increased UCC will only be deductible at the applicable rates of 5 or 20 percent. Alternatively, a non-capital loss carry forward can be deducted in full, as soon as the Companies have sufficient income to absorb it.

In certain circumstances, companies can effectively use a net capital loss balance even when non-capital losses have reduced Net Income For Tax Purposes to nil. More specifically, if an enterprise has net taxable capital gains for the year, they are permitted to deduct a net capital loss carry over from a nil Net Income For Tax Purposes, with the amount of the deduction being added to the non-capital loss balance.

In the case at hand, it would be necessary to elect a value of $600,000 on the Land in order to trigger the required taxable capital gain of $75,000 [(1/2)($600,000 - $450,000)]. The results would be as follows:

ITA 3(a)	Nil
ITA 3(b) Net Taxable Capital Gains	$ 75,000
ITA 3(c)	$ 75,000
ITA 3(d) Non-Capital Losses	(145,000)
Net Income For Tax Purposes	Nil
Net Capital Loss Carry Forward	($ 75,000)
Taxable Income	Nil

This would leave a non-capital loss carry forward from the short fiscal period of $145,000, calculated as follows:

Non-Capital Loss For The Short Fiscal Period	$145,000
Net Capital Loss Deducted	75,000
Subtotal	$220,000
Income Under ITA 3(c)	(75,000)
Non-Capital Loss Available For Carry Over	$145,000

The total non-capital loss carry forward of $465,000 is made up of the $320,000 carry forward from 2004 and 2005, plus the preceding short fiscal period loss of $145,000. There is no net capital loss carry forward.

Using LF's Losses   Without changing the structure of the two Companies, it may be possible to generate income for LF through transfer pricing between the Companies, or by selling some of OLC's profitable assets to LF.   Alternatively, to directly apply LF's losses against OLC's profits, it will be necessary to have a wind-up, amalgamation, or other form of corporate reorganization (See Chapter 19).

Solution to Self Study Problem Fifteen - 4

Net Income For Tax Purposes And Taxable Income Before Carry Overs   The income calculations for the four years, before any consideration of loss carry overs, would be as follows:

	2003	2004	2005	2006
Business Income (Loss)	$ 95,000	($205,000)	$ 69,500	$ 90,000
Taxable Capital Gains	Nil	Nil	4,500	5,000
Dividends	12,000	42,000	28,000	32,000
Net Income (Loss) For Tax Purposes*	$107,000	($163,000)	$102,000	$127,000
Dividends	(12,000)	(42,000)	(28,000)	(32,000)
Charitable Donations	(21,400)	Nil	(8,000)	(22,000)
Taxable Income (Loss) Before Carry Overs*	$ 73,600	($205,000)	$ 66,000	$ 73,000

*There is, of course, no concept of a negative Net Income For Tax Purposes or Taxable Income. However, showing the 2004 loss amount as negative is useful in problems involving loss carry overs.

2003 Analysis   The Taxable Income as reported in the 2003 tax return would be $73,600, as in the preceding schedule. There would be a carry forward at the end of the year as follows:

- 2003 Net Capital Loss [($10,000)(1/2)] $5,000

2004 Analysis   For 2004, Net Income For Tax Purposes and Taxable Income are nil. This would leave a non-capital loss carry over of $205,000, a portion of which could be carried back to 2003. This would result in the following amended 2003 Taxable Income:

2003 Taxable Income As Reported In 2003	$73,600
Non-Capital Loss Carry Back From 2004	(73,600)
Amended 2003 Taxable Income	$ Nil

This would leave the following carry over balances at the end of 2004:

- Charitable Donations $ 4,600
- Non-Capital Loss ($205,000 - $73,600) $131,400
- 2003 Net Capital Loss [($10,000)(1/2)] $5,000
  2004 Net Capital Loss [($14,000)(1/2)]   7,000 $ 12,000

2005 Analysis   As shown in the preceding schedule, 2005 Taxable Income before the application of carry overs was $66,000. The various balances carried forward from 2004 could be used in any order that Linden chooses. The following calculation uses the losses in inverse order to their time limits. As charitable donations expire after five years, we have deducted those first. This is followed by non-capital losses, which expire after ten or 20 years. As shown in the following calculation, this leaves no room for the deduction of net capital loss carry overs:

Taxable Income Before Carry Overs	$66,000
Carry Forward Of Charitable Donations	(4,600)
Carry Forward Of 2004 Non-Capital Loss	
(Maximum To Reduce 2005 Taxable Income To Nil)	(61,400)
Taxable Income	$ Nil

The order that we have used in deducting losses will generally be preferable, as long as the taxpayer anticipates future taxable capital gains. Note, however, that while net capital loss carry overs have an unlimited life, they can only be deducted against taxable capital gains. If Linden does not anticipate future taxable capital gains, they would probably deduct the maximum $4,500 of net capital losses, and make a corresponding reduction in the non-capital loss deduction.

After the preceding allocation of losses, the following balances remain:

• Charitable Donations ($4,600 - $4,600)		Nil
• Non-Capital Loss ($131,400 - $61,400)		$70,000
• 2003 Net Capital Loss [($10,000)(1/2)]	$5,000	
2004 Net Capital Loss [($14,000)(1/2)]	7,000	$ 12,000

2006 Analysis Using the same ordering of losses as in 2005, the 2006 Taxable Income would be as follows:

Taxable Income Before Carry Overs	$73,000
Remaining 2004 Non-Capital Loss Carry Over	(70,000)
Balance Available	$ 3,000
Carry Forward Of 2003 Net Capital Loss	
(Maximum To Reduce 2006 Taxable Income To Nil)	(3,000)
Taxable Income	$ Nil

The amount of the net capital loss carry forward used in this period is limited to the balance of income available after deducting the 2004 non-capital loss carryover. Note, however, if 2006 taxable capital gains had been less than $3,000, they would have been the limiting factor for deduction of the net capital loss carry over.

At the end of 2006, the only remaining carry forward is the balance of the net capital loss:

• 2003 Net Capital Loss [($10,000 - $6,000)(1/2)]	$2,000	
• 2004 Net Capital Loss [($14,000)(1/2)]	7,000	$ 9,000

Solution to Self Study Problem Fifteen - 5

From the descriptions in the problem, it would appear that each of the provincial warehouses of the Sundean Company would qualify as a permanent establishment. As a consequence, the allocation to each of the five provinces would be based on the following calculations:

Province	Gross Revenues		Salaries And Wages	
	Amount	Percent	Amount	Percent
Alberta	$ 1,886,940	18%	$ 261,870	21%
British Columbia	2,306,260	22%	274,340	22%
Nova Scotia	1,362,790	13%	174,580	14%
Saskatchewan	1,257,960	12%	99,760	8%
Ontario	3,669,050	35%	436,450	35%
Total	$10,483,000	100%	$1,247,000	100%

The province by province average of the two percentages calculated above, and the allocation of the total Taxable Income of $1,546,000 would be as follows:

Province	Revenues	Wages	Average	Taxable Income
Alberta	18%	21%	19.5%	$ 301,470
British Columbia	22%	22%	22.0%	340,120
Nova Scotia	13%	14%	13.5%	208,710
Saskatchewan	12%	8%	10.0%	154,600
Ontario	35%	35%	35.0%	541,100
Total	100%	100%	100.0%	$1,546,000

Solution to Self Study Problem Fifteen - 6

Part A   By virtue of ITA 256(1)(b), John Fleming and Eric Flame are related by the fact that they are married to persons who are connected by a blood relationship (their wives). Further, under ITA 256(1.5), a person who holds shares in two or more corporations shall be, as a shareholder of one of the corporations, deemed to be related to himself as a shareholder of the other corporation(s). Therefore, Fleming Ltd. and Lartch Inc. are associated under ITA 256(1)(d), as John Fleming controls Fleming Ltd., is a member of a related group (John Fleming and Eric Flame) that controls Lartch Inc., and owns more than 25 percent of the voting shares of Lartch Inc. In a similar fashion, Flame Ltd. is associated with Lartch Inc. under ITA 256(1)(d), as Eric Flame controls Flame Ltd., is a member of a related group (John Fleming and Eric Flame) that controls Lartch Inc., and owns more than 25 percent of Lartch Inc. Fleming Ltd. and Flame Ltd. are associated under ITA 256(2), as they are both associated with a third corporation, Lartch Inc.

Part B   Mr. and Mrs. Cuso are a group with respect to both Male Ltd. and Female Inc. [ITA 256(1.2)(a) - two or more persons holding shares in the same corporation]. As a group, they control both Male Ltd. and Female Inc. Therefore, the two Companies are associated under ITA 256 (1)(b). The fact that Mr. and Mrs. Cuso are related is not relevant.

Part C   Ms. Jones and Miss Lange are a group that controls Alliance Ltd. However, they do not control Breaker Inc., as Mrs. Kelly (not a member of the group that controls Alliance Ltd.) owns 50 percent of the shares. Therefore, Alliance Ltd. and Breaker Inc. are not associated.

Part D   Mr. Martin and Mr. Oakley constitute a group [ITA 256(1.2)(a)] with respect to both Martin Inc. and Oakley Ltd. ITA 256(1.2)(b)(i) indicates that where one person in a group controls a corporation, the group is considered to control that corporation. As the group Mr. Martin and Mr. Oakley control both corporations, the two Companies are associated under ITA 256(1)(b).

Solution to Self Study Problem Fifteen - 7

Assuming the net rental income is considered property income, the components to be used in the calculation of the manufacturing and processing profits deduction for Mason Industries are as follows:

Adjusted Active Business Income ($1,556,000 - $106,000)	$1,450,000
Cost Of Labour	$1,940,000
Cost Of Manufacturing Labour	$1,270,000

Cost Of Capital:

Rent Paid [(75%)($375,000 - $50,000)]	$ 243,750
Depreciable Assets [(10%)($6,850,000)]	685,000
Total Cost Of Capital	$ 928,750

Cost Of Manufacturing Capital:

Rent [(55%)($375,000 - $50,000)]	$ 178,750
Depreciable Assets [(10%)($5,560,000)]	556,000
Total Cost Of Manufacturing Capital	$ 734,750

Given the preceding, the base for the manufacturing and processing profits deduction is calculated as follows:

$$[\$1,450,000]\left[\frac{(^{100}/_{75})(\$1,270,000) + (^{100}/_{85})(\$734,750)}{(\$1,940,000 + \$928,750)}\right]$$

$$= [\$1,450,000]\left[\frac{\$2,557,745}{\$2,868,750}\right]$$

$$= \underline{\$1,292,804}$$

The manufacturing and processing profits deduction rate is 7 percent. The federal Tax Payable for Mason Industries Ltd. would be calculated as follows:

Taxable Income As Given	$1,556,000

Base Amount Of Part I Tax [(38%)($1,556,000)]	$ 591,280
Surtax [(4%)(28%)($1,556,000)]	17,427
Federal Tax Abatement [(10%)($1,556,000)]	(155,600)
M&P Deduction [(7%)($1,292,804)]	(90,496)
General Rate Reduction [(7%)($1,556,000 - $1,292,804)]	(18,424)
Federal Tax Payable	$ 344,187

Solution to Self Study Problem Fifteen - 8

The Taxable Income and Tax Payable for the Serendipity Shop Corp. for the year would be calculated as follows:

Net Income For Tax Purposes		$240,000
Deductions:		
Dividends	($20,000)	
Donations	(48,000)	(68,000)
Taxable Income		$172,000

Base Amount Of Part I Tax [(38%)($172,000)]	$ 65,360
Federal Surtax [(4%)(28%)($172,000)]	1,926
Federal Tax Abatement [(10%)($172,000)]	(17,200)
Small Business Deduction (Note)	(21,600)
General Rate Reduction [(7%)($172,000 - $135,000)]	(2,590)
Part I Federal Tax Payable	$ 25,896

Note   The small business deduction is based on the least of the following:

Active business income	$220,000
Taxable Income	172,000
Allocated annual business limit	135,000

The small business deduction is equal to $21,600 [(16%)($135,000)].

Solution to Self Study Problem Fifteen - 9

Part A   The minimum Net Income For Tax Purposes for Borscan Inc. would be calculated as follows:

Accounting Income Before Taxes		$1,375,000
Additions:		
Amortization Expense	$255,000	
Taxable Capital Gain [(1/2)($525,000 - $500,000)]	12,500	
Recaptured CCA ($500,000 - $350,000)	150,000	
Political Contributions	1,500	
Interest And Penalties - Late Payment	500	
Charitable Donations	12,000	431,500
		$1,806,500
Deductions:		
Capital Cost Allowance	($287,000)	
Extraordinary Gain	(125,000)	
Amortization Of Cumulative Eligible Capital [(7%)($85,000)]	(5,950)	(417,950)
Net Income For Tax Purposes		$1,388,550

Part B   The minimum Taxable Income for Borscan Inc. would be calculated as follows:

Net Income For Tax Purposes	$1,388,550
Dividends Received	(25,000)
Charitable Donations	(12,000)
Net Capital Loss Carry Forward (Note)	(12,500)
Non-Capital Loss Carry Forward	(35,000)
Taxable Income	$1,304,050

Note   The net capital loss carry forward can be used only to the extent of the taxable capital gain for the year, resulting in a deduction of $12,500. This leaves a remaining net capital loss carry forward of $17,500 ($30,000 - $12,500).

Part C   The minimum federal Tax Payable for Borscan Inc. is as follows:

Base Amount Of Part I Tax [(38%)($1,304,350)]	$495,539
Surtax [(4%)(28%)($1,304,050)]	14,605
Federal Tax Abatement [(10%)($1,304,050)]	(130,405)
General Rate Reduction [(7%)($1,304,050)]	(91,284)
Political Contributions Credit (Maximum Allowable)	(650)
Federal Tax Payable	$287,805

Solution to Self Study Problem Fifteen - 10

Taxable Income   The Company's Taxable Income would be calculated as follows:

Accounting Income Before Taxes	$523,000
Accounting Gain On Sale Of Shares	(22,900)
Taxable Capital Gain [(1/2)($22,900)]	11,450
Donations To Registered Canadian Charity	18,700
Contributions To Registered Political Party	7,400
Net Income For Tax Purposes	$537,650
Donations To Registered Canadian Charity	(18,700)
Dividends From Taxable Canadian Corporations	(9,400)
Non-Capital Loss Carry Forward	(21,950)
Net Capital Loss Carry Forward*	(11,450)
Taxable Income	$476,150

*Lesser of $11,450 [(1/2)($22,900)] and $13,500 [(1/2)($27,000)].

Part I Tax Payable   The Company's Part I Tax Payable would be calculated as follows:

Base Amount Of Part I Tax [(38%)($476,150)]	$180,937
Surtax [(4%)(28%)($476,150)]	5,333
Federal Tax Abatement (Note One)	(42,854)
General Rate Reduction [(7%)($476,150 - $410,406)]	(4,602)
Subtotal	$138,814
Small Business Deduction (Note Two)	Nil
Foreign Non-Business Tax Credit (Note Three)	(4,845)
Foreign Business Tax Credit (Note Four)	(20,700)
M&P Deduction (Note Five)	(28,728)
Political Contributions Tax Credit (Maximum)	(650)
Part I Tax Payable	$ 83,891

Note One   No income would be allocated to Manitoba as there are no permanent establishments in that province. However, the Manitoba sales would be included in the Ontario total, as the Manitoba customers are serviced through that province. Based on this, the allocation would be as follows:

Gross Revenues	Amount	Percent
Ontario (Including Manitoba)	$5,725,000	91.0
New York	565,000	9.0
Total	$6,290,000	100.0

Salaries And Wages	Amount	Percent
Ontario	$3,540,000	89.0
New York	438,000	11.0
Total	$3,978,000	100.0

Average Ontario Percent [(91.0% + 89.0%) ÷ 2]	90.0%
Average New York Percent [(9.0% + 11.0%) ÷ 2]	10.0%
Total	100.0%

Based on the preceding calculations, the federal tax abatement would be $42,854

[(10%)(90%)($476,150)].

Note Two There is no small business deduction in the calculation of Part I tax, as Mercury Manufacturing Company is not Canadian controlled.

Note Three The foreign non-business tax credit would be the lesser of:

- The Amount Withheld $4,845

- $\left(\dfrac{\text{Foreign Non - Business Income}}{\text{Adjusted Net Income}}\right)$(Part I Tax Otherwise Payable)

$$= \left(\dfrac{\$32,300}{\$537,650 - \$11,450 - \$9,400}\right)(\$138,814)$$ $8,676

The lesser figure would be the actual withholding of $4,845.

Note Four The foreign business tax credit would be the least of:

- The Amount Withheld $ 20,700

- $\left(\dfrac{\text{Foreign Business Income}}{\text{Adjusted Net Income}}\right)$(Part I Tax Otherwise Payable)

$$= \left(\dfrac{\$64,200}{\$537,650 - \$11,450 - \$9,400}\right)(\$138,814 + \$42,854)$$ $ 22,568

- Tax Otherwise Payable, Less The Foreign Non-Business Tax Credit
  ($138,814 + $42,854 - $4,845) $176,823

The least of these three figures would be the U.S. taxes withheld of $20,700.

Note Five The M&P deduction would be equal to $28,728. This amount is 7 percent of $410,406, which is the lesser of:

- M & P Profits (See Following Calculation) $410,406

- Taxable Income $476,150
  Less 3 Times The Foreign Business
     Tax Credit [(3)($20,700)]   (62,100) $414,050

Technically, a second calculation of the foreign tax credit, made without regard to the general rate reduction is required here. However, the result would be unchanged as the credit is based on the actual withholding.

The components used in the M & P profits formula would be calculated as follows:

Adjusted Business Income

Net Income For Tax Purposes	$537,650
Taxable Capital Gains [(1/2)($22,900)]	(11,450)
Dividends From Taxable Canadian Corporations	(9,400)
Interest Income From Canadian Sources	(7,800)
Dividends From U.S. Corporations	(32,300)
Foreign Business Income	(64,200)
Income From An Active Business In Canada	$412,500

Cost Of Capital

Gross Cost Of Business Property In Canada	$2,680,000
Applicable Percent	10%
Cost Of Capital Owned	$ 268,000
Canadian Rental Costs	67,200
Total Cost Of Capital	$ 335,200

Cost Of M & P Capital

Gross Cost Of Business Property Used In M & P [(75%)($2,680,000)]	$2,010,000
Applicable Percent	10%
Cost Of Capital Used In M & P	$ 201,000
M & P Rental Costs	67,200
Total Cost Of M & P Capital	$ 268,200
Gross Up Factor	100/85
Cost Of M & P Capital	$ 315,529

Cost Of Labour

Canadian Salaries And Wages (Total Cost Of Labour)	$3,540,000

Cost Of M & P Labour

Canadian Salaries And Wages Used In M & P	$3,250,000
Gross Up Factor	100/75
Cost Of M & P Labour*	$4,333,333

*As this grossed up amount exceeds the actual total cost of Canadian labour, the actual total cost of labour of $3,540,000 will be used in the formula.

Application Of The M & P Formula

$$\begin{bmatrix} \text{Adjusted} \\ \text{Active} \\ \text{Business} \\ \text{Income} \end{bmatrix} \left[\dfrac{\left(\begin{array}{c} [^{100}\!/_{75}] \text{ of Canadian} \\ \text{M\&P Labour Costs} \end{array} \right) + \left(\begin{array}{c} [^{100}\!/_{85}] \text{ of Canadian} \\ \text{M\&P Capital Costs} \end{array} \right)}{\left(\begin{array}{c} \text{Total Canadian} \\ \text{Labour Costs} \end{array} \right) + \left(\begin{array}{c} \text{Total Canadian Active} \\ \text{Business Income Capital Costs} \end{array} \right)} \right]$$

$$= [\$412,500] \left[\frac{(\$3,540,000 + \$315,529)}{(\$3,540,000 + \$335,200)} \right]$$

$$= \underline{\$410,406}$$

Chapter Fifteen Learning Objectives

After completing Chapter 15, you should be able to:

1. Calculate a corporation's Net Income For Tax Purposes (paragraphs 15-1 through 15-3).

2. List the deductions that are available to corporations in calculating Taxable Income (paragraphs 15-4 through 15-9).

3. Apply the treatment for different types of dividends received (paragraphs 15-10 through 15-24).

4. Apply the provisions related to loss carry forwards when there has been an acquisition of control (paragraphs 15-25 through 15-28).

5. Apply the treatment of unrecognized losses at a deemed year end resulting from an acquisition of control (paragraphs 15-31 through 15-53).

6. Calculate the non-capital loss carry over for a corporation (paragraphs 15-54 through 15-60).

7. Apply the concepts relating to the ordering of deduction of loss carry overs (paragraphs 15-61 through 15-66).

8. Allocate corporate Taxable Income to specific provinces (paragraphs 15-67 through 15-76).

9. Calculate Part I federal Tax Payable for a corporation (paragraphs 15-77 through 15-89).

10. Demonstrate a basic understanding of provincial Tax Payable for a corporation (paragraphs 15-90 through 15-101).

11. Demonstrate an understanding of the non-revenue raising goals of the corporate tax system (paragraphs 15-102 and 15-103).

12. Be aware of the federal large corporations tax phase out (paragraphs 15-104 through 15-106).

13. Explain the rules for determining which corporations and what amounts of income are eligible for the small business deduction (paragraphs 15-107 through 15-131).

14. Apply the associated companies rules (paragraphs 15-132 through 15-147).

15. Calculate the amount of the small business deduction (paragraphs 15-148 through 15-158).

16. Calculate the reduction in the small business deduction that is applicable to large CCPCs (paragraphs 15-159 through 15-170).

17. Identify personal services corporations and demonstrate an understanding of their tax treatment (paragraphs 15-171 through 15-176).

18. Identify professional corporations and management companies and demonstrate an understanding of their tax treatment (paragraphs 15-177 and 15-178).

19. Identify the types of income eligible for the manufacturing and processing profits deduction and calculate the amount of the manufacturing and processing profits deduction using the ITR 5200 formula (paragraphs 15-179 through 15-215).

20. Calculate the general rate reduction that is available to all corporations and the specific application of the general rate reduction to CCPCs (paragraphs 15-216 through 15-230).

21. Calculate the foreign non-business (property) income tax credit for corporations (paragraphs 15-231 through 15-237).

22. Calculate the foreign business income tax credit for corporations (paragraphs 15-238 through 15-241).

23. Apply the general rules applicable to investment tax credits (paragraphs 15-242 through 15-253).

24. Apply the provisions related to refundable investment tax credits (paragraphs 15-254 through 15-259).

25. Apply the carry over rules for investment tax credits, as well as the influence of an acquisition of control on their availability (paragraphs 15-260 through 15-265).

26. Apply the provisions associated with the special incentives for scientific research and experimental development expenditures (paragraphs 15-266 through 15-289).

CHAPTER SIXTEEN

How To Work Through Chapter Sixteen

We recommend the following approach in dealing with the material in this Chapter:

AN IMPORTANT NOTE

An understanding of dividend gross up and tax credit procedures is essential to comprehending the material in this Chapter and Chapters 17, 18, and 19. If you do not fully understand these procedures, you should review Paragraphs 9-70 through 9-99 in Chapter 9 of this text.

Integration
☐ Read the text pages 663 through 666 (paragraph 16-1 through 16-21).

☐ Complete Exercises Sixteen-1 and Sixteen-2 on page 666 and 667 of the text. The solutions are on page S-258.

Shareholders' Equity Under GAAP
☐ Read the text page 667 (paragraph 16-22 through 16-24).

Paid Up Capital
☐ Read the text pages 667 and 668 (paragraph 16-25 through 16-28).

☐ Complete Exercise Sixteen-3 on page 668 of the text. The solution is on pages S-258 and S-259.

Tax Basis Retained Earnings - Introduction
☐ Read the text pages 668 and 669 (paragraph 16-29 through 16-32).

Pre-1972 Capital Surplus On Hand (CSOH)
☐ Read the text page 669 (paragraph 16-33 through 16-37).

Capital Dividend Account
☐ Read the text pages 669 through 671 (paragraph 16-38 through 16-45).

☐ Complete Exercise Sixteen-4 on page 671 of the text. The solution is on page S-259.

Distributions Of Corporate Surplus Through Cash, Stock And In Kind Dividends
☐ Read the text pages 672 through 674 (paragraph 16-46 though 16-59).

Capital Dividends
☐ Read the text page 674 (paragraph 16-60 through 16-64).

ITA 84(1) Deemed Dividends - Increase In PUC
☐ Read the text pages 674 and 675 (paragraph 16-65 through 16-70).

☐ Complete Exercise Sixteen-5 on page 675 of the text. The solution is on page S-259.

ITA 84(2) Deemed Dividends - On Winding-Up
☐ Read the text pages 675 through 677 (paragraph 16-71 through 16-75).

☐ Complete Exercise Sixteen-6 on page 677 of the text. The solution is on pages S-259 and S-260.

ITA 84(3) Deemed Dividends - Redemption, Acquisition, Or Cancellation
☐ Read the text pages 677 and 678 (paragraph 16-76 through 16-78).

☐ Complete Exercise Sixteen-7 on page 678 of the text. The solution is on page S-260.

ITA 84(4) And ITA 84(4.1) Deemed Dividends
☐ Read the text pages 678 and 679 (paragraph 16-79 through 16-84).

☐ Complete Exercise Sixteen-8 on page 679 of the text. The solution is on page S-260.

☐ Complete Self Study Problem Sixteen-1 on page 706 of the text. The solution is on pages S-263 and S-264.

Refundable Tax On Aggregate Investment Income
☐ Read the text pages 679 through 681 (paragraph 16-85 through 16-97).

Additional Refundable Tax (ART) On Investment Income
☐ Read the text page 682 (paragraph 16-98 through 16-101).

☐ Complete Exercise Sixteen-9 on page 682 of the text. The solution is on pages S-260 and S-261.

☐ Read the text pages 682 and 683 (paragraph 16-102 through 16-105).

Refundable Portion Of Part I Tax
☐ Read the text pages 683 through 688 (paragraph 16-106 through 16-124).

☐ Complete Exercise Sixteen-10 on page 688 of the text. The solution is on page S-261.

Refundable Part IV Tax On Dividends Received
☐ Read the text pages 688 through 693 (paragraph 16-125 through 16-154).

☐ Complete Exercise Sixteen-11 on page 693 of the text. The solution is on page S-261.

☐ Read the text page 693 (paragraph 16-155 and 16-156).

Refundable Dividend Tax On Hand (RDTOH)
☐ Read the text pages 693 through 698 (paragraph 16-157 through 16-184).

☐ Complete Exercises Sixteen-12 and Sixteen-13 on pages 698 and 699 of the text. The solutions are on page S-262.

☐ Complete Self Study Problems Sixteen-2 through Sixteen-6 on pages 706 through 711 of the text. The solutions are on pages S-264 through S-273.

Designation Of Eligible Dividends
☐ Read the text pages 699 and 700 (paragraph 16-185 through 16-198).

CCPCs And Their GRIP
☐ Read the text pages 701 and 702 (paragraph 16-199 through 16-206).

Non-CCPCs And Their LRIP
☐ Read the text pages 702 and 703 (paragraph 16-207 through 16-213).

Sample Corporate Tax Return

☐ Read the Sample Corporate Tax Return found on pages S-244 through S-257 of this Study Guide. The complete sample tax return is available on the Student CD-ROM included with the text in two formats, a T1 ProFile return file and a .PDF file. To view the files, access your Student CD-ROM (not the ProFile Tax Suite CD-ROM) and under the heading "Textbook Support Files", select the option "Tax Return Files".

To Complete This Chapter

☐ Review the Key Terms Used In This Chapter on page 704 of the text. Consult the Glossary for the meaning of any key terms you do not know.

☐ Review the Glossary Flashcards and complete the Key Terms Self-Test for the Chapter. These features can be found in two places, on your Student CD-ROM under the heading "Key Term Practice" and on the web site.

☐ Review the Learning Objectives of the Chapter found on pages S-274 and S-275 of this Study Guide.

☐ As a review, we recommend that you view the PowerPoint Slides for Chapter Sixteen that are available on the web site. If you do not have access to the Microsoft PowerPoint program, the PowerPoint Viewer program can be installed from the Student CD-ROM.

Sample Corporate Tax Return

The following simplified example contains Schedules 200 (the jacket), 1 and the tax summary from a T2 corporate income tax return, completed using the ProFile T2 corporate tax preparation program from Intuit Canada. As this sample is designed to illustrate the corporate tax return calculations, no GIFI (General Index of Financial Information) data has been included.

At the time the Profile software release (version 2005.5.1) included on the CD-ROM was completed, the software did not support fiscal periods ending after October 31, 2006. As a result, we have used a December 31, 2005 year end in this example.

When the updated Intuit ProFile software is available in January, 2007, instructions on how to install the updated software program will be available on the web site at:

www.pearsoned.ca/byrdchen/ctp2007

Sample Files On Student CD-ROM

The complete sample tax return is available on the Student CD-ROM included with this book in two versions, a T2 ProFile return file and a .PDF file.

Installation Of ProFile, InTRA and Adobe Reader

In order to view the ProFile return files, you must first install the ProFile program from the ProFile Tax Suite CD-ROM (not the Student CD-ROM) that accompanies this book.

If you also install the InTRA Library, you will be able to right-click from a form in a ProFile return and jump directly to the InTRA commentary related to that form. See the installation instructions for both of these programs at the back of the textbook.

In order to view the complete return, including schedules, as a .PDF file, you must have the Adobe Reader program installed on your computer. If you do not have access to the Adobe Reader program, it can be downloaded and installed for free from the Adobe website (http://www.adobe.com).

To View The Tax Return Files

Insert your Student CD-ROM (not the ProFile Tax Suite CD-ROM) and you should see a splash page that allows you to access the contents of the Student CD-ROM.

Under the heading "Textbook Support Files", is the option to view "Tax Return Files ". Select this option and you will see two drop-down lists. To view the ProFile file, select the file "Sample - Chapter 16" from the ProFile drop-down list. To view the .PDF file, select the file "PDF Sample - Chapter 16" from the PDF drop-down list.

How To Increase The Benefits From Viewing The ProFile Files

To get the maximum benefit from using the ProFile program, we strongly advise that you do the T2 tutorial "Getting Started" that is included with the program. If you have not previously used ProFile for personal (T1) returns, we suggest that you also do the T1 tutorial "Using the Form Explorer". The data in the following sample tax return problem can be used in the tutorial.

Two Quick Reference Cards (for ProFile and InTRA) are available on the ProFile Tax Suite CD-ROM in .PDF format.

When viewing the sample return file, we offer the following suggestions:

- Press <F1> on any ProFile form or field to display related information in the help system. In ProFile dialog boxes, click the [?] symbol in the top right corner, then click any element for help on that item. Right-click within a form to see available links to the InTRA Library (if InTRA has been installed).

- By pressing <F4> you will open the Form Explorer. In the categories of forms appearing in the shaded box on the left, if you choose "A. Used" near the bottom of the column, all the forms that have calculations for the return will be shown. You can then double click on the form itself to view it.

- Right clicking on a number in a field shows a variety of options, including the form or schedule where the amount originated from.

- Clicking on "Show Auditor" under the "Audit" list will display any warnings or potential errors.

Sample Problem Data

Metro Inc. is a Canadian controlled private corporation based in Saskatoon that manufactures furniture. Most of its income is earned from active business in Canada. The Company has no associated corporations. Its Business Number is 111111118 RC 0001.

During the taxation year ending December 31, 2005, the condensed before tax Income Statement of Metro Inc. was prepared in accordance with the requirements of the *CICA Handbook*. In condensed form it is as follows:

Metro Inc.
Condensed Income Statement
Year Ending December 31, 2005

Sales	$3,980,000	
Gain On Building Sale	160,000	$4,140,000
Amortization Expense	$ 607,000	
Other Expenses Excluding Taxes	1,773,000	2,380,000
Accounting Income Before Taxes		$1,760,000

Other Information:

1. The Gain On Building Sale resulted from the sale of a building for proceeds of $692,000. The building had an adjusted cost base of $664,000 and was acquired on August 28, 1986. The head office of the Company had been located in this building and the head office has subsequently moved to leased space. As the Company leases all of its other buildings and equipment, the building was the only asset in Class 3. The Undepreciated Capital Cost of this class prior to the disposition of the building was $514,000. The land on which the building is situated was leased. The purchaser has assumed Metro's responsibilities under the lease.

2. Amortization expense included in the accounting expenses amounts to $607,000. The opening UCC balance was $905,000 for Class 8, $800,000 for Class 10 and $2,100,000 for Class 43. The only fixed asset acquisition was $200,000 in Class 43 assets. There were no dispositions in Classes 8, 10 or 43.

3. Expenses include interest and penalties of $2,300 resulting from late installments and a failure to file the 2004 tax return within the prescribed time period.

4. Revenues include dividends of $36,000 from Canadian Tax Save Inc., a taxable Canadian corporation. Metro Inc. has no association with Canadian Tax Save Inc. and considers the dividends portfolio dividends.

5. Expenses include a deduction for charitable donations to the Cancer Research Society in the amount of $15,000.

6. The Company has available a non-capital loss carry over from the previous year of $56,000. The net capital loss carry forward from 2002 is $22,500 (1/2 of $45,000).

7. Information related to Canadian manufacturing and processing activities for the year is as follows:

Cost of capital [(10% of $6,000,000) + ($200,000 in rental costs)]	$ 800,000
Portion of capital used in M&P activities	500,000
Cost of labour	1,000,000
Portion of labour used in M&P activities	760,000

8. During 2005, the Company earned $97,000 of interest income on bonds purchased in 2004 that mature in 2009.

9. The beginning balance in the Company's Cumulative Eligible Capital account is $90,000. There were no acquisitions or dispositions that affected this account during the year.

10. The beginning balance in the Company's capital dividend account is nil.

11. The Company paid $100,000 in taxable dividends during the year. There was no balance in the Refundable Dividend Tax On Hand account at December 31, 2004, and there was no dividend refund for 2004.

12. All of the common shares of Metro Inc. are held by the president, Jack Brown (SIN 527-000-582).

13. The Company paid no income tax instalments for 2005.

Notes On Metro Inc. Sample Tax Return

GIFI Requirements

In order to eliminate the warning messages generated by ProFile related to the GIFI, without completing all the GIFI requirements, the following GIFI information was input:

- On GIFI Schedule 125 (Income Statement), the total sales were input as "Trade sales of goods and services" (Code 8000) and the Gain On Building Sale was input as "Realized gains / losses on disposal of assets" (Code 8210) from the drop down menu under Revenues. The Amortization Expense was input as "Amortization of tangible assets" (Code 8670) and the Other Expenses were input as "Other expenses" (Code 9270) from the drop down menu under Operating Expenses.

- On GIFI Schedule 100 (Balance Sheet), the Net Income figure was input as "Cash and deposits" (Code 1000) in order to make the total assets equal to the total liabilities and equity.

Although this will not properly complete the GIFI statements, this will give the correct Net Income figure that will carry forward to the Schedule 1 and eliminate the warning messages that would otherwise be generated. This will have no effect on the calculations in the tax return.

Capital Dividend Account

The balance in the Capital Dividend Account is $14,000 [(1/2)($692,000 - $664,000)]. A tax free capital dividend of $14,000 could have been paid if form T2054 had been filed.

General Rate Reduction

Metro Inc. is eligible for the general rate reduction for CCPCs.

Building Expropriation

The $160,000 extraordinary gain is deducted on Schedule 1 as the tax effects of the disposition are included in Net Income For Tax Purposes. As calculated on Schedule 6, the taxable capital gain on the building expropriation is $14,000 [(1/2)($692,000 - $664,000)].

As calculated on Schedule 8, the recapture of CCA on the building is equal to $150,000 ($664,000 - $514,000). This is shown as an addition on Schedule 1.

Loss Carry Forwards

The losses of prior taxation years deducted in the calculation of Taxable Income consist of the non-capital loss of $56,000 and a $14,000 net capital loss. As calculated on Schedule 4, the net capital loss carry forward deduction is limited by the $14,000 taxable capital gain for the year and leaves a net capital loss carry forward of $8,500 ($22,500 - $14,000). There is no non-capital loss carry forward remaining.

Active Business Income

As calculated on Schedule 7, income from active business carried on in Canada of $1,154,000 [$1,301,000 - $14,000 - ($36,000 + $97,000)] is Net Income For Tax Purposes less:

- taxable capital gains, and
- net property income (dividends received plus interest income)

This figure is used in the small business deduction calculation and in Schedule 27 for the M&P deduction.

Investment Income

In calculating the refundable portion of Part I tax, the investment income of $97,000 consists of $97,000 in interest income, plus the $14,000 taxable capital gain, less the $14,000 net capital loss carry forward claimed. This calculation is on Schedule 7.

M&P Labour

As the grossed up M&P Labour of $1,013,333 [(100/75)($760,000)] is greater than the $1,000,000 Cost of Labour, M&P Labour in the Schedule 27 calculation is limited to $1,000,000.

As mentioned in the text, although the effect of the federal 7 percent M&P deduction has been negated by the 7 percent general rate reduction, there are still provincial M&P tax reductions available. In this example, Metro Inc. is eligible for the Saskatchewan M&P tax reduction. (See Schedule 5.)

Printed Return

On the following pages you will find Metro's Schedule 200 (Jacket), Schedule 1 and Tax Summary. The complete return can be found on the Student CD-ROM.

Metro Inc. CRA Business # 111111118 Year-end: 2005-12-31
Summary

Tax Summary

Corporation name   Metro Inc.

Tax year ending 2005-12-31

Taxable income

Net income for tax purposes		1,301,000
Charitable donations and gifts	-	15,000
Taxable dividends	-	36,000
Losses of prior years	-	70,000
Other adjustments	±	
Taxable income	=	1,180,000

Part I tax

38% of taxable income		448,400
Surtax	+	13,216
Refundable tax on CCPC investment income	+	6,467
Active business income	1,154,000	
Small business deduction	-	48,000
Federal tax abatement	-	118,000
Manufacturing and processing deduction	-	50,276
Additional deduction - credit unions	-	
Foreign tax credits	-	
Resource deduction	-	
Political contribution tax credit	-	
Investment tax credit	-	
Other deductions and credits	-	4,534
Part I tax	=	247,273

Tax payable

Part I tax		247,273
Part I.3 tax (large corporations tax)	+	
Taxable dividends received	36,000	
Part IV tax	+	12,000
Other federal tax payable	+	
Subtotal	=	259,273
Provincial and territorial tax (except QC,ON,AB)	+	114,324
Provincial tax on large corporations (NB,NS)	+	
Tax payable	+	373,597
Tax instalments paid	-	
Investment tax credit refund	-	
Taxable dividends paid	100,000	
Dividend refund	-	33,333
Other refundable credits	-	
Balance owing (refund) on federal return	=	340,264
Provincial income tax (ON,AB,QC)		
Capital and other provincial taxes	+	
Tax instalments and credits	-	
Other provincial taxes	=	
Total balance owing (refund)		340,264

Provincial tax

Provincial tax	% Provincial allocation	Taxable income	Income tax	Capital and other provincial taxes	Tax instalments and credits	Net provincial tax
Newfoundland						
Prince Edward Island						
Nova Scotia						
New Brunswick						
Manitoba						
Saskatchewan	100.0000	1,180,000	114,324			114,324
British Columbia						
Yukon Territory						
Northwest Territories						
Nunavut						
Schedule 5 provincial tax payable			114,324			
Ontario						
Alberta						
Québec						
Totals			114,324			114,324

Loss continuity

Loss continuity	Current year carry back	Carryforward end of year
Capital		17,000
Non-capital		
Farm		
Restricted farm		
Limited partnership		
Listed personal property		

Other carryforwards

Capital dividend account	14,000
Refundable dividend tax on hand (net of dividend refund)	4,534
Unused Part 1.3 tax credit	
Unused surtax credits	13,216
Foreign business tax credits	
Donations and gifts	
Investment tax credits	
Ontario CMT losses	
Ontario CMT credit	

Complete Return Available On Student CD-ROM

| Canada Customs and Revenue Agency | Agence des douanes et du revenu du Canada | **T2 CORPORATION INCOME TAX RETURN** | **Schedule 200** |

This form serves as a federal, provincial, and territorial corporation income tax return, unless the corporation is located in Quebec, Ontario or Alberta. If the corporation is located in one of these provinces, you have to file a separate provincial corporate return.

Parts, sections, subsections, and paragraphs mentioned on this return refer to the *Income Tax Act*. This return may contain changes that had not yet become law at the time of printing. If you need more information about items on the return, see the corresponding items in the *T2 Corporation - Income Tax Guide* (T4012).

Send one completed copy of this return, including schedules and the *General Index of Financial Information* (GIFI), to your tax services office or tax centre. You have to file the return within six months after the end of the corporation's taxation year. For more information on when and how to file T2 returns, refer to the Guide under the heading "Before you start."

055 Do not use this area

Identification

Business number (BN)   **001** 11111 1118 RC 0001

Corporation's name
002 Metro Inc.

Has the corporation changed its name since the last time we were notified?   **003** ☐ Yes   ☒ No

If *Yes*, do you have a copy of the articles of amendment?   **004** ☐ Yes   ☐ No

Address of head office
Has the address changed since the last time we were notified?   **010** ☐ Yes   ☒ No
011 340 - 3rd Avenue North
012

City	Province, territory, or state
015 Saskatoon	**016** SK
Country (other than Canada)	Postal code/Zip code
017	**018** S7K 0A8

To which taxation year does this return apply?
From **060** 2005-01-01   to   **061** 2005-12-31

Has there been an acquisition of control to which subsection 249(4) applies since the previous taxation year?   **063** ☐ Yes   ☒ No

If *Yes*, give the date control was acquired   **065** _____

Is the corporation a professional corporation that is a member of a partnership?   **067** ☐ Yes   ☒ No

Mailing address (if different from head office address)
Has the address changed since the last time we were notified?
020 Yes ☐   No ☒
021 C/o
022 340 - 3rd Avenue North
023

City	Province, territory, or state
025 Saskatoon	**026** SK
Country (other than Canada)	Postal code/Zip code
027	**028** S7K 0A8

Is this the first year of filing after:
Incorporation?   **070** ☐ Yes   ☒ No
Amalgamation?   **071** ☐ Yes   ☒ No
If *Yes*, complete lines 030 to 038 and attach Schedule 24.

Has there been a wind-up of a subsidiary under section 88 during the current taxation year?
If *Yes*, complete and attach Schedule 24   **072** ☐ Yes   ☒ No

Location of books and records
Has the location of books and records changed since the last time we were notified?   **030** ☐ Yes   ☒ No
031 340 - 3rd Avenue North
032

City	Province, territory, or state
035 Saskatoon	**036** SK
Country (other than Canada)	Postal code/Zip code
037	**038** S7K 0A8

Is this the final taxation year before amalgamation?   **076** ☐ Yes   ☒ No

Is this the final return up to dissolution?   **078** ☐ Yes   ☒ No

Is the corporation a resident of Canada?   **080** ☒ Yes   ☐ No
If *No*, give the country of residence on line 081 and complete and attach Schedule 97.   **081** _____

040 Type of corporation at end of taxation year
1 ☒ Canadian controlled private corporation (CCPC)
2 ☐ Other private corporation
3 ☐ Public corporation
4 ☐ Corporation controlled by a public corporation
5 ☐ Other corporation (specify, below)

If the type of corporation changed during the taxation year, provide the effective date of the change   **043** _____

Is the non-resident corporation claiming an exemption under an income tax treaty?   **082** ☐ Yes   ☒ No
If *Yes*, complete and attach Schedule 91

If the corporation is exempt from tax under section 149, tick one of the following boxes:
085 1 ☐   Exempt under paragraph 149(1)(e) or (l)
2 ☐   Exempt under paragraph 149(1)(j)
3 ☐   Exempt under paragraph 149(1)(t)
4 ☐   Exempt under other paragraphs of section 149

			Do not use this area		
091	**092**	**093**	**094**	**095**	**096**

T2 E (05) GP23 - **RETAIN ON FILE. DO NOT SUBMIT TO THE CRA.**

Page 1 of 8

Metro Inc. CRA Business # 111111118 Year-end: 2005-12-31

Attachments

Financial statement information: Use GIFI schedules 100, 125, and 141. * We do not print these schedules.

Schedules - Answer the following questions. For each *Yes* response, attach to the T2 return the schedule that applies.

Question		Yes	Schedule
Is the corporation related to any other corporations?	150	☐	9
Does the corporation have any non-resident shareholders?	151	☐	19
Is the corporation an associated Canadian-controlled private corporation (CCPC)?	160	☐	23
Is the corporation an associated CCPC that is claiming the expenditure limit?	161	☐	49
Has the corporation had any transactions, including section 85 transfers, with its shareholders, officers, or employees, other than transactions in the ordinary course of business? Exclude non-arm's length transactions with non-residents	162	☐	11
If you answered *Yes* to the above question, and the transaction was between corporations not dealing at arm's length, were all or substantially all of the assets of the transferor disposed of to the transferee?	163	☐	44
Has the corporation paid any royalties, management fees, or other similar payments to residents of Canada?	164	☐	14
Is the corporation claiming a deduction for payments to a type of employee benefit plan?	165	☐	15
Is the corporation claiming a loss or deduction from a tax shelter acquired after August 31, 1989?	166	☐	T5004
Is the corporation a member of a partnership for which an identification number has been assigned?	167	☐	T5013
Did the corporation, a foreign affiliate controlled by the corporation, or any other corporation or trust that did not deal at arm's length with the corporation have a beneficial interest in a non-resident discretionary trust?	168	☐	22
Did the corporation have any foreign affiliates during the year?	169	☐	25
Has the corporation made any payments to non-residents of Canada under subsections 202(1) and/or 105(1) of the federal *Income Tax Regulations*?	170	☐	29
Has the corporation had any non-arm's length transactions with a non-resident?	171	☐	T106
Has the corporation made payments to, or received amounts from, a retirement compensation plan arrangement during the year?	172	☐	-----
For private corporations: Does the corporation have any shareholders who own 10% or more of the corporation's common and/or preferred shares?	173	☒	50
Is the net income/loss shown on financial statements different from the net income/loss for income tax purposes?	201	☒	1
Has the corporation made any charitable donations; gifts to Canada, a province, or a territory; or gifts of cultural or ecological property?	202	☒	2
Has the corporation received dividends or paid taxable dividends for purposes of the dividend refund	203	☒	3
Is the corporation claiming any type of losses?	204	☒	4
Is the corporation claiming a provincial or territorial tax credit or does it have a permanent establishment in more than one jurisdiction?	205	☒	5
Has the corporation realized any capital gains or incurred any capital losses during the taxation year?	206	☒	6
i) Is the corporation claiming the small business deduction and reporting income from: a) property (other than dividends deductible on line 320 of the T2 return, b) a partnership, c) a foreign business, or d) a personal services business; or ii) is the corporation claiming the refundable portion of Part I tax?	207	☒	7
Does the corporation have any property that is eligible for capital cost allowance?	208	☒	8
Does the corporation have any property that is eligible capital property?	210	☒	10
Does the corporation have any resource-related deductions?	212	☐	12
Is the corporation claiming reserves of any kind?	213	☐	13
Is the corporation claiming a patronage dividend deduction?	216	☐	16
Is the corporation a credit union claiming a deduction for allocations in proportion to borrowing or an additional deduction?	217	☐	17
is the corporation an investment corporation or a mutual fund corporation?	218	☐	18
Was the corporation carrying on business in Canada as a non-resident corporation?	220	☐	20
Is the corporation claiming any federal or provincial foreign tax credits, or logging tax credits?	221	☐	21
Is the corporation a non-resident-owned investment corporation claiming an allowable refund?	226	☐	26 *
Does the corporation have any Canadian manufacturing and processing profits?	227	☒	27
Is the corporation claiming an investment tax credit?	231	☐	31
Is the corporation claiming any scientific research and experimental development (SR&ED) expenditures?	232	☐	T661
Is the corporation subject to Part 1.3 tax?	233	☐	33/34/35
Is the corporation a member of a related group with one or more members subject to gross Part 1.3 tax?	236	☐	36
Is the corporation claiming a surtax credit?	237	☐	37
Is the corporation subject to gross Part VI tax on capital of financial institutions?	238	☐	38
Is the corporation claiming a Part I tax credit?	242	☐	42
Is the corporation subject to Part IV.1 tax on dividends received on taxable preferred shares or Part VI.1 tax on dividends paid?	243	☐	43
Is the corporation agreeing to a transfer of the liability for Part VI.1 tax?	244	☐	45
Is the corporation subject to Part II - Tobacco Manufacturers' surtax?	249	☐	46
For financial institutions: Is the corporation a member of a related group of financial institutions with one or more members subject to gross Part VI tax?	250	☐	39
Is the corporation claiming a Canadian film or video production tax credit refund?	253	☐	T1131
Is the corporation claiming a film or video production services tax credit refund?	254	☐	T1177
Is the corporation subject to Part XIII.1 tax?	255	☐	92 *

Attachments Continued from page 2

Attachments - Continued from page 2

		Yes	Schedule
Did the corporation have any foreign affiliates that are not controlled foreign affiliates?	256		T1134-A
Did the corporation have any controlled foreign affiliates?	258		T1134-B
Did the corporation own specified foreign property in the year with a cost amount over $100,000?	259		T1135
Did the corporation transfer or loan property to a non-resident trust?	260		T1141
Did the corporation receive a distribution from or was it indebted to a non-resident trust in the year?	261		T1142
Has the corporation entered into an agreement to allocate assistance for SR&ED carried out in Canada?	262		T1145
Has the corporation entered into an agreement to transfer qualified expenditures incurred in respect of SR&ED contracts?	263		T1146
Has the corporation entered into an agreement with other associated corporations for salary or wages of specified employees for SR&ED?	264		T1174

Additional information

Is the corporation inactive?	280	1 Yes ☐	2 No ☒
Has the major business activity changed since the last return was filed? (enter *Yes* for first time-filers)	281	1 Yes ☐	2 No ☒

What is the corporation's major business activity? **282** _____
(Only complete if *Yes* was entered at line 281)

If the major activity involves the resale of goods, indicate whether it is wholesale or retail **283** 1 Wholesale ☐ 2 Retail ☐

Specify the principal product(s) mined, manufactured, sold, constructed, or service provided, giving the approximate percentage of the total revenue that each product or service represents.

284 Furniture manufacturing		**285**	100.000 %
286 _____		**287**	%
288 _____		**289**	%

Did the corporation immigrate to Canada during the taxation year?	291	1 Yes ☐	2 No ☒
Did the corporation emigrate from Canada during the taxation year?	292	1 Yes ☐	2 No ☒

Taxable income

Net income or (loss) for income tax purposes from Schedule 1, financial statements, or GIFI		**300**	1,301,000	A
Deduct: Charitable donations from Schedule 2	**311**	15,000		
Gifts to Canada or a province, or a territory from Schedule 2	**312**			
Cultural gifts from Schedule 2	**313**			
Ecological gifts from Schedule 2	**314**			
Taxable dividends deductible under section 112 or 113, or subsection 138(6) from Schedule 3	**320**	36,000		
Part VI.1 tax deduction from Schedule 43 *	**325**			
Non-capital losses of preceding taxation years from Schedule 4	**331**	56,000		
Net capital losses of preceding taxation years from Schedule 4	**332**	14,000		
Restricted farm losses of preceding taxation years from Schedule 4	**333**			
Farm losses of preceding taxation years from Schedule 4	**334**			
Limited partnership losses of preceding taxation years from Schedule 4	**335**			
Taxable capital gains or taxable dividends allocated from a central credit union	**340**			
Prospector's and grubstaker's shares	**350**			
Subtotal		121,000	121,000	B
Subtotal (amount A minus amount B) (if negative, enter "0")			1,180,000	C
Add: Section 110.5 additions and/or subparagraph 115(1)(a)(vii) additions		**355**		D
Taxable income (amount C plus amount D)		**360**	1,180,000	
Income exempt under paragraph 149(1)(t)		**370**		
Taxable income for a corporation with exempt income under paragraph 149(1)(t) (line 360 minus line 370)				Z

* This amount is equal to 3 times the Part VI.1 tax payable at line 724 on page 8.

Metro Inc.   CRA Business # 111111118   Year-end: 2005-12-31

Small business deduction

Canadian-controlled private corporations (CCPCs) throughout the taxation year

Income from active business carried on in Canada from Schedule 7 — **400** 1,154,000 A

Taxable income from line 360 on page 3, **minus** 10/3 of the amount on line 632* on page 7, **minus** 3 times the amount on line 636** on page 7, and **minus** any amount that, because of federal law, is exempt from Part I tax — **405** 1,180,000 B

Calculation of the business limit:

For all CCPCs, calculate the amount at line 4 below

$225,000 x (Number of days in the taxation year in 2003 / Number of days in the taxation year 365) = 1

$250,000 x (Number of days in the taxation year in 2004 / Number of days in the taxation year 365) = 2

$300,000 x (Number of days in the taxation year after 2004 365 / Number of days in the taxation year 365) = 300,000 3

Add amounts at line 1, 2, and 3 — 300,000 4

Business limit (see notes 1 and 2 below) — **410** 300,000 C

Notes: 1. For CCPCs that are not associated, enter the amount from line 4 on line 410. However, if the corporation's taxation year is less than 51 weeks, prorate the amount from line 4 by the number of days in the taxation year divided by 365, and enter the result on line 410.

2. For associated CCPCs, use Schedule 23 to calculate the amount to be entered on line 410.

Business limit reduction:

Amount C 300,000 X **415** *** D / 11,250 = E

Reduced business limit (amount C minus amount E) (if negative, enter "0") — **425** 300,000 F

Small business deduction – 16% of whichever amount is the least: A, B, C, or F . — **430** 48,000 G

(enter amount G of line 9 on page 7)

Accelerated tax reduction

Canadian-controlled private corporations throughout the taxation year that claimed the small business deduction

Reduced business limit (amount from line 425) x = a

Net active business income (amount from line 400)* — b

Taxable income from line 360 on page 3 **minus** 3 times the amount at line 636** on page 7, and **minus** any amount that, because of federal law, is exempt from Part I tax — c

Deduct:

Aggregate investment income (amount from line 440 of page 6) — d

Amount c minus amount d (if negative, enter "0") ▶ e

Amount a, b, or e above, whichever is less — f

Amount Z from Part 9 of Schedule 27 x 100 / 7 = g

Amount QQ from Part 13 of Schedule 27 — h

Taxable resource income from line 435 on page 5 — i

Amount used to calculate the credit union deduction (amount e in Part 3 of Schedule 17) — j

Amount on line 400, 405, 410 or 425 of the small business deduction, whichever is less — k

Total of amounts g, h, i, j, and k ▶ l

Amount f minus amount l (if negative, enter "0") — m

Accelerated tax reduction - 7% of amount m — n

(enter amount n on line 637 of page 7)

* If the amount at line 450 of Schedule 7 is positive, members of partnerships need to use Schedule 70 to calculate net active business income.

** Calculate the amount of foreign business income tax credit deductible at line 636 without reference to the corporate tax reductions under section 123.4.

Metro Inc. CRA Business # 111111118   Year-end: 2005-12-31

Resource deduction

Taxable resource income [as defined in subsection 125.11(1)] **435** _____ H

Amount H _____ x Number of days in the taxation year in 2003 / Number of days in the taxation year _____ 365 x 1% = _____ I

Amount H _____ x Number of days in the taxation year in 2004 / Number of days in the taxation year _____ 365 x 2% = _____ J

Amount H _____ x Number of days in the taxation year in 2005 / Number of days in the taxation year 365 / 365 x 3% = _____ K

Amount H _____ x Number of days in the taxation year in 2006 / Number of days in the taxation year _____ 365 x 5% = _____ L

Amount H _____ x Number of days in the taxation year after 2006 / Number of days in the taxation year _____ 365 x 7% = _____ M

Resource deduction – total of amounts I, J, K, L , and M **438** _____ N

(enter amount N on line 10 of page 7)

General tax reduction for Canadian-controlled private corporations
Canadian-controlled private corporations throughout the taxation year

Taxable income from line 360 page 3 1,180,000 A

Amount Z from Part 9 of Schedule 27 50,276 x 100 / 7 = 718,229 B

Amount QQ from Part 13 of Schedule 27 _____ C

Taxable resource income from line 435 above _____ D

Amount used to calculate the credit union deduction (amount E in Part 3 of Schedule 17) _____ E

Amounts on lines 400, 405, 410, and 425 on page 4, whichever is less 300,000 F

Aggregate investment income from line 440 of page 6 97,000 G

Amount used to calculate the accelerated tax reduction (amount m of page 4)

Subtotal 1,115,229 ▶ 1,115,229 H

Amount A minus amount H (if negative, enter "0") 64,771 I

Amount I 64,771 x Number of days in the taxation year in 2003 / Number of days in the taxation year 365 x 5% = _____ J

Amount I 64,771 x Number of days in the taxation year after 2003 / Number of days in the taxation year 365 / 365 x 7% = 4,534 K

General tax reduction for Canadian-controlled private corporations - total of amounts J and K 4,534 L

(enter amount L on line 638 of page 7)

General tax reduction
Corporations other than a Canadian-controlled private corporation, an investment corporation, a mortgage investment corporation, or a mutual fund corporation

Taxable income from line 360 on page 3 _____ M

Amount Z from Part 9 of Schedule 27 _____ x 100 / 7 = _____ N

Amount QQ from Part 13 of Schedule 27 _____ O

Taxable resource income from line 435 above _____ P

Amount used to calculate the credit union deduction (amount E in Part 3 of Schedule 17) _____ Q

Total of amounts N, O, P, and Q ▶ _____ R

Amount M **minus** amount R (if negative, enter "0") _____ S

Amount S _____ x Number of days in the taxation year in 2003 / Number of days in the taxation year _____ x 5% = _____ T

Amount S _____ x Number of days in the taxation year after 2003 / Number of days in the taxation year _____ x 7% = _____ U

General tax reduction - total of amounts T and U _____ V

(enter amount V on line 639 of page 7)

Metro Inc.   CRA Business # 111111118   Year-end: 2005-12-31

Refundable portion of Part I tax

Canadian-controlled private corporations throughout the taxation year

Aggregate investment income	**440**	97,000	X 26 2/3 % =	25,867 A

(Amount P from Part 1 of Schedule 7)

Foreign non-business income tax credit from line 632 on page 7

Deduct:

Foreign investment income	**445**		X 9 1/3 % =	
(Amount O from Part 1 of Schedule 7)		(if negative, enter "0")	▶	B

Amount A **minus** amount B (if negative, enter "0") — 25,867 C

Taxable income from line 360 on page 3 — 1,180,000

Deduct:

Amount on line 400, 405, 410, or 425 on page 4,
whichever is the least — 300,000

Foreign non-business income tax credit
from line 632 of page 7 — x 25/9 =

Foreign business income tax credit from
line 636 of page 7 — x 3 =

	300,000 ▶	300,000	
		880,000 X 26 2/3% =	234,667 D

Part I tax payable minus investment tax credit refund
(line 700 minus line 780 on page 8) — 247,273

Deduct: Corporate surtax from line 600 of page 7 — 13,216

Net amount — 234,057 ▶ 234,057 E

Refundable portion of Part I tax – Amount C, D, or E, whichever is the least   **450**   25,867 F

Refundable dividend tax on hand

Refundable dividend tax on hand at the end of the preceding tax year	**460**	
Deduct: Dividend refund for the previous taxation year	**465**	
		▶ G

Add the total of:

Refundable portion of Part I tax from line 450 above	25,867
Total Part IV tax payable from line 360 on page 2 of Schedule 3	12,000

Net refundable dividend tax on hand transferred from a predecessor
corporation on amalgamation, or from a wound-up subsidiary
corporation   **480**

	37,867 ▶	37,867 H

Refundable dividend tax on hand at the end of the taxation year - Amount G **plus** amount H   **485**   37,867

Dividend refund

Private and subject corporations at the time taxable dividends were paid in the taxation year

Taxable dividends paid in the taxation year from line 460 on page 2 of
Schedule 3 — 100,000 X 1/3 — 33,333 I

Refundable dividend tax on hand at the end of the taxation year from line 485 above — 37,867 J

Dividend refund – Amount I or J, whichever is less (enter this amount on line 784 of page 8) — 33,333

Metro Inc.   CRA Business # 111111118   Year-end: 2005-12-31

Part I tax

Base amount of Part I tax - 38% of taxable income (line 360 or amount Z, whichever applies)
from page 3   **550**   448,400   A

Corporate surtax calculation

Base amount from line A above	448,400	1

Deduct:

10% of taxable income (line 360 or amount Z, whichever applies) from page 3	118,000	2
Investment corporation deduction from line 620 below		3
Federal logging tax credit from line 640 below		4
Federal qualifying environment trust tax credit from line 648 below		5

For a mutual fund corporation or an investment corporation throughout
the taxation year, enter amount a, b, or c below on line 6, whichever is
the least:

28% of taxable income from line 360 on page 3		a	
28% of taxed capital gains		b	6
Part I tax otherwise payable (line A **plus** line C and D **minus** line F)	227,590	c	

Total of lines 2 to 6	118,000	7
Net amount (line 1 minus line 7)	330,400	8

Corporate surtax - 4% of the amount on line 8   **600**   13,216   B

Recapture of investment tax credit from line PPP in Part 21 of Schedule 31   **602** _____   C

Calculation for the refundable tax on Canadian-controlled private corporation's (CCPC) investment income
(if it was a CCPC throughout the taxation year)

Aggregate investment income from line 440 on page 6		97,000	i
Taxable income from line 360 on page 3	1,180,000		

Deduct:

Amount on line 400, 405, 410, or 425 of page 4, whichever is the least	300,000		
Net amount	880,000 ▶	880,000	ii

Refundable tax on CCPC's investment income – 6 2/3% of whichever is less: amount i or ii   **604**   6,467   D

Subtotal (add lines A, B, C, and D)   468,083   E

Deduct:

Small business deduction from line 430 on page 4		48,000	9
Federal tax abatement	**608**	118,000	
Manufacturing and processing profits deduction from amount BB or amount RR of Schedule 27	**616**	50,276	
Investment corporation deduction	**620**		
(taxed capital gains **624** _____)			
Additional deduction – credit unions from Schedule 17	**628**		
Federal foreign non-business income tax credit from Schedule 21	**632**		
Federal foreign business income tax credit from Schedule 21	**636**		
Accelerated tax reduction from amount n of page 4	**637**		
Resource deduction from line 438 of page 5			10
General tax reduction for CCPCs from amount L on page 5	**638**	4,534	
General tax reduction from amount V on page 5	**639**		
Federal logging tax credit from Schedule 21	**640**		
Federal political contribution tax credit	**644**		
Federal political contributions **646** _____			
Federal qualifying environmental trust tax credit	**648**		
Investment tax credit from Schedule 31	**652**		
Apprenticeship Job Creation Tax Credit (Applicable for salaries and wages paid to qualifying apprentices on or after May 2, 2006)			

Subtotal	220,810 ▶	220,810 F

Part I tax payable – Line E **minus** line F (enter amount G on line 700 of page 8)   247,273   G

S - 255

Metro Inc.   CRA Business # 111111118   Year-end: 2005-12-31

Summary of tax and credits

Federal tax

Part I tax payable from page 7	**700**	247,273
Part I.3 tax payable from Schedule 33, 34, or 35	**704**	
Part II surtax tax payable from Schedule 46	**708**	
Part IV tax payable from Schedule 3	**712**	12,000
Part IV.1 tax payable from Schedule 43	**716**	
Part VI tax payable from Schedule 38	**720**	
Part VI.1 tax payable from Schedule 43	**724**	
Part XIII.1 tax payable from Schedule 92	**727**	
Part XIV tax payable from Schedule 20	**728**	
	Total federal tax	259,273

Add provincial and territorial tax:

Provincial or territorial jurisdiction **750** SK		
(if more than one jurisdiction, enter "multiple" and complete Schedule 5)		
Net provincial and territorial tax payable (except Quebec, Ontario and Alberta)	**760**	114,324
Provincial tax on large corporations (New Brunswick and Nova Scotia)	**765**	
	114,324 ▶	114,324
	Total tax payable **770**	373,597 A

Deduct other credits:

Investment tax credit refund from Schedule 31	**780**		
Dividend refund from page 6	**784**	33,333	
Federal capital gains refund from Schedule 18	**788**		
Federal qualifying environmental trust tax credit refund	**792**		
Canadian film or video production tax credit refund (Form T1131)	**796**		
Film or video production services tax credit refund (Form T1177)	**797**		
Tax withheld at source	**800**		
Total payments on which tax has been withheld **801**			
Allowable refund for non-resident-owned investment corporations - Schedule 26	**804**		
Provincial and territorial capital gains refund from Schedule 18	**808**		
Provincial and territorial refundable tax credits from Schedule 5	**812**		
Royalties deductible under Syncrude Remission Order **815**			
Tax remitted under Syncrude Remission Order	**816**		
Tax instalments paid	**840**		
Total credits **890**		33,333	33,333 B

Refund Code **894** ☐ Overpayment _____	Balance (line A minus line B)	340,264 I

Direct Deposit Request

To have the corporation's refund deposited directly into the corporation's bank account at a financial institution in Canada, or to change banking information you already gave us, complete the information below.

☐ Start   ☐ Change information   **910** _____
Branch number

914 _____   **918** _____
Institution number   Account number

If the result is negative, you have an **overpayment**.
If the result is positive, you have a **balance unpaid**.
Enter the amount on whichever line applies.
We do not charge or refund a difference of $2 or less.

Balance unpaid	340,264
Enclosed payment **898**	

If the corporation is a Canadian-controlled private corporation throughout the taxation year, does it qualify for the one-month extension of the date the balance is due?   **896** 1 Yes ☒   2 No ☐   NA ☐

Certification

950 Brown	**951** Jack	**954** President
Surname	First name	Position, office or rank
955 2006-07-12	**956** (306) 975-4580	
Date	Telephone number	

Is the contact person the same as the authorized signing officer? If *no*, complete the information below.   **957** 1 Yes ☒   2 No ☐

958 _____	**959** ( ) ____ - ____
Name	Telephone number

Language of correspondence - Langue de correspondance

990   Language of choice/Langue de choix   1 English / Anglais ☒   2 Français / French ☐

Metro Inc.   CRA Business # 111111118   Year-end: 2005-12-31

Canada Revenue Agency   **Agence du revenu du Canada**   **NET INCOME (LOSS) FOR INCOME TAX PURPOSES**   **Schedule 1**

• The purpose of this schedule is to provide a reconciliation between the corporation's net income (loss) as reported on the financial statements and its net income (loss) for tax purposes.

Net income (loss) after taxes and extraordinary items per financial statements			A	1,760,000
Add:				
Interest and penalties on taxes	103	2,300		
Amortization of tangible assets	104	607,000		
Recapture of capital cost allowance - Schedule 8	107	150,000		
Charitable donations - Schedule 2	112	15,000		
Taxable capital gains - Schedule 6	113	14,000		
Total of fields 101 to 199	500	788,300 ▶		788,300
Deduct:				
Gain on disposal of assets per financial statements	401	160,000		
Capital cost allowance - Schedule 8	403	1,081,000		
Cumulative eligible capital deduction - Schedule 10	405	6,300		
Total of fields 401 to 499	510	1,247,300 ▶		1,247,300
Net income (loss) for income tax purposes (enter on line 300 of the T2 return)				1,301,000

S - 257

Solution to Chapter Sixteen Exercises

Exercise Sixteen - 1 Solution

If she incorporates, the corporation will pay taxes of $19,000 [(19%)($100,000)], leaving $81,000 to be distributed as dividends. Her individual Tax Payable on these non-eligible dividends would be calculated as follows:

Dividends Received	$ 81,000
Gross Up [(25%)($81,000)]	20,250
Grossed Up Dividends	$101,250
Personal Tax Rate	45%
Tax Before Credit	$ 45,563
Dividend Tax Credit [(2/3 + 25%)($20,250)]	(18,563)
Tax Payable On Dividends	$ 27,000

The net after tax retention would be $54,000 ($81,000 - $27,000). This compares to $55,000 [($100,000)(1 - .45)] retained if a corporation is not used. The use of a corporation is undesirable because the province's low dividend tax credit rate more than offsets the province's favourable corporate tax rate.

Exercise Sixteen - 2 Solution

If he incorporates, the corporation will pay taxes of $34,000 [(34%)($100,000)], leaving $66,000 to be distributed as dividends. His individual Tax Payable on these eligible dividends would be calculated as follows:

Dividends Received	$66,000
Gross Up [(45%)($66,000)]	29,700
Grossed Up Dividends	$95,700
Personal Tax Rate	42%
Tax Before Credit	$40,194
Dividend Tax Credit [(11/18 + 40%)($29,700)]	(30,030)
Tax Payable On Dividends	$10,164

The net after tax retention would be $55,836 ($66,000 - $10,164). This compares to $58,000 [($100,000)(1 - .42)] retained if a corporation is not used. The use of a corporation is undesirable because the effect of the province's high corporate tax rate outweighs the favourable dividend tax credit rate.

Exercise Sixteen - 3 Solution

The adjusted cost base of the shares would be determined as follows:

	Number of Shares	Cost/Share	Total Cost
First Purchase	2,400	$1.10	$2,640
Second Purchase	3,850	$1.82	7,007
Totals	6,250		$9,647

The adjusted cost base for all of the investor's shares is $9,647. The adjusted cost base per share would be $1.54 ($9,647 ÷ 6,250).

The PUC for the investor's shares would be calculated as follows:

	Number of Shares	PUC/Share	Total PUC
First Sale	100,000	$1.10	$110,000
Second Sale	50,000	$1.35	67,500
Third Sale	30,000	$1.82	54,600
Total PUC Of Outstanding Shares	180,000		$232,100

Number Of Shares	6,250
PUC Per Share [$232,100 ÷ 180,000 Shares]	$ 1.29
PUC For Investor's Shares	$8,063

Exercise Sixteen - 4 Solution

The balance in the capital dividend account as at December 31, 2006 would be as follows:

1987 Capital Gain [(1/2)($123,000 - $98,000)]	$12,500
1996 Capital Gain [(1/4)($98,000 - $86,000)]	3,000
Capital Dividend Received - 2005	8,200
2006 Sale Of Goodwill [(3/4)($42,000 - $37,000)(2/3)]	2,500
Capital Dividend Paid - 2006	(16,000)
Balance - End Of 2006	$10,200

Exercise Sixteen - 5 Solution

This transaction will result in an ITA 84(1) deemed dividend for all shareholders, calculated as follows:

PUC Of New Shares [(40,000)($12.70)]	$508,000
Increase In Net Assets	(450,000)
ITA 84(1) Deemed Dividend	$ 58,000

This would be allocated to all 166,000 shares outstanding, on the basis of $0.35 per share. This would be a taxable dividend, subject to either the 45 percent or the 25 percent gross up and tax credit procedures. The $0.35 per share dividend would also be added to the adjusted cost base of all 166,000 shares.

With the addition of $0.35 resulting from the ITA 84(1) deemed dividend to the original issue price of $10.50, the adjusted cost base of these shares is now $10.85. Mr. Uni's sale of 5,000 shares at $13.42 per share would result in a taxable capital gain of $6,425 [(1/2)(5,000)($13.42 - $10.85)].

Exercise Sixteen - 6 Solution

The analysis of the $2,350,000 distribution would be as follows:

Cash Distributed	$2,350,000
PUC Of Shares	(250,000)
ITA 84(2) Deemed Dividend	$2,100,000
ITA 83(2) Capital Dividend	(340,000)
ITA 88(2)(b) Wind-Up Dividend	$1,760,000

The $1,760,000 wind-up dividend would be subject to either the 45 percent or the 25 percent gross up and dividend tax credit procedures.

Proceeds Of Disposition	$2,350,000
ITA 84(2) Deemed Dividend	(2,100,000)
ITA 54 Proceeds Of Disposition	$ 250,000
Adjusted Cost Base	(250,000)
Capital Gain	$ Nil

As shown by the preceding calculation, there would be no capital gain on the disposition.

Exercise Sixteen - 7 Solution

The redemption transaction would have no tax consequences for Ms. Tandy. The tax consequences to Jesuiah Tandy resulting from the redemption of his shares would be as follows:

Proceeds Of Redemption [(15,000)($11.75)]	$176,250
PUC [(15,000)($8.25)]	(123,750)
ITA 84(3) Deemed Dividend	$ 52,500
Proceeds Of Redemption [(15,000)($11.75)]	$176,250
ITA 84(3) Deemed Dividend	(52,500)
ITA 54 Proceeds Of Disposition	$123,750
Adjusted Cost Base [(15,000)($10.57)]	(158,550)
Capital Loss	($ 34,800)
Inclusion Rate	1/2
Allowable Capital Loss	($ 17,400)

The deemed dividend of $52,500 would be subject to either the 45 percent or the 25 percent gross up and tax credit procedures. The allowable capital loss can be used in the current year, only to the extent of taxable capital gains realized in the current year.

Exercise Sixteen - 8 Solution

To the extent of the $225,000 PUC reduction, the dividend will be treated as a tax free distribution. The only tax consequence associated with this will be a reduction in the adjusted cost base of Mr. Jondo's shares to $400,000 ($625,000 - $225,000). The remaining $105,000 ($330,000 - $225,000) of the distribution will be an ITA 84(4) deemed dividend, subject to either the 45 percent or the 25 percent gross up and tax credit procedures. As it will be taxed as a dividend, this part of the distribution will not be subtracted from the adjusted cost base of the shares.

Exercise Sixteen - 9 Solution

Zircon's Taxable Income would be calculated as follows:

Net Income For Tax Purposes	$281,000
Dividends From Taxable Canadian Corporations	(22,000)
Net Capital Loss Carry Over	(26,000)
Non-Capital Loss Carry Over	(23,000)
Taxable Income	$210,000

Zircon's amount eligible for the small business deduction would be the least of active business income of $198,000, Taxable Income of $210,000, and the annual business limit of $300,000.

Given these calculations, Zircon's additional refundable tax on investment income would be calculated using the lesser of:

Aggregate Investment Income		
Taxable Capital Gains	$46,000	
Interest Income	15,000	
Net Capital Loss Deducted	(26,000)	$35,000
Taxable Income	$210,000	
Amount Eligible For SBD	(198,000)	$12,000

The additional refundable tax on investment income would be $800 [(6-2/3%)($12,000)].

Exercise Sixteen - 10 Solution

If Ms. Nicastro receives the income directly, she will retain $51,000 [($100,000)(1 - .49)]. Alternatively, if the investments are transferred to a corporation, the results would be as follows:

Corporate Investment Income	$100,000
Corporate Tax At 48 Percent	(48,000)
After Tax Income	$ 52,000
Dividend Refund ($1 For Each $3 Of Dividends Paid)	26,000
Non-Eligible Dividends Paid To Ms. Nicastro	$ 78,000
Non-Eligible Dividends Received	$ 78,000
Gross Up Of 25 Percent	19,500
Personal Taxable Income	$ 97,500
Personal Tax Rate	49%
Tax Payable Before Dividend Tax Credit	$ 47,775
Dividend Tax Credit [(2/3 + 40%)($19,500)]	(20,800)
Personal Tax Payable With Corporation	$ 26,975
Non-Eligible Dividends Received	$ 78,000
Personal Tax Payable	(26,975)
After Tax Cash Retained With Corporation	$ 51,025

There would be two tax advantages associated with using the corporation. First, as corporate taxes of $48,000 are less than the personal taxes of $49,000, there would be a small amount of tax deferral on income left in the corporation. Second, the after tax cash retained with a corporation of $51,025, is slightly higher than the $51,000 retained on direct receipt of the income. However, it is is unlikely that either of these small benefits would justify the costs associated with incorporation.

Exercise Sixteen - 11 Solution

The amount of Part IV Tax Payable would be calculated as follows:

Tax On Portfolio Investments [(1/3)($14,000)]	$4,667
Tax On Subsidiary Dividends	Nil
Tax On Ruby Inc. Dividends [(30%)($15,000)]	4,500
Part IV Tax Payable	$9,167

Exercise Sixteen - 12 Solution

The refundable amount of Debut Inc.'s Part I tax for the current year would be the least of the following three figures:

Foreign Non-Business Income (100 Percent)		$15,000
Taxable Capital Gains [(1/2)($38,250)]		19,125
Net Rental Income		6,500
Interest Income		9,200
Net Capital Loss Carry Forward Deducted [(1/2 ÷ 3/4)($13,500)]		(9,000)
Aggregate Investment Income Under ITA 129(4)		$40,825
Rate		26-2/3%
Amount Before Foreign Income Adjustment		$10,887
Deduct Excess Of:		
Foreign Non-Business Tax Credit	$ 750	
Over 9-1/3 Percent Of Foreign Non-Business		
Income [(9-1/3%)($15,000)]	(1,400)	Nil
ITA 129(3)(a)(i) Amount		$10,887

Taxable Income ($121,825 - $22,000 - $9,000)		$ 90,825
Deduct:		
Amount Eligible For The Small Business Deduction ($8,000 ÷ 16%)		(50,000)
[(25/9)($750)] Foreign Non-Business Tax Credit		(2,083)
Adjusted Taxable Income		$ 38,742
Rate		26-2/3%
Amount Under ITA 129(3)(a)(ii)		$ 10,331

Part I Tax Payable	$20,420
Deduct: Surtax	(1,017)
Amount Under ITA 129(3)(a)(iii)	$19,403

The least of these three amounts is $10,331, and this would be the refundable portion of Part I tax for the year.

Exercise Sixteen - 13 Solution

The balance in the RDTOH account of QIL would be as follows:

Opening Balance	$12,500	
Previous Year's Dividend Refund	(1,000)	$11,500
Part I Refundable Addition [(26-2/3%)($24,000)]	$ 6,400	
Part IV Tax On Portfolio Dividends [(1/3)($6,000)]	2,000	8,400
Closing Balance - RDTOH		$19,900

The dividend refund would be $5,000, the lesser of one-third of the $15,000 dividend paid and the $19,900 balance in the RDTOH account.

Solution to Self Study Problem Sixteen - 1

Part A(i)   There would be an ITA 84(1) deemed dividend calculated as follows:

Increase In PUC - Preferred Shares	$11,000
Increase In Net Assets (Decrease In Liabilities)	(10,000)
ITA 84(1) Deemed Dividend	**$ 1,000**

This $1,000 deemed dividend is applicable to all 1,000 of the Preferred Shares that are now outstanding. A pro rata share of the dividend, $1 per share, will be added to the adjusted cost base of all of the Preferred Shares that are outstanding. All of the preferred stock investors will be taxed on the deemed dividend of $1 per share which will be subject to the 25 percent gross up and tax credit procedures.

Part A(ii)   This investor's taxable capital gain would be calculated as follows:

Proceeds Of Disposition		$11,000
Adjusted Cost Base:		
Original Cost	($4,100)	
ITA 84(1) Dividend [(250)($1)]	(250)	(4,350)
Capital Gain		$ 6,650
Inclusion Rate		1/2
Taxable Capital Gain		**$ 3,325**

Part B   As noted in ITA 84(1)(a), a stock dividend is not considered to be a deemed dividend under ITA 84. However, the $780 addition to Paid Up Capital will be considered to be a regular dividend under the definition in ITA 248(1). The holders of the common shares will have a dividend of $1.30 ($780 ÷ 600) per share, and this will be grossed up to a taxable dividend of $1.63 [($1.30)(125%)] per share. For individuals holding the common shares, the adjusted cost base of their holding would be increased by $1.30, multiplied by the number of shares held.

Part C   As the increase in Paid Up Capital was less than the increase in net assets, there is no deemed dividend or any other tax consequences in this Part. This is verified in the following calculation:

Increase In PUC [(250/500)($11,000)]		$ 5,500
Increase In Net Assets:		
New Assets Acquired	$17,500	
Increase In Liabilities	(7,500)	(10,000)
ITA 84(1) Deemed Dividend		**Nil**

Part D   The ITA 84(3) deemed dividend would be calculated as follows:

Redemption Proceeds [(100 Shares)($32)]	$3,200
PUC [(100 Shares)($26)]	(2,600)
ITA 84(3) Deemed Dividend	$ 600
Gross Up Of 25 Percent	150
Taxable Dividend	**$ 750**

In addition, there would be a taxable capital gain calculated as follows:

Redemption Proceeds	$3,200
ITA 84(3) Deemed Dividend	(600)
Deemed Proceeds Of Disposition	$2,600
Adjusted Cost Base [(100)($15)]	(1,500)
Capital Gain	$1,100
Inclusion Rate	1/2
Taxable Capital Gain	$ 550

The total increase in Taxable Income would be $1,300 ($750 + $550). As all of this individual's shares have been redeemed, information on changes in the adjusted cost base is not relevant.

Solution to Self Study Problem Sixteen - 2

Part A   The ending RDTOH balance for FOL would be as follows:

Refundable Dividend Tax On Hand - Beginning	$2,000
Refundable Portion Of Part I Tax [(26-2/3%)($7,000)]	1,867
Refundable Dividend Tax On Hand - Ending	$3,867

As FOL has no foreign investment income or deductions for loss carry overs, the calculation of the addition to the RDTOH for the refundable portion of Part I tax is based solely on the interest income.

The dividend refund would be $3,867, the lesser of:

- One-Third Of Taxable Dividends Paid [(1/3)($75,000)] $25,000

- Refundable Dividend Tax On Hand - Ending $ 3,867

Part B   The Part IV tax for SHI would be calculated as follows:

Portfolio Dividends [(1/3)($8,000)]	$2,667
SHI's Share Of FOL's Dividend Refund (100%)	3,867
Part IV Tax Payable	$6,534

Part C   SHI's aggregate investment income totals $35,625, the sum of $12,000 in interest income and $23,625 [(1/2)($47,250)] in taxable capital gains. This means that the ending RDTOH balance for SHI would be as follows:

Refundable Dividend Tax On Hand - Beginning	$ 8,000
Refundable Portion Of Part I Tax [(26-2/3%)($35,625)]	9,500
Part IV Tax Payable (Part B)	6,534
Refundable Dividend Tax On Hand - Ending	$24,034

The dividend refund would be $16,667, the lesser of:

- One-Third Of Taxable Dividends Paid [(1/3)($50,000)] $16,667

- Refundable Dividend Tax On Hand - Ending $24,034

Solution to Self Study Problem Sixteen - 3

The Part IV Tax Payable for Burton Investments Ltd. would be calculated as follows:

Puligny's Dividend Refund	$12,500
Burton's Percentage Of Ownership	52%
Part IV Tax Payable On Puligny's Dividends	$ 6,500
Part IV Tax Payable On Portfolio Dividends From	
Bank Of Montreal [(1/3)($13,480)]	4,493
Part IV Tax Payable	$10,993

The end of year balance in the Refundable Dividend Tax On Hand account and refundable Part I tax can be calculated as follows:

Balance - End Of Preceding Year	$22,346
Dividend Refund For The Preceding Year	(7,920)
Opening Balance	$14,426
Part IV Tax Payable	10,993
Refundable Part I Tax On Capital Gain [(1/2)($18,000)(26-2/3%)]	2,400
Balance - End Of The Year	$27,819

As the interest received appears to be related to temporary balances resulting from the Company's normal business activities, it would be viewed as active business income, and would not influence the preceding calculations.

The dividends paid of $22,500 will generate a $7,500 [(1/3)($22,500)] dividend refund, as this is less than the $27,819 ending balance in the Refundable Dividend Tax On Hand account.

Solution to Self Study Problem Sixteen - 4

Part A   The Part I Tax Payable is calculated as follows:

Base Amount Of Part I Tax [(38%)($503,500)]	$191,330
Surtax [(4%)(28%)($503,500)]	5,639
ART [(6-2/3%)($43,250 + $55,000 + $24,500 - $12,300)]	7,363
Federal Tax Abatement [(10%)($503,500 - $38,200 - $98,000)]	(36,730)
Foreign Business Income Tax Credit (Given)	(34,000)
Foreign Non-Business Income Tax Credit (Given)	(8,250)
Small Business Deduction [(16%)($200,000)]	(32,000)
General Rate Reduction For CCPCs	
[(7%)($503,500 - $200,000 - $110,450)]	(13,514)
Part I Tax Payable	$ 79,838

Part B   To determine the dividend refund, the RDTOH balance must first be calculated. This requires the calculation of the refundable portion of Part I tax and the Part IV tax.

Refundable Part I Tax   The refundable portion of Part I tax would be the least of the following three amounts:

Interest On Loan To Subsidiary	$ 43,250
Taxable Capital Gains	24,500
Foreign Investment Income	55,000
Net Capital Losses Claimed	(12,300)
Aggregate Investment Income (Note One)	$110,450
Rate	26-2/3%
Total	$ 29,453

Deduct Excess Of:

Foreign Non-Business Tax Credit	$8,250	
Over 9-1/3% Of Foreign Non-Business Income		
[(9-1/3%)($55,000)]	(5,133)	(3,117)
Amount Under ITA 129(3)(a)(i)		$ 26,336

Taxable Income	$503,500
Deduct:	
Amount Eligible For The Small Business Deduction	(200,000)
[(25/9)($8,250)] Foreign Non-Business Tax Credit	(22,917)
[(3)($34,000)] Foreign Business Tax Credit	(102,000)
	$178,583
Rate	26-2/3%
Amount Under ITA 129(3)(a)(ii)	$ 47,622

Part I Tax Payable	$79,838
Deduct: Surtax	(5,639)
Amount Under ITA 129(3)(a)(iii)	$74,199

The least of these three amounts is $26,336, the amount calculated under ITA 129(3)(a)(i).

Note One   The definition contained in ITA 129(4.1) excludes income from property that is incidental to carrying on an active business and, as a consequence, we have left out the $5,050 of term deposit interest. With respect to the interest on the loan to the subsidiary, if the subsidiary had deducted the $43,250 in computing active business income eligible for the small business deduction, ITA 129(6) would have deemed this interest to be active business income rather than investment income. However, the subsidiary was not involved in the production of active business income and, as a consequence, the interest from the subsidiary is included in the above calculation of aggregate investment income.

Part IV Tax Payable   The Part IV Tax Payable would be calculated as follows:

One-Third Of Portfolio Dividends Received [(1/3)($19,600)]	$ 6,533
Share Of Dividend Refund Included In	
Dividends From Subsidiary [(75%)($12,750)]	9,563
Part IV Tax Payable	$16,096

Refundable Dividend Tax On Hand Balance   This balance would be calculated as follows:

RDTOH Balance - End Of The Preceding Year	$23,500	
Dividend Refund For The Preceding Year	(9,600)	$13,900
Refundable Portion Of Part I Tax	$26,336	
Part IV Tax Payable	16,096	42,432
RDTOH Balance - December 31, 2006		$56,332

Dividend Refund   The dividend refund for the year would be $36,333, the lesser of:

- One-third of taxable dividends paid during the year
  {[1/3][$25,000 + (3)($28,000)]} = $36,333

- RDTOH Balance - December 31, 2006 = $56,332

Solution to Self Study Problem Sixteen - 5

Part A - Taxable Income   The calculation of Acme Imports' Taxable Income would be as follows:

Accounting Income Before Taxes		$232,300
Additions:		
Amortization Expense	$20,000	
Charitable Donations	25,000	
Taxable Capital Gain On Sale Of Equipment		
[(1/2)($84,500 - $62,000)]	11,250	
Golf Club Membership	2,800	
50 Percent Of Business Meals And Entertainment	3,360	
Share Issue Costs [(80%)($950)]	760	
Costs Of Supplementary Letters Patent	7,000	
Interest On Mortgage For The Land	12,300	82,470
Deductions:		
CCA (Note One)	($38,800)	
Gain On Sale Of Equipment ($84,500 - $27,500)	(57,000)	
Cumulative Eligible Capital On Customer List		
And Letters Patent [($183,000 + $7,000)(3/4)(7%)]	(9,975)	(105,775)
Net Income For Tax Purposes		$208,995
Charitable Donations		(25,000)
Dividends From Sarco Ltd.		(24,000)
Taxable Income		$159,995

Note One   The maximum CCA on the equipment would be calculated as follows:

Opening UCC	$256,000
Disposition (Capital Cost)	(62,000)
CCA Base	$194,000
Rate - Class 8	20%
CCA	$ 38,800

Several of the items in this problem need further comment. These are as follows:

- **Item 4**   With respect to the costs of issuing shares, IT-341R3 indicates that these amounts are deductible under ITA 20(1)(e). However, such amounts have to be deducted over at least five years at a maximum rate of 20 percent per year. With respect to the costs of acquiring supplementary letters patent, they are considered to be an eligible capital expenditure, three-quarters of which must be added to the cumulative eligible capital account, and amortized at 7 percent.

- **Item 5**   As the loan to the shareholder has been included in two consecutive Balance Sheets, it will become income to the shareholder. However, this does not affect the Company's calculations.

- **Item 6**   Only 50 percent of the $6,720 in charges at the local golf and country club are deductible.

- **Item 7**   The cars provided to the principal shareholder and to the manager of the Company will result in their being assessed for a substantial taxable benefit. However, the costs are fully deductible to the Company.

- **Item 11**   The fees paid to the site consultant are deductible as indicated in ITA 20(1)(dd). ITA 18(3.1) disallows the deduction of interest on financing related to land during construction. The $12,300 interest on the $244,000 mortgage on the land would be capitalized and is not deductible.

Part B - Active Business Income   The active business income of Acme is as follows:

Net Income For Tax Purposes		$208,995
Dividends		(24,000)
Aggregate Investment Income:		
Inkterest Revenue	($10,000)	
Taxable Capital Gain	(11,250)	(21,250)
Active Business Income		$163,745

Part C - Tax Payable   The calculation of Acme Ltd.'s federal Tax Payable would be as follows:

Base Amount Of Part I Tax [(38%)($159,995]	$ 60,798
Corporate Surtax [(4%)(28%)($159,995)]	1,792
Refundable Tax On Investment Income (Note Three)	Nil
Federal Tax Abatement [(10%)($159,995)]	(16,000)
Small Business Deduction (Note Two)	(25,599)
General Rate Reduction (Note Four)	Nil
Part I Tax Payable	$ 20,991
Part IV Tax Payable (Note Five)	3,000
Federal Tax Payable	$ 23,991
Instalments Paid (From Balance Sheet)	(28,000)
Amount Payable (Refund)	($ 4,009)

Note Two   Since none of the annual business limit has been allocated to Sarco, the small business deduction is 16 percent of the least of the following three amounts:

1.   Active Business Income (Part B) $163,745

2.   Taxable Income (no foreign tax credit adjustment) $159,995

3.   Annual Business Limit $300,000

The lowest of these figures is the Taxable Income of $159,995 and this gives a small business deduction of $25,599 [(16%)($159,995)].

Note Three The ITA 123.3 refundable tax (ART) is 6-2/3 percent of the lesser of:

1. Aggregate Investment Income (Part B)	$21,250

2. Taxable Income	$159,995	
Deduct: Amount Eligible For The SBD	(159,995)	Nil

Since the income eligible for the small business deduction is not less than Taxable Income, there is no ITA 123.3 tax on investment income payable.

Note Four The general rate reduction under ITA 123.4(2) would be nil, calculated as follows:

Taxable Income	$159,995
Amount Eligible For The Small Business Deduction [(100/16)($25,599)]	(159,995)
Aggregate Investment Income (Part B)	(21,250)
Full Rate Taxable Income	Nil
Rate	7%
ITA 123.4(2) General Rate Reduction For CCPCs	Nil

Note Five Acme would have to pay a Part IV tax equal to its share of the dividend refund received from Sarco Ltd. This amount would be $3,000 [(60%)($5,000)].

Part D - Refundable Dividend Tax On Hand The ending balance in this account would be calculated as follows:

RDTOH, End Of The Preceding Year		$ -0-
Refundable Portion Of Part I Tax (Note Six)	$ -0-	
Part IV Tax Payable (Note Five)	3,000	3,000
RDTOH Balance - December 31, 2006		$3,000

Note Six The amount of refundable Part I tax will be the least of the following three amounts. In this problem, the calculation of these amounts is greatly simplified by the absence of foreign non-business income. The calculations are as follows:

ITA 129(3)(a)(i) This amount would be $5,667, 26-2/3 percent of aggregate investment income of $21,250 ($10,000 + $11,250).

ITA 129(3)(a)(ii) This amount would be nil, 26-2/3 percent of Taxable Income, reduced by the amount of income that is eligible for the small business deduction [(26-2/3%)($159,995 - $159,995)].

ITA 129(3)(a)(iii) This amount would be Part I Tax Payable, less the corporate surtax, for an amount of $19,199 ($20,991 - $1,792).

The least of these amounts is nil, so there would be no refundable portion of Part I tax.

Solution to Self Study Problem Sixteen - 6

Part A Brasco's Net Income For Tax Purposes and Taxable Income would be calculated as follows:

Active Business Income	$171,000
Taxable Capital Gains [($72,000)(1/2)]	36,000
Canadian Source Interest Income	2,200
Portfolio Dividends	15,800
Foreign Source Investment Income (Gross Amount)	4,500
Dividends From Subsidiary	37,800

Net Income For Tax Purposes		$267,300
Dividends Received:		
Portfolio	($15,800)	
Subsidiary	(37,800)	(53,600)
Charitable Donations		(11,900)
Non-Capital Loss Carry Forward Deducted		(25,800)
Net Capital Loss Carry Forward Deducted (Note One)		(36,000)
Taxable Income		$140,000

Note One Note that the net capital loss carry forward is limited to the taxable capital gains. This will leave a net capital loss carry forward of $28,500 ($64,500 - $36,000) for subsequent periods.

Part B Brasco's Tax Payable would be calculated as follows:

Base Amount Of Part I Tax [(38%)($140,000)]	$53,200
Corporate Surtax [(4%)(28%)($140,000)]	1,568
Additional Refundable Tax On Investment Income (Note Two)	447
Federal Tax Abatement [(10%)($140,000)]	(14,000)
Small Business Deduction (Note Three)	(20,000)
Foreign Non-Business Tax Credit (Amount Withheld)	(675)
General Rate Reduction For CCPCs (Note Four)	(581)
Part I Tax Payable	$19,959
Part IV Tax Payable (Note Five)	17,867
Total Tax Payable	$37,826
Dividend Refund (Note Six)	(13,000)
Net Tax Payable	$24,826

Note Two The aggregate investment income of $6,700 is calculated as follows:

Canadian Interest	$ 2,200
Taxable Capital Gains	36,000
Foreign Investment Income	4,500
Net Capital Loss Carry Forward Deducted	(36,000)
Aggregate Investment Income	$ 6,700

The ITA 123.3 refundable tax (ART) is 6-2/3 percent of the lesser of:

1. Aggregate Investment Income $ 6,700

2. Taxable Income $140,000
    Deduct: Amount Eligible For The SBD   (125,000) $15,000

The ITA 123.3 tax on aggregate investment income is $447 [(6-2/3%)($6,700)].

Note Three   The small business deduction is 16 percent of the least of the following three amounts:

1. Active Business Income $171,000

2. Taxable Income $140,000
    Deduct:
        [(10/3)($675)] Foreign Non-Business Tax Credit   (2,250) $137,750

3. Annual Business Limit (Given) $125,000

The lowest of these figures is the allocated annual limit of $125,000 and this gives a small business deduction of $20,000 [(16%)($125,000)].

Note Four   The general rate reduction would be calculated as follows:

Taxable Income	$140,000
Amount Eligible For The Small Business Deduction [(100/16)($20,000)]	(125,000)
Aggregate Investment Income (See Note Two)	(6,700)
Full Rate Taxable Income	$ 8,300
Rate	7%
ITA 123.4(2) General Rate Reduction For CCPCs	$ 581

Note Five   The calculation of Part IV Tax Payable would be as follows:

Part IV Tax Transfer From Masco [(60%)($21,000)]	$12,600
Part IV Tax On Portfolio Dividends [(1/3)($15,800)]	5,267
Part IV Tax Payable	$17,867

Note Six   The dividend refund would be equal to the lesser of:

*   One-third of taxable dividends paid [(1/3)($39,000)] = $13,000

*   RDTOH Balance - December 31, 2006 (Note Seven) = $26,399

The lesser of these two figures is $13,000 and that would be the refund for the year. Note that the payment of capital dividends does not generate a dividend refund.

Note Seven   The Balance in the RDTOH would be calculated as follows:

RDTOH Balance - End Of The Preceding Year	$ 7,000	
Dividend Refund For The Preceding Year	Nil	$ 7,000
Refundable Portion Of Part I Tax (Note Eight)	$ 1,532	
Part IV Tax (Note Five)	17,867	19,399
RDTOH Balance - December 31, 2006		$26,399

Note Eight   The refundable portion of Part I tax will be the least of the following three amounts:

Aggregate Investment Income (Note Two)		$ 6,700
Rate		26-2/3%
		$ 1,787
Deduct Excess Of:		
Foreign Non-Business Tax Credit	$675	
Over 9-1/3% Of Foreign Non-Business Income		
[(9-1/3%)($4,500)]	(420)	(255)
Amount Under ITA 129(3)(a)(i)		$ 1,532

Taxable Income	$140,000
Deduct:	
Amount Eligible For The Small Business Deduction	(125,000)
[(25/9)($675)] Foreign Non-Business Tax Credit	(1,875)
Adjusted Taxable Income	$ 13,125
Rate	26-2/3%
Amount Under ITA 129(3)(a)(ii)	$ 3,500

Part I Tax Payable	$ 19,959
Deduct: Surtax	(1,568)
Amount Under ITA 129(3)(a)(iii)	$ 18,391

The least of these three amounts would be $1,532, the amount calculated under ITA 129(3)(a)(i).

Part C   If you cannot assume that the foreign tax credit is equal to the amount withheld, the actual foreign tax credit is a complex calculation in this situation. The use of foreign taxes paid as credits against Canadian Tax Payable is limited by a formula that includes the "tax otherwise payable". In the case of foreign taxes paid on non-business income, the "tax otherwise payable" in the formula includes the ART that is assessed under ITA 123.3. This creates a problem in that the calculation of the ART includes the amount eligible for the small business deduction [ITA 123.3(b)]. In turn, the determination of the amount eligible for the small business deduction requires the use of the foreign tax credits for foreign taxes paid on non-business and business income [ITA 125(1)(b)(i) and (ii)].

To solve this circular calculation, for the purpose of calculating the small business deduction, the foreign tax credit for taxes paid on non-business income is calculated using a "tax otherwise payable" figure that does not include the ART under ITA 123.3. This means that in situations where foreign non-business income, the small business deduction, and the ART are involved, the following procedures should be used:

1. Calculate the foreign non-business tax credit using a "tax otherwise payable" that excludes the ART. This initial version of the foreign non-business tax credit will be used only for determining the small business deduction, with the actual credit to be applied calculated after the ART has been determined.

2. Calculate the amount eligible for the small business deduction using the numbers determined in step 1.

3. Calculate the ART, using the amount eligible for the small business deduction determined in step 2.

4. Calculate the actual foreign non-business tax credit using a "tax otherwise payable" figure that includes the ART.

The initial version of the foreign non-business tax credit will be the lesser of the actual tax paid of $675, and an amount determined by the following formula:

$$\left(\frac{\text{Foreign Non - Business Income}}{\text{Adjusted Net Income}}\right)(\text{Part I Tax Otherwise Payable Excluding The ART})$$

$$= \left(\frac{\$4,500}{\$267,300 - \$53,600 - \$36,000}\right)(\$53,200 + \$1,568 - \$14,000)$$

$$= \underline{\$1,032}$$

Part I tax otherwise payable in the preceding formula does not include the ART under ITA 123.3 or the general rate reduction under ITA 123.4. The ITA 123.4 reduction will also be excluded in the calculation of the regular foreign tax credit, as the definition of tax otherwise payable excludes this amount for CCPCs. Adjusted Net Income in the formula is Net Income For Tax Purposes minus deductible dividends and net capital loss carry overs claimed in the current year. In this case, the actual tax paid of $675 will be the credit. As a result, the small business deduction will be the same amount as calculated in Part A of this problem.

The actual foreign non-business tax credit, which takes into consideration the ART, will be the lesser of the actual taxes paid of $675 and an amount determined by the following formula:

$$\left(\frac{\text{Foreign Non - Business Income}}{\text{Adjusted Net Income}}\right)(\text{Part I Tax Otherwise Payable Including The ART})$$

$$= \left(\frac{\$4,500}{\$267,300 - \$53,600 - \$36,000}\right)(\$53,200 + \$1,568 + \$447 - \$14,000)$$

$$= \underline{\$1,044}$$

In this calculation, the actual taxes paid of $675 will again be the credit.

Chapter Sixteen Learning Objectives

After completing Chapter 16, you should be able to:

1. Explain the goal of integration in the design of the Canadian corporate tax system (paragraphs 16-1 through 16-5).

2. Calculate after-tax income retained from dividends received (paragraphs 16-6 through 16-13).

3. Demonstrate how the dividend gross up and tax credit procedures work to implement integration with respect to business income (paragraphs 16-14 through 16-21).

4. Explain the relationship between tax basis Shareholders' Equity and Shareholders' Equity as presented under GAAP (paragraphs 16-22 through 16-24).

5. Demonstrate an understanding of the concept of, and calculate the amount of, Paid Up Capital (paragraphs 16-25 through 16-28).

6. Identify and explain the major components of Tax Basis Retained Earnings (paragraphs 16-29 through 16-45).

7. List the various types of corporate surplus distributions (paragraphs 16-46 through 16-49).

8. Apply the procedures related to the declaration and payment of cash dividends (paragraphs 16-50 through 16-53).

9. Apply the procedures related to the declaration and payment of stock dividends (paragraphs 16-54 through 16-56).

10. Apply the procedures related to the declaration and payment of dividends in kind (paragraphs 16-57 through 16-59).

11. Apply the procedures related to the declaration and payment of capital dividends (paragraphs 16-60 through 16-64).

12. Explain and apply the procedures related to ITA 84(1) deemed dividends (paragraphs 16-65 through 16-70).

13. Explain and apply the procedures related to ITA 84(2) deemed dividends (paragraphs 16-71 through 16-75).

14. Explain and apply the procedures related to ITA 84(3) deemed dividends (paragraphs 16-76 through 16-78).

15. Explain and apply the procedures related to ITA 84(4) and 84(4.1) deemed dividends (paragraphs 16-79 through 16-84).

16. List the components of aggregate investment income as it is defined in ITA 129(4) (paragraphs 16-85 and 16-86).

17. Demonstrate an understanding of the basic concepts of the Part I refundable tax (paragraphs 16-87 through 16-97).

18. Calculate the additional refundable tax (ART) on the investment income of a CCPC (paragraphs 16-98 through 16-105).

19. Calculate the Part I refundable tax on the investment income of a CCPC (paragraphs 16-106 through 16-124).

20. Describe and apply the provisions related to the Part IV refundable tax on private corporations (paragraphs 16-125 through 16-156).

21. Calculate the balance in the Refundable Dividend Tax On Hand (RDTOH) account and the dividend refund (paragraphs 16-157 through 16-184).

22. Demonstrate an understanding of how eligible dividends improve integration when public company dividends are involved (paragraph 16-185 through 16-193).

24. Demonstrate an understanding of the Part III.1 tax on excessive eligible dividend designations (paragraph 16-194 through 16-198).

25. Explain and apply the eligible dividend designation procedures relevant to CCPCs and their GRIP (paragraph 16-199 through 16-205).

26. Explain and apply the eligible dividend designation procedures relevant to non-CCPCs and their LRIP (paragraph 16-206 through 16-213).

CHAPTER SEVENTEEN

How To Work Through Chapter Seventeen

We recommend the following approach in dealing with the material in this Chapter:

The Decision To Incorporate
☐ Read the text pages 721 and 722 (paragraph 17-1 through 17-9).

Other Advantages And Disadvantages Of Incorporation
☐ Read the text pages 722 and 723 (paragraph 17-10 through 17-11).

☐ Complete Self Study Problem Seventeen-1 on page 752 of the text. The solution is on pages S-283 and S-284.

Tax Reduction And Deferral - Basic Example Data
☐ Read the text pages 723 through 725 (paragraph 17-12 through 17-25).

Tax Reduction And Deferral For Public Companies
☐ Read the text pages 725 through 727 (paragraph 17-26 through 17-37).

Tax Reduction And Deferral For CCPCs - Active Business Income
☐ Read the text pages 727 through 729 (paragraph 17-38 through 17-53).

☐ Complete Exercise Seventeen-1 on page 730 of the text. The solution is on page S-279.

Tax Reduction And Deferral For CCPCs - Non-Dividend Investment Income
☐ Read the text pages 730 and 731 (paragraph 17-54 through 17-57).

☐ Complete Exercise Seventeen-2 on page 731 of the text. The solution is on page S-279.

Tax Reduction And Deferral For CCPCs - Dividend Income
☐ Read the text pages 731 and 732 (paragraph 17-58 through 17-63).

Tax Reduction And Deferral - Conclusions
☐ Read the text pages 732 through 734 (paragraph 17-64 through 17-66).

☐ Complete Exercises Seventeen-3 and Seventeen-4 on pages 734 and 735 of the text. The solutions are on pages S-279 through S-281.

Using Imperfections In The Integration System
☐ Read the text pages 735 through 737 (paragraph 17-67 through 17-81).

Income Splitting
☐ Read the text pages 737 through 739 (paragraph 17-82 through 17-90).

Management Compensation - General Principles
☐ Read the text pages 739 and 740 (paragraph 17-91 through 17-98).

Tax-Free Dividend Calculations
☐ Read the text pages 740 through 743 (paragraph 17-99 through 17-110).

Salary Vs. Dividend Decisions For The Owner-Manager

☐ Read the text pages 743 through 746 (paragraph 17-111 through 17-137).

☐ Complete Exercises Seventeen-5 and Seventeen-6 on pages 746 and 747 of the text. The solutions are on pages S-281 and S-282.

Salary Vs. Dividends - Use Of Tax Credits

☐ Read the text pages 747 through 750 (paragraph 17-138 through 17-153).

☐ Complete Exercises Seventeen-7 and Seventeen-8 on page 750 of the text. The solutions are on page S-282.

Salary Vs. Dividends - Conclusion

☐ Read the text pages 750 and 751 (paragraph 17-154 through 17-155).

☐ Complete Self Study Problems Seventeen-2 and Seventeen-3 on page 753 of the text. The solutions are on pages S-285 through S-287.

To Complete This Chapter

☐ Review the Key Terms Used In This Chapter on page 751 of the text. Consult the Glossary for the meaning of any key terms you do not know.

☐ Review the Glossary Flashcards and complete the Key Terms Self-Test for the Chapter. These features can be found in two places, on your Student CD-ROM under the heading "Key Term Practice" and on the web site.

☐ Review the Learning Objectives of the Chapter found on page S-288 of this Study Guide.

☐ As a review, we recommend that you view the PowerPoint Slides for Chapter Seventeen that are available on the web site . If you do not have access to the Microsoft PowerPoint program, the PowerPoint Viewer program can be installed from the Student CD-ROM.

Solution to Chapter Seventeen Exercises

Exercise Seventeen - 1 Solution

Mr. Slater's combined tax rate on income earned by the unincorporated business is 43 percent (29% + 14%). If he incorporates, all of the $126,000 will be eligible for the small business deduction. This means it will be taxed at a rate of 20.12 percent [(38% - 10%)(104%) - 16% + 7%]. There is clearly a significant amount of tax deferral with respect to income left in the corporation. His Tax Payable on direct receipt of the $126,000 of business income would be $54,180 [(43%)($126,000)], far higher than the $25,351 [(20.12%)($126,000)] that would be paid by the corporation.

Mr. Slater's tax rate on non-eligible dividend income is 28.75 percent [(125%)(43%) - (2/3 + 1/3)(25%)]. This means that the overall tax rate on income that is paid out as non-eligible dividends is 43 percent [20.12% + (100% - 20.12%)(28.75%)]. This is equal to the 43 percent rate applicable to income from the unincorporated business. As a consequence, there is no tax savings available on active business income that is paid out as non-eligible dividends.

Exercise Seventeen - 2 Solution

Mr. Slater's combined tax rate on interest income earned outside the corporation is 43 percent (29% + 14%). If he incorporates, the interest income will not be eligible for the small business deduction or the general rate reduction, and it will be subject to the ART. This means that, if the investments are transferred to a corporation, the interest will be taxed at a rate of 51.2 percent [(38% - 10%)(104%) + 6-2/3% + 15.4%]. As this is higher than the 43 percent rate applicable to the direct receipt of interest income, the corporation does not provide any deferral on amounts left within the corporation. In this case, incorporation requires prepayment of taxes.

After being taxed at 51.2 percent, the corporation would have $61,488 in after tax funds available. With the available refund, this would allow the payment of a dividend of $92,232 [(3/2)($61,488)]. Mr. Slater's tax rate on non-eligible dividends received is 28.75 percent [(125%)(43%) - (2/3 + 1/3)(25%)]. After payment of taxes at this rate, he would be left with $65,715 in after tax funds. If he does not incorporate, the $126,000 in interest income would be taxed at 43 percent, leaving an after tax amount of $71,820. There is clearly a tax cost as a result of transferring the investments to a corporation.

Exercise Seventeen - 3 Solution

Direct Receipt   If the income is received directly, the total Tax Payable will be as follows:

Non-Eligible Dividends Received ($46,000 + $87,000)	$133,000
Gross Up At 25 Percent	33,250
Taxable Dividends	$166,250
Interest Income	32,000
Taxable Income	$198,250
Personal Tax Rate (29% + 15%)	44%
Tax Payable Before Dividend Tax Credit	$ 87,230
Dividend Tax Credit [(2/3 + 1/3)($33,250)]	(33,250)
Personal Tax Payable	$ 53,980

The after tax retention can be calculated as follows:

Cash Received ($46,000 + $87,000 + $32,000)	$165,000
Tax Payable	(53,980)
After Tax Retention	$111,020

Transfer To Corporation   If the investments are transferred to a corporation, the corporate taxes will be as follows:

Part IV Tax On Dividends Received [(1/3)($46,000) + $23,000]	$38,333
Part I Tax On Interest Income	
{[$32,000][(38% - 10%)(104%) + 6-2/3% + 15%]}	16,252
Corporate Tax Payable Before Refund	**$54,585**

The RDTOH balance prior to the dividend refund would be calculated as follows:

Part IV Addition	$38,333
Part I Addition [(26-2/3%)($32,000)]	8,533
RDTOH Balance	**$46,866**

The cash available for paying dividends would be $110,415 ($165,000 - $54,585). This represents two-thirds of $165,623, a dividend that would generate a dividend refund of $55,208. However, as the balance in the RDTOH is only $46,866, the maximum dividend that can be paid is $157,281 ($110,415 + $46,866). This would result in personal taxes as follows:

Non-Eligible Dividends Received	$157,281
Gross Up At 25 Percent	39,320
Taxable Dividends	**$196,601**
Personal Tax Rate	44%
Tax Before Dividend Tax Credit	$ 86,504
Dividend Tax Credit [(2/3 + 1/3)($39,320)]	(39,320)
Tax Payable	**$ 47,184**

After tax retention with the use of a corporation would be $110,097 ($165,000 - $54,585 + $46,866 - $47,184). This is $923 less than the $111,020 that would be retained through the direct receipt of this income. You should advise your client not to form or use a corporation to hold these investments.

Note that, as the client needs all of the income produced by these investments, the use of a corporation to defer taxes is not an issue.

Exercise Seventeen - 4 Solution

The client's combined tax rate on direct receipt of income is 45 percent (29% + 16%). If she receives the capital gains directly, the Tax Payable will be $20,700 [($46,000)(45%)]. This will leave her with after tax cash of $71,300 ($92,000 - $20,700).

If the investments are transferred to a CCPC, the aggregate investment income will be $46,000. The applicable tax rate will be 51.8% [(38% - 10%)(104%)+ 6-2/3% + 16%]. Corporate Tax Payable will be $23,828 [(51.8%)($46,000)], leaving cash of $68,172 ($92,000 - $23,828). Of this total, $46,000 [(1/2)($92,000)] can be distributed as a tax free capital dividend. The remaining $22,172 ($68,172 - $46,000) must be distributed as a dividend subject to tax. This represents two-thirds of $33,258, a dividend that would generate a dividend refund of $11,086. As the balance in the RDTOH is $12,267 [(26-2/3%)($46,000)], a taxable dividend of $33,258 can be paid.

The client's tax rate on dividend income is 31.25 percent [(125%)(45%) - (2/3 + 1/3)(25%)], resulting in Tax Payable on the dividend received of $10,393 [(31.25%)($33,258)]. The overall after tax retention when a corporation is used would be as follows:

Capital Dividend Received	$46,000
Non-Eligible Dividend Subject To Tax Received	33,258
Tax Payable On Non-Eligible Dividend Received	(10,393)
After Tax Cash Retained	$68,865

As this is less than the $71,300 after tax cash retained on the direct receipt of the income, the use of a corporation to hold these investments is not an appropriate choice.

Note that, as the client needs all of the income produced by these investments, the use of a corporation to defer taxes is not an issue.

Exercise Seventeen - 5 Solution

If the full $333,000 is paid out as salary, it will be deductible and will reduce the Company's Taxable Income to nil. This means that no corporate taxes will be paid. This salary payment will result in Ms. Broad having Taxable Income of $333,000. Given this, her Tax Payable will be calculated as follows:

Federal Tax On First $118,285	$ 25,389
Federal Tax On Remaining $214,715 At 29%	62,267
Provincial Tax At 10 Percent Of $333,000	33,300
Tax Payable Before Credits	$120,956
Personal Tax Credits (Given)	(3,800)
Total Tax Payable	$117,156

Based on the preceding Tax Payable, Ms. Broad's after tax retention would be $215,844 ($333,000 - $117,156).

Exercise Seventeen - 6 Solution

As dividends are not deductible for tax purposes, corporate taxes will have to be paid prior to the payment of any dividends. While the $33,000 of income in excess of the annual business limit of $300,000 would not get the small business deduction, it would be eligible for the general rate reduction of 7 percent. Given this, the corporate rate on this income would be 39.12% [(38% - 10%)(104%) - 7% + 17%]. On income eligible for the small business deduction, the rate would be 21.12% [(38% - 10%)(104%) - 16% + 8%]. Using these rates, corporate taxes would be calculated as follows:

Income Not Eligible For SBD [(39.12%)($33,000)]	$12,910
Income Eligible For SBD [(21.12%)($300,000)]	63,360
Corporate Tax Payable	$76,270

After payment of these taxes, the maximum dividend that could be paid would be $256,730 ($333,000 - $76,270).

The fact that the corporation's Taxable Income was in excess of the 2006 annual business limit of $300,000 will create an addition to the GRIP of $22,440 [(68%)($333,000 - $300,000)]. Given this, $22,440 of the dividend can be designated as eligible, leaving a non-eligible dividend of $234,290 ($256,730 - $22,440). The grossed up taxable dividends would be calculated as follows:

Total Eligible And Non-Eligible Dividends Received	$256,730
Gross Up:	
Eligible Dividends [(45%)($22,440)]	10,098
Non-Eligible Dividends [(25%)($234,290)]	58,573
Taxable Dividends	$325,401

Personal taxes on this dividend would be calculated as follows:

Federal Tax On First $118,285	$ 25,389
Federal Tax On Remaining $207,116 At 29%	60,064
Provincial Tax At 10 Percent Of $325,401	32,540
Taxes Payable Before Credits	$117,993
Personal Tax Credits (Given)	(3,800)
Dividend Tax Credit:	
Eligible Dividends [(11/18 + 40%)($10,098)]	(10,210)
Non-Eligible Dividends [(2/3 + 40%)($58,573)]	(62,478)
Personal Tax Payable	$ 41,505

The after tax retention would be equal to $215,225 ($256,730 - $41,505).

Exercise Seventeen - 7 Solution

As the available cash is less than Taxable Income, some corporate taxes will have to be paid since there is insufficient cash to pay a salary equivalent to Taxable Income. To determine the maximum salary that can be paid (x), it is necessary to solve the following equation:

$$x = \$18,500 - [(\$21,500 - x)(17.3\%)]$$

$$x = \underline{\$17,872}$$

Given this salary, Mr. Fargo would be subject to the following personal Tax Payable:

Tax Payable Before Credits [(15.25% + 10%)($17,872)]	$4,513
Available Tax Credits (Given)	(3,950)
Personal Tax Payable	$ 563

Given the preceding Tax Payable, Mr. Fargo's after tax retention on salary would be $17,309 ($17,872 - $563).

As dividends are not deductible, corporate taxes would have to be paid on the full $21,500. These taxes would be $3,720 [(17.3%)($21,500)], leaving an amount available for dividends of $14,780 ($18,500 - $3,720). As no individual taxes would be payable on this amount of dividends, the full $14,780 would be retained.

Given these calculations, it is clear that the preferred approach is to pay the maximum salary. Note, however, some combination of dividends and salary may provide an even better result.

Exercise Seventeen - 8 Solution

Ms. Mortell's combined tax rate on additional salary is 45 percent (29% + 16%). In order to have $30,000 in after tax funds, she would have to receive salary of $54,545 [$30,000 ÷ (1 - .45)]. If the corporation pays this amount in deductible salary, it will pay taxes of $23,670 [(16.5%)($198,000 - $54,545)]. The combined cash outflow for salary and taxes would be $78,215 ($54,545 + $23,670).

Ms. Mortell's tax rate on non-eligible dividends is 33-1/3 percent [(125%)(45%) - (2/3 + 25%)(25%)]. In order to have $30,000 in after tax funds, she would have to receive dividends of $45,000 [$30,000 ÷ (1 - .3333)]. As none of this amount would be deductible, the corporation will pay taxes at 16.5 percent on the full $198,000 of Taxable Income, an amount of $32,670 [(16.5%)($198,000)]. The combined cash outflow would be $77,670 ($45,000 + $32,670).

As the cash outflows associated with the payment of salary are larger, the dividend alternative would be preferable.

Solution to Self Study Problem Seventeen - 1

Part A

Calculation Of Corporate Business Income   The business income of the corporation would be calculated as follows:

Management Fees		$82,900
Expenses:		
Mr. Ashley's Salary	($18,400)	
Office Salaries	(25,400)	
Office Rent	(8,180)	
CCA On Office And Dental Equipment	(5,700)	
Other Business Expenses	(2,170)	(59,850)
Business Income		$23,050
Rate On Active Business Income		20%
Tax Payable On Active Business Income		$ 4,610

Tax Payable on the dividends and investment income would be calculated as follows:

Interest Income	$21,600
Net Rental Income ($34,600 - $27,800)	6,800
Aggregate Investment Income	$28,400
Rate On Investment Income	51%
Part I Tax On Investment Income	$14,484
Part IV Tax On Dividends Received [(1/3)($13,900)]	4,633
Tax Payable On Property Income	$19,117

Given the preceding taxes on property income, the RDTOH balance is as follows:

Part I Refundable Amount [(26-2/3%)($28,400)]	$ 7,574
Part IV Refundable Amount [(1/3)($13,900)]	4,633
RDTOH Balance	$12,207

The eligible dividends received by the corporation will be added to the GRIP balance, leaving $13,900 in this account. This means that $13,900 in dividends could be designated as eligible for the enhanced dividend gross up and tax credit procedures.

Given the preceding calculations, the maximum eligible and non-eligible dividend that could be paid is as follows:

Business Income	$23,050
Interest Income	21,600
Net Rental Income	6,800
Eligible Dividends	13,900
Taxes On Business Income	(4,610)
Taxes On Property Income	(19,117)
Balance Before Refund	$41,623
Dividend Refund (RDTOH Balance)	12,207
Available For Dividends	$53,830
Eligible Dividends (GRIP Balance)	(13,900)
Non-Eligible Dividends (Remainder)	$39,930

With respect to the eligible dividends, $8,340 would go to Mr. Ashley (60 percent) and $5,560 would go to Dr. Ashley (40 percent). With respect to the non-eligible dividends, $23,958 would go to Mr. Ashley (60 percent) and $15,972 would go to Dr. Ashley (40 percent). The resulting Tax Payable would be as follows:

	Dr. Ashley	Mr. Ashley
Salary	Nil	$18,400
Eligible Dividends	$ 5,560	8,340
Gross Up At 45 Percent	2,502	3,753
Non-Eligible Dividends	15,972	23,958
Gross Up At 25 Percent	3,993	5,990
Taxable Income	$28,027	$60,441
Tax Rate	47%	30%
Tax Payable Before Dividend Tax Credit	$13,173	$18,132
Dividend Tax Credits:		
Eligible Dividends [(11/18 + 25%)(Gross Up)	(2,154)	(3,232)
Non-Eligible Dividends [(2/3 + 25%)(Gross Up)]	(3,660)	(5,491)
Tax Payable	$ 7,359	$ 9,409

This would leave after tax balances available to Dr. and Mr. Ashley as follows:

Ashley Management Services	Nil
Dr. Ashley ($5,560 + $15,972 - $7,359)	$14,173
Mr. Ashley ($18,400 + $8,340 + $23,958 - $9,409)	41,289
After Tax Retention	$55,462

Part B

Balances With No Corporation If Dr. Ashley had received all of the amounts involved directly, her Tax Payable and net retention could be calculated as follows:

Business Income (No Salary To Husband)	$41,450
Interest Income	21,600
Rental Income (Net)	6,800
Eligible Dividends	13,900
Gross Up At 45 Percent	6,255
Taxable Income	$90,005
Tax Rate	47%
Tax Before Dividend Credit	$42,302
Dividend Tax Credit [(11/18 + 25%)($6,255)]	(5,386)
Tax Payable	$36,916
Income Received ($41,450 + $21,600 + $6,800 + $13,900)	$83,750
Tax Payable	(36,916)
After Tax Retention	$46,834

It is clear from these calculations that the use of the management company has had a positive effect on after tax retention of income. Without the corporation, Dr. Ashley would have ended up with only $46,834. This compares to a total of $55,462 for Mr. and Dr. Ashley when the corporation is used, an improvement of over $8,500. Although personal tax credits were not taken into consideration, they would have made only a small difference, as Dr. Ashley would be able to claim the spousal credit in full if Mr. Ashley had no income.

Solution to Self Study Problem Seventeen - 2

Salary Alternative   In order to determine the amount of salary that would be required to produce $10,000 in after tax income, we need to know Ms. Lusk's effective tax rate on additional income. In this regard, her Taxable Income of $44,385 puts her in the 22 percent federal tax bracket. She will stay in this bracket for the next $28,371 ($72,756 - $44,385) of income. Any income in excess of $72,756 would be taxed at a 26 percent federal rate.

When the federal rates of 22 and 26 percent are combined with an additional 10 percent at the provincial level, Ms. Lusk's combined rates are 32 percent on the next $28,371 of income and 36 percent on any additional amounts. As $10,000 in after tax cash would only require $14,706 in additional salary [$10,000 ÷ (1 - .32)], the higher bracket does not have to be considered. With the additional salary of $14,706 being fully deductible to the corporation, the only tax cost associated with this alternative would be an additional $4,706 ($14,706 - $10,000) in personal taxes for Ms. Lusk.

Dividend Alternative   The dividend alternative involves a more complex analysis. The relevant tax rates on non-eligible dividends would be as follows:

$$[(125\%)(32\%) - (2/3 + 1/3)(25\%)] = 15\%$$

$$[(125\%)(36\%) - (2/3 + 1/3)(25\%)] = 20\%$$

With a tax rate of 15 percent on dividends, a dividend of $11,765 would be required to provide an after tax amount of $10,000 [$10,000 ÷ (1 - .15)]. This would create a taxable dividend of $14,706, and a total Taxable Income of $59,091. As this is below the threshold for the next bracket, the 20 percent rate on dividends can be ignored.

As dividends are not deductible for the corporation, any pre-tax corporate income that is used for the payment of dividends will be subject to the Company's Part I tax rate of 21 percent. This means that, in order to pay $11,765 in dividends to Ms. Lusk, $14,892 [$11,765 ÷ (1 - .21)] of pre-tax corporate income will be required.

The total personal and corporate tax cost of the dividend alternative can be calculated as follows:

Personal Taxes On Dividends ($11,765 - $10,000)	$ 1,765
Corporate Taxes ($14,892 - $11,765)	3,127
Total Tax Cost	$4,892

Conclusion   Since the salary alternative would require tax payments of only $4,706, while the dividend alternative would require tax payments of $4,892, the salary alternative is better.

Solution to Self Study Problem Seventeen - 3

Part A   As salary payments can be deducted by the corporation, the entire $27,500 can be paid as salary. Given this deduction, no taxes would be paid by the Company. With a salary payment of $27,500, Mr. Bedford's after tax cash balance would be as follows:

Salary Payment		$27,500
Tax Before Credits [(25%)($27,500)]	($ 6,875)	
Personal Tax Credits	3,750	(3,125)
After Tax Cash Retained		$24,375

Part B   The tax rate for Bedford Inc. would be 19.12% {[(38% - 10%)(1.04)] - 16% + 6%}. As dividend payments are not deductible to the Company, taxes of $5,258 [(19.12%)($27,500)] will have to be paid, leaving a maximum of $22,242 to be used for the payment of dividends. When this is paid, the after tax retention by Mr. Bedford will be as follows:

Non-Eligible Dividends Received	$22,242
Gross Up At 25 Percent	5,561
Taxable Dividends	$27,803

Tax At 25 Percent [(25%)($27,803)]	$ 6,951
Personal Tax Credits	(3,750)
Dividend Tax Credit [(2/3 + 30%)($5,561)]	(5,376)
Tax Payable	$ Nil

Dividends Received	$22,242
Tax Payable	Nil
After Tax Cash Retained	$22,242

Part C   While Mr. Bedford's Tax Payable is nil, subtracting personal and dividend tax credits from the tax balance gives a negative $2,175. This means that the all dividend approach leaves unused tax credits. While not conclusive, this suggests that there may be a better solution than either all salary or all dividends.

Part D   To examine the possibility of an optimum solution using both salary and dividends, consider the result that occurs when $1,000 in salary is paid in lieu of some dividends. Because the deductible salary payment would reduce corporate taxes, dividends would only have to be decreased by $808.80 [($1,000)(1 - .1912)]. The tax effects of this switch can be calculated as follows:

Increase In Salary	$1,000.00
Decrease In Dividend	(808.80)
Decrease In Dividend Gross Up	(202.20)
Decrease In Mr. Bedford's Taxable Income	($ 11.00)

Decrease In Tax At 25% [(25%)($11.00)]	($ 2.75)
Decrease In Dividend Tax Credit [(2/3 + 30%)($202.20)]	195.46
Increase In Personal Tax Payable	$ 192.71

The rate on a $1,000 increase in salary is 19.271% ($192.71 ÷ $1,000). Applying this rate to the unused credits of $2,175 (see Part C), gives a required increase in salary of $11,286 ($2,175 ÷ .19271).

Based on this payment of salary, corporate taxes and funds available for dividend payments would be calculated as follows:

Pre-Salary Corporate Taxable Income	$27,500
Salary	(11,286)
Corporate Taxable Income	$16,214
Corporate Tax At 19.12 Percent	(3,100)
Available For Dividends	$13,114

After tax retention at the personal level would be calculated as follows:

Non-Eligible Dividends Received	$13,114
Gross Up At 25 Percent	3,279
Taxable Dividends	$16,393
Salary	11,286
Mr. Bedford's Taxable Income	$27,679

Tax At 25 Percent [(25%)($27,679)]	$ 6,920
Personal Tax Credits	(3,750)
Dividend Tax Credit [(2/3 + 30%)($3,279)]	(3,170)
Tax Payable	$ Nil

Amounts Received ($11,286 + $13,114)	$24,400
Personal Tax Payable	Nil
After Tax Cash Retained	$24,400

This combination of salary and dividends will produce the maximum after tax cash retention for Mr. Bedford. While it is a significant improvement over the all dividend after tax retention of $22,242, it is only a very marginal improvement over the all salary after tax retention of $24,375.

Part E Other factors that might be considered include:

- Dividend payments are not Earned Income for purposes of making RRSP contributions.

- Salary payments incur the additional cost of CPP payments and, in some provinces, payroll taxes.

- If he has a CNIL balance, dividend payments will serve to reduce this constraint on the lifetime capital gains deduction.

- Mr. Bedford should consider declaring a bonus (a form of salary) to be paid after the end of the calender year. This would defer the personal taxes without affecting corporate taxes as long as the bonus was paid within 180 days of December 31.

Chapter Seventeen Learning Objectives

After completing Chapter 17, you should be able to:

1. Explain how a corporation can be used to reduce taxes, defer taxes, and facilitate income splitting (paragraphs 17-1 through 17-9).

2. Demonstrate a basic understanding of other advantages and disadvantages of incorporation (paragraphs 17-10 and 17-11).

3. Use various personal and corporate tax rates in the calculation of after-tax retention of earnings flowed through a corporation (paragraphs 17-12 through 17-25).

4. Calculate the amount of tax reduction and tax deferral that is available through the use of a public corporation (paragraphs 17-26 through 17-37).

5. Calculate the amount of tax reduction and tax deferral that is available through the use of a CCPC earning active business income (paragraphs 17-38 through 17-45).

6. Explain the advantages of bonusing down to the owner of a CCPC eligible for the small business deduction (paragraphs 17-46 through 17-53).

7. Calculate the amount of tax reduction and tax deferral that is available through the use of a CCPC earning investment income other than dividends (paragraphs 17-54 through 17-57).

8. Calculate the amount of tax reduction and tax deferral that is available through the use of a CCPC earning dividend income (paragraphs 17-58 through 17-63).

9. Summarize the tax reduction and tax deferral that is available through the use of various types of corporations earning different types of income (paragraphs 17-64 through 17-66).

10. Identify imperfections in the integration system that allow for enhanced tax reduction or enhanced tax deferral (paragraphs 17-67 through 17-81).

11. Describe and calculate the benefits that can be achieved by using a corporation to implement income splitting (paragraphs 17-82 through 17-90).

12. Explain the principles of management compensation in the context of an owner-managed corporation (paragraphs 17-91 through 17-98).

13. Explain why large amounts of dividends can be received on a tax free basis by individuals with no other source of income (paragraphs 17-99 through 17-110).

14. Describe the basic trade-off between the payment of salary and the payment of dividends (paragraphs 17-111 through 17-116).

15. Calculate the appropriate choice between salary and dividends, taking into consideration all of the relevant factors (paragraphs 17-117 through 17-153).

16. Summarize the various non-tax factors that must be taken into consideration in making salary vs. dividend decisions (paragraphs 17-154 and 17-155).

CHAPTER EIGHTEEN

How To Work Through Chapter Eighteen

We recommend the following approach in dealing with the material in this Chapter:

Rollovers Under Section 85 - General Rules For The Transfer
❏   Read the text pages 759 through 763 (paragraph 18-1 through 18-27).

Transfer Price Rules Applicable To All Assets
❏   Read the text page 763 (paragraph 18-28 through 18-33).

Transfer Price Rules - Accounts Receivable
❏   Read the text pages 763 and 764 (paragraph 18-34 through 18-37).

Transfer Price Rules - Inventories And Non-Depreciable Capital Property
❏   Read the text page 764 (paragraph 18-38 through 18-46).

❏   Complete Exercise Eighteen-1 on page 765 of the text. The solution is on page S-291.

Transfer Price Rules - Disallowed Capital Losses
❏   Read the text pages 765 through 767 (paragraph 18-47 through 18-57).

Transfer Price Rules - Depreciable Property
❏   Read the text pages 767 and 768 (paragraph 18-58 through 18-66).

❏   Complete Exercise Eighteen-2 on page 768 of the text. The solution is on page S-291.

Transfer Price Rules - Terminal Losses Disallowed
❏   Read the text page 769 (paragraph 18-67 through 18-70).

Transfer Price Rules - Eligible Capital Property
❏   Read the text pages 769 and 770 (paragraph 18-71 through 18-77).

❏   Complete Exercise Eighteen-3 on page 770 of the text. The solution is on page S-291.

Transfer Price Rules - Disallowed Deductions On CEC Dispositions
❏   Read the text page 771 (paragraph 18-78 through 18-86).

❏   Complete Self Study Problems Eighteen-1 and Eighteen-2 on pages 793 and 794 of the text. The solutions are on pages S-294 through S-296.

Consideration Received By The Transferor
❏   Read the text page 772 (paragraph 18-87 through 18-88).

❏   Complete Exercise Eighteen-4 on page 772 of the text. The solution is on page S-291.

Assets Acquired By The Corporation
❏   Read the text pages 772 through 774 (paragraph 18-89 through 18-98).

Paid Up Capital Of Issued Shares And PUC Reduction
❏   Read the text pages 774 through 776 (paragraph 18-99 through 18-109).

❏   Complete Exercise Eighteen-5 on page 776 of the text. The solution is on pages S-291 and S-292.

Section 85 Rollovers - Comprehensive Example

☐ Read the text pages 776 through 778 (paragraph 18-110 through 18-124).

☐ Complete Exercises Eighteen-6 and Eighteen-7 on pages 778 and 779 of the text. The solutions are on page S-292.

☐ Complete Self Study Problems Eighteen-3 through Eighteen-6 on pages 794 through 797 of the text. The solutions are on pages S-296 through S-301.

Gifts To Related Person - Section 85

☐ Read the text pages 779 and 780 (paragraph 18-125 through 18-133).

☐ Complete Exercise Eighteen-8 on page 780 of the text. The solution is on page S-292.

Benefit To Transferor - Section 85

☐ Read the text pages 780 and 781 (paragraph 18-134 through 18-135).

☐ Complete Exercise Eighteen-9 on page 781 of the text. The solution is on pages S-292 and S-293.

GST And Section 85 Rollovers

☐ Read the text page 782 (paragraph 18-136 through 18-139).

Dividend Stripping - ITA 84.1

☐ Read the text pages 782 through 786 (paragraph 18-140 through 18-172).

☐ Complete Exercise Eighteen-10 on page 787 of the text. The solution is on pages S-293 and S-294.

☐ Complete Self Study Problem Eighteen-7 on pages 797 and 798 of the text. The solution is on pages S-301 and S-302.

Capital Gains Stripping - ITA 55(2)

☐ Read the text pages 788 through 791 (paragraph 18-173 through 18-189).

☐ Complete Exercise Eighteen-11 on page 791 of the text. The solution is on page S-294.

To Complete This Chapter

☐ Review the Key Terms Used In This Chapter on page 791 of the text. Consult the Glossary for the meaning of any key terms you do not know.

☐ Review the Glossary Flashcards and complete the Key Terms Self-Test for the Chapter. These features can be found in two places, on your Student CD-ROM under the heading "Key Term Practice" and on the web site.

☐ Review the Learning Objectives of the Chapter found on pages S-303 and S-304 of this Study Guide.

☐ As a review, we recommend that you view the PowerPoint Slides for Chapter Eighteen that are available on the web site. If you do not have access to the Microsoft PowerPoint program, the PowerPoint Viewer program can be installed from the Student CD-ROM.

Solution to Chapter Eighteen Exercises

Exercise Eighteen - 1 Solution
With respect to the inventories, the $125,000 is both the floor and the ceiling, making this the only possible elected value. The transfer would result in a loss of $15,000 ($140,000 - $125,000), an amount that would be fully deductible as a business loss [ITA(23)]. With respect to the land, the floor would be the boot of $150,000 and the ceiling would be the fair market value of $350,000. Electing the minimum amount would result in a taxable capital gain of $12,500 [($150,000 - $125,000)(1/2)].

Exercise Eighteen - 2 Solution
With respect to the Class 1 property, the range would be from a floor of $250,000 (the boot to a ceiling of $475,000 (fair market value). Election of the $250,000 floor value would result in recapture of $70,000 ($220,000 - $150,000) and a taxable capital gain of $15,000 [($250,000 - $220,000)(1/2)].

The range for the Class 10 asset would be from a floor of $10,000 (the boot) to a ceiling of $12,000 (fair market value). Electing the minimum value of $10,000 would result in recapture of $2,000 ($10,000 - $8,000).

Exercise Eighteen - 3 Solution
The cumulative eligible capital balance before the 2005 deduction was $101,250 [($135,000)(3/4)]. The deduction for 2005 was $7,088 [($101,250)(7%)]. The cumulative eligible capital balance at the time of transfer would be $94,162 ($101,250 - $7,088). Four-thirds of this amount would be $125,549. However, the floor would be established by the boot of $135,000. The ceiling would be the fair market value of $175,000.

With the election at $135,000, three-quarters of this amount would be subtracted from the CEC balance, leaving a negative balance of $7,088 ($94,162 - $101,250). This would result in an income inclusion of $7,088. Since the elected amount was also the cost of the franchise, this full amount is included in income with no adjustment as it is equal to the CEC deducted in 2005.

Exercise Eighteen - 4 Solution
The adjusted cost base amounts would be calculated as follows:

Elected Value	$62,000
ACB Of Note (Fair Market Value)	(51,000)
Available For Shares	$11,000
ACB Of Preferred Shares*	(11,000)
ACB Of Common Shares (Residual)	$ Nil

*Remainder available as it is less than the fair market value of $53,000.

Exercise Eighteen - 5 Solution
The total PUC reduction would be calculated as follows:

Increase In Legal Stated Capital ($97,000 + $54,000)		$151,000
Less The Excess Of:		
Total Elected Value	($114,000)	
Over The Total Non-Share Consideration	83,000	(31,000)
PUC Reduction		$120,000

This PUC reduction would be split between the preferred and common shares on the basis of their fair market values, resulting in the following PUC values:

- Preferred Shares = $97,000 - [(97,000/151,000)($120,000)] = <u>$19,914</u>

- Common Shares = $54,000 - [(54,000/151,000)($120,000)] = <u>$11,086</u>

Note that the sum of these two figures equals $31,000, the difference between the elected value of $114,000 and the total non-share consideration of $83,000.

Exercise Eighteen - 6 Solution

The required information is as follows:

- Minimum and maximum transfer value = $33,783 [(4/3)($25,337)] and $86,000.

- If the minimum value of $33,783 is elected, there would be no income resulting from the transfer.

- As the PUC of the shares issued ($93,000) exceeds the fair market value of the net assets acquired ($86,000), there would be an ITA 84(1) deemed dividend of $7,000. This will be a non-eligible dividend and the grossed up dividend of $8,750 [(125%)($7,000)] would qualify for federal and provincial dividend tax credits.

- The adjusted cost base of the preferred shares will be $40,783, the elected value of $33,783, plus the $7,000 ITA 84(1) deemed dividend.

Exercise Eighteen - 7 Solution

The tax consequences to Mr. Savage and the corporation can be described as follows:

- Mr. Savage will have a taxable capital gain of $20,000 [(1/2)($160,000 - $120,000)].

- Mr. Savage will have recapture of CCA of $22,000 ($120,000 - $98,000).

- Mr. Savage will be holding shares with an adjusted cost base and a PUC of nil ($160,000 - $160,000).

- The corporation will have a depreciable asset with a capital cost of $160,000 and a value, for CCA and recapture purposes, of $140,000 [$120,000 + (1/2)($160,000 - $120,000)].

Exercise Eighteen - 8 Solution

As Ms. Bellows transferred property with a fair market value of $110,000 and received consideration with a fair market value of $65,000 ($50,000 + $15,000), she has made a gift to her daughter of $45,000 ($110,000 - $65,000). The tax consequences for Ms. Bellows and her daughter are as follows:

- The $45,000 gift will be added to the $50,000 elected value, giving Ms. Bellows a total proceeds of disposition of $95,000. This will result in a taxable capital gain of $22,500 [(1/2)($95,000 - $50,000)].

- The preferred shares issued to Ms. Bellows will have an adjusted cost base and a PUC of nil. A subsequent sale of these shares for fair market value will result in a taxable capital gain of $7,500 [(1/2)($15,000 - Nil)].

- The shares acquired by the daughter will have an adjusted cost base and a PUC of $1,000. However, because of the gift, they will have a fair market value of $46,000 ($1,000 + $45,000). This means that on a subsequent sale for fair market value, the daughter would have a capital gain of $45,000 (46,000 - $1,000), with a taxable amount of $22,500 [(1/2)($45,000)].

Exercise Eighteen - 9 Solution

By electing to transfer at the fair market value of $217,000, Mr. Custer will have a taxable capital gain of $47,000 [(1/2)($217,000 - $123,000)]. There will be a PUC reduction of $53,000 calculated as follows:

Increase In Legal Stated Capital		$75,000
Less Excess, If Any, Of:		
Total Elected Value	($217,000)	
Over The Non-Share Consideration	195,000	(22,000)
ITA 85(2.1) PUC Reduction		$53,000

This will leave a PUC of $22,000 ($75,000 - $53,000).

There is an ITA 84(1) deemed dividend of $22,000, the excess of the increase in PUC of the preferred shares ($22,000) over the related increase in net assets (Nil). This is a non-eligible dividend and the taxable amount will be $27,500 [(125%)($22,000)]. The $22,000 ITA 84(1) deemed dividend will be added to the adjusted cost base of the preferred shares.

There is an ITA 15(1) shareholder benefit calculated as follows:

Fair Market Value Of Total Consideration		$270,000
Fair Market Value Of Property	($217,000)	
ITA 84(1) Deemed Dividend	(22,000)	(239,000)
ITA 15(1) Shareholder Benefit		$ 31,000

The total effect on Net Income For Tax Purposes is as follows:

Taxable Capital Gain	$ 47,000
Grossed Up Non-Eligible Deemed Dividend	27,500
Shareholder Benefit	31,000
Total Addition To Net Income For Tax Purposes	$105,500

The deemed dividend would qualify for federal and provincial dividend tax credits.

Exercise Eighteen - 10 Solution

Miss Cole (an individual) has sold shares of a subject corporation to a purchasing corporation, both corporations do not deal with Miss Cole at arm's length, and the two corporations are connected subsequent to the sale. As a consequence, ITA 84.1 is applicable. Given this, the tax consequences of this transaction to Miss Cole are as follows:

Increase In Legal Stated Capital		$317,000
Less Excess, If Any, Of:		
PUC And ACB Of Subject Shares	($125,000)	
Over The Non-Share Consideration	450,000	Nil
PUC Reduction		$317,000

PUC Of New Shares ($317,000 - $317,000)	Nil

Increase In Legal Stated Capital		$317,000
Non-Share Consideration		450,000
Total		$767,000
Less The Sum Of:		
PUC And ACB Of Subject Shares	($125,000)	
PUC Reduction	(317,000)	(442,000)
ITA 84.1 Deemed Dividend (Non-Eligible)		$325,000

Proceeds Of Disposition For Subject Shares	$625,000
ITA 84.1 Deemed Dividend	(325,000)
Proceeds For Capital Gains Purposes	$300,000
ACB Of Subject Shares	(125,000)
Capital Gain	$175,000
Inclusion Rate	1/2
Taxable Capital Gain	$ 87,500

ACB Of New Shares ($625,000 - $450,000)	$175,000

The grossed up non-eligible dividend of $406,250 [(125%)($325,000)] would qualify for federal and provincial dividend tax credits. In addition, there would be a taxable capital gain of $87,500. However, as the new preferred shares have a fair market value of $317,000, there is still a deferred gain of $142,000 ($317,000 - $175,000).

Exercise Eighteen - 11 Solution

A deductible dividend has been paid in conjunction with an arm's length sale of shares, and it would appear that the dividend payment served to eliminate the potential capital gain on the transaction. As a consequence, ITA 55 is applicable and the tax consequences of the transaction are as follows:

Dividend Payment (Tax Free)	$750,000
Safe Income	(225,000)
Deemed Proceeds Of Disposition	$525,000
Actual Proceeds Of Disposition	90,000
Total Proceeds Of Disposition	$615,000
Adjusted Cost Base Of Shares	(75,000)
Capital Gain	$540,000
Inclusion Rate	1/2
Taxable Capital Gain	$270,000

Solution to Self Study Problem Eighteen - 1

Part A   The disposition of a business is a capital transaction and, in the absence of special provisions, any resulting gain or loss must be treated as a capital gain or loss. With respect to the Inventories, a special provision in ITA 23 indicates that, when such assets are sold as part of the disposition of a business, the sale is deemed to be in the ordinary course of carrying on business and any resulting gain or loss is considered business in nature. ITA 23 automatically applies in the disposition of a business and no election is required on the part of the vendor. ITA 22 provides for a similar treatment of Accounts Receivable. However, a joint election by the vendor and purchaser is required before this business income treatment is applicable. In the absence of this election, losses on Accounts Receivable are treated as capital losses.

If the assets are transferred at fair market values, the Taxable Income resulting from the transfer can be calculated as follows:

Inventories - Business Income ($88,000 - $73,000)	$15,000
Furniture And Fixtures - Recaptured CCA ($45,000 -$38,000)	7,000
Goodwill [(3/4)($150,000 - Nil)(1/2 ÷ 3/4)]	75,000
Taxable Income	$97,000

When the $112,500 [(3/4)($150,000)] proceeds for the goodwill is subtracted from the Cumulative Eligible Capital balance, a business income inclusion is created. As no amounts have been deducted under ITA 20(1)(b), this amount is reduced from a three-quarters inclusion to a one-half inclusion, by multiplying the negative balance by (1/2 ÷ 3/4).

There is also an allowable capital loss of $3,000 [(1/2)($51,000 - $45,000)] on the disposition of the Accounts Receivable. However, ITA 40(2)(g) would disallow this loss as the accounts are being transferred to a corporation that is controlled by the transferor. This loss would be added to the tax cost of the Accounts Receivable on the corporation's books.

Part B   The cash can, of course, be transferred to the corporation with no tax consequences. All of the other assets can be transferred at elected values under ITA 85. Under the provisions of this Section, the tax consequences would be as follows:

> **Accounts Receivable**   If the Accounts Receivable are transferred under ITA 85, the maximum value that can be elected is the fair market value of $45,000. This will result in a capital loss of $6,000 (allowable amount of $3,000). However, this loss will be disallowed under ITA 40(2)(g) because the transfer is to a corporation that will be controlled by Ms. Flack.

> **Inventories**   The Inventories can be transferred at an elected value of $73,000, resulting in no Taxable Income on the transfer.

> **Furniture And Fixtures**   The Furniture And Fixtures can be transferred at their UCC of $38,000, resulting in no Taxable Income on the transfer.

> **Goodwill**   The Goodwill can be transferred at a nominal value of $1, resulting in no significant Taxable Income on the transfer.

An alternative with respect to the Accounts Receivable would be to transfer these assets under the provisions of ITA 22. If Ms. Flack and her corporation were to make this joint election, the $6,000 loss resulting from transferring these assets to the corporation would be fully deductible as a business loss. As it is not a capital loss, it would not be disallowed and Ms. Flack would be able to deduct the full $6,000 against any other source of income in the year of transfer. Using the ITA 22 election is the preferable approach to the transfer of these Accounts Receivable.

Solution to Self Study Problem Eighteen - 2

Part A   Of the assets in the Balance Sheet, Cash is not among the eligible assets listed in ITA 85(1.1). This is of no consequence as the tax value of cash is always equal to its carrying value.

Accounts Receivable could be transferred under Section 85, but are usually transferred to the corporation under the provisions of ITA 22. ITA 22 is used for two reasons. First, it means that any loss on the transfer will be a fully deductible business loss, rather than a capital loss that will be disallowed on a transfer to a corporation controlled by the transferor under ITA 40(2)(g). In addition, the use of the ITA 22 joint election to make the transfer will permit the transferee corporation to deduct any additional bad debts as business losses, rather than capital losses.

There will be a terminal loss on the transfer of the equipment. This loss will be disallowed on a transfer to an affiliated person. This is the case, without regard to whether Ms. Speaks makes the transfer directly or under the provisions of ITA 85(1). Given this, there is no reason to use ITA 85(1) for this transfer.

Part B The minimum transfer values for the assets to be included in the rollover would be as follows:

Inventories (Cost)	$261,000
Land (Adjusted Cost Base)	196,000
Building (UCC)	103,600
Goodwill (Nominal Value)	1

Note The Goodwill has been given a nominal elected value to ensure that it is specifically included in the transfer. A failure to do this could result in the Goodwill being assessed on the basis of a transfer at fair market value.

Part C The tax consequences of the Section 85 transfers with respect to both Ms. Speaks and Speaks Inc. can be described as follows:

Inventories The cost of the Inventories to Speaks Inc. would be the transfer price of $261,000. As this was the cost of the Inventories, there would be no tax consequence to Ms. Speaks.

Land The cost of the Land to Speaks Inc. would be the transfer price of $196,000. As this was the adjusted cost base of the Land, there would be no tax consequence to Ms. Speaks.

Building The capital cost of the Building to Speaks Inc. would be $155,500, and Speaks Inc. would be deemed to have taken CCA in the amount of $51,900. As the net value of the transfer is equal to UCC, there would be no tax consequence to Ms. Speaks.

Goodwill The cost of the Goodwill to Speaks Inc. will be $1, and three-quarters of this amount will be added to the Company's Cumulative Eligible Capital balance. There would be no material tax consequence to Ms. Speaks resulting from this transfer.

If Ms. Speaks chose to include the Equipment in the rollover, the capital cost of the Equipment to Speaks Inc. would be its fair market value of $32,500. Ms. Speaks will have a terminal loss of $34,500 ($67,000 - $32,500) that she will not be able to deduct. The $34,500 loss will be placed in the same CCA class as the Equipment was, and Ms. Speaks will continue to take CCA on this class until the Equipment is disposed of by Speaks Inc. or there is no balance left in the class.

Solution to Self Study Problem Eighteen - 3

Part A As the $1,241,100 elected price was equal to the sum of the capital cost of the Land and the UCC of the Building ($315,000 + $926,100), there would be no tax consequences associated with the transfer of these assets. However, the corporation will be deemed to have acquired these assets at their old tax values to Mr. Dix, not at their fair market values at the time of transfer.

Under ITA 85(1)(f), the adjusted cost base of the non-share consideration is equal to its fair market value of $1,241,100. The problem does not specify whether preferred shares, common shares, or a combination of both were issued. Under ITA 85(1)(g), the adjusted cost base of any preferred shares received is the lesser of their fair market value and the total elected value, reduced by the non-share consideration. As the $1,241,100 elected value is equal to the non-share consideration provided by the corporation, the adjusted cost base of any preferred shares would be nil. Under ITA 85(1)(h), the adjusted cost base of any common shares issued would be the elected value, reduced by any non-share consideration and any amounts allocated to preferred stock. This value would also be nil.

Part B   As the debt was paid off at face value, this amount would be equal to Mr. Dix's adjusted cost base, and he would have no gain or loss. However, the shares have an adjusted cost base of nil and, as a consequence, he would have a capital gain equal to the entire proceeds of disposition of $894,000. This would result in a taxable capital gain of $447,000 [(1/2)($894,000)].

It is likely that the corporation is a "qualified small business corporation". If this is the case, Mr. Dix would be eligible for the $500,000 ($250,000 taxable amount) lifetime capital gains deduction. To qualify, the corporation must be a Canadian controlled private corporation with at least 90 percent of the fair market value of its assets being used in an active business operating primarily in Canada. The 24 month holding period requirement would be met as no other taxpayer has owned the business in the preceding 24 months.

Even if Mr. Dix is eligible for the full lifetime capital gains deduction, he would still have to pay taxes on a $197,000 ($447,000 - $250,000) taxable capital gain. Whether or not he can use the lifetime capital gains deduction, he may need to pay alternative minimum tax.

Solution to Self Study Problem Eighteen - 4

Part A   The adjusted cost base of the shares would be as follows:

Total Elected Value	$467,000
Non-Share Consideration ($122,000 + $128,000)	(250,000)
Adjusted Cost Base Preferred And Common Shares	$217,000
Allocated To Preferred Shares (FMV)	(150,000)
Adjusted Cost Base Of Common Shares (Residual)	$ 67,000

Part B   The legal stated capital of the preferred and common shares would be their respective fair market values of $150,000 and $326,000. The PUC reduction required under ITA 85(2.1) would be calculated as follows:

Increase In Legal Stated Capital ($150,000 + $326,000)		$476,000
Less Excess Of:		
Total Elected Value	($467,000)	
Over The Total Non-Share Consideration	250,000	(217,000)
Reduction In Paid Up Capital		$259,000

Note that this total reduction is equal to the deferred gain on the election ($726,000 - $467,000). This total will be allocated to the two classes of shares on the basis of their relative fair market values. The relevant calculations are as follows:

Preferred Shares = [($150,000 ÷ $476,000)($259,000)] = **$81,618**

Common Shares = [($326,000 ÷ $476,000)($259,000)] = **$177,382**

The PUC of the two classes of shares after the ITA 85(2.1) reduction is as follows:

	Preferred Shares	Common Shares
Legal Stated Capital	$150,000	$326,000
PUC Reduction	(81,618)	(177,382)
PUC	$ 68,382	$148,618

Part C   The tax consequences to Mr. Lardner, if the corporation redeemed both classes of shares at their respective fair market values, would be calculated as follows:

	Preferred Shares	Common Shares
Redemption Proceeds	$150,000	$326,000
PUC (See Preceding Calculations)	(68,382)	(148,618)
ITA 84(3) Deemed Dividend	$ 81,618	$177,382
Redemption Proceeds	$150,000	$326,000
ITA 84(3) Deemed Dividend	(81,618)	(177,382)
Deemed Proceeds Of Disposition	$ 68,382	$148,618
Adjusted Cost Base	(150,000)	(67,000)
Capital Gain (Loss)	($ 81,618)	$ 81,618

Mr. Lardner would have a deemed non-eligible dividend of $259,000 ($81,618 + $177,382) that would be subject to the usual gross up and tax credit procedures for non-eligible dividends. He has a net capital gain of nil ($81,618 - $81,618).

Solution to Self Study Problem Eighteen - 5

Part A   Accounts Receivable could be transferred under Section 85, but are usually transferred to the corporation under the provisions of ITA 22. ITA 22 is used for two reasons. First, it means that any loss on the transfer will be a fully deductible business loss, rather than a capital loss that will be disallowed on a transfer to a corporation controlled by the transferor under ITA 40(2)(g). In addition, the use of the ITA 22 joint election to make the transfer will permit the transferee corporation to deduct any additional bad debts as business losses, rather than capital losses. As a result, the Accounts Receivable should be transferred at $75,000 using the ITA 22 joint election. This will result in a fully deductible business loss of $3,000 for Miss Brock. Although the corporation will have to add the $3,000 to income, any difference between the $78,000 face value and amounts actually collected will be fully deductible.

The values that should be elected under ITA 85 on the other assets in order to eliminate any current Tax Payable on the transfer, are as follows:

Inventory	$174,000
Equipment	234,000
Goodwill	1
Total Elected Value	$408,001

Part B   The total elected value would become the adjusted cost base of the consideration received by Miss Brock. It would be allocated to the individual items as follows:

Total Elected Value	$408,001
Non-Share Consideration ($95,000 + $75,000)	(170,000)
Available For Preferred And Common Stock	$238,001
Adjusted Cost Base - Preferred Stock (Maximum Of Fair Market Value)	(225,000)
Adjusted Cost Base - Common Stock (Residual)	$ 13,001

Part C   The calculation of PUC would begin with the legal stated capital associated with the two classes of shares, which is their fair market value. This would be $225,000 for the preferred stock and $480,000 for the common stock, a total of $705,000. ITA 85(2.1) would require a reduction in this total as follows:

Increase In Legal Stated Capital		$705,000
Less Excess Of:		
Total Elected Value	($408,001)	
Over The Total Non-Share Consideration	170,000	(238,001)
Reduction In PUC		$466,999

This reduction in PUC would be allocated to the two classes of shares on the basis of their fair market values. The calculations would be as follows:

Preferred Stock = [($225,000 ÷ $705,000)($466,999)] = <u>$149,042</u>

Common Stock = [($480,000 ÷ $705,000)($466,999)] = <u>$317,957</u>

Using this allocation, the Paid Up Capital of the two classes of shares would be as follows:

Preferred Stock = $225,000 - $149,042 = <u>$75,958</u>

Common Stock = $480,000 - $317,957 = <u>$162,043</u>

Note that the total PUC of $238,001 ($75,958 + $162,043) is equal to the difference between the total elected value for the assets of $408,001 and the non-share consideration received by Miss Brock of $170,000.

Part D   The tax consequences for Miss Brock on the redemption of the preferred and common shares would be calculated as follows:

	Preferred Stock	Common Stock
Redemption Proceeds	$225,000	$480,000
Paid Up Capital	(75,958)	(162,043)
ITA 84(3) Deemed Dividend	$149,042	$317,957
Redemption Proceeds	$225,000	$480,000
ITA 84(3) Deemed Dividend	(149,042)	(317,957)
ITA 54 - Deemed Proceeds Of Disposition	$ 75,958	$162,043
Adjusted Cost Base	(225,000)	(13,001)
Capital Gain (Loss)	($149,042)	$149,042

Miss Brock would have a deemed non-eligible dividend of $466,999 ($149,042 + $317,957), which would be subject to the usual gross up and tax credit procedures for non-eligible dividends. This is also the amount of the gain that was deferred through the use of Section 85 ($208,000 + $317,000 + $350,000 - $408,001). There would be a net capital gain of nil ($149,042 - $149,042).

Solution to Self Study Problem Eighteen - 6

Part A Given the stated wishes of Mr. Fleck, he should transfer the following assets using the indicated elected values:

	Elected Values	Fair Market Values
Cash	$ 20,000	$ 20,000
Equipment (At Tax Value)	62,000	66,000
Land (At Cost Plus $40,000)	146,000	185,000
Building (At Tax Value)	178,000	323,000
Goodwill*	Nil	95,000
Totals	$406,000	$689,000

*It would be equally acceptable to transfer the goodwill at an elected value of $1.

The following explanations are required:

Cash While there is no advantage to transferring the cash under ITA 85(1), Mr. Fleck indicated that he wished to transfer all assets "unless there is some tax reason not to". This would indicate that the cash should be included in the election.

Accounts Receivable Accounts Receivable should never be transferred under ITA 85(1) as the result will be a capital loss, which will be disallowed under ITA 40(2)(g). Rather, the Accounts Receivable should be transferred using a joint election under ITA 22. This will result in a fully deductible business loss on the transfer.

Land The Land is transferred at a value that is $40,000 in excess of cost in order to create a taxable capital gain that will allow the deduction of Mr. Fleck's net capital loss carry forward. The same $40,000 gain could have been created by electing to transfer the Building at a value $40,000 in excess of its cost. However, this would have resulted in recapture and this would not be consistent with Mr. Fleck's desire not to have other tax consequences resulting from the transfer of assets to Fleck Ltd.

Other Assets The other assets (Equipment, Building, and Goodwill) have been transferred at their tax values in order to avoid other tax consequences resulting from the transfer.

Part B The total non-share consideration received by Mr. Fleck was $200,000 (the Corporation's assumption of $123,000 in old debt, plus its issuance of $77,000 in new debt). As the fair market value of the assets transferred was $689,000, the fair market value of the common shares issued would be $489,000 ($689,000 - $200,000).

The adjusted cost base of the shares would be calculated as follows:

Total Elected Value	$406,000
Fair Market Value Of Non-Share Consideration	(200,000)
Adjusted Cost Base Of Common Shares	$206,000

The PUC reduction for the shares would be calculated as follows:

Increase In Legal Stated Capital (Fair Market Value)		$489,000
Less Excess Of:		
Total Elected Value	($406,000)	
Over The Non-Share Consideration	200,000	(206,000)
PUC Reduction For Common Shares		$283,000

This reduction would leave the PUC of the shares at $206,000 ($489,000 - $283,000).

Part C   If one-half of the shares were redeemed for their fair market value of $244,500 [(1/2)($489,000)], the tax consequences would be as follows:

Redemption Proceeds	$244,500
PUC [(1/2)($206,000)]	(103,000)
ITA 84(3) Deemed Dividend	$141,500

Redemption Proceeds	$244,500
ITA 84(3) Deemed Dividend	(141,500)
Proceeds Of Disposition	$103,000
Adjusted Cost Base [(1/2)($206,000)]	(103,000)
Capital Gain	Nil

This $141,500 deemed dividend is consistent with an economic analysis of the transaction. Assets with a total fair market value of $689,000 were transferred at an elected value of $406,000. This resulted in the deferral of a gain of $283,000 ($689,000 - $406,000). With the sale of one-half of the common shares, $141,500 [(1/2)($283,000)] of this gain must be recognized.

The deemed non-eligible dividend would be subject to the usual dividend gross up and tax credit procedures for non-eligible dividends.

Solution to Self Study Problem Eighteen - 7

Part A   In the absence of ITA 84.1, the Section 85 rollover would have resulted in a capital gain of $500,000. This is based on the elected value of $575,000, less the adjusted cost base of $75,000 [(75%)($100,000)]. However:

- There has been a sale by a Canadian resident (Ms. Chisholm) of shares in a subject corporation (DML).

- The purchaser of the subject corporation (Dorlaine Inc.) does not deal at arm's length with the Canadian resident (Ms. Chisholm).

- Immediately after the disposition, the subject corporation (DML) and the purchaser corporation (Dorlaine Inc.) are connected (Dorlaine Inc. controls DML).

As a consequence, the provisions of ITA 84.1 are applicable. This means that there will be a reduction of Paid Up Capital under ITA 84.1(1)(a) as follows:

Increase In Legal Stated Capital Of Dorlaine Inc.		$400,000
Less Excess, If Any, Of:		
Greater Of PUC And ACB Of DML Shares	($ 75,000)	
Over The Non-Share Consideration	500,000	Nil
PUC Reduction		$400,000

The PUC of the Dorlaine Inc. shares would be nil ($400,000 - $400,000).

The transfer would result in an ITA 84.1(1)(b) deemed dividend that would be calculated as follows:

Increase In Legal Stated Capital Of Dorlaine Inc.		$400,000
Non-Share Consideration		500,000
Total		$900,000
Less The Sum Of:		
PUC Of DML Shares	($ 75,000)	
PUC Reduction Under ITA 84.1(1)(a)	(400,000)	(475,000)
ITA 84.1(1)(b) Deemed Dividend (Non-Eligible)		$425,000

The capital gain on the disposition of the DML shares would be calculated as follows:

Proceeds Before Adjustment Of DML Shares (Elected Value)	$575,000
Deemed ITA 84.1(1)(b) Dividend	(425,000)
Adjusted Proceeds Of Disposition (ITA 54)	$150,000
ACB Of DML Shares	(75,000)
Capital Gain	$ 75,000
Inclusion Rate	1/2
Taxable Capital Gain	$ 37,500

The tax consequences of transferring the DML shares are:

- a deemed non-eligible dividend of $425,000, which would qualify for the usual gross up and tax credit procedures for non-eligible dividends; and

- a taxable capital gain of $37,500, which would be eligible for the lifetime capital gains deduction as long as DML is a qualified small business corporation.

Note that, if Ms. Chisholm had elected the same $575,000 value, but limited her non-share consideration to $75,000 (the PUC and ACB of the DML shares), there would have been no deemed dividend. Under this approach, she would have realized a $500,000 capital gain, which would potentially be eligible for the lifetime capital gains deduction, and still retained control of her Company.

Part B At Ms. Chisholm's death, there would be a deemed disposition of all of her capital property at its fair market value, $400,000 in the case of the Dorlaine Inc. shares. The adjusted cost base of these shares would be $75,000, calculated as follows:

Value Elected In Section 85 Rollover	$575,000
Fair Market Value Of Non-Share Consideration	(500,000)
Adjusted Cost Base Of Dorlaine Inc. Shares	$ 75,000

Given this, the taxable capital gain on the deemed disposition would be calculated as follows:

Deemed Proceeds Of Disposition (Fair Market Value)	$400,000
Adjusted Cost Base	(75,000)
Capital Gain	$325,000
Inclusion Rate	1/2
Taxable Capital Gain	$162,500

Since Dorlaine Inc. is holding various investments, it would not be a qualified small business corporation. As a result, none of the taxable capital gain would be eligible for the lifetime capital gains deduction.

Chapter Eighteen Learning Objectives

After completing Chapter 18, you should be able to:

1. Describe the type of situation where ITA 85 is applicable (paragraphs 18-1 through 18-3).

2. Explain the general rules that are applicable to the transferor and the transferee under ITA 85 (paragraphs 18-4 through 18-9).

3. Describe the types of consideration that can be received by the transferor under ITA 85 (paragraphs 18-10 and 18-11).

4. Describe the procedures required for making the ITA 85 election (paragraphs 18-12 through 18-14).

5. Calculate the range of values that can be used in a transfer under the provisions of ITA 85 (paragraphs 18-15 through 18-27).

6. Apply the general rules applicable to all assets that determine the range of values that can be used in a transfer under the provisions of ITA 85 (paragraphs 18-28 through 18-33).

7. Apply the detailed rules for the transfer of accounts receivable, inventories, and non-depreciable capital property under ITA 85 (paragraphs 18-34 through 18-46).

8. Describe the rules related to the disallowance of capital losses arising on transfers of non-depreciable capital property to affiliated persons and associated tax planning issues (paragraphs 18-47 through 18-57).

9. Apply the detailed rules for the transfer of depreciable assets under ITA 85 (paragraphs 18-58 through 18-66).

10. Describe the rules related to the disallowance of terminal losses arising on transfers of depreciable capital property to affiliated persons and associated tax planning issues (paragraphs 18-67 through 18-70).

11. Apply the detailed rules for the transfer of eligible capital property under ITA 85 (paragraphs 18-71 through 18-77).

12. Describe the rules related to the disallowance of deductions arising on transfers of eligible capital property to an affiliated person and associated tax planning issues (paragraphs 18-78 through 18-86).

13. Calculate the amount of the elected value that will be allocated to each component of the consideration received by the transferor under ITA 85 (paragraphs 18-87 and 18-88).

14. Calculate the amount of the elected value that will be allocated to each of the assets acquired by the transferee under ITA 85 (paragraphs 18-89 through 18-98).

15. Calculate the Paid Up Capital of the shares received by the transferor in an ITA 85 rollover (paragraphs 18-99 through 18-109).

16. Apply the ITA 85 rules to situations involving the incorporation of an unincorporated business (paragraphs 18-110 through 18-124).

17. Identify situations where the ITA 85 rules on gifts to related persons are applicable and make the appropriate adjustments that are required by these rules (paragraphs 18-125 through 18-133).

18. Identify situations where the ITA 85 rules on benefits to the transferor are applicable and make the appropriate adjustments that are required by these rules (paragraphs 18-134 and 18-135).

19. Be aware that there are GST rules related to transfers under ITA 85 and that these will be covered in Chapter 19 (paragraphs 18-136 through 18-139).

20. Identify situations where ITA 84.1 (dividend stripping rules) is applicable (paragraphs 18-140 through 18-149).

21. Apply the ITA 84.1 rules to situations involving shares issued after December 31, 1971 (paragraphs 18-150 through 18-158).

22. Apply the ITA 84.1 rules to situations involving shares issued before January 1, 1972 (paragraphs 18-159 through 18-172).

23. Identify situations where ITA 55(2) (capital gains stripping rules) is applicable (paragraphs 18-173 through 18-179).

24. Apply the ITA 55(2) rules to situations involving capital gains stripping (paragraphs 18-180 through 18-189).

CHAPTER NINETEEN

How To Work Through Chapter Nineteen

We recommend the following approach in dealing with the material in this Chapter:

Introduction
☐ Read the text page 805 (paragraph 19-1 through 19-3).

Share For Share Exchanges (ITA 85.1)
☐ Read the text pages 805 and 806 (paragraph 19-4 through 19-10).

☐ Complete Exercise Nineteen-1 on page 806 of the text. The solution is on page S-307.

Exchange Of Shares In A Reorganization (ITA 86)
☐ Read the text pages 807 through 810 (paragraph 19-11 through 19-26).

☐ Complete Exercises Nineteen-2 through Nineteen-4 on pages 810 and 811 of the text. The solutions are on pages S-307 and S-308.

☐ Complete Self Study Problem Nineteen-1 on page 845 of the text. The solution is on page S-311.

Gift To Related Part (Benefit Rule)
☐ Read the text pages 811 through 813 (paragraph 19-27 through 19-36).

☐ Complete Exercise Nineteen-5 on page 813 of the text. The solution is on pages S-308 and S-309.

☐ Complete Self Study Problem Nineteen-2 on pages 845 and 846 of the text. The solution is on pages S-312 through S-314.

Using ITA 86 - Practical Considerations
☐ Read the text pages 813 and 814 (paragraph 19-37).

Using ITA 86 - Advantages And Disadvantages
☐ Read the text page 814 (paragraph 19-38 through 19-43).

Amalgamations
☐ Read the text pages 814 through 817 (paragraph 19-44 through 19-61).

☐ Complete Exercise Nineteen-6 on page 817 of the text. The solution is on page S-309.

Winding-Up Of A 90 Percent Owned Subsidiary
☐ Read the text pages 818 through 819 (paragraph 19-62 through 19-77).

☐ Complete Exercise Nineteen-7 on page 820 of the text. The solution is on page S-310.

☐ Read the text pages 820 and 821 (paragraph 19-78 through 19-80).

☐ Complete Exercise Nineteen-8 on page 821 of the text. The solution is on page S-310.

☐ Read the text page 821 (paragraph 19-81 through 19-82).

☐ Complete Self Study Problem Nineteen-3 on page 846 of the text. The solution is on page S-314.

Tax Planning - Amalgamation Vs. Winding-Up
☐ Read the text pages 822 and 823 (paragraph 19-83 through 19-89).

Winding-Up Of A Canadian Corporation
☐ Read the text pages 823 through 825 (paragraph 19-90 through 19-103).

☐ Complete Exercise Nineteen-9 on page 825 of the text. The solution is on page S-310.

☐ Complete Self Study Problem Nineteen-4 on pages 846 and 847 of the text. The solution is on pages S-315 and S-316.

Convertible Properties
☐ Read the text page 826 (paragraph 19-104 through 19-110).

The Valuation Of A Business
☐ Read the text pages 826 through 829 (paragraph 19-111 through 19-131).

Sale Of An Incorporated Business
☐ Read the text pages 829 through 837 (paragraph 19-132 through 19-169).

☐ Complete Self Study Problem Nineteen-5 on pages 847 and 848 of the text. The solution is on pages S-316 through S-318.

GST Implications
☐ Read the text pages 837 through 839 (paragraph 19-170 through 19-182).

Tax Shelters
☐ Read the text pages 839 through 843 (paragraph 19-183 through 19-208).

To Complete This Chapter
☐ Review the Key Terms Used In This Chapter on page 843 of the text. Consult the Glossary for the meaning of any key terms you do not know.

☐ Review the Glossary Flashcards and complete the Key Terms Self-Test for the Chapter. These features can be found in two places, on your Student CD-ROM under the heading "Key Term Practice" and on the web site.

☐ Review the Learning Objectives of the Chapter found on pages S-319 and S-320 of this Study Guide.

☐ As a review, we recommend that you view the PowerPoint Slides for Chapter Nineteen that are available on the web site. If you do not have access to the Microsoft PowerPoint program, the PowerPoint Viewer program can be installed from the Student CD-ROM.

Solution to Chapter Nineteen Exercises

Exercise Nineteen - 1 Solution

It would appear that, in this example, there is a share for share exchange that meets the conditions of ITA 85.1. Unless Ms. Alee elects out of this rollover provision in her income tax return, the tax consequences of this transaction for Ms. Alee would be as follows:

- Ms. Alee would be deemed to have disposed of her Aayee Ltd. shares at a value equal to their adjusted cost base of $450,000. As a consequence, there would be no capital gain on the disposition.
- Ms. Alee would be deemed to have acquired her Global Outreach Inc. shares at a cost equal to the adjusted cost base of the Aayee Ltd. shares, or $450,000.

With respect to Global Outreach Inc., they would be deemed to have acquired the Aayee Ltd. shares at the lesser of their fair market value and their paid up capital. In this case, the $450,000 paid up capital amount is the lower figure.

Exercise Nineteen - 2 Solution

The required PUC reduction on the redeemable preferred shares would be calculated as follows:

Increase In Legal Stated Capital		$1,300,000
Less The Excess, If Any, Of:		
PUC Of Common Shares	($1,000,000)	
Over The Non-Share Consideration	1,000,000	Nil
PUC Reduction		$1,300,000

This means that the redeemable preferred shares would have a PUC of nil ($1,300,000 - $1,300,000).

The adjusted cost base of the redeemable preferred shares would be calculated as follows:

Adjusted Cost Base Of Common Shares	$1,000,000
Non-Share Consideration	(1,000,000)
Adjusted Cost Base Of Redeemable Preferred Shares	Nil

The proceeds of redemption of the common shares would be $1,000,000 ($1,000,000 + Nil new PUC), resulting in an ITA 84(3) deemed dividend of nil ($1,000,000 - $1,000,000 old PUC). The proceeds of disposition would also be $1,000,000 ($1,000,000 cash + Nil new ACB), resulting in a capital gain of nil ($1,000,000 - $1,000,000).

Exercise Nineteen - 3 Solution

The required PUC reduction on the redeemable preferred shares would be calculated as follows:

Increase In Legal Stated Capital		$1,300,000
Less The Excess, If Any, Of:		
PUC Of Common Shares	($1,000,000)	
Over The Non-Share Consideration	1,000,000	Nil
PUC Reduction		$1,300,000

This means that the redeemable preferred shares would have a PUC of nil ($1,300,000 - $1,300,000).

The adjusted cost base of the redeemable preferred shares would be calculated as follows:

Adjusted Cost Base Of Common Shares	$1,250,000
Non-Share Consideration	(1,000,000)
Adjusted Cost Base Of Redeemable Preferred Shares	$ 250,000

The proceeds of redemption of the common shares would be $1,000,000 ($1,000,000 + Nil new PUC), resulting in an ITA 84(3) deemed dividend of nil ($1,000,000 - $1,000,000 old PUC). The proceeds of disposition would be $1,250,000 ($1,000,000 cash + $250,000 new ACB), resulting in a capital gain of nil ($1,250,000 - $1,250,000).

Exercise Nineteen - 4 Solution

The required PUC reduction on the redeemable preferred shares would be calculated as follows:

Increase In Legal Stated Capital		$1,100,000
Less The Excess, If Any, Of:		
PUC Of Common Shares	($1,000,000)	
Over The Non-Share Consideration	1,200,000	Nil
PUC Reduction		$1,100,000

This means that the redeemable preferred shares would have a PUC of nil ($1,100,000 - $1,100,000).

The adjusted cost base of the redeemable preferred shares would be calculated as follows:

Adjusted Cost Base Of Common Shares	$1,250,000
Non-Share Consideration	(1,200,000)
Adjusted Cost Base Of Redeemable Preferred Shares	$ 50,000

Because the non-share consideration was greater than the PUC of the old shares, the resulting ITA 84(3) deemed dividend and the capital loss would be calculated as follows:

Non-Share Consideration	$1,200,000
PUC Of New Shares	Nil
Proceeds Of Redemption Under ITA 84(5)(d)	$1,200,000
PUC Of Old Shares	(1,000,000)
ITA 84(3) Deemed Dividend (Non-Eligible)	$ 200,000

Adjusted Cost Base Of New Shares	$ 50,000
Plus Non-Share Consideration	1,200,000
Proceeds Of Disposition Under ITA 86(1)(c)	$1,250,000
ITA 84(3) Deemed Dividend	(200,000)
Adjusted Proceeds	$1,050,000
Adjusted Cost Base Of Old Shares	(1,250,000)
Capital Gain (Loss)	($ 200,000)

The taxable amount of the non-eligible dividend would be $250,000 [(125%)($200,000)]. It would qualify for a federal dividend tax credit of $33,333 [(2/3)(25%)($200,000)]. The allowable capital loss would be $100,000 [(1/2)($200,000)].

Exercise Nineteen - 5 Solution

Ms. Reviser gave up shares with a fair market value of $1,280,000 [(80%)($1,600,000)], in return for consideration of $1,100,000 ($300,000 + $800,000). As her daughter holds common shares, it would appear that there is a gift to her daughter of $180,000. This means that ITA 86(2) is applicable.

The PUC reduction on the new shares would be calculated as follows:

Increase In Legal Stated Capital		$800,000
Less The Excess, If Any, Of:		
PUC Of Common Shares [(80%)($250,000)]	($200,000)	
Over The Non-Share Consideration	300,000	Nil
PUC Reduction		$800,000

This means that the redeemable preferred shares would have a PUC of nil ($800,000 - $800,000).

Under ITA 86(2)(e), the adjusted cost base of the redeemable preferred shares would be calculated as follows:

Adjusted Cost Base Of Common Shares [(80%)($250,000)]		$200,000
Deduct:		
Non-Share Consideration	($300,000)	
Gift	(180,000)	(480,000)
Adjusted Cost Base Of Preferred Shares		Nil

Given the $180,000 gift, the ITA 84(3) deemed dividend and the capital gain would be calculated as follows:

Non-Share Consideration	$300,000
PUC Of New Shares	Nil
Proceeds Of Redemption Under ITA 84(5)(d)	$300,000
PUC Of Old Shares	(200,000)
ITA 84(3) Deemed Dividend (Non-Eligible)	$100,000
ITA 86(2)(c) Proceeds Of Disposition:	
Non-Share Consideration	$300,000
Gift	180,000
Total Proceeds Of Disposition	$480,000
ITA 84(3) Deemed Dividend	(100,000)
Adjusted Proceeds	$380,000
Adjusted Cost Base Of Old Shares	(200,000)
Capital Gain	$180,000

The taxable amount of the non-eligible dividend would be $125,000 [(125%)($100,000)] and the taxable capital gain would be $90,000 [(1/2)($180,000)].

Exercise Nineteen - 6 Solution
As Upton Inc. has a clear majority of the shares in Amalgo Inc., it would appear that they have acquired control of Downer Ltd. As the acquisition of control rules would be applicable, there would be a deemed year end for both Companies that coincides with the amalgamated year end. The non-capital loss carry forward of Downer Ltd. will be flowed through to the amalgamated company, Amalgo Inc. However, because of the acquisition of control, the net capital loss carry forward cannot be used. In addition, for the non-capital loss to be used, Amalgo Inc. would have to continue the business in which the loss occurred and the loss carry forward could only be applied against profits in that business.

Exercise Nineteen - 7 Solution

Subsequent to the beginning of an ITA 88(1) winding-up, the parent company can deduct subsidiary losses in its first taxation year beginning after that date. This would be the year beginning on September 16, 2006.

Side's loss is deemed to occur in Park's taxation year that includes Side's year end. This would be the year ending September 15, 2002. This means that it will expire, after seven taxation years, at the end of Park's taxation year ending September 15, 2008 (the winding-up creates a deemed year end which counts as an additional year).

Exercise Nineteen - 8 Solution

Under ITA 88(1), a limited bump-up of non-depreciable assets is available. The basic limit would be calculated as follows:

Adjusted Cost Base Of Lorne Inc. Shares	$1,200,000
Tax Values Of Lorne Inc.'s Net Assets	
At Winding-Up ($500,000 - $75,000)	(425,000)
Dividends Paid By Lorne Since Acquisition	Nil
Excess	$ 775,000

However, this basic amount cannot exceed the difference between the fair market value of the non-depreciable assets at the time of the share acquisition and their tax cost at that time. This amount would be $130,000 ($270,000 - $140,000). The bump-up in the Land value is limited to that amount, resulting in the following tax values for Lorne's assets at the time of the ITA 88(1) winding-up:

Cash	$120,000
Land ($140,000 + $130,000)	270,000
Depreciable Assets - At UCC	240,000
Total Assets	$630,000

Exercise Nineteen - 9 Solution

Given the size of the proceeds, the balance in the RDTOH account will clearly be less than one-third of the dividends to be declared. Given this, the total distribution to shareholders will be $912,000 ($865,000 + $47,000).

The taxable dividend component of the total distribution to the shareholders is as follows:

Total Distribution	$912,000
Paid Up Capital	(88,000)
ITA 84(2) Deemed Dividend On Winding-Up	$824,000
Capital Dividend Account (Election Required)	(26,000)
Non-Eligible Dividend Subject To Tax	$798,000

The dividend subject to tax will qualify for the usual gross up and tax credit procedures for non-eligible dividends. As a disposition of shares has occurred, we must also determine whether there is a capital gain or loss. The calculations are as follows:

Total Distribution To Shareholders	$912,000
ITA 84(2) Deemed Dividend	(824,000)
Deemed Proceeds Of Disposition	$ 88,000
Adjusted Cost Base Of Shares	(88,000)
Capital Gain	Nil

Solution to Self Study Problem Nineteen - 1

Part A   The PUC of the new shares would be reduced under ITA 86(2.1) as follows:

Increase In Legal Stated Capital Of New Shares		$99,000
PUC - Old Shares	($99,000)	
Non-Share Consideration	69,000	(30,000)
Reduction In PUC		$69,000

Given this reduction, the resulting PUC of the new preferred shares would be as follows:

Increase In Legal Stated Capital Of New Shares	$99,000
Reduction In PUC	(69,000)
PUC - New Shares	$30,000

Part B   The adjusted cost base of the new preferred shares would be calculated as follows:

Adjusted Cost Base - Old Shares	$99,000
Non-Share Consideration	(69,000)
Adjusted Cost Base - New Shares	$30,000

Part C   The proceeds of disposition for the old common shares would be calculated as follows:

Adjusted Cost Base And PUC - New Shares	$30,000
Non-Share Consideration	69,000
Proceeds Of Disposition - Old Shares	$99,000

As the PUC of the old shares is equal to their ACB, this would be the proceeds of disposition under both ITA 86(1)(b) and ITA 84(5)(d).

Part D   As the proceeds of disposition is equal to both the adjusted cost base and PUC of the old shares, there would be no ITA 84(3) deemed dividend and no capital gain for Mr. Farnsworth at the time of the reorganization transaction.

Part E   If the preferred shares were redeemed for $381,000, the tax consequences would be as follows:

Redemption Proceeds	$381,000
Paid Up Capital - Preferred Shares	(30,000)
ITA 84(3) Deemed Dividend (Non-Eligible)	$351,000
Proceeds Of Disposition	$381,000
ITA 84(3) Deemed Dividend	(351,000)
Adjusted Proceeds Of Disposition	$ 30,000
Adjusted Cost Base - Preferred Shares	(30,000)
Capital Gain	Nil

There would be a taxable non-eligible dividend of $438,750 [(125%)($351,000)], which would qualify for a federal dividend tax credit of $58,500 [(2/3)(25%)($351,000)].

Solution to Self Study Problem Nineteen - 2

Approach One

Gift The fair market value of the common shares given up is $810,000 [(90%)($900,000)] and this is equal to the fair market value of the consideration received ($90,000 + $720,000). Given this, no gift is involved in the rollover and ITA 86(1) applies.

Adjusted Cost Base Of New Preferred Shares The adjusted cost base of these shares is calculated as follows:

Adjusted Cost Base Of Old Common Shares [($360,000)(90%)]	$324,000
Fair Market Value Of Boot	(90,000)
Adjusted Cost Base Of Preferred Shares	$234,000

PUC Reduction - New Shares The PUC reduction on the new shares would be calculated as follows:

Increase In Legal Stated Capital Of New Shares		$234,000
PUC Of Common Shares [(90%)($100,000)]	($90,000)	
Fair Market Value Of Boot	90,000	Nil
PUC Reduction		$234,000

PUC Of New Preferred Shares Giving the preceding PUC reduction, the PUC of the new shares would be nil ($234,000 - $234,000).

Redemption Of Common Shares For purposes of determining any ITA 84(3) dividend, the calculation would be as follows:

Non-Share Consideration	$90,000
PUC Of New Shares	Nil
Proceeds Of Redemption - ITA 84(5)(d)	$90,000
PUC Of Common Shares Redeemed [(90%)($100,000)]	(90,000)
ITA 84(3) Deemed Dividend	$ Nil

For purposes of determining any capital gain or loss, the calculation would be as follows:

Proceeds Of Disposition - ITA 86(1)(c) ($90,000 + $234,000)	$324,000
Deduct: ITA 84(3) Deemed Dividend	Nil
Adjusted Proceeds Of Disposition - ITA 54	$324,000
Adjusted Cost Base [(90%)($360,000)]	(324,000)
Capital Gain	$ Nil

Net Economic Effect No current income would be assessed to Mr. Long as a result of this reorganization transaction. He would retain the $90,000 note along with the preferred stock with a fair market value of $720,000. The $486,000 ($720,000 - $234,000) deferred capital gain on these shares would be the same as the deferred capital gain that was present on his previous holding of common shares ($810,000 - $324,000). He has accomplished the goal of freezing the value of his estate with no immediate tax consequences.

Approach Two

Gift   There is a gift involved in this approach, calculated as follows:

FMV Of Common Shares [(90%)($900,000)]		$810,000
FMV Of Boot	($ 50,000)	
FMV Of Preferred Shares	(660,000)	(710,000)
Gift		$100,000

As Mr. Long's daughter holds the remaining common shares, it is reasonable to assume that this $100,000 in value accrues to her. This means that the provisions of ITA 86(2) will be applicable if this approach is used.

Adjusted Cost Base Of New Preferred Shares   Under the provisions of ITA 86(2), the adjusted cost base of the new preferred shares would be calculated as follows:

Adjusted Cost Base Of Old Common Shares [(90%)($360,000)]		$324,000
Fair Market Value Of Boot	($ 50,000)	
Amount Of Gift	(100,000)	(150,000)
Adjusted Cost Base Of Preferred Shares		$174,000

PUC Reduction - New Shares   The PUC reduction on the new shares would be calculated as follows:

Increase In Legal Stated Capital Of New Shares		$40,000
PUC Of Common Shares	($90,000)	
Fair Market Value Of Boot	50,000	(40,000)
PUC Reduction		$ Nil

PUC Of New Preferred Shares   As there is no PUC reduction, the PUC of the new shares would be $40,000.

Redemption Of Common Shares   For purposes of determining any ITA 84(3) deemed dividend, the calculation would be as follows:

Fair Market Value Of The Boot	$50,000
PUC Of Preferred Shares	40,000
Proceeds Of Redemption - ITA 84(5)(d)	$90,000
PUC Of Common Shares Redeemed	(90,000)
ITA 84(3) Deemed Dividend	$ Nil

For purposes of determining any capital gain or loss, the calculation would be as follows:

Fair Market Value Of The Boot	$ 50,000
Gift	100,000
Proceeds Of Disposition - ITA 86(2)(c)	$150,000
ITA 84(3) Deemed Dividend	Nil
Adjusted Proceeds Of Disposition - ITA 54	$150,000
Adjusted Cost Base [(90%)($360,000)]	(324,000)
Capital Loss [Disallowed By ITA 86(2)(d)]	$ Nil

Net Economic Result   No current income would be assessed to Mr. Long as a result of this reorganization transaction. He would retain the $50,000 note along with the preferred stock with a fair market value of $660,000. The $486,000 ($660,000 - $174,000) deferred capital gain on these shares would be the same as the deferred capital gain that was present on his previous holding of common shares. However, the value of his investment has been reduced by $150,000 ($810,000 - $660,000). While he has received $50,000 of this reduction in non-share consideration, there is no corresponding reduction in tax values for the remaining $100,000. In addition, the fair market value of his daughter's shares has increased by $100,000 with no corresponding increase in their tax value. In effect, this approach will result in the amount of the $100,000 gift being subject to tax in his daughter's hands, with no compensating benefit available to either his daughter or himself.

Solution to Self Study Problem Nineteen - 3

Section 87   If ITA 87 is used, the tax consequences are as follows:

- Lynn will have proceeds of disposition equal to the adjusted cost base of the land of $175,000. No capital gain or loss will be recorded.

- Ricon Ltd. will be deemed to have acquired the land at its adjusted cost base of $175,000. As the subsidiary is less than 100 percent owned by Ricon, the bump-up provision from ITA 88(1) is not available if ITA (87) is used.

Section 88(1)   If ITA 88(1) is used, the tax consequences are as follows:

- Lynn will have proceeds of disposition equal to the adjusted cost base of the land of $175,000. No capital gain or loss will be recorded.

- Ricon Ltd. will have a "bump-up" in the tax value of the land that is the lesser of:

Adjusted Cost Base Of Lynn Shares		$380,000
Deduct:		
Cost Of Lynn's Assets	$175,000	
Dividends Paid By Lynn	Nil	(175,000)
Maximum Bump-Up		$205,000
Fair Market Value Of Land When Lynn Shares Acquired (90 Percent)		$351,000
Adjusted Cost Base Of Land (90 Percent)		(157,500)
Maximum Increase In Land Value		$193,500

The amount of the bump-up will be limited to $193,500, resulting in an adjusted cost base of the land of $368,500 ($175,000 + $193,500).

Conclusion   ITA 88(1) is the preferable approach as it adds $193,500 to Ricon's adjusted cost base for the land. This will serve to reduce any future capital gain on an arm's length disposition of the land. Note that this solution does not consider the tax consequences to the minority shareholders of Lynn.

Solution to Self Study Problem Nineteen - 4

The taxable capital gains and active business income (recapture) at the corporate level can be calculated as follows:

Asset	Taxable Capital Gains	Active Business Income
Inventories	Nil	Nil
Taxable Capital Gains:		
On Land [(1/2)($1,553,750 - $778,750)	$387,500	Nil
On Building [(1/2)($1,591,250 - $1,093,750)	248,750	
Recapture On Building ($1,093,750 - $732,500)		$361,250
Totals	$636,250	$361,250

The taxable capital gains will result in an addition to the Refundable Dividend Tax On Hand account. This will leave a balance in this account as follows:

RDTOH Balance Prior To Asset Dispositions	$ 33,750
Additions [(26-2/3%)($636,250)]	169,667
Ending RDTOH Balance	$203,417

The Taxable Income resulting from the sale of assets equals $997,500 ($636,250 + $361,250). This will create a General Rate Income Pool balance of $41,650 [(68%)($997,500 - $300,000 - $636,250)]. This will provide a basis for designating $41,650 of the taxable dividends as eligible for the enhanced gross up and tax credit procedures.

The amount available for distribution to the shareholders, after the payment of all taxes at the corporate level, can be calculated as follows:

Fair Market Values:	
Inventories	$ 43,750
Land	1,553,750
Building	1,591,250
Gross Proceeds	$3,188,750
Tax On Income Eligible For Small Business Deduction [(18%)($300,000)]	(54,000)
Tax On Remaining Active Business Income [(37%)($361,250 - $300,000)]	(22,663)
Tax On Taxable Capital Gains [(50-2/3%)($636,250)]	(322,367)
Dividend Refund (Note)	203,417
Funds Available For Distribution	$2,993,137

Note The dividend refund is equal to the balance in the RDTOH account. As will be shown in a subsequent calculation, the taxable dividends paid on the wind-up are well in excess of the amount needed to trigger the refund of the balance in the RDTOH account.

With respect to the capital dividend account, the final balance is calculated as follows:

Balance Before Dispositions	$268,750
Disposition Of Land	387,500
Disposition Of Building	248,750
Ending Balance	$905,000

Assuming an election has been made to declare the maximum capital dividend, the taxable dividend component of the total distribution to the shareholders can be calculated as follows:

Distribution To Shareholders	$2,993,137
Paid Up Capital	(68,750)
ITA 84(2) Deemed Dividend	$2,924,387
ITA 83(2) Capital Dividend (Balance In Account)	(905,000)
Deemed Dividend Subject To Tax	$2,019,387

In order to maximize the after tax retention by the shareholders, the Company should designate $41,650 of this dividend as eligible for the enhanced 45 percent gross up and tax credit procedures. This leaves a non-eligible dividend of $1,977,737 ($2,019,387 - $41,650).

With respect to capital gains, ITA 54 indicates that the proceeds of disposition for purposes of determining any capital gain on the disposition of shares does not include any amount paid out as ITA 84(2) deemed dividends. Given the preceding calculation, the capital gain to the shareholders would be calculated as follows:

Distribution To Shareholders	$2,993,137
ITA 84(2) Deemed Dividend	(2,924,387)
Deemed Proceeds	$ 68,750
Adjusted Cost Base Of Shares	(68,750)
Capital Gain	$ Nil

Solution to Self Study Problem Nineteen - 5

Sale Of Shares   If the shares are sold for $455,000, the after tax results are as follows:

Proceeds Of Disposition	$455,000
Adjusted Cost Base	(52,500)
Capital Gain	$402,500
Inclusion Rate	1/2
Taxable Capital Gain	$201,250
Tax Rate For Mr. Brock	47%
Tax Payable	$ 94,588
Proceeds Of Disposition	$455,000
Tax Payable	(94,588)
After Tax Proceeds	$360,412

Sale Of Assets   This more complex transaction begins with a calculation of the Tax Payable at the corporate level, subsequent to the sale of assets:

	Business Income	Taxable Capital Gains
Inventory ($109,500 - $105,000)	$ 4,500	$ Nil
Land	Nil	17,500
Building	87,500	7,000
Equipment (Note One)	(21,000)	Nil
Goodwill (Note Two)	82,250	Nil
Taxable Amounts	$153,250	$24,500
Tax Rate	18%	47%
Tax Payable	$ 27,585	$11,515

Note One   There is a terminal loss of $21,000 ($63,000 - $42,000).

Note Two   Business income in the amount of $82,250 [(3/4)($164,500)(1/2 ÷ 3/4)] will have to be recognized on the disposition of the business assets.

Given the preceding calculations, the amount that would be available for distribution to Mr. Brock would be as follows:

Gross Proceeds (Given)	$491,000
Tax Payable ($27,585 + $11,515)	(39,100)
Dividend Refund (Note)	6,533
Available For Distribution	$458,433

Note   The dividend refund would be the lesser of the ending balance in the RDTOH and an amount equal to $1 for every $3 in taxable dividends paid. There was no opening balance in the RDTOH and the only addition during the year was $6,533 [(26-2/3%)($24,500)]. This leaves a balance of $6,533, which is significantly less than one-third of the dividends that will be paid.

With respect to the capital dividend account, the final balance is calculated as follows:

Balance Before Dispositions	$ 70,000
Disposition Of Land [(1/2)($70,000 - $35,000)]	17,500
Disposition Of Building [(1/2)($136,500 - $122,500)]	7,000
Disposition Of Goodwill [($164,500)(1/2)]	82,250
Ending Balance	$176,750

Assuming an election has been made to declare the maximum capital dividend, the taxable dividend component of the total distribution to Mr. Brock can be calculated as follows:

Funds Available For Distribution	$458,433
Paid Up Capital	(52,500)
ITA 84(2) Deemed Dividend	$405,933
ITA 83(2) Capital Dividend (Balance In Account)	(176,750)
Deemed Dividend Subject To Tax (Non-Eligible)	$229,183

The gain or loss resulting from the disposition of shares on winding-up the corporation is calculated as follows:

Funds Distributed	$458,433
ITA 84(2) Deemed Dividend	(405,933)
Deemed Proceeds Of Disposition For Shares	$ 52,500
Adjusted Cost Base	(52,500)
Capital Gain	Nil

The total cash retained, after the deemed dividends and winding-up of the corporation, can be calculated as follows:

Funds Distributed	$458,433
Tax On Deemed Non-Eligible Dividend Subject To Tax [(31%)($229,183)]	(71,047)
After Tax Proceeds	$387,386

As this result is more favourable than the $360,412 in after tax proceeds resulting from the sale of shares, Mr. Brock should sell the assets rather than the shares.

Chapter Nineteen Learning Objectives

After completing Chapter 19, you should be able to:

1. Identify situations where the ITA 85.1 rollover provision is applicable (paragraph 19-1 through 19-10).

2. Identify situations where the ITA 86(1) rollover provision is applicable (paragraph 19-11 through 19-14).

3. List the conditions that must be met in order to use the ITA 86(1) rollover provision (paragraph 19-15 through 19-16).

4. Explain the procedures that are required in implementing an ITA 86(1) rollover (paragraph 19-17 through 19-20).

5. Apply the ITA 86(1) rollover procedures to specific examples (paragraph 19-21 through 19-26).

6. Identify situations where the ITA 86(2) benefit rule is applicable and apply the required procedures to specific examples (paragraph 19-27 through 19-36).

7. Describe the practical factors that must be given consideration in implementing an ITA 86(1) rollover (paragraph 19-37).

8. Describe some of the advantages and disadvantages associated with the use of ITA 86(1) (paragraph 19-38 through 19-43).

9. Explain the nature of an ITA 87 amalgamation (paragraph 19-44 through 19-46).

10. Describe the position of the amalgamated company subsequent to an ITA 87 amalgamation (paragraph 19-47 through 19-51).

11. Describe the position of the shareholders of the amalgamated company subsequent to an ITA 87 amalgamation (paragraph 19-52).

12. Identify the specific considerations involved in vertical amalgamations (paragraph 19-53 through 19-57).

13. Explain both the non-tax and tax planning considerations related to ITA 87 amalgamations (paragraph 19-58 through 19-61).

14. Explain the nature of an ITA 88(1) winding-up of a 90 percent owned subsidiary (paragraph 19-62 through 19-69).

15. Apply the procedures for recording the assets acquired by the parent company in an ITA 88(1) winding-up of a 90 percent owned subsidiary (paragraph 19-70 through 19-80).

16. Apply the procedures required for the disposition of shares that occurs in the winding-up of a 90 percent owned subsidiary (paragraph 19-81 through 19-82).

17. Compare the results of applying ITA 87 vs. the results of applying ITA 88(1) and any associated tax planning issues (paragraph 19-83 through 19-89).

18. Apply the procedures required in an ITA 88(2) winding-up of a Canadian corporation (paragraph 19-90 through 19-103).

19. Explain the procedures used under ITA 51 when there is a conversion of a corporation's debt securities (paragraph 19-104 through 19-110).

20. Describe the alternative methods of business valuation (paragraph 19-111 through 19-115).

21. Demonstrate an understanding of the asset based methods of business valuation (paragraph 19-116 through 19-121).

22. Demonstrate an understanding of the income based methods of business valuation (paragraph 19-122 through 19-131).

23. Explain the basic alternatives for the sale of an incorporated business (paragraph 19-132 through 19-133).

24. Demonstrate an understanding of the provisions relating to restrictive covenants (a.k.a. non-competition agreements) (paragraph 19-134 through 19-138).

25. Describe the procedures used when the individual assets of a business are sold (paragraph 19-139 through 19-141).

26. Describe the procedures used when the assets of a business are sold as a going concern (paragraph 19-142 through 19-151).

27. Describe the procedures used when the shares of a business are sold (paragraph 19-152 through 19-156).

28. Compare an offer to purchase the shares of a business and an offer to purchase its assets and determine the preferable alternative (paragraph 19-157 through 19-169).

29. Describe the GST implications resulting from the sale of an incorporated business (paragraph 19-170 through 19-182).

30. Explain the meaning of the term tax shelter and describe the basic types of tax shelters (paragraph 19-183 through 19-206).

31. List the factors to consider in evaluating investments in tax shelters (paragraph 19-207 through 19-208).

CHAPTER TWENTY

How To Work Through Chapter Twenty

We recommend the following approach in dealing with the material in this Chapter:

Partnerships - Introduction
☐ Read the text pages 857 and 858 (paragraph 20-1 through 20-6).

Partnerships Defined
☐ Read the text pages 858 through 860 (paragraph 20-7 through 20-23).

☐ Complete Self Study Problem Twenty-1 on page 882 of the text. The solution is on pages S-325 and S-326.

Co-Ownership, Joint Ventures, And Syndicates
☐ Read the text pages 860 through 862 (paragraph 20-24 through 20-38).

Determining Partnership Income, Losses, And Tax Credits
☐ Read the text pages 862 through 864 (paragraph 20-39 through 20-52).

☐ Complete Exercise Twenty-1 on page 864 of the text. The solution is on page S-323.

☐ Read the text page 865 (paragraph 20-52).

☐ Complete Exercises Twenty-2 and Twenty-3 on pages 865 and 866 of the text. The solutions are on page S-323.

Allocations To Partners And Partner Expenses
☐ Read the text pages 866 through 868 (paragraph 20-53 through 20-64).

☐ Complete Exercise Twenty-4 on page 868 of the text. The solution is on page S-323.

☐ Complete Self Study Problem Twenty-2 on pages 882 and 883 of the text. The solution is on pages S-326 and S-327.

The Partnership Interest
☐ Read the text pages 868 and 869 (paragraph 20-65 through 20-74).

☐ Complete Exercise Twenty-5 on page 869 of the text. The solution is on pages S-323 and S-324.

Adjustments To The ACB Of A Partnership Interest
☐ Read the text pages 869 through 872 (paragraph 20-75 through 20-91).

☐ Complete Exercise Twenty-6 on pages 872 and 873 of the text. The solution is on page S-324.

☐ Complete Self Study Problem Twenty-3 on pages 883 and 884 of the text. The solution is on pages S-327 and S-328.

☐ Complete Self Study Problem Twenty-6 on pages 885 and 886 of the text. The solution is on pages S-330 and S-331.

Limited Partnerships And Limited Partners

☐ Read the text pages 873 through 875 (paragraph 20-92 through 20-103).

☐ Complete Exercise Twenty-7 on page 875 of the text. The solution is on page S-324.

☐ Complete Self Study Problem Twenty-4 on page 884 of the text. The solution is on pages S-328 and S-329.

Transfers Of Property To And From A Partnership - No Rollover

☐ Read the text pages 875 and 876 (paragraph 20-104 through 20-109).

☐ Complete Exercise Twenty-8 on page 876 of the text. The solution is on page S-325.

☐ Read the text page 876 (paragraph 20-110).

☐ Complete Exercise Twenty-9 on pages 876 and 877 of the text. The solution is on page S-325.

Common Partnership Rollovers

☐ Read the text pages 877 through 879 (paragraph 20-111 through 20-127).

☐ Complete Self Study Problem Twenty-5 on pages 884 and 885 of the text. The solution is on pages S-329 and S-330.

Partnerships And GST

☐ Read the text page 880 (paragraph 20-128 through 20-134).

To Complete This Chapter

☐ Review the Key Terms Used In This Chapter on page 881 of the text. Consult the Glossary for the meaning of any key terms you do not know.

☐ Review the Glossary Flashcards and complete the Key Terms Self-Test for the Chapter. These features can be found in two places, on your Student CD-ROM under the heading "Key Term Practice" and on the web site.

☐ Review the Learning Objectives of the Chapter found on page S-332 of this Study Guide.

Solution to Chapter Twenty Exercises

Exercise Twenty - 1 Solution

Net Accounting Income	$146,000
Interest On Partners' Capital Accounts	4,400
Salaries To Partners	37,000
Net Income For Tax Purposes	$187,400

Note that the salaries paid to the spouses of the partners would be deductible, provided the amounts were reasonable for the work that was done.

Exercise Twenty - 2 Solution

A. Deductible - Office rent expense is deductible if incurred to earn property or business income.
B. Not deductible - Political contributions eligible for the tax credit are flowed through to the individual partners.
C. Deductible - Interest can be deducted if the loan is a bona fide arrangement and the proceeds are used by the partnership to earn property or business income.
D. Not deductible - Donations to registered Canadian charities are flowed through to the individual partners.

Exercise Twenty - 3 Solution

Net Accounting Loss	($71,600)
Qualifying Political Contributions	16,000
Personal Expenditures Of Partner	8,000
Rental Expenses	(12,000)
Net Loss For Tax Purposes	($59,600)

Exercise Twenty - 4 Solution

The required first $40,000 of partnership income should be allocated to Ruth. The remaining negative balance of $5,000 should be allocated equally between Emily and Ruth, as follows:

	Emily	Ruth	Total
Guaranteed income allocation (salary)	Nil	$40,000	$40,000
Share of remainder ($35,000 - $40,000)	($2,500)	(2,500)	(5,000)
Net allocations	($2,500)	$37,500	$35,000

This solution follows the recommendations in the CRA's "Guide For The Partnership Information Form". This is the recommended treatment when salaries are considered as part of the allocation process to partners.

Exercise Twenty - 5 Solution

Alan and Balan will each have a disposition of one-third of their partnership interests for $40,000. The adjusted cost base of each third is $16,000 [(1/3)($48,000)], so Alan and Balan will each have a $24,000 ($40,000 - $16,000) capital gain, of which one-half, or $12,000, will be a taxable capital gain.

The partner capital account transactions and ending balances will be:

	Alan	Balan	Caitlin
Opening Capital Accounts	$48,000	$48,000	Nil
Adjustment For Caitlin's Admission	(16,000)	(16,000)	$32,000
Ending Capital Accounts (Accounting Values)	$32,000	$32,000	$32,000
ACB Of Partnership Interest	$32,000	$32,000	$80,000

Exercise Twenty - 6 Solution

The ACB of Robert's partnership interest on December 31, 2006 and January 1, 2007 would be determined as follows:

Original Capital Contribution	$12,500
Additional Contribution	7,200
Drawing	(4,000)
ACB - December 31, 2006	$15,700
Adjustment For 2006 Income [(40%)($11,600 + $3,100 + $46,700)]	24,560
ACB - January 1, 2007	$40,260

Robert's inclusion in Net Income For Tax Purposes would be as follows:

Taxable Capital Gain [(1/2)($11,600)]	$5,800
Taxable Dividends [($3,100)(145%)]	4,495
Net Business Income	46,700
Subtotal	$56,995
Robert's Share Of Profits	40%
Inclusion In 2006 Net Income For Tax Purposes	$22,798

Note that this is not the same $24,560 that was added to the ACB of Robert's partnership interest to reflect his share of 2006 partnership income. The dividends would qualify for a federal dividend tax credit of $852 [(11/18)($3,100)(45%)].

Exercise Twenty - 7 Solution

ACB Of Partnership Interest		$200,000
Share Of Partnership Income For Current Period		Nil
Subtotal		$200,000
Amounts Owed To The Partnership	($150,000)	
Other Amounts Intended To Reduce Investment Risk	Nil	(150,000)
At-Risk Amount - December 31, 2006		$ 50,000

The loss is only deductible to the extent of the $50,000 at-risk amount. The $25,000 ($75,000 - $50,000) excess is his limited partnership loss for 2006.

Exercise Twenty - 8 Solution

Part A   Charles is considered to have disposed of the land for $100,000, resulting in a $33,500 [(1/2)($100,000 - $33,000)] taxable capital gain. LIU will be considered to have acquired the land for $100,000. Charles is considered to have made a capital contribution of $100,000 that will be added to the ACB of his partnership interest.

Part B   Charles will have the same $33,500 taxable capital gain as in Part A and LIU will be considered to have acquired the land for $100,000. The capital contribution and the addition to the ACB of the partnership interest is equal to $75,000. This is the difference between the fair market value of the land transferred to LIU of $100,000 and the $25,000 in other consideration received by Charles on the property transfer.

Part C   Charles will have the same $33,500 taxable capital gain as in Part A and LIU will be considered to have acquired the land for $100,000. No capital contribution is made. As Charles withdrew $12,000 ($112,000 - $100,000) more from LIU than he transferred in, Charles will be considered to have made a net withdrawal. The ACB of his partnership interest will be reduced by $12,000.

Exercise Twenty - 9 Solution

ITA 98(2) deems DG to have disposed of the share investments for the fair market value of $94,000, resulting in an $55,000 ($94,000 - $39,000) capital gain. One-fifth of the capital gain, or $11,000, will be allocated to Darlene. One-half of this amount, or $5,500, will be a taxable capital gain that she will be required to include in her income for 2006. Darlene will also be considered to have acquired the share investments for $18,800 [(20%)($94,000)]. The adjusted cost base of her partnership interest on December 31, 2006 and on January 1, 2007 is calculated as follows:

Adjusted Cost Base Prior To The Distribution	$30,000
Drawings	(18,800)
Adjusted Cost Base - December 31, 2006	$11,200
Allocated Capital Gain	11,000
Adjusted Cost Base - January 1, 2007	$22,200

Solution to Self Study Problem Twenty - 1

The determination of the existence of a partnership is a mixed question of fact and law, based upon the intention of the parties that may be expressed clearly through a valid written partnership agreement or inferred from actions. In Canada, the relevant provincial partnership legislation is applicable to answering this question.

In this case, an analysis of the three elements of a partnership is as follows:

1. **Was a business carried on by the partnership?**

   A business has a beginning and an end. Ongoing profitable activity within the business may actually only occur between these two extremes, but the activity remains a business throughout the period. In other words, profitability is generally irrelevant to a finding that a business exists. In this case, the selling off of store property will likely occur as part of the wind up process of the two stores. Accordingly, there are arguments that support the carrying on of a business.

2. **Was the business carried on in common by two or more persons?**

The details of the partnership agreement contain many of the necessary ingredients that the courts will look to in support of this element. Accordingly, it appears that this element has also been met.

3. **Was there a view to profit?**

This element will be satisfied if there is a potential for profit even though one may never be realized. The facts clearly lead to a conclusion that there is no hope of profit. The additional fact that the partnership will be terminated once the property is sold and that losses are not only expected, but anticipated, speaks for itself. A tax motivation that predominates, such as this, will not invalidate a partnership as long as there is a profit potential and the other elements are met. This is not the case.

Conclusion: A partnership was not created. As a result, no losses can be allocated to the investors. The losses belong to Wayout Ltd.

Solution to Self Study Problem Twenty - 2

Partnership Net Income   The income of the partnership, calculated as if the partnership were a separate person resident in Canada, is as follows:

Net Income As Per Income Statement		$192,100
Additions:		
Partners' Salaries [(2)($44,000)]	$88,000	
Depreciation Deducted	12,500	
Charitable Donations	7,200	
Closing Accounts Receivable (Note One)	56,000	163,700
Deductions:		
Opening Accounts Receivable (Note One)	($27,000)	
Capital Gains On Securities (Note Two)	(14,000)	
Dividends Received (Note Three)	(48,000)	
CCA:		
Class 8 [(20%)($26,000)]	(5,200)	
Class 45 {[45%][$14,000 + ($8,500)(1/2)]}	(8,213)	(102,413)
Net Business Income		$253,387

Note One   The addition of closing accounts receivable and the deduction of the opening accounts receivable are required to adjust the cash based income figure to an accrual based income figure.

Note Two   The total capital gain is deducted in the calculation of net business income. The taxable one-half of these gains is included on a flow through basis in the income of the individual partners.

Note Three   The dividends received are deducted in the calculation of net business income. They are flowed through as taxable Canadian dividends in the income of the individual partners.

Mr. Caldwell's Personal Income   The amount to be included in Mr. Caldwell's personal tax return would be calculated as follows:

Partnership Income [(1/2)($253,387)]	$126,694
Automobile Costs:	
CCA [($13,500)(30%)(75%)]	(3,038)
Operating Costs [($4,000)(75%)]	(3,000)
Net Business Income From Professional Practice	$120,656
Taxable Capital Gains [(1/2)($14,000)(1/2)]	3,500
Eligible Dividends Received From Canadian	
Corporations [($48,000)(145%)(1/2)]	34,800
Net Income For Tax Purposes	$158,956

Mr. Caldwell's $3,600 [(1/2)($7,200)] share of the charitable donations can be used as the basis for a credit against his personal Tax Payable. The amount of the credit would be $1,017 [(15.25%)($200) + (29%)($3,400)].

He is also entitled to a federal dividend tax credit of $6,600 [(11/18)($48,000)(45%)(1/2)].

Solution to Self Study Problem Twenty - 3

The adjusted cost base of Eric Beam's partnership interest on the date he withdrew from the partnership is calculated as follows:

Initial Investment	$225,000
Share Of Business Income [(1/3)($195,000)]	65,000
Share Of Capital Gains (Note One) [(1/3)($66,000)]	22,000
Share Of Charitable Donations (Note Two) [(1/3)($12,000)]	(4,000)
Drawings From The Partnership	(43,000)
Additional Capital Contributions	54,000
Adjusted Cost Base On January 1, 2006	$319,000

Note One   Only one-half of the capital gain is included in the partner's income on the flow through of capital gains realized by a partnership. However, the remaining one-half is included in the assets of the partnership and, in the absence of a special provision to deal with this situation, the realization of this amount would be added to any capital gain realized on the disposition of the partnership interest. ITA 53(1)(e)(i) provides such a provision, indicating that the full amount of any capital gains must be added to the ACB of a partnership interest.

Note Two   Charitable donations cannot be deducted in the calculation of partnership income for tax purposes. Instead, they are allocated to the individual partners to be used by them as the basis for credits against their personal Tax Payable. Given this, ITA 53(2)(c)(iii) requires that these amounts be deducted from the ACB of the partnership interest.

Given the preceding calculation, the gain on the disposition of the partnership interest can be calculated as follows:

Proceeds Of Disposition		$355,000
Adjusted Cost Base:		
From Preceding Calculation	($319,000)	
Legal And Accounting Fees	(1,800)	(320,800)
Capital Gain		$ 34,200
Inclusion Rate		1/2
Taxable Capital Gain		$ 17,100

This amount would be included in Eric Beam's Net Income For Tax Purposes for 2006 as a taxable capital gain. He would not include any partnership income for the period January 1 to February 1, 2006, as he was not allocated any of this income.

Solution to Self Study Problem Twenty - 4

Note The addition of the share of the partnership income amounts to the at-risk balance as at December 31 is intended to ensure that this amount is taken into consideration in determining the amount that is actually at risk on that date. Notice, however, losses are not deducted at this time in the determination of the at-risk amount. We would remind you that in calculating the adjusted cost base of the partnership interest, a partner's share of either a loss or a gain is not added until the first day of the following taxation year.

The required amounts for Melanie's investment in the Cross Your Fingers Partnership are as follows:

Adjusted Cost Base - December 31, 2006		$20,000
Add: Share Of Partnership Income (Not Losses) For		
The Current Period [(4%)($12,000 + $17,500 + $20,000)]		1,980
Total		$21,980
Less:		
Amounts Owed To The Partnership		
($16,800 - $2,100)	$ 14,700	
Other Amounts Intended To		
Reduce The Investment Risk	1,500	(16,200)
At-Risk Amount - December 31, 2006		$ 5,780

The share of partnership income that is added to the at-risk amount is the amount that will be added to the ACB. It does not include the dividend gross up and it is not reduced by the non-taxable half of the capital gain.

Allocated 4 Percent Share Of 2006 Partnership Income (Loss)	
[(4%)($180,000)]	($ 7,200)
At-Risk Amount - December 31, 2006	5,780
Limited Partnership Loss For 2006	($ 1,420)
Allocated 4 Percent Share Of 2006 Partnership Income (Loss)	($ 7,200)
Limited Partnership Loss For 2006	1,420
Deductible Loss For 2006	($ 5,780)

There is a limited partnership loss carry forward of $1,420 at the end of 2006.

Adjusted Cost Base - December 31, 2006	$20,000
Add: Share Of Partnership Income For The Current Period	
[(4%)($12,000 + $17,500 + $20,000)]	1,980
Deductible Loss For 2006	(5,780)
Adjusted Cost Base - January 1, 2007	$16,200

Solution to Self Study Problem Twenty - 5

Cash With all non-share consideration, the ACB is equal to its fair market value. In the case of cash, the fair market value is equal to the face value. These amounts would be $78,000 for Porter, $222,000 for Quinn, and $422,000 for Roberts.

Preferred Shares With respect to the preferred shares received by each partner, ITA 85(3)(e) indicates that their ACB will be the lesser of:

- Their fair market value, which would be $180,000 for each of the three partners.

- The ACB of each partnership interest, reduced by the amount of non-share consideration received by the partner.

This latter value would be calculated as follows for each of the three partners:

	Porter	Quinn	Roberts
ACB	$382,000	$526,000	$726,000
Cash Received	(78,000)	(222,000)	(422,000)
Balance	$304,000	$304,000	$304,000

For each of the three partners, the lower figure would be the fair market value of $180,000 and, as a consequence, this would be the ACB of their preferred shares.

Common Shares Under ITA 85(3)(f), the ACB of the common shares received by each partner would be the ACB of their partnership interest, less the sum of the value of the non-share consideration received and the value assigned to the preferred shares received. These amounts would be calculated as follows:

	Porter	Quinn	Roberts
ACB - Partnership Interest	$382,000	$526,000	$726,000
Cash Received	(78,000)	(222,000)	(422,000)
ACB - Preferred Shares	(180,000)	(180,000)	(180,000)
ACB - Common Shares	$124,000	$124,000	$124,000

Capital Gain Or Loss As the non-share consideration had a value that was less than the value of the assets transferred, there will be no immediate gain or loss on this rollover. This can be demonstrated with the following calculation:

	Porter	Quinn	Roberts
Proceeds Of Disposition:			
Cash	$ 78,000	$222,000	$422,000
Preferred Shares	180,000	180,000	180,000
Common Shares	124,000	124,000	124,000
Total Proceeds	$382,000	$526,000	$726,000
ACB	(382,000)	(526,000)	(726,000)
Capital Gain (Loss)	Nil	Nil	Nil

From an economic point of view the gain is still present. The partners have simply deferred recording it for tax purposes by placing a value on the common shares of $372,000 [(3)($124,000)]. This is significantly below their current fair market value of $1,080,000. Note that the difference of $708,000 ($1,080,000 - $372,000) is also the difference between the $2,342,000 fair market value of the total consideration given and the $1,634,000 value for the total ACB of the partnership interests.

Solution to Self Study Problem Twenty - 6

Part A The Net Income For Tax Purposes of the partnership would be calculated as follows:

Accounting Net Income		$571,000
Add:		
Depreciation	$12,000	
One-Half Meals And Entertainment	11,500	
Charitable Donations	17,000	
Taxable Capital Gain [(1/2)($14,000)]	7,000	47,500
Deduct:		
Accounting Gain	($14,000)	
CCA	(19,000)	(33,000)
Net Income For Tax Purposes		$585,500

Matt's Taxable Income resulting from the partnership activities would be calculated as follows:

Share Of Partnership Income [(1/2)($585,500)]	$292,750
Gross Up On Partnership Dividends [(45%)(1/2)($8,000)]	1,800
Matt's Income From Partnership	$294,550

Matt's Taxable Income for the year ending December 31, 2006 would be calculated as follows:

Income From Partnership	
(Including $1,800 Dividend Gross Up)	$294,550
Dividends Received Personally	34,000
Gross Up On Dividends Received Personally [(45%)($34,000)]	15,300
2006 Taxable Income	$343,850

Based on the preceding calculation, Matt's 2006 federal Tax Payable would be calculated as follows:

Tax On The First $118,285	$25,389
Tax On Additional $225,565 At 29 Percent	65,414
Tax Payable Before Credits	$90,803
Basic Personal Credit [(15.25%)($8,839)]	(1,348)
Dividend Tax Credit [($1,800 + $15,300)(11/18)]	(10,450)
Charitable Donations:	
[(15.25%)($200)] $ 31	
[(29%)($8,500 - $200)] 2,407	(2,438)
2006 Tax Payable	$76,567

Part B   The adjusted cost base of Matt's partnership interest on January 1, 2007 would be calculated as follows:

Capital Contribution	$280,000
2005 Partnership Income [(1/2)($180,000)]	90,000
2005 Drawings	(23,000)
2006 Partnership Income (Excludes Dividend Gross Up)	292,750
2006 Drawings	(290,000)
2006 Charitable Contributions [(1/2)($17,000)]	(8,500)
Untaxed Portion Of Capital Gain [(1/2)(1/2)($14,000)]	3,500
January 1, 2007 Adjusted Cost Base	$344,750

Given this calculation, the taxable capital gain on Matt's sale of the partnership interest would be calculated as follows:

Proceeds Of Disposition	$435,000
Adjusted Cost Base	(344,750)
Capital Gain	$ 90,250
Inclusion Rate	1/2
Taxable Capital Gain	$ 45,125

Chapter Twenty Learning Objectives

After completing Chapter 20, you should be able to:

1. Explain the basic approach of Canadian income tax legislation to the taxation of partnerships (paragraphs 20-1 through 20-6).

2. Define, for income tax purposes, a partnership arrangement (paragraphs 20-7 through 20-17).

3. List the various types of partnership arrangements that are used in Canada (paragraphs 20-18 through 20-23).

4. Describe the difference between partnership arrangements and such other forms of organization as co-ownership, joint ventures, and syndicates (paragraphs 20-24 through 20-38).

5. Explain the basic concepts that are involved in the determination of partnership income, losses, and tax credits (paragraphs 20-39 through 20-50).

6. Calculate partnership Net Income For Tax Purposes (paragraphs 20-51 and 20-52).

7. Calculate the amount of partnership income that will be allocated to each partner under the terms of a partnership agreement (paragraphs 20-53 through 20-64).

8. Explain the concept of the adjusted cost base of a partnership interest (paragraphs 20-65 through 20-67).

9. Apply the procedures related to recording the acquisition of a partnership interest (paragraphs 20-68 through 20-74).

10. Calculate the amount of the adjusted cost base of a partnership interest (paragraphs 20-75 through 20-91).

11. Define a limited partnership arrangement (paragraphs 20-92 through 20-94).

12. Apply the at-risk rules to limited partnership arrangements (paragraphs 20-95 through 20-103).

13. Outline the various types of transfers that may take place between a partnership and its partners (paragraphs 20-104 through 20-107).

14. Apply the procedures related to transfers between a partnership and its partners when no rollover provision is used (paragraphs 20-108 through 20-110).

15. List and apply the common rollover provisions for transfers between a partnership and its partners (paragraphs 20-111 through 20-127).

16. Describe the GST implications related to partner expenses, dispositions of partnership interests, transfers between a partnership and its partners, and reorganizations of partnerships (paragraphs 20-128 through 20-134).

CHAPTER TWENTY-ONE

On-Line Survey

We would appreciate your feedback on this text. Your comments will help us to improve it. In addition, students who complete the survey will have their name entered in a draw for a $100 cash prize.

To complete a brief, on-line survey, visit the "Student And General Resources" web page on our web site at:

www.pearsoned.ca/byrdchen/ctp2007/

We recommend the following approach in dealing with the material in this Chapter:

How To Work Through Chapter Twenty-One

Introduction
- [ ] Read the text pages 893 and 894 (paragraph 21-1 through 21-7).

Basic Concepts
- [ ] Read the text pages 894 and 895 (paragraph 21-8 through 21-19).

Establishing A Trust
- [ ] Read the text pages 895 and 896 (paragraph 21-20 through 21-23).
- [ ] Complete Exercise Twenty-One-1 on page 896 of the text. The solution is on page S-336.

Non-Tax Reasons For Using Trusts
- [ ] Read the text pages 896 and 897 (paragraph 21-24 through 21-25).

Classification Of Trusts
- [ ] Read the text pages 897 through 899 (paragraph 21-26 through 21-36).

Taxation Of Trusts - The Basic Model
- [ ] Read the text pages 899 and 900 (paragraph 21-37 through 21-38).
- [ ] Complete Exercise Twenty-One-2 on page 900 of the text. The solution is on page S-336.

Rollovers To A Trust
- [ ] Read the text pages 900 and 901 (paragraph 21-39 through 21-47).
- [ ] Complete Exercise Twenty-One-3 on page 901 of the text. The solution is on page S-336.
- [ ] Read the text page 902 (paragraph 21-48 through 21-51).
- [ ] Complete Exercise Twenty-One-4 on page 902 of the text. The solution is on page S-336.

Rollovers To Capital Beneficiaries

☐ Read the text page 903 (paragraph 21-52 through 21-56).

21 Year Deemed Disposition Rule

☐ Read the text page 903 (paragraph 21-57 through 21-59).

Net Income For Tax Purposes And Taxable Income Of A Trust

☐ Read the text pages 904 and 905 (paragraph 21-60 through 21-69).

☐ Complete Exercise Twenty-One-5 on page 906 of the text. The solution is on page S-337.

Income Allocations To Beneficiaries

☐ Read the text pages 906 through 908 (paragraph 21-70 through 21-84).

☐ Complete Exercise Twenty-One-6 on page 908 of the text. The solution is on page S-337.

Allocation Of CCA, Recapture of CCA, And Terminal Losses

☐ Read the text page 908 (paragraphs 21-85 and 21-86).

☐ Complete Exercise Twenty-One-7 on pages 908 and 909 of the text. The solution is on page S-338.

Principal Residence Exemption

☐ Read the text page 909 (paragraph 21-87).

Tax Payable Of Personal Trusts

☐ Read the text pages 909 and 910 (paragraph 21-88 through 21-97).

☐ Complete Exercise Twenty-One-8 on page 910 of the text. The solution is on page S-338.

☐ Complete Self Study Problems Twenty-One-1 through Twenty-One-4 on pages 923 through 925 of the text. The solutions are on pages S-339 through S-343.

Trust Tax And Information Returns

☐ Read the text pages 910 and 911 (paragraph 21-98).

Income Attribution

☐ Read the text page 911 (paragraph 21-99 through 21-101).

☐ Complete Exercise Twenty-One-9 on page 911 of the text. The solution is on page S-338.

☐ Read the text page 912 (paragraphs 21-102 and 21-103).

Purchase Or Sale Of An Interest In A Trust

☐ Read the text pages 912 and 913 (paragraph 21-104 through 21-109).

☐ Complete Exercise Twenty-One-10 on page 913 of the text. The solution is on page S-339.

Tax Planning

☐ Read the text pages 913 and 914 (paragraph 21-110 through 21-117).

☐ Complete Exercise Twenty-One-11 on page 914 of the text. The solution is on page S-339.

☐ Read the text pages 915 and 916 (paragraph 21-118 through 21-122).

Objectives Of Estate Planning And An Estate Freeze

☐ Read the text pages 916 through 918 (paragraph 21-123 through 21-129).

Estate Freeze Techniques Not Involving Rollovers

☐ Read the text pages 918 through 919 (paragraph 21-130 through 21-137).

Section 86 Share Exchange

☐ Read the text pages 919 through 920 (paragraph 21-138 through 21-146).

Rollover Provisions - Section 85 vs. Section 86

☐ Read the text page 920 (paragraph 21-147 through 21-149).

GST And Trusts

☐ Read the text page 921 (paragraphs 21-150 through 21-152).

To Complete This Chapter

☐ Review the Key Terms Used In This Chapter on page 921 of the text. Consult the Glossary for the meaning of any key terms you do not know.

☐ Review the Glossary Flashcards and complete the Key Terms Self-Test for the Chapter. These features can be found in two places, on your Student CD-ROM under the heading "Key Term Practice" and on the web site.

☐ Review the Learning Objectives of the Chapter found on pages S-343 and S-344 of this Study Guide.

Solution to Chapter Twenty-One Exercises

Exercise Twenty-One - 1 Solution

Case A   While Mr. Black has transferred property, it is not clear that his intention was to create a trust. No trust would be created by his transfer.

Case B   Jane's "friends" cannot be considered to be an identifiable class. As a consequence, there is no certainty as to beneficiaries and no trust would be created by her transfer.

Case C   Robert's "children" would be an identifiable class. It would appear that a trust has been created.

Case D   While Suzanne has signed the agreement, it does not appear that the property has been transferred. This means that no trust has been created.

Exercise Twenty-One - 2 Solution

With respect to Joanne's transfer of her securities to the trust, the transaction would be deemed to take place at fair market value. This would result in a taxable capital gain to Joanne of $10,000 [(1/2)($220,000 - $200,000)]. There would be no tax consequences to Jocelyn or the trust as a result of this transfer.

As the trust distributed all of its income during the year, none of the interest would be taxed in the trust. All of the interest would be included in Jocelyn's income and, because she is an adult, there would be no income attribution to Joanne.

Under ITA 107(2), the transfer from the trust to Jocelyn on January 1, 2007 would take place at the trust's tax cost of $220,000. There would be no tax consequences for Joanne, Jocelyn, or the trust as a result of this transfer.

Exercise Twenty-One - 3 Solution

As there is a rollover available on transfers to a qualifying spousal trust, the accrued $30,000 gain ($90,000 - $60,000) will not be recognized until her husband or the spousal trust eventually disposes of the land. The spousal trust acquires the land (a non-depreciable capital asset) at Louise's adjusted cost base of $60,000, which will be her husband's adjusted cost base if the trust transfers the asset to him personally rather than selling it.

Exercise Twenty-One - 4 Solution

Scenario	Taxable Capital Gain (Settlor)	Adjusted Cost Base (Trust)
1. Inter vivos trust for adult child	$300	$1,600
2. Inter vivos trust for minor child	300	1,600
3. Testamentary trust for friend	300	1,600
4. Inter vivos spousal trust	Nil	1,000
5. Testamentary spousal trust	Nil	1,000
6. Joint spousal trust	Nil	1,000
7. Alter ego trust	Nil	1,000

Exercise Twenty-One - 5 Solution

The required calculations are as follows:

Business Income	$220,000
Preferred Beneficiary Election	(50,000)
Distributions To Other Beneficiaries	(170,000)
Designation Under ITA 104(13.1)	35,000
Net Income For Tax Purposes	$ 35,000
Business Loss Carry Forward	(35,000)
Taxable Income	$ Nil

The preferred beneficiary election would mean that the $50,000 would be taxed in the hands of the disabled beneficiary even though the funds are retained in the trust. Since this is an inter vivos trust, without the election, the $50,000 would be taxed at the maximum rate in the trust. As the disabled beneficiary has no other source of income, the $50,000 would be subject to tax at lower rates than would be the case if it was taxed in the trust.

By designating $35,000 as amounts not paid, the trust can absorb the loss carry forward. As a result, the beneficiaries will not pay tax on this amount even though it has been distributed to them.

Exercise Twenty-One - 6 Solution

The Net Income For Tax Purposes of the trust would be calculated as follows:

Eligible Dividends From Canadian Public Corporations	$100,000	
Distribution To Bryan	(60,000)	$ 40,000
Non-Eligible Dividends From CCPC	$ 30,000	
Distribution To Bryan	(30,000)	Nil
Taxable Capital Gain [(1/2)($20,000)]	$ 10,000	
Distribution To Bryan	(10,000)	Nil
Gross Up Of Retained Eligible Dividends [(45%)($40,000)]		18,000
Net Income For Tax Purposes - Trust		$ 58,000

The corresponding calculation for Bryan would be as follows:

Eligible Dividends From Canadian Public Corporations	$ 60,000
Gross Up Of Eligible Dividends At 45 percent	27,000
Non-Eligible Dividends From CCPC	30,000
Gross Up Of Non-Eligible Dividends At 25 Percent	7,500
Taxable Capital Gains [(1/2)($20,000)]	10,000
Subtotal	$134,500
Split Income Deduction - ITA 20(1)(ww)	(37,500)
Net Income For Tax Purposes - Bryan	$ 97,000

Note that the dividends from Canadian controlled private corporations, while not included in regular Net Income For Tax Purposes or Taxable Income, would be subject to the tax on split income. The non-taxable one-half of the capital gain would be received by Bryan on a tax free basis. Both the trust and Bryan will be able to deduct a dividend tax credit against Tax Payable.

Exercise Twenty-One - 7 Solution

If the rental property is not sold and all of the income is distributed to Martin, he will have to include $6,000 ($32,000 - $26,000) in his 2006 Net Income For Tax Purposes. The trust's 2006 Net Income For Tax Purposes will be nil.

Alternatively, if the property is sold on December 31, 2006, no CCA will be deducted. Provided the rental income is distributed to Martin, he would have to include $32,000 in his 2006 Net Income For Tax Purposes. In addition, as there is no provision to allocate recapture to beneficiaries, the trust would have a 2006 Net Income For Tax Purposes of $65,000. As this is an intro vivos trust, this amount would be taxed at the maximum federal rate of 29 percent.

Exercise Twenty-One - 8 Solution

Taxable Income and federal Tax Payable for the trust would be calculated as follows:

Income From Dividends	$20,000
Deduction For Distribution To Beneficiary	(15,000)
Net Dividend Income	$ 5,000
Dividend Gross Up [(45%)($5,000)]	2,250
Taxable Income For The Trust	$ 7,250
Federal Tax Rate (Inter Vivos Trust)	29%
Federal Tax Before Credits	$ 2,103
Federal Dividend Tax Credit [(11/18)($2,250)]	(1,375)
Federal Tax Payable - Trust	$ 728

Taxable Income and federal Tax Payable for the son would be calculated as follows:

Dividend Income From The Trust	$15,000
Dividend Gross Up [(45%)($15,000)]	6,750
Taxable Income For The Son	$21,750
Federal Tax Rate	15.25%
Federal Tax Before Credits	$ 3,317
Basic Personal Credit [(15.25%)($8,839)]	(1,348)
Federal Dividend Tax Credit [(11/18)($6,750)]	(4,125)
Federal Tax Payable - Son	Nil

Exercise Twenty-One - 9 Solution

Income on the bonds is subject to the attribution rules to the extent that the income is allocated to Trevor's spouse, Carmen, and to their minor son, Mitch. This means that two-thirds of the interest will be attributed back to Trevor. With respect to the capital gain, the attribution rules do not apply on transfers to minors. This means that only Carmen's one-third share of the gain will be attributed back to Trevor.

	Carmen	Mitch	Rhonda
Interest Income ($27,000 ÷ 3)	$9,000	$9,000	$ 9,000
Taxable Capital Gain ($3,000 ÷ 3)	1,000	1,000	1,000
Interest Attribution To Trevor	(9,000)	(9,000)	Nil
Capital Gain Attribution To Trevor	(1,000)	Nil	Nil
Allocated Trust Income	Nil	$1,000	$10,000

The total amount attributed to Trevor would be $19,000 ($9,000 + $9,000 + $1,000).

Exercise Twenty-One - 10 Solution

With respect to Sam, he has acquired a capital interest for consideration of $190,000. This will be the adjusted cost base of the interest he has acquired.

With respect to Mehrdad, he has disposed of a capital asset for proceeds of disposition of $190,000. Since he did not purchase the interest in the trust, his adjusted cost base as usually determined would be nil. However, for this disposition, the adjusted cost base of the capital interest is the greater of nil and the cost amount as determined under ITA 108(1). The cost amount would be $125,000, one-half of the tax cost of the assets in the trust. The result would be a taxable capital gain of $32,500 [(1/2)($190,000 - $125,000)].

Exercise Twenty-One - 11 Solution

As Sarah's other income places her in the maximum federal tax bracket of 29 percent, her tax savings resulting from transferring the assets to the family trust would be $31,900 [($110,000)(29%)]. The federal tax that would be payable on the additional $55,000 received by each of her two children is as follows:

Jerri

Tax On First $36,378	$5,548
Tax On Additional $18,622 ($55,000 - $36,378) At 22 Percent	4,097
Tax Before Credit	$9,645
Personal Credit	(1,348)
Tax Payable	$8,297

Mark

Marginal Tax At 22 Percent [(22%)($72,756 - $45,000)]	$ 6,106
Additional Tax At 26 Percent [($55,000 + $45,000 - $72,756)]	7,083
Additional Tax Payable (See Note)	$13,189

Note   As Mark would be in a position to use all of his tax credits prior to receiving the additional $55,000 in income, they are not relevant to the determination of his marginal increase in taxes.

The total tax paid by the two children would $21,486 ($8,297 + $13,189). This is $10,414 ($31,900 - $21,486) per year less than the amount that would be paid by Sarah without the trust. When combined with a reduction in provincial taxes, the total value of establishing a family trust would be over $15,000 per year. This is more than enough to cover the costs of establishing and maintaining this trust.

Solution to Self Study Problem Twenty-One - 1

A.   The following schedule allocates income as per the trust agreement:

Income Allocation	Trust	Spouse	Son
Business Income	$ Nil	$12,000	$ 8,000
Interest	Nil	1,800	1,200
Eligible Dividends Received	25,000	15,000	10,000
Dividend Gross Up (45%)	11,250	6,750	4,500
Net Rental Income (Note)	Nil	2,400	1,600
Net Income And Taxable Income	$36,250	$37,950	$25,300

	Trust	Spouse	Son
Federal Income Tax			
On First $36,378 At 15.25 Percent	$5,528	$5,548	$3,858
On Remaining $1,572 At 22 Percent	Nil	346	Nil
Basic Personal Credit	N/A	(1,348)	(1,348)
Federal Dividend Tax Credit			
[(11/18)(Gross Up)]	(6,875)	(4,125)	(2,750)
Federal Tax Payable	Nil	$ 421	Nil

Note The $4,000 net rental income is calculated as the rent receipts of $12,000, less the operating expenses of $6,000 and CCA of $2,000. The CCA is claimed at the trust level, and is flowed through as a deduction in calculating the income of the beneficiaries.

B. The following income allocation assumes that all of the trust's income will be allocated to Mrs. Rowand and Roger. This means that the Taxable Income and federal Tax Payable of the trust will be nil. The calculations for Mrs. Rowand and Roger are as follows:

Income Allocation	Spouse	Son
Business Income	$12,000	$ 8,000
Interest	1,800	1,200
Dividends	30,000	20,000
Dividend Gross Up (45%)	13,500	9,000
Net Rental Income	2,400	1,600
Net And Taxable Income	$59,700	$39,800

	Spouse	Son
Federal Income Tax		
On First $36,378 At 15.25 Percent	$5,548	$5,548
On Remaining $23,322 At 22 Percent	5,131	Nil
On Remaining $3,422 At 22 Percent	Nil	753
Basic Personal Credit	(1,348)	(1,348)
Federal Dividend Tax Credit		
[(11/18)(Gross Up)]	(8,250)	(5,500)
Federal Tax Payable	$1,081	Nil

C. The total basic federal Tax Payable in Part B is $1,081, which is $660 higher than the total of $421 in Part A. This excess tax bill of $660 is the net effect of two offsetting factors:

- In Case B, a significant portion of Mrs. Rowand's income is taxed at 22 percent. In contrast, in Case A only $1,572 is taxed at 22 percent.

- Partially offsetting this higher rate is the fact that, in Case A, over $1,500 of the available tax credits could not be used. In contrast in Case B, the only unused credits are the son's $547.

Solution to Self Study Problem Twenty-One - 2

Calculation Of Taxable Income The Taxable Income of the two beneficiaries and the trust would be calculated as shown in the following table. With the exception of the recapture on the sale of the rental property, all amounts are allocated 30 percent to Ms. Robinson's son, 50 percent to her daughter, and 20 percent to the trust.

	Son	Daughter	Trust
Interest On Government Bonds	$ 19,500	$ 32,500	$ 13,000
Dividends On Canadian Stocks	75,000	125,000	50,000
Gross Up Of 45 Percent	33,750	56,250	22,500
Rental Revenues	147,600	246,000	98,400
Rental Expenses	(102,600)	(171,000)	(68,400)
Taxable Capital Gain On Land [(1/2)($2,300,000 - $1,430,000)]	130,500	217,500	87,000
Taxable Capital Gain On Building [(1/2)($4,560,000 - $3,840,000)]	108,000	180,000	72,000
Recaptured CCA On Building (Note)	Nil	Nil	460,000
Net And Taxable Income	$411,750	$686,250	$734,500

Note   The recapture of CCA on the Building is calculated as follows:

Capital Cost	$3,840,000
UCC	(3,380,000)
Recaptured CCA	$ 460,000

As noted in the text, recapture must be included in the Taxable Income of the trust.

Calculation Of Tax Payable   Based on the preceding Taxable Income, the federal Tax Payable of the trust can be calculated as follows:

Federal Tax [(29%)($734,500)]	$213,005
Federal Dividend Tax Credit [(11/18)($22,500)]	(13,750)
Federal Tax Payable	$199,255

Solution to Self Study Problem Twenty-One - 3

The various components of the trust's income would be allocated as follows:

	Daughter	Son	Trust
Canadian Dividends Received	$26,100	$43,500	$17,400
Gross Up Of 45 Percent	11,745	19,575	7,830
British Interest (Gross Amount Of $110,000)	33,000	55,000	22,000
Net Rental Income	18,300	30,500	12,200
Capital Cost Allowance	(13,500)	(22,500)	(9,000)
Net And Taxable Income	$75,645	$126,075	$50,430
British Taxes Paid ($16,500)	$ 4,950	$ 8,250	$ 3,300

The CCA is claimed at the trust level, and is flowed through as a deduction in calculating the Taxable Income of the beneficiaries. Except for the fact that the ITA 118 personal tax credits are not available, income that remains in a testamentary trust is taxed in the same general manner as would apply to an individual. Given this, Tax Payable for the trust would be calculated as follows:

Federal Tax Payable:	
On First $36,378 At 15.25 Percent	$5,548
On Remaining $14,052 At 22 Percent	3,091
Federal Tax Payable Before Credits	$8,639
Federal Dividend Tax Credit [(11/18)($7,830)]	(4,785)
Foreign Tax Credit (See Note)	(3,300)
Tax Payable	$ 554

Note The amount that can be deducted for the foreign tax credit is the lesser of the amount of foreign taxes withheld and an amount determined by the following formula:

[(Foreign Non-Business Income ÷ Adjusted Net Income)(Tax Payable Before Credits)]

= [($22,000 ÷ $50,430)($8,639)]

= $3,769

As this amount is more than the actual foreign taxes of $3,300 allocated to the trust, the actual foreign taxes paid would be the lesser amount, and would be the foreign tax credit.

You should also note that, if the foreign taxes had exceeded 15 percent of the gross amount of foreign income, the excess would have been available as a deduction under ITA 20(11), rather than as an additional amount of tax credit.

Solution to Self Study Problem Twenty-One - 4

Part A   Trust For Daughter   The first trust created is a testamentary trust for the benefit of Mrs. Turner's daughter, Melanie. When there is a transfer of assets at death to any taxpayer other than a spouse or a spousal trust, there is a deemed disposition with proceeds equal to fair market value. Capital gains on all of the assets transferred would need to be realized along with recapture of CCA on the warehouse building.

The principal residence exemption could be used to eliminate the gain on the residence. Melanie will not have a taxable benefit from use of the residence. However, since the trust pays for the upkeep and maintenance of the residence, the trust can deduct the costs and they are taxable as income to Melanie.

The capital gain and recapture on the disposition of the warehouse building would have to be included in Mrs. Turner's final tax return. The taxable capital gain on the warehouse land is $10,000 [(1/2)($75,000 - $55,000)]. As the fair market value of the warehouse is equal to its capital cost, there is no capital gain on the warehouse building. However, there would be recapture of CCA in the amount of $40,000 ($85,000 - $45,000). This amount would have to be included in Mrs. Turner's final tax return.

The trust will be deemed to acquire all of the assets at their fair market values. In the case of the warehouse building, the new UCC will be the fair market value of $85,000.

Part A   Trust For Husband   The second trust appears to be a qualifying spousal trust. Where there is a transfer at death to a qualifying spousal trust, the transfer is deemed to be a disposition with proceeds equal to the deceased taxpayer's tax cost. This would be the capital cost of the cottage and stock portfolio and, as a consequence of using this value, the transfer of assets to the trust will have no tax consequences for Mrs. Turner's final tax return.

The trust will be deemed to have acquired all of the assets at the same capital cost values that were used as proceeds of disposition by Mrs. Turner.

Part B Death Of Husband Unless Mr. West has remarried with great haste and can pass these assets on to a new spouse or qualifying spousal trust, his death will result in a deemed disposition of the trust's assets for proceeds equal to fair market value. In the case of the cottage, a taxable capital gain of $5,000 [(1/2)($72,000 - $62,000)] will result, while on the stock market portfolio there will be a taxable capital gain of $3,000 [(1/2)($28,000 - $22,000)].

Chapter Twenty-One Learning Objectives

After completing Chapter 21, you should be able to:

1. Explain the basic concepts of trusts (paragraphs 21-1 through 21-15).

2. Explain the difference between a trust and an estate (paragraphs 21-16 through 21-19).

3. Describe the procedures required to establish a trust (paragraphs 21-20 through 21-23).

4. Demonstrate an understanding of the non-tax reasons for using trusts (paragraphs 21-24 and 21-25).

5. Demonstrate an understanding of the different classifications of trusts (paragraphs 21-26 through 21-36).

6. Explain the basic model for the taxation of trusts (paragraphs 21-37 and 21-38).

7. Demonstrate an understanding of the available rollovers to a trust (paragraphs 21-39 through 21-51).

8. Demonstrate an understanding of the available rollovers to the capital beneficiaries of a trust (paragraphs 21-52 through 21-56).

9. Apply the 21 year deemed disposition rule (paragraphs 21-57 through 21-59).

10. Calculate the Net Income For Tax Purposes and Taxable Income of a trust (paragraphs 21-60 through 21-69).

11. Demonstrate an understanding of the provisions relating to income allocations to beneficiaries (paragraphs 21-70 through 21-87).

12. Calculate the Tax Payable for testamentary and inter vivos trusts (paragraphs 21-88 through 21-97).

13. Describe the procedures applicable to the filing of trust tax and information returns (paragraph 21-98).

14. Explain how the income attribution rules may be applicable to trusts and any associated tax planning considerations (paragraphs 21-99 through 21-103).

15. Explain the tax treatment of the purchase of an interest in a trust (paragraphs 21-104 through 21-109).

16. Demonstrate an understanding of tax planning involving various types of trusts (paragraphs 21-110 through 21-122).

17. Demonstrate an understanding of the objectives of estate planning (paragraphs 21-123 through 21-127).

18. Demonstrate an understanding of the objectives of an estate freeze (paragraphs 21-128 and 21-129).

19. Demonstrate an understanding of the estate freeze techniques that do not involve roll-overs (paragraphs 21-130 through 21-137).

20. Apply ITA 86(1) to the implementation of an estate freeze (paragraphs 21-138 through 21-146).

22. Demonstrate a basic understanding of the considerations involved in choosing between Section 85 and Section 86 when implementing an estate freeze (paragraphs 21-147 through 21-149).

23. Explain the applicability of GST legislation to trusts (paragraphs 21-150 through 21-152).

CHAPTER TWENTY-TWO

How To Work Through Chapter Twenty-Two

We recommend the following approach in dealing with the material in this Chapter:

International Taxation - Introduction
☐   Read the text pages 929 and 930 (paragraph 22-1 through 22-7).

Neutrality In International Taxation
☐   Read the text pages 930 and 931 (paragraph 22-8 through 22-14).

☐   Complete Exercise Twenty-Two-1 on page 931 of the text. The solution is on page S-348.

The Role Of Tax Treaties
☐   Read the text pages 931 and 932 (paragraph 22-15 through 22-19).

☐   Complete Exercise Twenty-Two-2 on page 932 of the text. The solution is on page S-348.

Residence And Dual Residence
☐   Read the text pages 933 through 934 (paragraph 22-20 through 22-31).

☐   Complete Exercises Twenty-Two-3 and Twenty-Two-4 on pages 934 and 935 of the text. The solutions are on page S-348.

☐   Complete Self Study Problem Twenty-Two-1 on page 964 of the text. The solution is on page S-352.

The Problem Of Double Taxation
☐   Read the text pages 935 through 938 (paragraph 22-32 through 22-48).

☐   Complete Exercise Twenty-Two-5 on page 938 of the text. The solution is on page S-349.

☐   Complete Self Study Problems Twenty-Two-2 and Twenty-Two-3 on pages 964 and 965 of the text. The solutions are on pages S-352 through S-354.

Non-Residents Earning Canadian Source Income - Basic Approaches
☐   Read the text pages 938 and 939 (paragraph 22-49 through 22-54).

Non-Residents Earning Employment Income - General Rules
☐   Read the text page 939 (paragraphs 22-55 through 22-57).

☐   Complete Exercise Twenty-Two-6 on page 939 of the text. The solution is on pages S-349 and S-350.

Canada/U.S. Tax Treaty On Employment Income
☐   Read the text page 940 (paragraph 22-58 through 22-59).

☐   Complete Exercise Twenty-Two-7 on page 940 of the text. The solution is on page S-350.

Non-Residents Carrying On Business In Canada
☐   Read the text pages 940 and 941 (paragraph 22-60 through 22-66).

☐   Complete Exercise Twenty-Two-8 on page 942 of the text. The solution is on page S-350.

Dispositions Of Taxable Canadian Property By Non-Residents

☐ Read the text page 942 and 943 (paragraphs 22-67 through 22-70).

☐ Complete Exercise Twenty-Two-9 on page 943 of the text. The solution is on pages S-350 and S-351.

Non-Residents Earning Income From Property And Other (Passive) Sources

☐ Read the text pages 943 and 944 (paragraph 22-71 through 22-74).

☐ Complete Exercise Twenty-Two-10 on page 944 of the text. The solution is on page S-351.

Non-Residents Receiving Royalties And Rents

☐ Read the text pages 944 and 945 (paragraph 22-75 through 22-80).

☐ Complete Exercise Twenty-Two-11 on pages 945 and 946 of the text. The solution is on page S-351.

Non-Residents Receiving Dividend Income

☐ Read the text page 946 (paragraph 22-81).

Non-Residents Receiving Pension Income And Other Retirement Benefits

☐ Read the text page 946 (paragraph 22-82 through 22-85).

Foreign Source Employment Income

☐ Read the text pages 947 (paragraph 22-86 through 22-88).

☐ Complete Self Study Problem Twenty-Two-4 on page 965 of the text. The solution is on page S-354.

Foreign Source Business Income

☐ Read the text page 947 (paragraph 22-89 through 22-90).

Foreign Source Capital Gains

☐ Read the text pages 947 and 948 (paragraphs 22-91 through 22-92).

Foreign Source Investment Income

☐ Read the text page 948 (paragraph 22-93 through 22-97).

Foreign Investment Reporting

☐ Read the text page 949 (paragraph 22-98 through 22-102).

☐ Complete Exercise Twenty-Two-12 on page 949 of the text. The solution is on page S-351.

☐ Complete Self Study Problem Twenty-Two-5 on pages 965 and 966 of the text. The solution is on page S-354.

Non-Resident Entities - Basic Issues

☐ Read the text pages 949 through 951 (paragraph 22-103 through 22-110).

Foreign Affiliates

☐ Read the text pages 951 and 952 (paragraph 22-111 through 22-117).

Controlled Foreign Affiliates

☐ Read the text page 952 (paragraph 22-118 through 22-121).

Foreign Accrual Property Income (FAPI)

☐ Read the text pages 952 through 954 (paragraph 22-122 through 22-128).

☐ Complete Exercise Twenty-Two-13 on page 954 of the text. The solution is on page S-351.

☐ Complete Self Study Problem Twenty-Two-6 on page 966 of the text. The solution is on page S-354.

Dividends From FAPI

☐ Read the text page 954 (paragraph 22-129).

☐ Complete Exercise Twenty-Two-14 on page 955 of the text. The solution is on page S-352.

Foreign Affiliate Dividends

☐ Read the text pages 955 through 957 (paragraph 22-130 through 22-137).

Foreign Investment Entities

☐ Read the text pages 957 through 959 (paragraph 22-138 through 22-149).

Dividends From Foreign Non-Affiliated Companies

☐ Read the text page 959 (paragraph 22-150 through 22-152).

Transfer Pricing

☐ Read the text pages 959 through 961 (paragraph 22-153 through 22-160).

To Complete This Chapter

☐ Review the Key Terms Used In This Chapter on page 948 of the text. Consult the Glossary for the meaning of any key terms you do not know.

☐ Review the Glossary Flashcards and complete the Key Terms Self-Test for the Chapter. These features can be found in two places, on your Student CD-ROM under the heading "Key Term Practice" and on the web site.

☐ Review the Learning Objectives of the Chapter found on pages S-306 and S-307 of this Study Guide.

Solution to Chapter Twenty-Two Exercises

Exercise Twenty-Two - 1 Solution

1. Capital export neutrality.

2. Capital import neutrality.

3. Neither. Under capital export neutrality only the U.S. would have the right to tax the interest. The Canadian withholding taxes are clearly contrary to that approach. Under capital import neutrality, only the source country (e.g. Canada) would have the right to tax the amount, applying tax rates equal to that of Canadian residents earning interest. Although withholding tax ensures that non-residents pay some tax, the tax rates applied to non-residents are different from the rates applied to residents. In addition, the U.S. taxes the interest income of its residents.

Exercise Twenty-Two - 2 Solution

The *Income Tax Act* and tax treaty are in conflict. Such inconsistencies are always resolved in favor of the tax treaty. Melissa will be subject to a 15 percent Part XIII withholding rate.

Exercise Twenty-Two - 3 Solution

Case 1 As it appears that Dizzy has a permanent home in Los Angeles, the tie-breaker rules would indicate that he is a resident of the United States. As he has been in Canada for more than 183 days in 2006, the sojourner rules might have made him a deemed Canadian resident. However, the tie-breaker rules in the international tax treaty would likely override this.

The boarding rooms and hotels would not be considered to be a permanent home given that Dizzy never intended to stay for a long period of time.

Case 2 As Donna was in Canada for more than 183 days in 2006, she is a deemed resident through the application of the sojourner rule, and therefore a dual resident. In applying the tie-breaker rules, the first factor that is considered is in which country the individual has a permanent home. With respect to this criteria, Donna would not be considered to have a permanent home in either country. She gave up her lease on the New York property and, given that she only planned to stay for a short period of time, the Toronto apartment would not be considered a permanent home. In the absence of a permanent home in either country, the next factor to consider would be the location of Donna's "centre of vital interests". This would appear to be the U.S. and, given this, the tie-breaker rules would make Donna a resident of the U.S. and a non-resident of Canada.

Exercise Twenty-Two - 4 Solution

Case 1 Taxco would be considered a deemed resident of Canada by ITA 250(4) since it was incorporated in Canada after April 26, 1965. Taxco would also be considered a factual resident of the U.S. since its mind and management are located there. Article IV(3) of the Canada/U.S. tax treaty however breaks the tie in favor of the place of the location of incorporation. Taxco would therefore be considered a resident of Canada for treaty purposes.

Case 2 Junko would be considered a factual resident of Canada since its mind and management are situated in Canada. Junko would also be considered a resident of the U.S. since it was incorporated there. Article IV(3) of the Canada/U.S. tax treaty however breaks the tie in favor of the place of incorporation. Junko would therefore be considered a resident of the U.S. for treaty purposes.

Exercise Twenty-Two - 5 Solution

The Deduction Method

Gross Foreign Income	$18,000
Foreign Tax Withheld	(1,800)
Foreign Interest Income Received	$16,200
Canadian Tax Payable At 44 Percent	$ 7,128
Foreign Tax Withheld	1,800
Total Taxes Payable	$ 8,928
After Tax Retention ($18,000 - $8,928)	$ 9,072
Overall Tax Rate ($8,928 ÷ $18,000)	49.6%

The Exemption Method

Gross Foreign Income	$18,000
Canadian Tax Payable	$ Nil
Foreign Tax Withheld	1,800
Total Taxes Payable	$ 1,800
After Tax Retention ($18,000 - $1,800)	$16,200
Overall Tax Rate ($1,800 ÷ $18,000)	10.0%

The Credit Method

Foreign Interest Received ($18,000 - $1,800)	$16,200
Foreign Tax Withheld	1,800
Taxable Income Inclusion	$18,000
Canadian Tax Payable At 44 Percent	$ 7,920
Foreign Tax Credit = Foreign Tax Withheld	(1,800)
Net Canadian Tax Payable	$ 6,120
Foreign Tax Withheld	1,800
Total Taxes Payable	$ 7,920
After Tax Retention ($18,000 - $7,920)	$10,080
Overall Tax Rate ($7,920 ÷ $18,000)	44.0%

Exercise Twenty-Two - 6 Solution

Dawn is an individual who has become a resident of another country, but continues to receive remuneration from a resident Canadian taxpayer. Given that the tax treaty exempts her salary from taxation in Egypt, ITA 115(2) deems her to be employed in Canada and, as a consequence, she would be subject to Canadian taxes.

Exercise Twenty-Two - 7 Solution

Case 1   The employment income is taxable in Canada. The Canada/U.S. tax treaty allows Canada to tax employment income earned in Canada unless either of two exceptions is applicable. The first exception is the $10,000 rule. This exception however does not apply since David earned $11,200 Canadian in 2006 [($2,800)(4 months)]. The second exception is the 183 day rule. Although David was in Canada for only 122 days during 2006 and therefore met the first part of the test, he failed the remaining part of the test since the employer was a Canadian resident and could deduct the payments.

Case 2   The employment income is not taxable in Canada. The 183 day rule exempts the income from Canadian taxation because the employer was not resident in Canada, nor had a fixed base of operations in Canada, and could not deduct the payments for Canadian tax purposes.

Case 3   The employment income is taxable in Canada. The Canada/U.S. tax treaty would exempt the income from Canadian tax if the amount was less than $10,000 Canadian, or if Sandra spent less than 183 days in Canada. As she earned $50,000 Canadian and spent 238 days at her job in Canada, neither of these exceptions are applicable.

Exercise Twenty-Two - 8 Solution

Case 1   Jazzco is not carrying on business in Canada and would not be subject to Canadian taxes.

Case 2   Jazzco is carrying on business in Canada in a permanent establishment located in Toronto. Therefore, Jazzco is taxable in Canada under ITA 2(3) on the profits attributable to the Canadian factory.

Case 3   The tax treaty allows Canada to tax business income only if such income is attributable to a permanent establishment in Canada. The warehouse constitutes a fixed place of business regardless of whether it is owned or leased. However, since it appears to be used exclusively to maintain an inventory for delivery, it would be an excluded activity and would therefore not be considered to be a permanent establishment. Jazzco would not be taxable under ITA 2(3) on its Canadian profits. The fact that the employee acts on behalf of the non-resident employer, would not alter the conclusion since the employee does not have the authority to conclude contracts.

Case 4   In this Case, because the employee has authority to conclude contracts on behalf of a non-resident enterprise, the employee is deemed to be a permanent establishment. This means that Jazzco is taxable in Canada under ITA 2(3) on its business profits attributable to the permanent establishment, i.e., the employee.

Exercise Twenty-Two - 9 Solution

Case 1   Nancy is not taxable on the gain. As a non-resident, Nancy is only taxable in Canada on the disposition of taxable Canadian property. Shares of a resident public company are only taxable Canadian property if Nancy had owned more than 25 percent of the issued shares of any class of the company in the 60 months preceding the disposition.

Case 2   Joe is taxable on the gain. The condo is taxable Canadian property since it is real property (e.g. land and buildings) situated in Canada. The Canada/U.S. tax treaty gives Canada the right to tax such gains. The property is not exempt from Canadian tax as a principal residence since Joe did not acquire the condo for his own habitation.

Case 3   Joe would be taxable on the gain on the shares. Shares of an unlisted Canadian corporation are taxable Canadian property. In addition, the Canada/U.S. tax treaty allows Canada to tax gains on the disposition of shares if the value of the shares is principally derived from real property situated in Canada.

Case 4 Joe would not be taxable on the gain on the shares. The shares are taxable Canadian property because they represent shares of an unlisted non-resident corporation that, at some time in the 60 months preceding the disposition, derived more than 50 percent of their value from taxable Canadian property. However, the Canada/U.S. tax treaty does not list this as one of the items where Canada is allowed to tax U.S. residents.

Exercise Twenty-Two - 10 Solution

Case 1 Jason's interest would be subject to Part XIII tax. However, under the treaty, it would be taxed at the reduced rate of 10 percent.

Case 2 Such interest would generally be subject to Part XIII tax, however, ITA 212(1)(b) contains an exemption from tax where the interest is earned on government of Canada bonds. The treaty is irrelevant since there is no Part XIII tax.

Case 3 Such interest would generally be subject to Part XIII tax. However, ITA 212(1)(b) contains an exemption from tax where the interest relates to real property situated outside of Canada and the funds are not used in a Canadian business or used to earn any property income except property income from the foreign real property. In this Case, there is no Part XIII tax.

Case 4 The interest would be subject to Part XIII tax. It would not be eligible for the exception since the funds were used in a Canadian business. The tax treaty would not override Part XIII tax, but would reduce the withholding to 10 percent.

Exercise Twenty-Two - 11 Solution

Case 1 Rentco appears to be carrying on business in Canada through a permanent establishment. As a result, no Part XIII tax is payable. However, Rentco would be subject to Part I tax on its income attributable to the permanent establishment in Saskatchewan.

Case 2 Jack would be subject to Part XIII tax of $10,500 [(25%)($42,000)]. This represents an effective tax rate of 37.5 percent on his net rental income of $28,000. Alternatively, Jack could elect under ITA 216 to be taxed under Part I on the net rental income of $28,000 ($42,000 - $14,000). If we assume that the net rental income represents a small portion of his worldwide income and his marginal tax rate is less than 37.5 percent ($10,500 ÷ $28,000), the Part I option would be preferable.

Case 3 Jack would be subject to Part XIII tax on the gross rents received for the boats unless he would be considered to be carrying on a business. However, the Canada/U.S. tax treaty reduces the withholding tax to 10 percent of the gross rents received, or $800. Note that Jack would not be eligible to elect under ITA 216 on the boat rents, since this election is generally restricted to real property.

Exercise Twenty-Two - 12 Solution

Simon's total foreign investments of £65,000 (£30,000 + £35,000) push him over the $100,000 Canadian reporting limit [(£65,000)($2.4) = $156,000]. Therefore, he should report foreign investments held during the year by filing Form T1135. He is also required to report any foreign interest income that he earns on the same form.

Exercise Twenty-Two - 13 Solution

Since Forco is a controlled foreign affiliate of Canco, Canco must report its proportionate share (100%) of Forco's investment income:

FAPI [ITA 91(1)]	$100,000
Deduct Lesser Of:	
• FAPI = $100,000	
• ITA 91(4) Deduction [(3.2258)(18%)($100,000)]	(58,064)
Addition To Net Income For Tax Purposes	$41,936

Exercise Twenty-Two - 14 Solution

Foreign Source Dividend – ITA 90(1)	$ 82,000
Deduct Lesser Of:	
• Previous FAPI = $100,000	
• Dividend Received = $82,000	(82,000)
Addition To Net Income For Tax Purposes	Nil

Had there been any withholding taxes on the dividend, then Canco would have been eligible for an increased deduction under ITA 113. Withholding taxes on dividends to corporate shareholders of foreign affiliates are not eligible for a foreign tax credit.

Solution to Self Study Problem Twenty-Two - 1

Paragraph 15 of IT-221R3 indicates that, in general, the CRA will view an individual as becoming a non-resident on the latest of three dates:

- The date the individual leaves Canada.
- The date the individual's spouse or common-law partner and dependants leave Canada.
- The date the individual becomes a resident of another country.

As Paul's wife and daughter did not leave Canada, it would appear that the CRA would take the position that Paul did not stop being a resident of Canada.

As he purchased a house in the U.S., it is possible that he will also be viewed as a resident of that jurisdiction. If this is the case, the tie breaker rules that are contained in the Canada/U.S. tax treaty must be applied. As Paul has a permanent home available in both locations, we need to apply the center of vital interests criterion. The personal ties appear to be stronger in Canada, so it is likely that the CRA would conclude that the center of vital interests is Canada. Given this, Paul would not be considered to be resident in the U.S.

Based on this conclusion, Paul should report his worldwide income in Canada, and claim a foreign tax credit for any U.S. tax paid on his employment income while he was living and working in the U.S.

Solution to Self Study Problem Twenty-Two - 2

The residence jurisdiction approach applies to Malcolm since it appears that he is a resident of Canada. All of Malcolm's sources of income are subject to Canadian tax regardless of where the income is earned.

From a Canadian point of view, the source jurisdiction approach applies to Melissa. While she is not a resident of Canada, she would be taxed on her Canadian dividends (under Part XIII), as well as on her sale of taxable Canadian property. This same jurisdiction concept would prevent her from being taxed on her employment income as it is not sourced in Canada.

Solution to Self Study Problem Twenty-Two - 3

Debbie will have a deemed disposition of all property except Canadian real estate and RRSPs. The deemed dispositions should result in the following gains, which will likely be capital gains.

Gains On Deemed Dispositions Of Capital Assets

Description	ACB	FMV	Gain (Loss)
Interest in CCPC (10 percent)	$ 90,000	$140,000	$ 50,000
Sports car (Note 1)	18,000	15,000	-0-
Paintings	50,000	175,000	125,000
10 percent interest in Sorrento Co., a Canadian public company	180,000	110,000	(70,000)
Net Capital Gains			$105,000
Inclusion Rate			1/2
Taxable Capital Gains			$ 52,500
Personal Tax Rate			45%
Personal Tax Payable (Note 2)			$ 23,625

Note 1   Losses on personal use property are not deductible.

Note 2   If Debbie continues to own the above assets, the CRA will accept security in lieu of cash for the related personal Tax Payable. The unpaid tax is due when the assets are eventually disposed of.

Deferred Gains On Real Estate

Description	ACB	FMV	Gain
House	$150,000	$225,000	$75,000
Whistler ski chalet	125,000	185,000	60,000

As the $20,000 ($60,000/3) annual gain on the Whistler ski chalet is much greater than the $7,500 ($75,000/10) annual gain on the house, Debbie should designate the ski chalet as the family's principal residence for 2005 and 2006 thereby eliminating the entire gain on this property (because of the plus one year rule for principal residences, only two years need to be designated to eliminate all three years of the gain). The house can then be designated as the principal residence from 1997 to 2004. This results in only one year of the gain on the house being taxable (again, due to the plus one year rule for principal residences, designating eight years will eliminate nine years of the gain).

Report Of Assets Held
As Debbie owns assets exceeding $25,000, she is obliged to provide a list to the CRA of all assets owned on her departure date and their related costs. Personal use property up to $10,000 can be excluded. The list of assets owned (Form T1161) should be attached to her tax return for the year of departure.

Other Planning Points   The following factors should also be considered:

Non-Resident Date   As Debbie's husband may defer his move for six months, the deemed date of non-residence will be when he finally moves to Hong Kong. This may be undesirable for Debbie, as the Hong Kong tax rates are less than Canadian rates. Until Debbie is officially a non-resident, all of her income will have to be reported in Canada, and will be subject to the relatively high Canadian tax rates. As Debbie's husband will be commuting anyway, it could be more advantageous for him to work from his Hong Kong base, and to wind up his Canadian client affairs. In this way, the non-resident date could be advanced and a tax savings would be realized.

Moving Expenses   The $50,000 moving allowance may be taxable in Canada, depending on the date she ceases to be a resident. It might be simpler for Debbie to be reimbursed for specific moving costs. Such reimbursements are not a taxable benefit and would not have to be included in her tax return, regardless of the date that she ceases to be a resident.

RRSP   Debbie will have relatively high income in 2006, so she should not collapse her RRSP while resident in Canada in 2006. If the departure from Canada is deferred to 2007, she could collapse some of the RRSP early that year, to be taxed at the low personal tax rates. This assumes that Debbie has no other Canadian income in 2007. It may be more advantageous for Debbie to collapse the RRSP after becoming a non-resident. At that time, a 25 percent Part XIII tax would apply in Canada, and there would likely not be any applicable Hong Kong income tax. Alternatively, Debbie can leave the RRSP invested in Canada and withdraw amounts, after withholding taxes are applied, in later years.

Rental Income   If the house and ski chalet are rented, a 25 percent Part XIII tax will apply to the gross rents received. Debbie can also elect to have the rental income taxed under Part I of the *Income Tax Act*. This is may be preferable in that she can deduct expenses against the gross rents if she makes this election.

Solution to Self Study Problem Twenty-Two - 4

A. With respect to the Florida school, the US$7,000 fee is less than the US$10,000 limit for exempting employment income that is specified in the treaty. Therefore, he would be exempt from U.S. taxation on his work in that country. While this is not discussed in the text, there is a separate limit of $15,000 for artists and athletes. As the individual appears to be a Canadian resident for tax purposes, all of the earnings will be taxable in Canada.

B. While we do not know the amount of remuneration, presumably it exceeds the US$10,000 limit. Regardless, the employment is exempt as the total number of days employed in the U.S. is 180 days [(60 days)(3 periods)], less than the cut-off of 183 days. In addition, the Canadian employer is not resident in the U.S. nor does it operate through a permanent establishment in the U.S. While the earnings would not be subject to U.S. taxation, they would be taxable in Canada.

Solution to Self Study Problem Twenty-Two - 5

A. The term deposits do not need to be reported because the total amount is less than $100,000.

B. If the Florida condominium is primarily for personal use, then reporting of the asset is not required. On the other hand, if it is rented out to third parties, it would need to be reported, as the total cost amount is greater than $100,000.

C. As the total cost of the Arizona condominium is $102,000, reporting is required if the condominium is not personal use property.

D. No foreign investment reporting is required when assets are used in an active business.

Solution to Self Study Problem Twenty-Two - 6

Operation As A Branch   As a branch, any profits will be taxed in the United States. In addition, they will be taxed in Canada as part of worldwide income earned by the Canadian company. However, any Canadian Tax Payable will be reduced by foreign tax credits for U.S. taxes paid on branch profits.

As the earnings of the branch will not be active business income earned in Canada, no small business deduction will be available to Tritec. However, any loss suffered in the U.S. operation will be deductible in arriving at Taxable Income for Canadian tax purposes.

Operation As A Subsidiary   A subsidiary will be subject to U.S. taxes on its worldwide income and, if the subsidiary earns investment income, the foreign accrual property income (FAPI) rules will result in this income being taxed in Canada as the investment income is earned. Subsidiary losses will not be deductible in Canada and, in addition, the U.S. taxation authorities will assess a withholding tax on any management fees, interest, or dividends paid to the Canadian parent.

Chapter Twenty-Two Learning Objectives

After completing Chapter 22, you should be able to:

1. Describe the principles of international taxation (paragraphs 22-1 through 22-7).

2. Demonstrate an understanding of the concepts associated with tax neutrality (paragraphs 22-8 through 22-14).

3. Describe the role of tax treaties in international taxation (paragraphs 22-15 through 22-19).

4. Determine the residency, for tax purposes, of individuals, corporations, trusts, and partnerships (paragraphs 22-20 through 22-31).

5. Demonstrate an understanding of the problem of double taxation in international taxation (paragraphs 22-32 through 22-38).

6. Explain the legislative approaches used to resolve source vs. residence issues (paragraphs 22-39 through 22-48).

7. Demonstrate an understanding of the basic approaches used for taxing non-residents earning Canadian source income (paragraphs 22-49 through 22-54).

8. Apply the appropriate tax treatment for non-residents earning Canadian source employment income (paragraphs 22-55 through 22-59).

9. Apply the appropriate tax treatment for non-residents carrying on a business in Canada (paragraphs 22-60 through 22-66).

10. Apply the appropriate tax treatment for gains realized by non-residents on the disposition of taxable Canadian property (paragraphs 22-67 through 22-70).

11. Apply the appropriate tax treatment for property income earned by a non-resident (paragraphs 22-71 though 22-74).

12. Apply the appropriate tax treatment for Canadian source royalties and rents received by non-residents (paragraphs 22-75 through 22-80).

13. Apply the appropriate tax treatment for Canadian source dividends received by non-residents (paragraph 22-81).

14. Apply the appropriate tax treatment for Canadian source pension benefits and other retirement related benefits received by non-residents (paragraphs 22-82 through 22-85).

15. Apply the appropriate tax treatment for foreign source employment income earned by Canadian residents (paragraphs 22-86 through 22-88).

16. Apply the appropriate tax treatment for foreign source business income earned by Canadian residents (paragraphs 22-89 and 22-90).

17. Apply the appropriate tax treatment for foreign source capital gains realized by Canadian residents (paragraphs 22-91 and 22-92).

18. Describe the basic concepts behind the taxation of foreign source investment income (paragraphs 22-93 through 22-97).

19. Demonstrate an understanding of the requirements of foreign investment reporting (paragraphs 22-98 through 22-102).

20. Describe the basic issues associated with the taxation of non-resident entities (paragraphs 22-103 through 22-110).

21. Identify situations where the rules associated with foreign affiliates are applicable (paragraphs 22-111 through 22-117).

22. Explain the concept of a controlled foreign affiliate (paragraphs 22-118 through 22-121).

23. Apply the rules associated with, and the appropriate tax treatment of, foreign property accrual income (FAPI) (paragraphs 22-122 through 22-129).

24. Apply the appropriate tax treatment for dividends received from foreign affiliates (paragraphs 22-130 through 22-137).

25. Apply the appropriate tax treatment for foreign investment entities (paragraphs 22-138 through 22-149).

26. Explain the tax treatment for dividends received from non-affiliated foreign companies (paragraphs 22-150 through 22-152).

27. Demonstrate a basic understanding of transfer pricing, including the models used to establish transfer prices (paragraphs 22-153 through 22-160).

GLOSSARY

Note that the Glossary is also available on the Student CD-ROM as part of the Folio version of Canadian Tax Principles in FITAC.

A

Accrual Basis A method of accounting for Income based on recording assets when the right to receive them is established and liabilities when the obligation to pay them arises.

Acquisition Of Control Acquisition of sufficient voting shares of a corporation, by a Person, or Group Of Persons, that they have the right to elect a majority of the board of directors of the Corporation.

Active Business A business carried on by a Taxpayer, other than a Specified Investment Business or a Personal Services Business.

Active Business Income Income earned by an Active Business.

Additional Refundable Tax On Investment Income (ART) A 6-2/3 percent tax on the Aggregate Investment Income of a CCPC.

Adjusted Active Business Income A term used in calculating the M&P Deduction, defined as the excess of a Corporation's Income from Active Business, less a Corporation's losses from Active Business. It does not appear to be a different concept than Active Business Income of a Corporation.

Adjusted Cost Base (Depreciable Capital Property) The cost of the property to the Taxpayer.

Adjusted Cost Base (Non-Depreciable Capital Property) The cost of the property to the Taxpayer, subject to ITA 53 adjustments (e.g., deduction of government grants on land purchase).

Adjusted Taxable Income Regular Taxable Income, adjusted to remove certain tax preferences. Used to calculate the Alternative Minimum Tax.

Adoption Expenses Tax Credit A credit against Tax Payable that is available to individuals with eligible adoption expenses.

Advance Tax Ruling Interpretations provided, at the request of a taxpayer, by the Income Tax Rulings Directorate as to how a particular transaction will be treated for tax purposes. Such interpretations are not binding on the CRA.

Affiliated Person [ITA 251.1(1)] For an Individual, an Affiliated Person is that individual's Spouse or Common-Law Partner. For a Corporation, an Affiliated Person is a Person or an Affiliated Group Of Persons who Controls the Corporation, or the Spouse or Common-Law Partner of either the Person who Controls, or a member of the group that Controls. More complex rules apply to determine affiliation between two Corporations.

Affiliated Group Of Persons A Group Of Persons each member of which is affiliated with every other member.

Age Tax Credit A credit against Tax Payable that is available to Individuals who are 65 years of age or older.

Aggregate Investment Income As defined in ITA 129(4), this concept of investment income includes net Taxable Capital Gains for the year reduced by any Net Capital Loss carry overs deducted in the year, Interest Income, rents, and royalties.

Alimony A term that was used at an earlier point in time to refer to both Spousal Support and Child Support.

Allowable Business Investment Loss The deductible portion, currently one-half, of a Business Investment Loss.

Allowable Capital Loss The deductible portion (currently one-half) of a Capital Loss.

Allowance An amount paid by an employer to an Employee to provide for certain types of costs incurred by the Employee, usually travel costs or automobile costs.

Alter Ego Trust　An Inter Vivos Trust established by an Individual aged 65 years or more, subject to the conditions that the Individual must be entitled to all of the Trust's Income during his/her lifetime, and the Individual must be the only Person who can access the capital of the Trust during his/her lifetime.

Alternative Minimum Tax (AMT)　A tax, calculated at the minimum federal rate on Adjusted Taxable Income, less a basic $40,000 exemption.

Amalgamation　A Rollover provision which allows two Taxable Canadian Corporations to be combined into a single Taxable Canadian Corporation, without tax consequences.

Annual Business Limit　The amount of Active Business Income that is eligible for the Small Business Deduction in a particular taxation year (e.g., $300,000 for calendar 2006).

Annual Child Care Expense Amount
The annual per child limit for deductible Child Care Expense. The amount is $4,000, $7,000, or $10,000, depending on the age and health of the child.

Annual Gains Limit　Taxable Capital Gains for the current year on qualifying assets, less the sum of Allowable Capital Losses and Net Capital Loss Carry Overs deducted during the current year, plus Allowable Business Investment Losses realized during the current year. Used to determine the Lifetime Capital Gains Deduction for the current year.

Annuitant　This term is used to describe a Person who is receiving an Annuity. However, in tax publications this term is often (and incorrectly) used to refer to the Beneficiary of an RRSP or RPP.

Annuity　A series of periodic payments that continues for a specified period of time, or until the occurrence of some event (e.g., the death of the Annuitant).

Anti-Avoidance Provision　A provision in the *Income Tax Act* that is designed to prevent a Taxpayer from taking some action that would allow him to avoid taxes.

Apprenticeship Job Creation Tax Credit　A tax credit that is available to eligible employers (individuals and corporations) for salaries and wages paid to qualifying apprentices.

ART　An acronym for "additional refundable tax on investment income".

Assessment　A formal determination of taxes to be paid or refunded. A Reassessment is a form of Assessment

Associated Corporations　Two or more Corporations that have an ownership/control arrangement that falls into one of the categories described in ITA 256(1) (e.g., two Corporations controlled by the same Person).

At-Risk Rules　A set of rules, directed largely at Limited Partners, designed to prevent an investment from creating tax deductions that exceed the amount invested (the At-Risk Amount).

At-Risk Amount　A defined measure that limits the amount of deductions that can be flowed through to a Limited Partner.

B

Basic Federal Tax Payable　An amount of individual Tax Payable that has been reduced by some, but not all of the Tax Credits available to individuals. Used in the calculation of Tax Payable of Canadian Residents who do not live in a province.

Beneficiary　The Person who will receive the benefits from a Trust.

Billed Basis　A method of determining Net Business Income based on recording inclusions when the relevant amounts are billed. Can only be used by certain specified types of professionals (e.g., accountants).

Bonus Arrangement　As used in this material, a tax planning arrangement for Employees. A Corporation declares and deducts a bonus near the end of its fiscal year. It is usually designed to be paid to the Employee early in the following calendar year. As Employment Income is taxed on a Cash Basis, the bonus will not be taxed in the employee's hands until that year.

Bonusing Down　A process of paying deductible salary to the owner-manager of a CCPC, or related parties, in order to eliminate corporate Taxable Income that is not eligible for the Small Business Deduction.

Boot　A colloquial term used by tax practitioners to refer to Non-Share Consideration.

Business Combination　A transaction in which an enterprise acquires net assets that constitute a business, or acquires an equity interest in a Corporation that gives the enterprise Control over the operating, financing, and investing decisions of that Corporation.

Business Income　Income that is earned through Active Business activity. This would include amounts earned by producing goods, selling goods or services, or delivering services. While usage is not always consistent, this term usually refers to a net amount (i.e., inclusions less deductions, or revenues less expenses).

Business Investment Loss A loss resulting from the Disposition of shares or debt of a Small Business Corporation.

C

Canada Education Savings Grants
A system of grants under which the federal government makes contributions to an Individual's RESP based on a percentage of the contributions to that Individual's RESP that have been made by others.

Canada Learning Bonds A system of grants under which the federal government makes contributions to an Individual's RESP based on the number of years in which the Individual's family is eligible for the National Child Benefit supplement.

Canada Employment Credit A credit against Tax Payable that is available to individuals with employment income.

Canada Pension Plan (CPP) A pension plan sponsored by the federal government. Individuals with Employment or Business Income must make contributions based on their income and, in return, receive benefits in future years.

Canada Pension Plan Tax Credit A credit against Tax Payable that is available to Individuals making contributions to the Canadian Pension Plan.

Canadian Controlled Private Corporation
A Corporation that is controlled by Persons Resident in Canada and that does not have any of its shares listed on a prescribed stock exchange.

Canadian Corporation A Corporation that is resident in Canada.

Canadian Partnership A Partnership, all of the members of which are Residents of Canada at the time the term is relevant.

Canadian Surtax Paid For purposes of calculating the Large Corporations Tax, this is the regular corporate Surtax, multiplied by the percentage of the corporation's activity at Permanent Establishments in Canada as determined under ITR 402.

Capital Asset An asset that is held for the purpose of producing Income.

Capital Cost The amount paid to acquire a depreciable asset. The tax equivalent of acquisition cost in accounting.

Capital Cost Allowance (CCA) A deduction in the determination of Business or Property Income based on the capital cost of capital assets. The tax equivalent of accounting amortization.

Capital Dividend A Dividend paid out of a Private Corporation's Capital Dividend Account. It is received on a tax free basis.

Capital Dividend Account A group of items, defined in ITA 89(1), that can be distributed by Private Corporations to shareholders as a tax free Capital Dividend (e.g., the non-taxable portion of realized Capital Gains).

Capital Export Neutrality The concept that the taxation system of a particular country does not encourage or discourage the export of capital.

Capital Gain The excess of proceeds resulting from the Disposition of a capital asset, over the sum of the Adjusted Cost Base of the asset plus any costs of disposition.

Capital Gains Reserve A Reserve that is deductible against Capital Gains. It is available when some part of the Proceeds Of Disposition is not collected in the period of disposition.

Capital Gains Stripping Procedures designed to allow a Corporation to convert a taxable capital gain resulting from the Disposition of investment shares to an arm's length party, into a tax free intercorporate Dividend.

Capital Import Neutrality The concept that the taxation system of a particular country does not encourage or discourage the import of capital.

Capital Interest (In A Trust) All rights of the Taxpayer as a Beneficiary under the trust, other than those that are an Income Interest in the Trust.

Capital Loss The excess of the sum of the Adjusted Cost Base of a capital asset plus any costs of disposition, over the proceeds resulting from the Disposition of the asset.

Capital Tax A tax assessed on the capital of a Corporation, without regard to its Income.

Caregiver Tax Credit A credit against Tax Payable that is available to an Individual who provides home care for an adult relative.

Carry Over As used in tax work, the ability to apply current year losses against Income in earlier or later years.

Charitable Gifts Donations to a registered charity, a registered Canadian amateur athletic association, a housing corporation resident in Canada that is exempt from tax under ITA 149(1)(i), a Canadian municipality, the United Nations or an agency thereof, a university outside of Canada which normally enrolls Canadian students, and a charitable organization outside of

Canada to which Her Majesty in right of Canada has made a gift in the year or in the immediately preceding year.

Cash Basis A method of accounting for Income based on cash receipts and cash disbursements.

Cash Damming Situations in which a separate bank account is established to receive all deposits of borrowed funds. Expenditures from this account are then limited to those which qualify for interest deductibility. This procedure facilitates linking the borrowed money to income producing investments.

CCPC An acronym for "Canadian controlled private corporation".

Charitable Donations Tax Credit A credit against Tax Payable that is available to Individuals making donations to qualifying charitable organizations.

Child Care Expenses Costs associated with caring for an Eligible Child.

Child Support A support amount that is not identified as being for the benefit of a Spouse or Common-Law Partner, or a former Spouse or Common-Law Partner.

Child Tax Benefit A monthly payment that is available to Individuals with children. The payments may be reduced or eliminated by a deduction of Income in excess of a threshold amount.

Children's Fitness Tax Credit
A credit against Tax Payable that is available to individuals for fees paid for the enrollment of a child under 16 in an eligible program of physical activity.

Class As used in tax work, a defined group of depreciable assets for which the *Income Tax Regulations* specify the CCA rate to be applied, as well as the method to be used in applying the rate.

Clawback An income tested taxing back, or reduction, in the payment of Old Age Security benefits and Employment Insurance benefits.

Commercial Activity This is a GST term which refers to any business or trade carried on by a Person, or any supply of real property made by a Person. Commercial Activity does not include any activity involved with making an exempt supply or any activity engaged in by an Individual without a Reasonable Expectation Of Profit.

Commodity Tax A type of Transaction Tax that is applied to the sale of certain types of commodities (e.g., taxes on the sale of tobacco products).

Common Shares Corporate shares that normally have all of the rights which are provided for under the relevant corporate enabling legislation. While there may be variations in the rights of such shares, at a minimum, voting rights would have to be present for the shares to be considered Common Shares.

Common-Law Partner A Person who cohabits in a conjugal relationship with the Taxpayer and (a) has so cohabited with the Taxpayer for a continuous period of at least one year, or (b) is a parent of a child of whom the Taxpayer is also a parent.

Comparable Uncontrolled Price A Transfer Pricing method that bases transfer prices on the prices used in comparable transactions between arm's length buyers and sellers, operating in the same market and under the same terms and conditions.

Competent Authority An authorized representative of a country's tax organization that helps resolve taxpayer disputes by negotiating with the other country on matters not adequately addressed by the tax treaty.

Connected Corporation Corporation A is connected with Corporation B if Corporation B Controls Corporation A, or if Corporation B owns more than 10 percent of the voting shares of Corporation A and more than 10 percent of the fair market value of all issued shares of Corporation A.

Consent Form A form that is used when a taxpayer wishes to have a different person represent him in dealing with the CRA. This form (T1013) authorizes the CRA to disclose information to and deal with a specified representative.

Consumption Tax A tax levied on the consumption of some product or service. This type of tax is also called a sales tax.

Contributed Capital In accounting usage, the amount of a Corporation's Shareholders' Equity that was received in return for issuing the shares that are currently outstanding.

Control [ITA 251.1(1)] Under ITA 251.1(1), Control means controlled, directly or indirectly in any manner whatever. [The reference here is to de facto control, which does not necessarily require majority ownership of shares.]

Control [ITA 256(1.2)(c)] A Corporation, Person or Group Of Persons has Control of a Corporation if that Corporation, Person or Group Of Persons owns either more than 50 percent of the Common Shares of that Corporation or, alternatively, owns shares (common and/or preferred) with a fair market value that exceeds 50 percent of the fair market value of all of the outstanding shares of that Corporation.

Control (CICA Handbook) The continuing power to determine strategic operating, investing and financing policies of an enterprise without the co-operation of others.

Controlled Foreign Affiliate A Foreign Affiliate of the Taxpayer that was controlled by (a) the Taxpayer, (b) the Taxpayer and not more than four other Persons Resident in Canada, (c) not more than four Persons Resident in Canada, other than the Taxpayer, (d) a Person or Persons with whom the Taxpayer does not deal at arm's length, or (e) the Taxpayer and a Person or Persons with whom the Taxpayer does not deal at arm's length.

Convertible Property A debt or equity financial instrument of a Corporation that can be exchanged for a different debt or equity financial instrument of the same Corporation, without the payment of additional consideration.

Co-Ownership Ownership of a single real or personal property by two or more Persons.

Corporation An artificial legal entity created through either federal or provincial legislation.

Cost Of Capital (M&P) For purposes of calculating the M&P Deduction, this amount is 10 percent of the Gross Cost of Capital Assets used by the corporation, plus 100 percent of rents paid for Capital Assets used by the Corporation.

Cost Of Labour (M&P) For purposes of calculating the M&P Deduction, this is the total cost of salaries and wages, plus non-salary amounts paid for employee-like services.

Credit Method A method for relieving a potential for Double Taxation on foreign source income by allowing a credit against Canadian Tax Payable for foreign income taxes assessed and withheld.

Crown Gifts Gifts made to Her Majesty in right of Canada or to Her Majesty in right of a province.

Cultural Gifts Gifts of objects that the Canadian Cultural Property Export Review Board has determined meet the criteria of the *Cultural Property And Import Act*.

Cumulative Eligible Capital (CEC) This term is used to refer to the amortized balance of Eligible Capital Expenditures. The amortization of this amount that is deducted under ITA 20(1)(b) is usually referred to as the cumulative eligible capital amount.

Cumulative Net Investment Loss (CNIL) The amount by which the aggregate of investment expenses for the current year and prior years ending after 1987, exceeds the aggregate of investment income for that period.

Cumulative Gains Limit Taxable Capital Gains on qualifying assets that have been realized since 1984, less the sum of Allowable Capital Losses and Net Capital Loss Carry Overs deducted after 1984, plus Allowable Business Investment Losses realized after 1984, capital gains deductions claimed in previous taxation years, and the Cumulative Net Investment Loss at the end of the year. Used to determine the Lifetime Capital Gains Deduction for the current year.

Customs Duties A tax imposed on the importation or exportation of certain goods or services.

D

Death Benefit All amounts in excess of $10,000 that are received by a Taxpayer in a taxation year, on or after the death of an Employee, in recognition of the Employee's service in an office or employment.

Declining Balance Method A method of calculating CCA in which a specified rate is applied to the ending UCC balance in a depreciable asset Class in order to determine the CCA for the period.

Deduction Method A method for relieving a potential for Double Taxation on foreign source income by allowing a deduction against Canadian Taxable Income for foreign income taxes assessed and withheld.

Deemed Disposition A requirement to assume that a Disposition has taken place when, in fact, a disposition transaction has not occurred (e.g., a change in use is deemed to be a Disposition).

Deemed Dividends A group of capital transactions and distributions, as specified in ITA 84(1), that are deemed to be Dividend payments.

Deemed Resident An Individual who is considered a Resident of Canada because of some factor other than physical presence in Canada (e.g., members of the Canadian armed forces are deemed to be Canadian Residents under ITA 250 without regard to where they are physically located).

Deemed Year End A requirement to have a taxation year end at a specified date, or as the result of a specified event.

Deeming Rule Rules that are used to require that an item or event be given a treatment for tax purposes that is not consistent with the actual nature of the item or event (e.g., members of the Canadian armed forces are deemed to be Canadian Residents even if they are not present in Canada at any time during the year).

Deferred Income Plans   A group of plans that allow Individuals to receive Income on a tax deferred basis.   These include Registered Pension Plans, Deferred Profit Sharing Plans, Registered Retirement Savings Plans, and Registered Retirement Income Funds.

Deferred Profit Sharing Plan (DPSP)
A trusteed plan to which employers can make deductible contributions, the amount of which is related to the profits of the enterprise, and which do not create a Taxable Benefit for the recipient employees.   Earnings accumulate tax free within the plan.   Withdrawals from the plan are subject to tax.

Defined Benefit Plan   A retirement savings plan in which the plan sponsor (usually an employer) promises a known or determinable retirement benefit and assumes financial responsibility for providing that benefit.

Defined Contribution Plan (a.k.a., Money Purchase Plan)   A retirement savings plan in which the plan sponsor (employer or individual) makes known or determinable contributions.   The retirement benefit is based on the accumulated contributions and earnings on investments within the plan.

Dependant   As defined in ITA 118(6), an Individual who, at any time during the year, is dependent on the taxpayer for support and is the child or grandchild of the Individual or of the individual's Spouse or Common-Law Partner, the parent, grandparent, brother, sister, uncle, aunt, niece, or nephew, if resident in Canada at any time in the year, of the Individual or of the individual's Spouse or Common-Law Partner.

Depreciable Capital Property   Capital property, such as equipment or furniture and fixtures, that is subject to depreciation or amortization.

Disability Tax Credit   A credit against Tax Payable that is available to Individuals with a doctor certified severe mental or physical disability.   Can be transferred to a supporting Individual.

Disability Tax Credit Supplement   A supplement to the Disability Tax Credit that is available for individuals who are under 18 years of age at the end of the year.

Disability Supports Deduction   A deduction available to individuals for attendant care and other disability support expenses, incurred to allow the disabled individual to work or to attend a designated educational institution.

Disappearing Source Rules   Rules designed to provide relief to investors who have borrowed money to make an investment and subsequently sold the investment for less than the related borrowings.   These rules provide that any amount of debt that remains after the proceeds of the sale are used to pay off a portion of the total balance is deemed to be debt that is used to produce income.

Discretionary Trust   A Trust for which the Settlor has given the Trustee discretion to decide the amounts of income or capital to be allocated to each Beneficiary.

Disposition   The disposal of an asset through sale, gift, physical destruction, conversion, expropriation, or other means.

Dividends   Amounts declared and paid, at the discretion of management, as a return on equity investments.

Dividend Gross Up   The 25 percent (non-eligible dividends) or 45 percent (eligible dividends) amount that must be added to Dividends received from Taxable Canadian Corporations before their inclusion in the Net Income For Tax Purposes of Individuals.

Dividend Stripping   Procedures designed to allow an Individual to remove accumulated Income from a Corporation in the form of tax-free capital gains, while still retaining Control of the Corporation.

Dividend Tax Credit   A credit against the Tax Payable of an Individual.   At the federal level it is equal to 11/18 of the Dividend Gross Up.   At the provincial level, its value varies from province to province.

Dividends In Kind   Dividends paid in corporate assets other than cash.

Division B Income   An alternative name for Net Income For Tax Purposes.

Double Taxation   A reference to situations in which the same stream of Income is subject to tax a second time.

Dual Resident   A taxpayer who is considered to be a Resident of two countries.

E

Earned Capital (a.k.a. Retained Earnings)
In accounting usage, the amount of a Corporation's Shareholders' Equity that resulted from the retention of earnings in the corporation.

Earned Income (Child Care Expenses)   For purposes of determining the deductible amount of Child Care Expenses, Earned Income is defined as Employment Income (gross), Business Income (losses), and Income from scholarships, training allowances, and research grants.

Earned Income (RRSP Deduction Limit)
The sum of Employment Income (without the RPP deduction), Business Income (losses), royalties (if the taxpayer is the author, inventor, or composer), taxable (deductible) support payments, supplementary unemployment benefits, income (loss) as an active partner, net rental income (loss), research grants (net of certain expenses), and CPP disability benefits.

Earned Surplus
An archaic accounting description of what now is called Retained Earnings. However, the term continues to be found in the *Income Tax Act*.

Ecological Gifts
Gifts of land certified by the Minister of the Environment to be ecologically sensitive land, the conservation and protection of which is important to the preservation of Canada's environmental heritage.

Education Tax Credit
A credit against Tax Payable that is available to Individuals attending a designated educational institution on a full or part time basis.

EFILE
EFILE is a service that lets authorized service providers send income tax return information to the CRA by Internet.

Election
A choice that is available to a Taxpayer with respect to a particular tax outcome (e.g., a Taxpayer can elect to have the spousal Rollover provision not be applicable).

Eligible Capital Expenditure
An amount expended to acquire an intangible asset that is not eligible for either write-off through CCA deductions or as a deduction in the period in which it is incurred.

Eligible Child
With respect to the deductibility of Child Care Expenses, an Eligible Child is a child of the Taxpayer, his Spouse, or a child who is dependent on the Taxpayer or his Spouse, and whose Income does not exceed the basic personal tax credit. An Eligible Child must either be under 16 years of age at some time during the year, or dependent on the Taxpayer or his Spouse by reason of physical or mental infirmity.

Eligible Dependant Tax Credit
A credit against Tax Payable that is available to a single Individual supporting a Dependant in a self-contained domestic establishment.

Eligible Dividends
Dividends that have been designated by the payor as eligible for the enhanced 45 percent gross up and tax credit procedure.

Emigration
Leaving a country, usually in order to establish permanent residency in another country.

Employee
An Individual who has an employment relationship with an entity that provides remuneration. Whether or not an Individual is working as an Employee or a Self-Employed Individual is dependent on such factors as control, ownership of tools, chance of profit or risk of loss, and integration with the entity making payments to the Individual.

Employer/ Employee Relationship
A written, verbal, or tacit agreement in which an Employee agrees to work on a full-time or part-time basis for an employer for a specified or indeterminate period of time, in return for Salary or wages. The employer has the right to decide where, when, and how the work will be done. In this type of relationship, a contract of services exists.

Employment Income
The Salary, wages, and other remuneration, including gratuities, received by an Employee in the year (see Employer/Employee Relationship).

Employment Insurance (EI)
A federal insurance plan designed to provide benefits to unemployed Individuals. In order to receive benefits, Employees must make contributions when they are employed.

Employment Insurance Tax Credit
A credit against Tax Payable that is available to Employees making payments to the federal Employment Insurance plan.

Estate
As the term is used in the *Income Tax Act*, the property of a deceased Individual.

Estate Freeze
Procedures undertaken by an Individual in order to fix a tax value for all or part of the Individual's property, and to Transfer future growth in the value of this property to other Individuals.

Estate Planning
Tax planning directed towards the distribution of an Individual's property at death.

Exchange Of Shares In A Reorganization (ITA 86)
A Rollover provision that allows one class of shares in a Corporation to be exchanged for a different class of shares, without tax consequences.

Executor
A Person appointed by an Individual in their Will to oversee the administration of the Estate on their death in accordance with the terms of that Will.

Exempt Goods And Services
Goods and services that are not subject to the GST. Registrants who sell Exempt Goods And Services are not eligible for Input Tax Credits for GST paid. Examples include sales of used residential housing, most medical services, and most financial services.

Exempt Surplus   A surplus account that tracks certain sources of income of a Foreign Affiliate.

Exemption Method   A method for relieving a potential for Double Taxation on foreign source income by exempting that income from inclusion in Taxable Income in the country of residence.

Excessive Eligible Dividend Designations (EEDD)   A balance, subject to Part III.1 tax, which reflects an inappropriate designation of an amount of dividends paid as an Eligible Dividend.

F

Family Trust   An Inter Vivos Trust, established by an Individual, with family members as Beneficiaries.

Fairness Package   A group of Information Circulars (IC 92-1, 92-2, and 92-3) which are designed to allow the CRA to make certain types of decisions on the basis of fairness to the Individual Taxpayer. An example would be a waiver of late filing interest and penalties because the Individual suffered a serious illness.

Farm Property   Farm Property includes real estate that is used in farming activities, a share of a Corporation that is carrying on a farming business, or an interest in a Partnership that is carrying on a farming business.

Federal Tax Abatement   A 10 percentage point reduction in the federal tax rate on Corporations, applicable to Income earned in a province.

Final Tax Return   A term used to describe the tax return filed for an Individual for the year of their death.

First Year Rules   See Half-Year Rules.

Fiscal Period   A taxation year that does not exceed 53 weeks.

Fishing Property   Fishing Property includes real estate and property that is used in fishing activities, a share of a Corporation that is carrying on a fishing business, or an interest in a Partnership that is carrying on a fishing business.

Fixed Term Annuity   An Annuity that is paid for a specified number of periods.

Flat Tax System   A tax on Income that is applied at the same rate to all Taxpayers, without regard to the level of their Income.

Foreign Accrual Property Income (FAPI)   Income of a Controlled Foreign Affiliate from property (interest, Dividends, rents, royalties), Income from inactive businesses, Taxable Capital Gains from properties not used in an Active Business, and Income from an investment business, defined as a business the principal purpose of which is to earn Property Income.

Foreign Affiliate   A non-resident Corporation in which a Canadian Taxpayer has an equity percentage of at least 1 percent. As well, the aggregate equity percentages of the Taxpayer and each Person related to the Taxpayer must be at least 10 percent.

Foreign Investment Entity   A non-resident entity that is largely devoting its activities to the production of investment or Property Income.

Foreign Taxes Paid Credit   A credit against Tax Payable based on taxes withheld by a foreign taxing authority on foreign source income.

Former Business Property   Real property that is used in the operation of a business.

Fringe Benefits   Non-cash benefits provided to Employees by an employer (e.g., contributions to an Employee's Registered Pension Plan).

Full Rate Taxable Income   For purposes of calculating the General Rate Reduction, Taxable Income reduced by amounts which have received preferential treatment under some other provision (e.g., the Small Business Deduction).

Fully Taxable Goods And Services   Goods and services that are taxable at the full 6 percent GST rate. Registrants who sell Fully Taxable Goods And Services are entitled to Input Tax Credits for GST paid. Examples include clothing, furniture, legal fees, hydro services, building materials, and restaurant meals.

G

GAAP   An acronym for "generally accepted accounting principles".

GAAR   An acronym for "general anti-avoidance rule". This ITA 245 provision attempts, in a very generalized manner, to limit the ability of Taxpayers to avoid tax through certain types of transactions that have no bona fide purpose other than to obtain a tax benefit.

General Partner   A Partner who has all of the rights and assumes all of the obligations that are specified by the General Partner provisions of the relevant provincial legislation.

General Partnership   A Partnership, all of the members of which are General Partners.

General Rate Income Pool (GRIP)   A notional account that tracks amounts of a CCPC's income that can be used for the payment of Eligible Dividends.

General Rate Reduction   A 7 percentage point deduction in the calculation of corporate Tax Payable that is designed to reduce the general corporate tax rate of 38 percent.

Gift   A voluntary Transfer of goods or services without remuneration.

Goods And Services Tax (GST)   A type of Transaction Tax that is assessed on the sale of goods and services. As it is assessed at all stages of the production/distribution chain, the tax that an enterprise must collect and pay to the government is offset by Input Tax Credits for the tax paid on the various inputs required to produce or distribute the goods and services.

Goodwill   The excess, if any, of the total fair value of a business enterprise, over the sum of the fair values of its identifiable tangible and intangible assets.

Gross Cost   For purposes of calculating Capital Cost in the determination of the M&P Deduction, this is the cost of Capital Assets, without the deduction of government grants or Investment Tax Credits.

Group Of Persons   For purposes of determining Control of a Corporation, a Group Of Persons is any two or more Persons, each of whom owns shares in the Corporation.

GST   An acronym for the "goods and services tax".

GST Tax Credit   A Refundable Tax Credit that is available to all Resident Individuals aged 19 or older who file a T1 tax return. May be reduced or eliminated by a deduction of Income in excess of a threshold amount.

H

Half-Year Rules (a.k.a. First Year Rules)   A group of rules which require, for most CCA Classes, the subtraction of one-half of the year's net additions (additions, less the amount subtracted from the class because of disposals) from the Class, prior to calculating the CCA for the year.

Harmonized Sales Tax (HST)   A combined federal/provincial sales tax that is assessed on the same basis as the federal Goods And Services Tax (GST). The combined rate is currently 14 percent and is notionally a combination of the 6 percent Goods And Services Tax and an 8 percent provincial sales tax.

Head Tax   A tax levied on the Individuals that are included in a specified classification.

Hobby Farmer   A part-time farmer who does not have a Reasonable Expectation Of Profit.

Home Buyers' Plan (HBP)   A provision that allows Individuals to make a temporary, non-taxable withdrawal from their RRSP for purposes of acquiring a residence.

Home Relocation Loan   A loan provided by an employer to an Employee to assist that Employee in acquiring a home at a new work location.

I

Identical Property Rules   Rules which require that, for a group of identical Capital Assets (e.g., Common Shares) acquired at different prices, the Adjusted Cost Base used to determine the gain or loss will be the average cost of the group. The rules are used when there is a partial Disposition of the group.

Immigration   Entering a new country, usually for purposes of establishing permanent residence.

Imputed Interest   Interest on outstanding debt calculated at a specified interest rate without regard to the actual interest rate being paid. This concept is used to determine the Taxable Benefit on loans to Employees and Shareholders.

Inadequate Consideration   A term used to refer to a situation where a non-arm's length transfer of property has been made and the Proceeds Of Disposition are not equal to the fair market value.

Income   A measure of either how much an entity has earned during a period or, alternatively, how much its net worth has increased during a period. As the term is used in accounting and tax, it is a rules-based calculation. In the case of accounting, the rules are referred to as generally accepted accounting principles (GAAP), while in tax the rules are found in the *Income Tax* Act and other sources.

Income Attribution   The allocation of some types of Income, on assets that have been transferred to a Spouse or related minors, back to the Transferor for inclusion in the Transferor's Net Income For Tax Purposes.

Income Interest (In A Trust)   A right of the Taxpayer as a Beneficiary under a Personal Trust to receive all or any part of the Income of the Trust.

Income Splitting   A group of Tax Planning techniques designed to divide a given stream of Income among family members or other related parties. The value of these techniques is based on progressive tax rates which means that, if a stream of Income can be divided into a group of smaller streams, a larger portion of it will be taxed at lower rates, resulting in aggregate tax savings.

Income Tax   A tax on the Income of certain defined entities.

Income Tax Application Rules A set of rules designed to deal with transitional problems associated with the introduction of Capital Gains taxation in 1972. While these rules were very important in the years immediately after 1971, they are of declining importance at this point in time.

Income Tax Regulations A set of rules concerning administration and enforcement of the *Income Tax Act*. One of the major issues covered here is Capital Cost Allowance rates and procedures.

Income Tax Technical News An irregularly published newsletter prepared by the Income Tax Rulings Directorate.

Indexation The process of adjusting tax brackets and some Tax Credits to reflect changes in the consumer price index.

Indexed Debt Obligations A debt obligation, the terms or conditions of which provide for an adjustment to an amount payable that is determined by reference to a change in the purchasing power of money.

Individual A single human being.

Information Circulars A group of separate publications that provides information regarding procedural matters that relate to both the *Income Tax Act* and the provisions of the Canada Pension Plan.

Information Return ITA 221(1)(d) gives the CRA the right to require any class of Taxpayer to file a return providing any class of information that it would like to have. A common example of an Information Return would be the T4 which employers are required to file in order to provide information on their Employees' earnings and withholdings.

Input Tax Credit (ITC) An amount, claimable by a registrant, for GST paid or payable on goods or services that were acquired or imported for consumption, use, or supply in the course of the Registrant's Commercial Activity.

Instalment Threshold An amount, currently $2,000, of net tax owing that is used to determine the need for Individuals to make Instalment payments (i.e., Individuals are required to make Instalment payments if their Net Tax Owing in the current year and one of the two preceding years exceeds the Instalment Threshold of $2,000).

Instalments Payments made during a taxation year by both Individuals and Corporations. They are designed to accumulate to an amount sufficient to cover the tax liability for the year. Individuals make quarterly Instalments, while Corporations are required to remit monthly.

Integration An approach to the taxation of Corporations that attempts to ensure that amounts of Income that are flowed through a Corporation to its Individual shareholders, are subject to the same amount of tax as would be the case if the Individuals had received the Income directly from its source.

Inter Vivos Transfer A Transfer made by a living Individual, as opposed to a Transfer made subsequent to that Individual's death.

Inter Vivos Trust A Trust that is not a Testamentary Trust.

Interest Income An amount that represents compensation for the use of money, is calculated with reference to a principal sum, and that accrues on a continuous basis.

International Taxation Income and other types of taxation related to transactions and events that take place in multiple jurisdictions.

International Tax Treaty (a.k.a., International Tax Convention) A bilateral agreement between two countries which establishes rules for dealing with cross-jurisdictional tax issues.

Interpretation Bulletins A group of over 500 individual publications which provides the CRA's interpretation of the various laws that they administer.

Investment Tax Credit A credit against Tax Payable, calculated as a percentage of some specified type of expenditure made by the Taxpayer.

Involuntary Disposition A Disposition of a capital property resulting from theft, destruction through natural causes, or expropriation by a statutory authority.

J

Joint Spousal Or Common-Law Partner Trust An Inter Vivos Trust established by an Individual aged 65 years or more, subject to the conditions that the Individual and his/her Spouse or Common-Law Partner must be entitled to all of the Trust's Income during their lifetimes, and the Individual and his Spouse or Common-Law Partner must be the only Individuals who can access the capital of the Trust during his/her lifetime.

Joint Tenancy A holding of property, either real or personal, by two or more Persons with each sharing the undivided interest that cannot be sold without the consent of all joint tenants.

Joint Venture   An arrangement in which two or more Persons work together in a limited and defined business undertaking, which does not constitute a Partnership, a Trust, or a Corporation, the expenses and revenues of which will be distributed in mutually agreed portions.

L

Labour Sponsored Funds Tax Credit
A credit against Tax Payable that is available to Individuals making investments in prescribed labour sponsored venture capital corporations.

Large Corporations Tax   A Capital Tax assessed on large corporations by the federal government.

Legal Stated Capital   An amount that is specified in corporate enabling legislation. In general, it is equal to the amount of consideration received for the issuance of shares.

Life Annuity   An Annuity that continues until the death of the Annuitant.

Lifelong Learning Plan (LLP)   A provision that allows Individuals to make temporary, non-taxable withdrawals from their RRSP when they are enrolled in a qualifying education program at a qualifying educational institution.

Lifetime Capital Gains Deduction   A deduction in the calculation of the Taxable Income of an Individual. It permits the deduction of a cumulative lifetime amount of up to $500,000 in Capital Gains resulting from the Disposition of Qualified Small Business Corporation shares or Qualified Farm Property.

Limited Liability   A reference to the fact that the liability of investors in equity shares of a Corporation is limited to the amount of their invested capital.

Limited Liability Partnerships   A Partnership, all of the members of which are legislatively specified professionals. The members of such Partnerships are relieved of any personal liability arising from the wrongful or negligent action of their professional Partners, as well as Employees, agents, or representatives of the Partnership who are conducting partnership business.

Limited Partner   As defined in most provincial legislation, a Partner whose liabilities for partnership debts is limited to the amount of his contribution to the Partnership, and who is not permitted to participate in the management of the Partnership.

Limited Partnership   A Partnership composed of at least one General Partner and at least one Limited Partner.

Limited Partnership Loss   The excess of losses allocated to a Limited Partner (other than farming or capital losses), over his At-Risk Amount.

Liquidating Dividend   A Dividend that represents a return of invested capital, as opposed to a distribution from earnings.

Listed Personal Property   A defined subset of Personal Use Property. The included items are works of art, jewelry, rare books, stamps, and coins.

Loss Carry Back   The application of a loss incurred in the current taxation year against the Income reported in a previous taxation year, resulting in a refund of taxes paid in that previous year.

Loss Carry Forward   The application of a loss incurred in the current taxation year against Income reported in a subsequent taxation year, resulting in a reduction of Tax Payable in that subsequent year.

Low Rate Income Pool   A notional account that tracks amounts of a non-CCPC's income that cannot be used for the payment of Eligible Dividends.

Lump-Sum Payments   Retroactive payments for Spousal or Child Support, pension benefits, EI benefits, and Employment Income (including payments for termination), that relate to prior years. Qualifying amounts of such payments are eligible for an alternative Tax Payable calculation.

M

M&P   An acronym for "manufacturing and processing" usually used in connection with the calculation of the Manufacturing And Processing Profits Deduction.

M&P Capital   100/85 of the Cost Of Capital related to Qualified Activities for M&P.

M&P Labour   100/75 of the Cost Of Labour related to Qualified Activities for M&P.

M&P Profits   A concept of Income based on M&P Capital and M&P Labour, applied in a formula contained in ITR 5200.

Manufacturing And Processing Profits Deduction (M&P Deduction)   A deduction in the calculation of corporate Tax Payable equal to 7 percentage points of M&P Profits.

Median Rule   A rule applicable to Capital Assets acquired before 1972. For purposes of calculating Capital Gains on Dispositions of these assets, the Adjusted Cost Base is equal to the median of the cost of the asset, the Valuation Day value of the asset, and the Proceeds Of Disposition.

Medical Expense Tax Credit A credit against Tax Payable that is available to Individuals with qualifying medical expenses.

Merger A combination of two or more business enterprises. While widely used in the *Income Tax Act*, this term does not have a formal definition in that legislation.

Money Purchase Limit An amount, specified in tax legislation that represents the maximum amount of Employee and employer contributions that can be added, for the benefit of a given Employee, to an RPP in the specified taxation year.

Money Purchase Plan (a.k.a., Defined Contribution Plan) A retirement savings plan in which the plan sponsor (employer or Individual) makes known or determinable contributions. The retirement benefit is based on the accumulated contributions and earnings on investments within the plan.

Moving Expenses Costs, as described in ITA 62(3), that can be deducted when an Individual is moving; to a new work location, to commence full-time attendance at a post-secondary institution, to a new work location after ceasing to be a full-time student at a post-secondary institution, or to a new location to take up employment, if unemployed prior to the move.

MUSH An acronym which stands for "municipalities, universities, schools, and hospitals". It is used in GST work to refer to the special rules applicable to these organizations.

N

"Negative" Adjusted Cost Base A term used to refer to situations where negative adjustments to the Adjusted Cost Base of a Capital Asset exceed its original cost plus positive adjustments. While, in general, such amounts must be taken into Income, an exception is made for Partnership Interests, for which such amounts can be carried forward.

Net Assets Assets minus the liabilities of a business enterprise.

Net Business Income As used in this text, the net of inclusions less deductions, related to Business Income, with all amounts determined as per Division B, Subdivision b, of the *Income Tax Act*.

Net Capital Loss The excess of Allowable Capital Losses over Taxable Capital Gains for the current year.

Net Income As used in this text, the net of revenues plus gains, less expenses plus losses, with all amounts determined through the application of GAAP.

Net Income For Tax Purposes The sum of Employment Income, Business and Property Income, net Taxable Capital Gains, other sources of income, and other deductions from income, determined using income tax procedures and concepts. These amounts are combined as per the rules in ITA 3. This amount is also referred to as Division B Income or simply Net Income. However, we tend to use the full Net Income For Tax Purposes title in order to avoid confusion with Net Income as determined by accounting rules.

Net Property Income As used in this text, the net of inclusions less deductions, related to Property Income, with all amounts determined as per Division B, Subdivision b, of the *Income Tax Act*.

Net Tax Owing A term, applicable to Taxpayers who are Individuals, used to describe the sum of federal and provincial taxes owing for the year, less amounts withheld for the year.

NETFILE An electronic filing system that requires the use of an approved software program. The Individual can use the Internet to transmit it directly to the CRA, without the use of a third party.

Non-Capital Loss The sum of employment losses (for Individuals), business losses, property losses, Net Capital Losses deducted, and deductible Dividends received (for Corporations), less Income as calculated under ITA 3(c).

Non-Depreciable Capital Property Capital property, such as land or holdings of securities, that are not subject to depreciation or amortization.

Non-Discretionary Trust A Trust for which the Trust documents have specified the amounts of Income and capital to be allocated to each Beneficiary.

Non-Refundable Tax Credit A Tax Credit that can only be used against the Tax Payable of an Individual. It will not be "refunded" to Individuals without sufficient Tax Payable to make use of it.

Non-Resident A Corporation, Trust, or any other type of entity that exists, was formed or organized, or was last continued under the laws of a country, or a political subdivision of a country, other than Canada.

Non-Share Consideration Consideration received by a Taxpayer from a Corporation that is in the form of assets other than shares of the Corporation.

Northern Residents Deductions Deductions from the Taxable Income of residents of prescribed areas in northern Canada, designed to compensate them for the higher costs of living in these regions.

Notice Of Assessment   A form that the CRA sends to all Taxpayers after they process their returns. It tells Taxpayers whether there were any changes to the returns and, if so, what they are. It also informs Taxpayers if they owe more tax or what the amount of their refund will be.

Notice Of Objection   A statement made to the CRA, which provides a statement of facts and reasons, detailing why a Taxpayer or Registrant disagrees with an Assessment. The notice can be filed using Form T400A or by simply writing a letter to the CRA.

O

OAS Clawback   A taxing back, or reduction, in the payment of Old Age Security benefits. The federal government taxes back, or retains, an amount of these payments equal to 15 percent of the Individual's Income in excess of an indexed threshold amount.

Old Age Security Benefits (OAS)   A monthly payment to Residents of Canada who are 65 years of age or older (see also OAS Clawback).

Operating Cost Benefit   A Taxable Benefit assessed to Employees whose employers pay the operating costs of an automobile provided to the Employee. It is designed to reflect, on a notional basis, the value of these operating costs.

Ordering Rule   Rules which establish the sequence or order in which a group of deductions must be made.

P

Paid Up Capital   A balance that is, in general, equal to Legal Stated Capital as determined under the legislation governing the particular Corporation. The equivalent of Contributed Capital in accounting usage.

Parent Company   A Corporation that Controls one or more Subsidiaries.

Part IV Tax   A refundable tax, applicable to Private Corporations and Subject Corporations, and assessed on Portfolio Dividends received as well as some Dividends received from Connected Corporations.

Part Year Resident   An Individual who either enters Canada during the year and becomes a Resident or, alternatively, an Individual who departs from Canada during the year and gives up their Resident status. In either case, the Individual will be taxed on their worldwide income for the part of the year that they were considered to be a Resident of Canada.

Partner   A Person who is a member of a Partnership.

Partnership   Two or more Persons who combine forces to carry on a business together for the purpose of making a profit by contributing their skills, knowledge, labour, experience, time, or capital.

Partnership Interest   A Non-Depreciable Capital Property that reflects the Partner's original cost, adjusted for earnings, withdrawals, and other factors.

Past Service Cost   The cost of starting a pension plan and extending the benefits/contributions to years of service prior to the inception of the plan or, alternatively, amending the benefit/contribution formula of an existing plan and extending the change retroactively to years of service prior to the amendment.

Past Service Pension Adjustment (PSPA)
An adjustment to reflect the past service benefits/contributions allocated to an Employee for years of service prior to the current year.

Penalties   Amounts taxpayers or GST registrants must pay if they fail to file returns or remit or pay amounts owing on time, or if they try to evade paying or remitting tax by not filing returns. Penalties must also be paid by people who knowingly, or under circumstances amounting to gross negligence, participate in or make false statements or omissions in their returns, and by those who do not provide the information required on a prescribed form.

Pension Adjustment Reversal (PAR)
An adjustment for amounts of benefits/contributions that were included in previously issued Pension Adjustments, but have subsequently been lost to the Individual (e.g., benefits earned during a pre-vesting period that did not ultimately vest).

Pension Adjustment (PA)   An adjustment reported by employers which reflects, for each Employee, the Employee's and employer's contributions to RPPs and DPSPs for the previous year (in the case of Defined Benefit RPPs, benefits are converted to an equivalent amount of contributions).

Pension Income Tax Credit   A credit against Tax Payable that is available to Individuals with qualifying pension income.

Periodic Child Care Expense Amount
A weekly limit on deductible child care costs, defined as 1/40 of the annual child care expense limit.

Permanent Establishment   A fixed place of business of a Corporation, including an office, a branch, a mine, an oil well, a farm, a timberland, a factory, a workshop, or a warehouse.

Person   A term used in the *Income Tax Act* to refer to taxable entities. For income tax purposes, the three taxable entities are Individuals, Corporations, and Trusts.

Personal Services Business   A Corporation that provides the services of a Specified Shareholder [ITA 248(1)] who could reasonably be regarded as an officer or Employee of the business, and that does not have five or more other full time Employees throughout the year.

Personal Tax Credits   A group of credits against Tax Payable that are specified in ITA 118(1). They provide credits for Individuals, Spouses and Common-Law Partners, Eligible Dependants, and Dependants 18 and over who are dependent because of a mental or physical infirmity.

Personal Trust   A Testamentary or Inter Vivos Trust in which no beneficial interest was acquired for consideration paid to the Trust or to a Person who contributed property to the Trust.

Personal Use Property   Any property that is owned by the Taxpayer and used primarily for his enjoyment, or for the enjoyment of one or more Individuals Related to the Taxpayer.

Political Contributions Tax Credit   A credit against Tax Payable that is available to persons (individuals and corporations) who have made contributions to a registered federal political party or to a candidate at the time of a federal election.

Portfolio Dividend   A Dividend received from a Corporation to which the recipient is not connected (see Connected Corporation). Usually applicable if 10 percent or less of the voting shares are owned.

Post-1971 Undistributed Surplus   Amounts earned by a Corporation after 1971 and retained in the Corporation.

Pre-1972 Capital Surplus On Hand   Capital Gains accrued before 1972 that have been realized as the result of a Disposition after 1971, less Capital Losses that accrued before 1972 that have been realized as the result of a Disposition after 1971.

Pre-1972 Undistributed Surplus   Amounts earned by a Corporation prior to 1972 and retained in the Corporation.

Pre-Acquisition Surplus   A surplus account that tracks certain sources of Income of a Foreign Affiliate.

Preferred Beneficiary   An Individual who is a Beneficiary of a Trust and who is either eligible for the Disability Tax Credit or, alternatively, 18 years of age or older and can be claimed by another Individual for purposes of the dependant tax credit for Individuals who are dependant because of mental or physical infirmity.

Preferred Beneficiary Election   An Election which allows trust Income to be allocated to a Preferred Beneficiary without being distributed to that Beneficiary by the Trust.

Preferred Shares   Shares that do not have all the rights which are provided for under the relevant corporate enabling legislation. While there are many variations in the rights that such securities have, Preferred Shares would normally have a fixed or determinable Dividend and would not have voting rights.

Prescribed Debt Obligations   A group of non-standard debt contracts that are defined in ITR 7001 (e.g., a debt contract with no interest stipulated as payable).

Prescribed Proxy Amount   An alternative basis for calculating Scientific Research And Experimental Development overhead costs. Instead of calculating actual overhead costs, a Prescribed Proxy Amount, based on 65 percent of the Salaries and wages of Employees involved in Scientific Research And Experimental Development activities, can be used.

Prescribed Rate   An interest rate which, as described in ITR 4301, changes quarterly and is based on the average interest rate paid on 90 day Treasury Bills during the first month of the preceding quarter. The basic rate is used for a variety of purposes (e.g., calculation of the Taxable Benefits on interest free loans to Employees). The basic rate, plus 2 percentage points, is used to calculate interest owing from the government to Taxpayers (e.g., interest on late payment of a tax refund). The basic rate, plus 4 percentage points, is used to calculate interest owed by Taxpayers to the government (e.g., interest on late Instalment payments).

Principal Residence   Any accommodation owned by the Taxpayer that was ordinarily inhabited in the year by the Taxpayer, his Spouse, a former Spouse, or a dependent child, and is designated by the Taxpayer as a Principal Residence.

Private Corporation   A Corporation that is a resident of Canada, but is not a Public Corporation.

Proceeds Of Disposition   Amounts received as the result of a Disposition. Usually related to a capital property Disposition.

Profit Sharing Plan   A trusteed plan to which employers can make deductible contributions, the amount of which is related to the profits of the enterprise. Both the contributions and the earnings resulting from their investment are taxed in the hands of the Employees as they occur. Payments from the plan are received by the Employees on a tax free basis.

Progressive Tax System   A tax system that applies higher effective rates for Individuals with higher Incomes and lower effective rates for Individuals with lower Incomes (e.g., personal income taxes).

Property Income   Income that is earned through the passive ownership of property. It would include rents, interest, Dividends, and some royalties (i.e., royalties paid on assets that have been purchased). While usage is not always consistent, this term usually refers to a net amount (i.e., inclusions less deductions, or revenues less expenses).

Property Tax   A tax on the ownership of some particular set of goods.

Public Corporation   A Corporation that has at least one class of its shares listed on a prescribed stock exchange in Canada.

Public Transit Passes Tax Credit   A credit against Tax Payable that is available to individuals who purchase monthly or longer public transit passes.

PUC   An acronym for "paid up capital".

Purification Of A Small Business Corporation   A process of disposing of corporate assets that are not being used to produce Active Business Income, so that the Corporation meets the 90 percent of assets test required to qualify as a Small Business Corporation.

Q

Qualified Activities   Types of activity, as defined in ITR 5202, that are considered to be manufacturing and processing activities.

Qualified Farm Property   A Qualified Farm Property is a Farm Property that, prior to its Disposition was owned by the Taxpayer, his Spouse, or his Common-Law Partner, or their children for a period of 24 months or more.

Qualified Fishing Property
A Qualified Fishing Property is a Fishing Property that, prior to its Disposition was owned by the Taxpayer, his Spouse, or his Common-Law Partner, or their children for a period of 24 months or more.

Qualified Property   Certain specified types of property that, when acquired, qualify the Taxpayer for an Investment Tax Credit.

Qualified Scientific Research And Experimental Development Expenditures
Scientific Research And Experimental Development expenditures that qualify the Taxpayer for Investment Tax Credits.

Qualified Small Business Corporation
A Small Business Corporation that, at the time of its Disposition, has been owned by no one other than the Taxpayer or a related party during the preceding 24 months, and during that 24 month period, more than 50 percent of the fair market value of its assets were used in an Active Business carried on primarily in Canada.

Qualifying Acquisition   An acquisition of publicly traded shares through the exercise of Stock Options that is eligible for the ITA 7(8) deferral of the recognition of Employment Income from the time the options are exercised until the time the shares are sold.

Qualifying Corporation   A CCPC throughout the year with Taxable Income in the immediately preceding year of no more than $300,000, thereby qualifying for the additional 15 percent tax credit on the first $2,000,000 of Qualified Scientific Research And Development Expenditures.

Qualifying Spousal Or Common-Law Partner Trust   A Spousal Or Common-Law Partner Trust that qualifies for the Rollover of assets into the Trust under ITA 73(1.01) for Inter Vivos Trusts or ITA 70(6) for Testamentary Trusts.

Qualitative Characteristics   This term is used in our text to refer to non-quantitative characteristics of a tax system that are considered to be desirable (e.g., fairness).

Quick Method   A method of determining GST amounts available to businesses with annual GST taxable sales, including those of associated businesses, of $200,000 or less. Specified percentages are applied to the GST inclusive sales figures to determine the GST payable or the refund. Accounting for Input Tax Credits on non-capital expenditures is not required. Input Tax Credits on capital expenditures are tracked separately.

R

RDTOH   An acronym for "refundable dividend tax on hand".

Reasonable Expectation Of Profit (REOP)
A test that involves the determination of whether a business or an investment is likely to have a profit. The CRA has tried to use this test to limit the ability of Taxpayers to deduct losses resulting from businesses and investments that fail their REOP test.

Reassessment   A revision of an original Assessment (see Assessment and Notice Of Assessment).

Recapture Of CCA An inclusion in Business and Property Income that arises when deductions from a CCA Class, engendered by disposals, leave a negative balance in that Class at the end of the taxation year.

Redemption Of Shares A transaction in which a Corporation purchases some of its own outstanding shares, either in the open market, or through a direct purchase from shareholders.

Refundable Dividend Tax On Hand A balance made up of refundable taxes paid, less refunds received as the result of paying Dividends.

Refundable Investment Tax Credit (RDTOH) An Investment Tax Credit that will be paid to the Taxpayer, even if the amount resulting from the Investment Tax Credit exceeds the Taxpayer's Tax Payable.

Refundable Medical Expense Supplement A refundable credit against Tax Payable that adds to the amounts available to certain low income individuals for their eligible medical expenses.

Refundable Part I Tax The portion of Part I tax that is applicable to a notional amount of Aggregate Investment Income earned by a CCPC.

Refundable Tax Credit An amount, based on a Tax Credit calculation, that will be paid to an Individual even if the amount resulting from the Tax Credit calculation exceeds the Individual's Tax Payable.

Refundable XI.3 Tax A 50 percent tax that is assessed on contributions to a Retirement Compensation Arrangement and on the earnings of amounts invested in the plan. It is fully refundable when amounts are distributed from the arrangement and taxed in the hands of the recipient Employees.

Registered Education Savings Plan (RESP) A trusteed arrangement that allows Individuals to make non-deductible contributions that will be invested on a tax-free basis, with the accumulated funds being used to provide for the post-secondary education of a child.

Registered Pension Plan (RPP) A retirement savings plan sponsored by an employer, to which the employer will make contributions which are not taxable to the Employee, and the Employee may make contributions which are deductible. Earnings accumulate tax free within the plan. Withdrawals from the plan are subject to tax.

Registered Retirement Income Fund (RRIF) A trusteed plan to which a Resident Individual can transfer balances from retirement savings plans on a tax free basis. Earnings accumulate tax free within the plan. Withdrawals from the plan are subject to tax. Unlike RRSPs, a minimum withdrawal is required each year.

Registered Retirement Savings Plan (RRSP) A trusteed plan to which a Resident Individuals can make deductible contributions. Earnings accumulate tax free within the plan. Withdrawals from the plan are generally subject to tax.

Registrant An entity who is registered to collect and remit the GST.

Regressive Tax System A tax system that applies higher effective rates for Individuals with lower Incomes and lower effective rates for Individuals with higher Incomes (e.g., most sales taxes).

Related Persons ITA 251(2)(a) indicates that two Individuals are related if they are connected by blood relationship, marriage or common-law partnership, or adoption. ITA 251(2)(b) describes various situations in which a Corporation would be related to other Persons (e.g., a Corporation is related to the Person who Controls it). ITA 251(2)(c) describes various situations in which two Corporations would be related to each other (e.g., the two Corporations are controlled by the same Person).

Reorganization Of Capital (ITA 86) A Rollover provision that allows one class of shares in a Corporation to be exchanged for a different class of shares, without tax consequences.

Replacement Property Rules A set of rules which provide for the deferral of both Recapture and Capital Gains on Involuntary Dispositions and some voluntary Dispositions of capital property. Deferral is conditional on replacing the property within a specified period after the Proceeds Of Disposition are received.

Resale Price Method A Transfer Pricing method generally used where fair market value comparables are unavailable because of the uniqueness of the products. It also applies to situations where the purchaser adds little or no value and effectively acts as a distributor or sales agent.

Reserve A deduction in the calculation of net Business Income or net Taxable Capital Gains.

Resident A Person who is located in a place. This is the basis on which Canadian income taxes are assessed. That is, Canadian Resident Persons are liable for the payment of Canadian income tax, without regard to their citizenship or the source of their Income. While not defined in the *Income Tax Act*, IT-221R3 provides guidance on the determination of residency for Individuals and IT-447 provides similar guidance for Trusts.

Residential Ties   Factors that will be considered in determining whether or not an Individual is a Resident of Canada.   While there are many such ties, IT-221R3 indicates that the most commonly used would be the maintenance of a dwelling in Canada, having one's Spouse or Common-Law Partner remain in Canada, and having one's Dependants remain in Canada.

Restricted Farm Loss   A farmer whose chief source of Income is not farming or a combination of farming and some other source of Income, but who has a reasonable expectation of long-run profitability, can only deduct losses to the extent of the first $2,500, plus one-half of the next $12,500.   Losses in excess of this deductible amount are referred to as Restricted Farm Losses.

Retained Earnings (a.k.a. Earned Capital)   In accounting usage, the amount of a Corporation's Shareholders' Equity that resulted from the retention of earnings in the Corporation.

Retirement Compensation Arrangement   An unregistered plan to which employers make deductible contributions to provide Employees with benefits subsequent to their retirement.   Both contributions and earnings are subject to a Part XI.3 Refundable Tax.

Retiring Allowance   Amounts received at retirement as recognition for long service, or as the result of loss of employment.

Revenue Jurisdiction Approach   An international taxation approach under which a country taxes all Income earned by its Residents, without regard to the country in which that Income is earned.

Reversionary Trust   A trust agreement under which the property held by the Trustee can revert to the Settlor.

Rights Or Things   With respect to a deceased Taxpayer, these are amounts that are due, but have not been received (e.g., wages to the end of a pay period prior to death, but not yet received).

Rollover   As this term is used in tax work, it refers to a tax free Transfer of assets under circumstances that, in the absence of a Rollover provision, would be considered a taxable Transfer.

RRSP Deduction Limit   The amount that is the sum of the Unused RRSP Deduction Room at the end of the preceding year, plus the amount by which the lesser of the RRSP Dollar Limit and 18 percent of Earned Income for the preceding year exceeds the Pension Adjustment for the preceding year.   This sum is adjusted for any Past Service Pension Adjustment or Pension Adjustment Reversal.   In simplified terms, it represents the maximum amount of contributions that have been made to an RRSP that can be deducted for a year.

RRSP Deduction Room   The excess of the RRSP Deduction Limit, over the amount of RRSP contributions that have been deducted.

RRSP Dollar Limit   For years other than 1996 and 2003, the Money Purchase Limit for the preceding year.

S

Safe Income   For purposes of applying ITA 55(2) to Capital Gains Stripping, Safe Income is made up of amounts earned by a Corporation after 1971, or if the investment shares in that Corporation were acquired after that date, amounts earned after the acquisition.

Salary   The amount an employer pays an Employee for work done.   An employer records this type of Employment Income on a T4.   A common component of Employment Income.

Salary Deferral Arrangement   An arrangement, whether funded or not, under which an Individual who has the right to receive compensation postpones the receipt of that compensation, and it is reasonable to assume that one of the main purposes of this postponement was to defer the payment of taxes.

Scientific Research And Experimental Development (SR&ED)   Activities related to systematic investigation or search that is carried out in a field of science or technology by means of experiment or analysis.

Self-Employed Individual   An Individual who has a business relationship with a Taxpayer.   Whether or not an Individual is working as an Employee or a Self-Employed Individual is dependent on such factors as control, ownership of tools, chance of profit or risk of loss, and integration with the Person making payments to the Individual.

Separate Class Rules   Rules that require certain types of assets that would, in the absence of these special rules, be included in a single Class, be allocated to a separate balance for that Class (e.g., each rental property with a cost greater than $50,000 must be placed in a different Class 3).

Settlor   The Individual who creates a Trust by contributing property to be managed and administered by a Trustee for the Beneficiaries.

Share For Share Exchange (ITA 85.1)
A Rollover provision that allows one Corporation to acquire shares in another Corporation by issuing its own shares, without tax consequences to either of the Corporations or their shareholders.

Shared Use Capital Equipment   Capital Assets that are used more than 50 percent, but less than 90 percent, in Scientific Research And Experimental Development activities.

Shareholders' Equity   The residual interest of the shareholders of a Corporation in the Net Assets of the Corporation.

Short Fiscal Period   A taxation year that is less than 12 months in duration. Can occur in the first and last years of operation, as well as certain other situations.

Simplified Accounting   A simplified method of determining Input Tax Credits available to small businesses, charities, not-for-profit organizations, and certain public service bodies. The organization must have annual GST taxable sales, including those of associated businesses, of less than $500,000 and annual GST taxable purchases of less than $2,000,000. Input Tax Credits are determined by multiplying all GST inclusive purchases, except real property purchases, by 6/106 rather than using the actual GST paid. Input Tax Credits on real property are tracked separately.

Small Business Corporation   A Corporation that is a Canadian Controlled Private Corporation that uses all or substantially all (90 percent or more) of the fair market value of its assets in an Active Business that is carried on primarily (more than 50 percent) in Canada.

Small Business Deduction   A deduction in the calculation of corporate Tax Payable equal to 16 percentage points on the first $300,000 (2006 figure) of Active Business Income earned by a CCPC.

Small Suppliers Exemption   An exemption from the requirement to register for the collection and remittance of GST for those entities with less than $30,000 in taxable supplies.

Social Benefits Repayment (a.k.a., Clawback)   An income tested taxing back, or reduction, in the payment of Old Age Security Benefits and Employment Insurance Benefits.

Sojourner   An Individual who is deemed under ITA 250 to be a Canadian Resident for the full taxation year as the result of having sojourned (i.e., been temporarily present) in Canada for 183 days or more.

Source Deductions   Amounts that are withheld by an employer from the Income of Employees. The withholdings for income taxes, Canada Pension Plan contributions, and Employment Insurance premiums must be remitted to the government.

Source Jurisdiction Approach   An international taxation approach under which a country taxes all Income earned within its borders, without regard to whether it is earned by Residents or Non-Residents.

Specified Class [ITA 256(1.1)]   A class of shares that has certain specified terms and conditions, including a fixed or determinable Dividend and an absence of voting rights. Would generally be referred to as Preferred Shares.

Specified Employee   An Employee who owns 10 percent or more of the shares of the Corporation, or who does not deal at arm's length with the Corporation.

Specified Individual   An Individual who has not attained the age of 17 before the beginning of the year and who has a parent who is Resident in Canada.

Specified Investment Business   A Corporation that does not have five or more full time Employees throughout the year, whose principal purpose is to derive Income from property.

Specified Member   A Limited Partner or a General Partner who is not actively involved in partnership business activity.

Specified Non-Resident Shareholder
A specified shareholder who is a non-resident Person or non-resident investment company.

Specified Shareholder [ITA 18(5)]   A shareholder of a Corporation who holds shares which give him either 25 percent or more of the votes to be cast at the annual meeting, or 25 percent or more of the market value of all outstanding shares.

Specified Shareholder [ITA 248(1)]   A shareholder of a Corporation who owns, directly or indirectly, at any time in the year, not less than 10 percent of the issued shares of any class of the capital stock of the Corporation, or of any other Corporation that is related to the Corporation.

Split Income   Certain types of Income received by a Specified Individual from non-arm's length sources that will be taxed at the maximum federal rate of 29 percent.

Spousal Support   A Support Amount that is for the benefit of a Spouse or Common-Law Partner, or a former Spouse or Common-Law Partner.

Spousal RRSP   An RRSP to which the Spouse or Common-Law Partner of the Annuitant (i.e., Beneficiary of the RRSP) has made contributions that the Spouse or Common-Law Partner can deduct in calculating Net Income For Tax Purposes.

Spouse   An Individual to whom a Taxpayer is legally married.

Spousal Or Common-Law Partner Trust
An Inter Vivos or Testamentary Trust that has an individual's Spouse or Common-Law Partner as a Beneficiary (see also Qualifying Spousal Or Common-Law Partner Trust).

Standby Charge   A Taxable Benefit assessed to Employees who have been provided with an automobile by their employer. It is designed to reflect, on a notional basis, the value of having the car available on a standby basis for personal usage.

Stock Dividend   A pro rata distribution of a Corporation's shares to its existing shareholders.

Stock Option   A contractual arrangement which gives the holder the right to purchase a specified number of shares for a specified period of time at a specified acquisition price.

Stop Loss Rules   A group of rules which, under specified conditions, prevent the deduction of a loss.

Straight-Line Method   A method of calculating CCA in which a specified or determinable rate is applied to the Capital Cost of acquired assets in order to determine the CCA for the period.

Subject Corporation   For purposes of the Part IV Tax, a Public Corporation that is controlled by, or for the benefit of, an Individual or a related group of Individuals. Also used in the determination of Dividend Stripping (ITA 84.1) and share sales to non-residents (ITA 212.1) to describe a Corporation, the shares of which have been sold.

Subsidiary   An enterprise that is controlled by another enterprise (the Parent Company). The Parent Company has the right and ability to obtain future economic benefits from the resources of the Subsidiary and is exposed to the related risks.

Superficial Loss (ITA 54)   A loss on the Disposition of property that is disallowed for tax purposes because the Taxpayer has acquired an identical property, either 30 days before the Disposition or, alternatively, 30 days after the Disposition.

Supply   A broad range of transactions between Persons. To "make a supply of property or a service" means to provide it in any way, including sale, transfer, barter, exchange, licence, rental, lease, gift, or Disposition.

Support Amount   Amounts paid as the result of the separation or divorce of two Individuals who were Spouses or Common-Law Partners. Can be divided into Spousal Support and Child Support.

Surtax   An additional or extra tax on something already taxed.

Syndicates   A group of Persons combined or making a joint effort to undertake some specific project or to carry out a specific transaction.

T

Tariffs   A tax imposed on the importation or exportation of certain goods or services.

Tax Avoidance   The undertaking of transactions or arrangements with a view to avoiding or minimizing the payment of taxes. As the term is generally used, it refers to legitimate procedures that could also be described as Tax Planning.

Tax Base   The income source, class of transaction, type of property, or other factor on which tax is assessed (e.g., sales tax is assessed on sales).

Tax Court Of Canada   A court that hears appeals about income tax and GST/HST assessments. In addition, the Court has jurisdiction to hear appeals under the Canada Pension Plan Act, Employment Insurance Act, and several other Acts. The Tax Court maintains four offices (Vancouver, Ottawa, Toronto, and Montréal) and regularly conducts hearings in major centres across Canada.

Tax Credit   A credit against Tax Payable.

Tax Deferral   An important type of Tax Planning. The basic idea here is to find procedures that will put off the payment of taxes until a later taxation year. The value of these procedures reflects the time value of money. That is, there is a value associated with making a payment later, rather than sooner.

Tax Evasion   The commission or omission of an act knowingly, the conspiracy to commit such an act, or involvement in the accommodation of such an act, which can result in a charge being laid in the Criminal Court under Subsection 239(1) of the *Income Tax Act*.

Tax Expenditures   Foregone tax revenues due to special exemptions, rate reductions, rebates, and credits that reduce the amount of tax that would otherwise be payable. Often designed to encourage certain kinds of activities or to serve other objectives, such as providing assistance to lower-income or elderly Canadians.

Tax Haven   A foreign country used to avoid or reduce income taxes, especially by investors from another country.

Tax Incidence   The Person who ultimately pays a tax, regardless of the legal basis of assessment (e.g., taxes paid by Corporations may be passed on to either Employees or customers).

Tax Neutrality   As applied to a tax system, the concept that the various features of that system do not influence business or other economic decisions.

Tax Planning   The undertaking of legitimate transactions or arrangements with a view to avoiding or minimizing the payment of taxes. Some or all of such efforts could also be referred to as Tax Avoidance.

Tax Shelter (ITA 237.1)   A property where the purchaser will likely be entitled to deduct losses or other amounts, in the four years following the acquisition of the investment, that are in excess of the cost of the investment.

Tax Shelter (Other Meaning 1)
An investment that shelters Income from other sources (e.g., Employment Income) by producing tax losses.

Tax Shelter (Other Meaning 2)
An investment with a positive cash flow that is sheltered by sufficient non-cash deductions (e.g., CCA) to produce a nil Taxable Income.

Taxable Allowance   An allowance provided by an employer to an Employee that must be included in the Employee's Employment Income. The amount is included on the Employee's T4.

Taxable Benefit   An amount of money, or the value of goods or services, that an employer pays or provides in addition to Salary.

Taxable Canadian Corporation   A Canadian Corporation that is not exempt from Canadian income tax by way of a statutory provision.

Taxable Canadian Property   A group of assets that are listed under the definition of Taxable Canadian Property in ITA 248(1). These assets are distinguished by the fact that gains on their Disposition are taxable without regard to the residence of the selling Taxpayer. For example, if a U.S. Resident sells Canadian real estate, Canadian income tax will be assessed on any gain resulting from the sale.

Taxable Capital   For purposes of calculating the Large Corporations Tax, this is the Total Capital of the Corporation, less the allowance for investments in other Corporations.

Taxable Capital Employed In Canada
For purposes of calculating the Large Corporations Tax, this amount is Taxable Capital, multiplied by the percentage of the Corporation's activity at Permanent Establishments in Canada as determined under ITR 402.

Taxable Capital Gain   The taxable portion (currently one-half) of a Capital Gain.

Taxable Entity   A defined organization or Individual that is subject to tax (e.g., Corporations are taxable entities for income tax purposes).

Taxable Income   Net Income For Tax Purposes, less certain deductions that are largely specified in Division C of Part I of the *Income Tax Act*. These deductions include loss carry overs, the Lifetime Capital Gains Deduction, and for Corporations, Dividends and charitable contributions.

Taxable Surplus   A surplus account that tracks certain sources of Income of a Foreign Affiliate.

Taxation Year   The period that is covered by a Taxpayer's return. As defined in ITA 249, it is equal to a calendar year for Individuals and Inter Vivos Trusts, and a Fiscal Period for Corporations and Testamentary Trusts.

Taxpayer   An entity that is required to file a tax return and pay taxes. For income tax purposes, a Taxpayer is an Individual, a Corporation, or a Trust.

TELEFILE   An electronic system for filing tax returns that uses telephone lines rather than the Internet to submit returns to the CRA. It is available to any Individual with a touch tone telephone, but can only be used for filing relatively simple tax returns.

Tenancy In Common   A holding of property, either real of personal, by two or more Persons, with each having a divisible interest that can be sold.

Term Preferred Shares   Preferred Shares which have a provision which allows them to be redeemed by the issuer or redeemed at the request of the holder.

Terminal Loss   A deduction in the calculation of Business and Property Income which arises when the last asset in a CCA Class is retired and a positive balance is left in the Class.

Testamentary Trust   A Trust that arises on, and as a consequence of, the death of an Individual.

Textbook Tax Credit   A credit against Tax Payable that is available to individuals who qualify for the education credit.

Thin Capitalization   A reference to situations where a non-resident Specified Shareholder is receiving interest on an amount of debt that exceeds two times the sum of his share of contributed capital plus 100 percent of Retained Earnings.

Tie-Breaker Rules   Provisions in International Tax Treaties that are designed to prevent the Double Taxation of Dual Residents.

Transaction Tax A tax that is assessed on specified types of transactions. Such taxes are most commonly applied to transactions involving the sale of goods or services.

Transfer To convey or move from one Taxpayer to a different Taxpayer.

Transfer Pricing An expression used to describe the price at which services, tangible property, and intangible property are traded across international borders between related or non-arm's length parties.

Transfer Tax A tax on the Transfer of property from one owner to another.

Transferee A Taxpayer to whom a Transfer is made.

Transferor A Taxpayer who makes a Transfer.

Trust A relationship in which one Person holds the title to property for the benefit of another Person.

Trustee An Individual or trust institution that holds legal title to property in trust for the benefit of the Trust Beneficiaries.

Tuition Tax Credit A credit against Tax Payable that is available to Individuals making qualifying tuition payments.

Twenty-One (21) Year Deemed Disposition Rule A requirement, applicable to some types of Personal Trusts, that requires a deemed disposition of the Trust's capital property at the end of every twenty-one years.

U

Undepreciated Capital Cost (UCC)
The Capital Cost of a depreciable asset class, less the cumulative CCA that has been taken to date. The tax equivalent of net book value in accounting.

Universal Child Care Benefit A $100 monthly payment that is available to Canadian families for each of their children under the age of 6 years.

Unused RRSP Deduction Room The cumulative total of all RRSP Deduction Limits, less amounts deducted in those years. The end of the preceding year balance is used when calculating the RRSP Deduction Limit.

V

Valuation Day (V-Day) December 22, 1971 for publicly traded assets and December 31, 1971 for other assets.

Value Added Tax (VAT) A tax based on the value added to a product at each stage of production or distribution by a particular entity. It is generally based on some accounting measurement of Income.

Vertical Amalgamation An Amalgamation of a Parent Company and one or more of its Subsidiaries.

Vested Benefit A benefit is vested if the beneficiary has an irrevocable right to receive it.

Vested Contribution A contribution is vested if the Individual making the contribution has an irrevocable right to either the amount of the contribution or a benefit of equivalent value.

Wholly Dependent Person A Dependant who lives with the Taxpayer (this requirement is not applicable if the Dependant is the Taxpayer's child) in a self-contained domestic establishment and is eligible for the Eligible Dependant Tax Credit (a.k.a., equivalent to spouse tax credit).

Will A document that is a legal declaration of an Individual's wishes as to the Disposition of his or her property after death.

Winding-Up Of A Canadian Corporation A series of transactions that result in substantially all of the assets of a Canadian Corporation being distributed to the shareholders of that Corporation.

Winding-Up Of A 90 Percent Owned Subsidiary A Rollover provision that allows a 90 percent or more owned Subsidiary to be combined with its Parent Company without tax consequences.

Zero-Rated Goods And Services Goods and services that are taxable at a zero GST rate. The fact that they are designated as "taxable" means that Registrants who sell such goods and services are eligible for Input Tax Credits for the GST that they pay. Examples include basic groceries (e.g., milk, bread, and vegetables), prescription drugs, and exports.